FEAR OF BEING FAT

Fear of Being Fat

THE TREATMENT OF ANOREXIA NERVOSA AND BULIMIA

Revised Edition

Edited by C. Philip Wilson, M.D.
with the assistance of
Charles C. Hogan, M.D., D.Med.Sc.
and Ira L. Mintz, M.D.

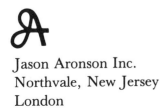

Jason Aronson Inc.
Northvale, New Jersey
London

It is well known that there is a neurosis in girls which occurs . . . at the time of puberty or soon afterwards, and which expresses aversion to sexuality by means of anorexia. This neurosis will have to be brought into relation with the oral phase of sexual life.

SIGMUND FREUD
From the History
of an Infantile Neurosis

CONTENTS

CONTRIBUTORS

GERALD V. FREIMAN, M.D.
  Clinical Associate Professor of Psychiatry
  Faculty, The Psychoanalytic Institute
  New York University Medical Center

CHARLES C. HOGAN, M.D., D.Med.Sc.
  Assistant Clinical Professor of Psychiatry
  Albert Einstein College of Medicine
  Lecturer, Columbia University College of Physicians and Surgeons
  Faculty, Columbia University Center for Psychoanalytic Training and
    Research

IRA L. MINTZ, M.D.
  Associate Clinical Professor of Psychiatry
  New Jersey College of Medicine
  Supervising Child Psychoanalyst
  Columbia University Center for Psychoanalytic Training and Research
  Consultant, Hackensack Medical Center

CHARLES A. SARNOFF, M.D.
  Lecturer, Columbia University College of Physicians and Surgeons

MELITTA SPERLING, M.D. (Deceased)
  Clinical Professor of Psychiatry
  Training Analyst and Supervisor
  Chairman, Postgraduate Study Group
  Division of Psychoanalytic Education
  Downstate Medical Center

HOWARD K. WELSH, M.D.
  Assistant Clinical Professor of Psychiatry
  Columbia University College of Physicians and Surgeons
  Faculty, The Psychoanalytic Institute
  New York University Medical Center

C. PHILIP WILSON, M.D.

Assistant Clinical Professor of Psychiatry
Columbia University College of Physicians and Surgeons
Faculty, Columbia University Center for Psychoanalytic Training and
    Research
Attending Psychiatrist
St. Luke's-Roosevelt Hospital Center
Faculty, The Psychoanalytic Institute
New York University Medical Center

PREFACE

In this book, Dr. C. Philip Wilson presents a major new hypothesis: as a diagnostic term, anorexia nervosa is a medical misnomer and should be replaced by "fat phobia" or "phobic fear of fat," which are true psychodynamic descriptions of this syndrome. Every analytic interpretation is focused on a conflict that is masked by the fear-of-being-fat complex and by the associated body-image disturbance—the obsession with being thin. The result of successful analysis is a decathexis of the complex, a resolution of the food phobia, and a complete, healthy alteration of the pathological body image.

The contributors to this volume are all members of the Psychosomatic Study Group of the Psychoanalytic Association of New York, Inc., which is composed of psychoanalytically trained psychiatrists specializing in the treatment of psychosomatic disorders. The group was led by Dr. Melitta Sperling from 1965 until 1973, the year of her death. Since that time, the moderator has been Dr. Wilson. In this long-term research, we have had the unique opportunity to review and discuss the analyses of numerous psychosomatic cases. Particularly important has been the presentation of the psychodynamic treatment of the mother, the father, the siblings, and the spouses of these patients, which has given us an in-depth understanding of the family psychodynamics.

This volume provides a blueprint for the treatment of abstaining and bulimic anorexics. The clinical papers detail the psychodynamics, etiology, and technique of analysis in children, adolescents, and adults. Basing our conclusions on a large number of analyzed cases, we attempt to provide a clinically documented understanding of the psychodynamics of the various personality disorders that are masked by the anorexic symptoms and to trace their ontogenesis back to the preoedipal years, when the predisposition for the development of the disease is first established. We explore the structure of the ego and superego, and the nature of the object relations in these cases. The special difficulties encountered in treatment are detailed, particularly the technique of analysis of the anorexic crisis, transference and countertransference, and the management of the characteristic provocative acting-out behavior.

We emphasize a technique of treatment that focuses on pregenital conflicts, part-object relations, and the central issue of the transference. Our findings closely parallel those of other analysts in their work with nonpsychosomatic patients who have severe preoedipal conflicts. We hope that we will be able to make it clear that psychoanalysis is the treatment of choice for abstaining and bulimic anorexics.

ACKNOWLEDGMENTS

We would like to express our appreciation to the founder of the Psychosomatic Study Group of the Psychoanalytic Association of New York, Dr. Melitta Sperling, for her pioneer psychosomatic research and publications. We are indebted to the other members of this study group for their thoughtful discussions of many of the topics explored in this book, particularly Drs. Leonard Barkin, Lawrence Deutsch, Cecilia K. Karol, Henry I. Schneer, and Otto Sperling. Our thanks are due to Drs. Stanley Friedman, Robert Langs, Robert A. Savitt, and Howard Schwartz for their critiques of the fear-of-being-fat hypothesis. Many of the chapters in this volume were originally presented in the form of lectures, symposiums, and papers at the Department of Psychiatry of St. Luke's-Roosevelt Hospital Center, Albert Einstein College of Medicine, the Downstate Psychoanalytic Institute, and the Center for Psychoanalytic Training and Research of Columbia University College of Physicians and Surgeons. We are in debt to the staffs and faculties of these institutions, especially Drs. John M. Cotton, David M. MacDonald, Byram Karasu, Stanley Heller, Clarice Kestenbaum, Donald I. Meyers, Helen C. Meyers, John W. Rosenberger, and John A. Sours. Drs. Norman Atkins, L. Bryce Boyer, Peter L. Giovacchini, and Samuel Ritvo have acquainted us with their techniques of treatment of patients with preoedipal psychopathology, and, since the early days of the study group, Dr. Cecil Mushatt has most generously shared with us his parallel research in the treatment of psychosomatic disorders.

Introduction

There is a widespread fear of being fat in our culture. In certain individuals it develops into a phobic avoidance of food with self-starvation. When this occurs, the diagnosis of abstaining anorexia nervosa is made. In other individuals the ego structure is different; they attempt self-starvation but cannot control their voraciousness and give in to the impulse to gorge. They then try to reestablish control by vomiting and using laxatives. These are the bulimic anorexics.

Both historically and currently, anorexia nervosa is a generic term that includes the bulimic as well as the abstaining syndromes. Anorexia has been known to medicine for almost three centuries, and its incidence is now increasing. It was first described by Morton in 1689, and he recorded exactly the same signs and symptoms that characterize the syndrome today. Even the pursuit of academic excellence that is ubiquitous among contemporary patients was noted in his 17th century patient. In 1868 the symptom complex was more precisely and carefully detailed by Gull. Articles by Gull (1868, 1873a, b, 1888) in England and Lasegue (1873) in France drew international medical attention to the illness. Subsequent investigators have been impressed with the emotional conflicts involved in the genesis of the symptomatology, with one relatively short exception in the years following Simmonds's publications in 1914 and 1916 on pituitary anorexia. During this period a number of observers, particularly in Germany, erroneously included cases of anorexia nervosa among patients suffering from Simmonds's Disease. Fortunately, this is no longer the case. The differential diagnosis is clear and in most cases unequivocal, both from the standpoint of history and from biochemical studies.*

Since the beginning of the century, the literature on this illness has been voluminous. In 1918 Freud noted a neurosis in pubertal and adolescent girls that "expresses aversion to sexuality by means of anorexia" (p. 106). Anna Freud (1968) noted the resistance aspect of the anorexic's self-starvation. Extensive bibliographic studies can be found in Bliss and Branch (1960), Bruch (1973), Dally (1969), Kaufman and Heiman (1964), Selvini Palazzoli (1978), Sours (1980), M. Sperling (1978), and Thomä (1967). L. Deutsch (1980) has explored the neglect of psychodynamics in his comprehensive book review of biochemical, endocrinological, ecological, sociological, and psychological research in psychosomatics. Summarizing current psychoanalytic theories of

---

*This historical review is the work of Dr. Charles C. Hogan.

1

somatization, he underscores the crucial importance of psychoanalysis in re-search and treatment. Wilson (1980c) recently noted that the technique of analysis of psychosomatic patients is similar to that of analysts (Boyer and Giovacchini 1980, Kernberg 1975, Volkan 1976) who treat nonpsychosomatic patients suffering from a preponderance of preoedipal conflicts. Sperling largely based her hypotheses on the treatment of children and adolescents. Her find-ings have been confirmed, refined, and expanded in the analyses of adolescents (Karol 1980, Mintz 1980) and adults (Wilson 1968, 1971, 1973, 1974, 1980c, d, 1982; Chapters 1 and 2). The structure of the ego, the split in the ego, the archaic superego, separation-individuation, and the defense of projective identi-fication are among the many areas of research that have been explored since Sperling's death in 1973.

All the contributors to this volume are impressed with the heterogeneity of anorexic patients—by the great dynamic, structural, and genetic variability under the coating of a relatively uniform symptomatology. We recognize that constitutional factors of infancy, variations in drive endowment, and gender differences affect each child's development, but we believe it is the domineering and controlling personality of the mother (and/or the father) that profoundly warps and inhibits the normal development of the anorexia-prone child. All the phases of separation-individuation described by Mahler (1968, 1972) are pro-foundly affected by parental attitudes. In no clinical case have we observed the constitutional lack of aggression suggested by Kramer (1974) in anorexia-prone children. On the contrary, ample clinical evidence demonstrates excess drive repression in these patients, which causes the frequent appearance of habits such as teeth-grinding, head-banging, nail-biting, and thumb-sucking.

As far as psychiatric diagnosis is concerned, anorexia nervosa is a neurotic symptom complex that occurs in a variety of character disorders: hysterical, obsessive compulsive, borderline, and, in some cases, conditions close to psy-choses. However, even in the most disturbed cases there is a split in the ego, with areas of relatively intact ego functioning and a capacity for a transference relationship. Sperling differentiates anorexia nervosa from the other psycho-somatic diseases because part of the patient's conflicts are conscious and there is no demonstrable tissue change in an organ system. Although we agree with this distinction, we classify anorexia as a psychosomatic illness because the symptoms are all emotionally caused. That the psyche can stop menstruation is to us patently psychosomatic.

We concur with Thomä's delineation of the syndrome (1967): (1) the age of onset is usually puberty; (2) the patients are predominantly female (although male cases have been reported by Falstein et al. [1956], Mintz [Chapter 13], and Sours [1974]); (3) the reduction in nutritional intake is psychically determined; (4) spontaneous or self-induced vomiting can occur, usually in secret; (5) amenorrhea (which is psychically caused) generally appears either before or, more rarely, after the beginning of the weight loss; (6) constipation, sometimes an excuse for excessive consumption of laxatives, speeds up weight loss; (7) the physical effects of undernourishment are present, and, in severe cases, death may ensue (7 to 15 percent die [Sours 1969]). Hogan added three further obser-vations: (8) there is commonly a tendency toward hyperactivity which may be extreme; (9) in females there is often a disproportionate loss of breast tissue early in the disease; and (10) the symptom complex is often accompanied by or alternates with other psychosomatic symptoms (or psychogenic equivalents such as depressions, phobias, or periods of self-destructive acting out that may include implusive sexual behavior, stealing, or accident-prone behavior). In agreement with Sours (1969, 1974), we have found that all the physical signs and symptoms of anorexia nervosa, including hypothermia, lanugo hair, hypotension, brady-cardia, anemia, and leukocytosis, subside when patients resume normal eating as a result of psychodynamic treatment; however, menstruation may not resume even though the patient's weight returns to normal limits if significant unconscious conflicts about pregnancy have not been resolved.

Throughout this volume, the clinical features, psychodynamics, and technique of treatment of adolescent female and male bulimic anorexics are described; Hogan, Mintz, and Wilson detail the analysis of adult cases. Wilson and Mintz confirm and elaborate on Wilson's hypothesis (Wilson 1982, Wilson and Mintz 1982) that the bulimic's ego, although perfectionistic, does not have the strict control of impulses that is characteristic of the abstainer's. They note that the behavior of the families of bulimic anorexics correlates with the anorexic family psychological profile (Wilson 1980a), but that there is a greater incidence of parental conflict, addiction, and instability. Elaborating on differences between bulimic and abstaining anorexics made by Hogan and Mintz, Wilson contrasts the analysis of a bulimic and an abstaining anorexic, with special emphasis on the countertransference (Chapter 8). Although Hogan notes little difference prognostically, Mintz and Wilson agree with Sours (1980) that the prognosis is more guarded for the chronic bulimic anorexic.

Psychoanalysts cannot offer large numbers of cases owing to the limitations of their practice, but the contributors to this volume are able to report on a broad spectrum. In Part I, Predisposing Factors, Wilson unfolds the many unconscious conflicts that are displaced onto the fear-of-being-fat complex by neurotic and anorexic patients. He underscores the important secondary role of the cultural factors such as fashion and medical diets in augmenting the general cultural fear of being fat. The psychodynamics of anorexia nervosa are related to problems of female psychology to explain both the greater incidence of anorexia in women and the increased incidence of cases in our culture. Wilson then applies an understanding of neurotic family interactions to the technique of treatment of the parents, which is often necessary with adolescent patients.

Attempts to classify anorexia nervosa patients have been made by Crisp (1968), Dally (1969), Bruch (1973), and Sours (1974, 1980). Part II, Psychodynamic Structure, opens with Melitta Sperling's review of classification, concepts, and treatment. Mintz goes on to discuss the clinical syndrome and its diagnostic implications. He subdivides patients into six different categories based on the severity of the presenting clinical symptoms and illustrates his hypothesis with specific case material. Hogan demonstrates the overdetermination of anorexic symptoms, which is ignored by nonanalytic therapists. For the first time in the analytic literature, he unfolds the complex puzzle of the anorexic's object relations. Particularly important is his description of how these patients attempt to control their internal object representations, their external object perceptions, and their impulses, and how this defense of control is manifested in the transference. The difficult problems of transference and countertransference are explored by Hogan in Part III, The Analytic Relationship.

Part IV is a comprehensive section on treatment. Hogan reviews the controversial issues of hospitalization and family therapy, resistances that prevent free association, and the characteristic anorexic lying and stealing. Mintz graphically describes a psychodynamic technique that achieved symptom resolution and characterological change in a hospitalized, emaciated, suicidal patient. Wilson addresses the interpretation of dreams, and Freiman presents the psychoanalysis of an anorexic with a hysterical character structure.

Unlike Sperling, we would include males under the diagnostic category of anorexia. Mintz's and Welsh's chapters show that male anorexics have oedipal and preoedipal fixations and unresolved problems in separation-individuation, severe latent homosexual conflicts and a feminine identification, and the same fear-of-being-fat complex seen in females, which is caused by an identification with the mother's and/or father's fear of being fat.

Part IV closes with Mintz's presentation of an analytic approach to hospital and nursing care in the treatment of anorexia nervosa. In the final section, Special Issues, Sarnoff shows the early derivatives of anorexia, and Mintz details the relationship between starvation and amenorrhea in anorexia, concluding that the refusal to eat can reflect an unconscious refusal to menstruate.

Currently there are four psychotherapeutic approaches to the treatment of anorexia nervosa—*psychotherapy* (Bruch 1961, 1962, 1965, 1970, 1973, 1974, 1975, 1978a), *psychoanalysis* (Mintz 1980; Mushatt 1975, 1980, 1982; Sours 1969; O. Sperling 1978a; Thomä 1967; Wilson, Chapters 1 and 2; Wilson and Mintz 1982), *family systems therapy* (Minuchin et al. 1978; Selvini Palazzoli 1978), and *object relations therapy* (Bettelheim 1975, Cohler 1975). Bruch offers many excellent case presentations and family histories that correlate closely with our clinical case histories. She treated 70 cases psychotherapeutically (1973), rejecting psychoanalysis as a method of treatment. Although Bruch (1975) seems to have become more sanguine about the psychoanalytic treatment of anorexia, we are particularly opposed to her insistence on early weight gain by medical treatment and on hospitalization. Hospitalization should be reserved for true emergencies. As Wilson illustrates (Chapter 8), a chronic anorexic in office analysis may be at less than one-half body weight if there is an ongoing transference relationship. We do not agree with Sours (1980) that "a degree of coercion to eat is necessary if the self-starving anorexic is going to start eating and reverse the hormonal inactivity of the hypothalamic pituitary axis and correct the psychological effects of starvation" (p. 363). Neither do we concur with Bruch (1982) that "the patient's persistent malnutrition creates psychological problems that are biologically, not psychodynamically, determined" (p. 1535).

As regards family systems therapy, Minuchin and his colleagues summarize their results in *Psychosomatic Families: Anorexia Nervosa in Context* (1978), reporting the rapid resolution of severe symptomatology. We feel that serious neurotic problems remain in these patients and that these so-called psychosocial recoveries are probably transference cures. We have the same criticism of Selvini Palazzoli's *Self-Starvation* (1978). We do not agree with her idea that "anorexia nervosa is a special defense structure midway between schizoparanoia and depression" (p. 93), as the majority of anorexic patients are in the neurotic diagnostic category. In our opinion, the successful resolution of symptoms in Bettelheim's and Cohler's (1975) residential treatment of anorexics, which they term object-relations therapy, also is a form of transference "cure" without a resolution of the underlying personality disorder.

The reported use of anti-depressant medication in the treatment of bulimic anorexics has been increasing recently. The contributors of this volume feel that psychoanalysis or analytic psychotherapy represent the most comprehensive approach to the treatment of restrictive and bulimic anorexics because the central focus of these treatments is on the resolution of the underlying personality disorder. Wilson demonstrates (Chapter 18) that while there may be situations in which medication, particularly anti-depressants, are appropriate (i.e. life threatening electrolyte imbalance, severe states of starvation, treatment stalemates or where cost and therapist availability are problems), the use of drugs may be a trade-off with potentially disadvantageous consequences.

On the basis of our belief that all the symptoms of anorexia nervosa are emotionally caused, the main theme of this volume is the psychodynamic treatment of anorexia. From the theoretical point of view, we stress that an understanding of the split in the ego in these patients clarifies metapsychological issues. Although Schur (1955) emphasizes ego regression, we are in agreement with O. Sperling's formulations (1978a) that

> ego regression is not the central problem. Most psychosomatic patients display age adequate ego functions; for example, reality testing, synthetic function, memory and intelligence. Regression is important but not to the extreme of infancy. Even more important . . . is object relationship in all its aspects, not just from the point of view of separation (Schmale 1958) or object loss (Engel 1962). (p. 10)

In anorexics, as in other patients with psychosomatic symptoms, a part of the ego is regressed. It is primitive, magical, and omnipotent, and manifests preoedipal conflicts and fantasies. This split-off, regressed part of the ego is vehemently denied by the patient. In some patients, this split is partly conscious and is described by the patient. It is true that some anorexics starve themselves to the brink of death and appear to deny the possibility of dying; in this ego state, there may be impairment of various ego functions.

In addition to splitting (Boyer and Giovacchini 1980, Kernberg 1975, M. Klein 1946), the anorexic makes extensive use of the defense of projective identification (Bion 1956; Boyer and Giovacchini 1980; Carpinacci et al. 1963; Carter and Rinsley 1977; Cesio 1963, 1973; Giovacchini 1975; Grinberg 1972, 1976, 1979; M. Klein 1955; Ogden 1978; Perestrello 1963; D. Rosenfeld and Mordo 1973; H. A. Rosenfeld 1952; Searles 1965b). As Hogan (Chapters 5 and 7) and Wilson (Chapter 8) demonstrate, the anorexic projects unacceptable aspects of the personality—impulses, self-images, superego introjects—onto other people, particularly the analyst, with a resulting identification based on these projected self-elements. The extreme psychoticlike denial of conflict of the anorexic is caused by primitive projective identification onto others of archaic destructive superego introjects.

As Freud showed us, thorough psychodynamic understanding of one patient is more valuable than limited psychological scrutiny of many patients. In the great majority of our cases, analysis achieved both a clearing of the anorexic symptoms and a resolution of the underlying personality disorder. Time and the vicissitudes of life will show us whether these patients will develop further psychopathology. While the mortality rate for anorexia nervosa is from 1 to 10 percent (Asbeck et al. 1972, Crisp 1979, Sours 1968), none of our patients died from suicide, starvation, or other illness-related causes.

PART I

Predisposing Factors

1
The Fear of Being Fat in Female Psychology

C. PHILIP WILSON, M.D.

Once analytic patients with anorexia nervosa return to their normal weight and begin menstruating again, their complex and pathological body image emerges more clearly. This body image is manifested consciously by an intense fear of being fat. Scrutiny of nonanorexic women in analysis showed a less intensely cathected fear-of-being-fat body-image disturbance, and observation and questioning of normal women in our culture showed that they also have the fear. As a result of their unconscious feminine identification, male homosexuals and men with severe latent homosexual conflicts also have the fear of being fat; in contrast, other men do not evidence the fear. The fear-of-being-fat body image is greatly overdetermined, and clinical material will be presented to demonstrate that conflicts from every level of development—preoedipal, oedipal, adolescent, and adult—are displaced onto and masked by the fear.

It is a central hypothesis of this chapter that anorexia nervosa symptoms are caused by the ego's attempt to defend itself against an overwhelming terror of being fat which has been caused primarily by an identification with a parent or parents with a similar, but less intense, fear. The symptom complex is secondarily reinforced by a general fear of being fat among most women in our culture. "Normal" women readily admit to the fear; no matter how "perfect" a woman's figure may be, if she is told she looks fat, she will have an emotional reaction out of all proportion to reality. On the other hand, if she is told she looks thin or has lost weight, she usually will be inordinately pleased.

The research that produced this hypothesis came from the following sources:

1. My 25 years of analysis and psychotherapy with anorexic patients and the parents of anorexic adolescents in therapy with colleagues. As is well known, anorexics strive to be thin, are afraid of being fat, and, unless treated effectively, go over to phases of obesity. Many have a childhood history of chubbiness or obesity.

2. My many years of supervising the therapy of anorexic patients in private practice and as a member of hospital liaison staffs.

3. The deliberations of the psychosomatic workshop of the Psychoanalytic Association of New York, which in recent years has focused on anorexia nervosa.

4. My presentations to the discussion group of the American Psychoanalytic Association on late adolescent girls.

5. My analyses of obese patients and of one patient with an intense fear of being fat who had an impulse disorder—nail-biting—which dated from early years.

6. My analyses of neurotic women with "normal" figures who had a fear of being fat.

7. My analyses of overt and latent homosexual men who evidenced the fear.

8. In analyzing the fear of being fat, I viewed it partly as a mannerism of speech (see Wilson 1968a). In addition, other research on stone and sand symbolism (Wilson 1967b, 1980b) alerted me to the developmental vicissitudes of the oral incorporative conflicts underlying the fear of being fat.

To my knowledge there has been no in-depth psychoanalytic exploration of the fear of being fat. Bruch (1978a) observes that the fear of being fat in anorexic girls has many different meanings, e.g., sensitivity to criticism, fear of growing up, fear of loss of control, and fear of superconformity. However, Bruch does not use the structural hypothesis or the concept of the unconscious in her formulations.

In a recent book for the lay public, "Fat is a Feminist Issue" (1978), Orbach, a social worker, mentions some psychological meanings of the fear without giving their deeper psychodynamic causes. Orbach concludes that compulsive eating is an individual protest against the inequality of the sexes, but does not substantiate her hypothesis with clinical analytic data, as her experience lies with group therapy. Intimately related to the fear of being fat is the wish to be thin, which has been noted in anorexics by many researchers, among them Bruch (1973b) and M. Sperling (1978). Bruch (1973b) observes that "thin fat people" have the same conflicts as obese patients and that millions of young women in our culture are obsessed with being thin. She also notes (1978a) that often the mothers of anorexics are overly preoccupied with weight and diet. Melitta Sperling (1978) emphasizes the etiologic role that parental attitudes about food and dieting play in predisposing a child to develop anorexic symptoms. However, she does not explore the psychodynamic and genetic meanings of the fear of being fat in normal, neurotic, and anorexic women.

CLINICAL MATERIAL

Anxiety and the affects of shame, guilt, humiliation, and fear associated with the fear of being fat in patients are defended against by the ego with the defense of denial, which in certain cases reaches an almost psychotic intensity. As this primitive defense is analyzed, a large variety of conflicts emerge; some of these are described in the following clinical material. To protect the anonymity of patients, identifying data have been changed. In no instance were patients asked about the fear of being fat (i.e., it was not induced). The first five cases were patients in analysis for neurotic conflicts; the next seven suffered from anorexia nervosa.

Neurotic Patients

CASE 1   *Displacement of Sexual-Moral Conflicts*

Sara, a married woman with a mixed neurosis and intermittent depressions, was 15 lbs. overweight and had fears of being fat. At a stage in her analysis when she had made considerable improvement, she reported a fight with her great aunt. Sara's 11-year-old daughter, dressed in a leotard, was standing on her head to the amused admiration of everyone except the great aunt, who said that the grandniece was too thin to do such exercises. Sara said that her daughter was healthy, that exercise was good for one, and that she herself did similar exercises. The great aunt snapped, "You do *that* in a leotard with your figure! You're *too fat* to do that!" Sara retorted, "You'd do well to do exercises yourself, it would be good for your arthritis." The great aunt rejoined that she got plenty of exercise doing housework. She then asked what size the patient was. The analysand replied that she was a size 9, which she felt was good for a woman with her build. The great aunt said, "I don't believe it. You must be size 11 or more." Sara asked, "Are you calling me a liar?" The great aunt then gave a weak apology which was received in hostile silence.

In her associations, Sara said that she and her daughter had exhibited their genitals by standing on their heads dressed in leotards and that her great aunt had expressed moral disapproval by telling her that she was too fat and that her daughter was too thin. Sara thought her great aunt was jealous of her; she always would try on Sara's new clothes. Angrily, Sara reflected that the great aunt never did anything pleasurable such as calisthenics or tennis. All she ever did was housework, which was tiresome. Sara laughed at how hypocritical women are, since all they talk about is dieting when they really want to be sexy and beautiful. In this case, sexual conflicts and moral disapproval were displaced onto the fear-of-being-fat quarrel.

CASE 2   *Displacement of Heterosexual and Latent Homosexual Conflicts*

Ron, a compulsive married man with intense latent homosexual conflicts, came to analysis for marital conflicts. His father had been killed in a car accident when Ron was six years old. He had grown up dominated by his mother, a teacher, who was overweight, addicted to cigarettes, and preoccupied with the fear of being fat and with diets. He was becoming aware in analysis that he was as controlling and disapproving with his wife and children as his Bible-quoting, hypermoral mother had been with him. He was very proud of his "figure," keeping his weight by diet and exercise at exactly 150 lbs. One day, his wife, a model, burst a seam in her dress and he told her it was because she was too fat. In his session the next day, he said his wife had not gotten over her anger at him for his criticism. He felt his concern with her weight was unreasonable, since she was only 10 lbs. overweight and actually was sexier now than when she was thinner. However, he feared that she would get fewer modeling jobs unless she dieted. He realized his comment about her being fat was "bitchy," that 99 out of 100 women would be upset if someone told them they looked fat. He realized he would have to watch his tongue, which was as mean as his mother's.

In this case, heterosexual and latent homosexual conflicts were displaced onto the fear of being fat. Ron's fear of being fat reflected his identification with his mother.

CASE 3   *Displacement of Anal Conflicts*

Anal components of the fear of being fat were graphically illustrated by the pantaloon dream of Myra, a divorced woman in analysis for a compulsive neurosis. It occurred when she was in the process of analyzing her intense, irrational fear of being fat. In her dream, she had no fresh clothes for her 6-year-old daughter to wear. Hung up to dry on a clothesline were frilly pink pantaloons that her daughter had dirtied. In the dream, Myra was confused with her daughter. There was also a classroom and a feeling that there was no teaching structure. There was an outspoken woman from the Bronx in the dream.

In her associations, Myra said she was proud of her legs, but was ashamed of her hips and thighs, which she felt were fat. The lumpy flesh on her thighs reminded her of indulgence and of lumps of feces. She knew that Titian and Rubens had painted voluptuous women whose figures were like hers. The previous day, she had purchased a sexy leotard cut high on the buttocks at a lingerie store that sold "beautifully made pants and bikinis." When asked why she had said "pants," she replied that the word "panty" was sexy and exciting, and she feared being embarrassed if she said it. She was afraid the analyst and her boyfriend would be disgusted with her if she wore her leotard. An interpretation was made that she felt it was dirty to exhibit her hips and buttocks which were hidden in the dream by pink pantaloons, that she had conflicts about asserting herself as a woman and wanted to hide behind a front of being an innocent little girl.

Myra confirmed the interpretation in a recollection of being on a beach on her honeymoon wearing a bikini. A man had stared at her and she had been afraid she looked fat. She realized now from the man's behavior that he had been admiring her sexy figure. Further associations were to childhood confusion about her mother's vagina and anus—that the area was dirty and mysterious like a cloaca, and that her adult figure was like her mother's (her mother also had had a fear of being fat and anxieties about "lumpy" thighs). In this case, anal conflicts were displaced onto the fear of being fat.

CASE 4   *Displacement of Aggression*

Margaret, a married businesswoman, came to analysis for sexual conflicts and phobias of airplanes, elevators, and subways. A dietician, she was obsessed with weight and dieting, and fantasies of being young and beautiful. She kept her figure zealously on the thin side, 10 lbs. underweight. Her mother had been chronically 15 lbs. overweight, whereas her father, a beautician, had been obsessed with dieting and weight control. In associating to the scales that she weighed herself on daily, Margaret referred to them as her "conscience" and "the law of her father." With the analysis of the transference neurosis in the context of a strong therapeutic alliance, her severe phobic symptoms subsided, but she reported that her 12-year-old daughter was amenorrheic and had symptoms of anorexia.

The analysis of the mother's fear of being fat revealed many conflicts, a most important one being her inability to tolerate any aggression in her daughter. Associations to fat led to a childhood memory of her father telling her she had a "fat lip"; he used to slap her for "sassing him." By the defense of identification with the aggressor, she was repeating the same harsh discipline with her daughter. All roundings of the female breasts, buttocks, or "tummy" in herself or her daughter repelled her. As these and other conflicts that had been displaced onto the fear of being fat were analyzed and the mother could accept her own, as well as her daughter's, femininity, the latter's anorexic symptoms disappeared.

CASE 5   Displacement of Oral Impulses

Linda, a narcissistic 25-year-old female patient in analysis for a severe character disorder, complained of obesity and nail-biting that dated from the time of weaning. Her mother had developed a progressively more incapacitating mental illness culminating in hospitalization when the patient was 10 years old. The mother was of little use to Linda, who described her as always "moping around the house"; the father, maids, and two aunts had raised Linda. As Linda interrupted her intense nail-biting during analytic sessions, fantasies of a breast and nipple, affects of depression and anger, and wishes for maternal love and tenderness emerged in the transference. Linda's intense fear of being fat was out of proportion to her weight, which at most was 15 lbs. above normal. She often woke up at night in panic states, which she relieved by drinking a mixture she concocted of milk and sugar; she recognized its similarity to mother's milk. She was aware that she kept herself overweight to avoid being sexy, which made her anxious. Fears of her oral impulses, nail-biting, and overeating, as well as her shame at the regressive affects and fantasies masked by these oral habits, were all displaced onto her fear of being fat.

Anorexic Cases

CASE 6   Displacement of Sexual Conflicts and Loss of Impulse Control

Sandra, an anorexic patient, came to her session angry. Since beginning analysis, she had gained 20 lbs. and she was expressing wishes to menstruate again, to master her sexual fears, and to get pregnant. She said that she had gone to a cocktail party wearing a revealing dress to show off her "new" figure. The hostess exclaimed, "Why Sandra, you've gained 50 lbs.!" In telling this, Sandra burst into tears of rage, saying, "She is so smug. She has two beautiful children. Her whole life she has been made to feel loved. She has everything. How could she say anything like that!" Actually, the changes in Sandra were startling. Her figure was beginning to be voluptuous. The hostess's hostile and envious comment triggered a dream of a fluffy puppy. Associating to this dream, Sandra thought that she wanted to have a puppy because she was afraid of childbirth.

She realized that her feelings about her hostess were akin to her childhood idealization of her mother. Her mother had had everything—a husband, children, a beautiful home, and everyone's love. When Sandra was five, the family collie had had two puppies and a baby had been born next door. She recovered repressed memories of being frightened on seeing mother's and grandmother's genitals in the bathroom and thinking they had been mutilated by childbirth. She knew that she had denied the female genitals and by displacement had replaced the fear-provoking birth process with fantasies of oral impregnation and birth.

Sandra's oedipal incestuous rivalry with her mother was repeated in her anger with her hostess. Her anorexic gorging had expressed fantasies of oral impregnation, and her vomiting, of giving birth. Her fear of being fat masked fears of being voluptuous and sexy, which could cause her to be impregnated; and, to her, impregnation meant vaginal mutilation. The hostess's comment seemed to contain the critical idea that Sandra had lost all control over herself and/or might be pregnant. Sandra did look beautiful, voluptuous, and feminine, which was in sharp contrast to her previous anorexic figure. In this case, sexual conflicts and loss of impulse control were displaced onto the fear of being fat.

CASE 7   *The Wish to Be Ethereal*

In anorexics, the wish to be ethereal generally accompanies, and is hidden by, the fear of being fat. This wish was expressed graphically by Gina, a married anorexic woman. She dreamed that a doctor gave her a pill. Then she was in a garden with Mrs. S. and a plain-looking girl wearing a sunbonnet. In her associations, the patient thought that she was jealous of Mrs. S., a wealthy, beautiful, divorced, jet-set woman whose teenage daughter was a "mess," unorganized and inhibited. The daughter had large doelike eyes. In the dream, only the girl's face could be seen. The lack of a body reminded Gina of how she had wanted to be a beautiful, ethereal child with no body and no fat. As a child, she had studied ballet. The bonnet reminded her that she wanted to buy a winter hat. The child made her think that her husband would "go bananas" about a baby; she would be jealous of a baby if she had one. The pill made her think of my giving her a magical cure, of an oral impregnation. As a child, she used to want a pill that would give her complete knowledge of everything. The night before, Gina had avoided intercourse; she prevented pregnancy by her anorexic amenorrhea. She kept her figure at around 90 lbs., although her normal weight was 120 lbs. People often asked her if she was a dancer as she had a gliding, graceful, lighter-than-air walk. Once, when crying silently, she got up from the couch and took a Kleenex from a box on a table by my analytic chair and resumed her position on the couch in such a swift, graceful, synchronous, silent fashion that if I had not been looking at her, I would not have noticed her. Even after seeing her, it was as if it had not happened. She was ethereal.

The dream wish was to divorce her husband and become a wealthy, beautiful, pleasure-loving princess who could have a magical oral pregnancy. Among the other meanings of the dream was the wish to be a doelike, innocent, ethereal child with no fleshly desires, no body, and no fat.

CASE 8   *Fear of Losing Control and of a Disfiguring Pregnancy*

The opposite of the wish to be ethereal was expressed by the dream of Wendy, another anorexic woman. In the dream, she was looking at her mother-in-law, who was dressed in a brassiere and panties. Someone referred to her as a fat pig. Her associations were that her mother-in-law was an overweight, sensual woman. The dream reminded her of how, at age five, she would watch, fascinated, as her mother dressed and undressed. A new baby had been born next door; she had adored the baby, but had not understood how pregnancy or birth occurred. She felt that the "fat pig" represented her terror of losing all controls—particularly her fears of multiple pregnancies, of being blown up fat by pregnancy.

Wendy was another anorexic who gorged and vomited, and she had long since realized that she was trying to get a magical pregnancy in her eating, that her full belly was a pregnancy, and that her vomiting was a giving-birth fantasy. There were many other meanings to this dream, an important one being her childhood idea that women had periodic seizures of uncontrollable sexual arousal like animals. Two conflicts were masked by the fear of being fat: a fear of losing all controls and a fear of a disfiguring multiple-birth pregnancy.

CASE 9   *Displacement of Menstruation Fears*

Cathy, an anorexic woman, had the following dream: "I started my periods, but realized that the red color was not from the vagina, but came from a red lollipop I had eaten."

The previous night, Cathy had been depressed and wished she could get her periods back. In her association, she recalled at six years of age finding wrapped, stained menstrual pads in the bathroom and asking her mother about them. She thought they had something to do with her older sister, who had been sick. Her mother replied that she would have to tell Cathy's older sister to be more careful, but she did not explain menstruation. Cathy then recalled having heavy menstrual flows in adolescence and not seeing a doctor until she was dangerously anemic.

Interpretations were made of her intense denial of fears about menstruation, which to her meant bleeding to death and castration. She noted that she loved to eat red cherry candies. A dream wish was that the periods were caused by something she ate. She was beginning to understand that her denial derived from her mother's denial. At this stage of her analysis, her fear of being fat was less intense; she wanted her menses and was gaining weight. She was beginning to be aware that an aspect of her fear of being fat was her fear of menstruating (i.e., that she had displaced the latter fear onto the former one).

CASE 10   *Breast-Penis Fantasies*

Another preoedipal fantasy masked by the fear of being fat is that of the breast–penis, which is illustrated by the following dream of Karen, an anorexic analysand: "My boyfriend made love to me. I was turned on, but his penis turned into a celery stalk. It was a long thing; there were no testicles. He was lying next to me making love, then his penis went down." This dream occurred at a point in her analysis when Karen was trying to spend time on her own without clinging to her boyfriend or to food, which she substituted for him. The previous night she had returned home late from an art class to find that her boyfriend was still at his office working. Although hungry, she waited to eat dinner with him and was angry with him when he came home.

Although she had intended to have intercourse, she picked a fight with him and they went to bed angry. Other associations were to "freezing" when doctors examined her as a child. The celery stalk reminded her of the penis of a horse she had seen mounting a mare when she was six years old. She knew they were doing something sexual, but was not sure what it was, what the sexual organs were, or whether the vagina or anus was entered.

The interpretation was made that, as a child, she had feared mutilation by a tremendous phallus that would enter her a tergo as she had witnessed with the horses, and that she covered this fear with the wish that the penis was something to be eaten. In trying to stop relating to her boyfriend as if he were a female with a phallus, Karen dreamt of the breast–phallus (the penis turning into celery).

Parenthetically, I (1967a,b) have found that when a patient dreams of a penis-like object that does not include testicular representations, the regression is to early (18–30 months) developmental levels, to a time before the child's ego can conceptualize the functions of the penis and testicles or the vagina, tubes, and uterus. The fantasies are oral and anal. This is the early phallic phase described by Galenson and Roiphe (1976).

CASE 11   Penis-Envy Conflicts

Donna, a married anorexic woman, had a nightmare in which a big penis was being thrust down on her face. Her associations were to her father having the money and controlling her mother; everyone had to go to him for everything and she hated him and having to take money from him. Her fantasy was that mother did not love her father, but was forced to have sex with him to please him and for the sake of the children, i.e., mother had to "suck father off."

Donna avoided intercourse, a pleasure (something fat) that her strict conscience forbade her. She had sex to please her husband and often avoided intercourse by fellating him. However, fellatio disgusted and frightened her as it revived repressed incestuous fantasies about her father's and brother's genitals, which she had frequently seen as a child, particularly in the bathroom where there was no privacy. The forbidden oral sucking fantasies associated with fellatio were repressed into the fear of being fat.

As Grossman and Stewart (1976) point out in discussing penis envy:

> The meaning of the discovery of the "anatomical distinction" will depend upon a complex variety of preparatory experiences. . . . The child's cognitive and libidinal levels will naturally play a part in his interpretation of this new information. To narcissistically oriented patients, "penislessness" can at any time in the psychosexual development become a prime example of deprivation, and they experience this in the same way as when they were eighteen months old. (pp. 206–207)

Analysis revealed that, like other anorexics, Donna had a body-phallus equation. She said that she knew she was vain and proud of her thin figure, straight back, and small waist. She did many exercises to keep in perfect shape.

Anorexia ablated her breasts, hips, and buttocks. The analysis of dreams in which she beat up her husband uncovered an identification with her father, who frequently had exhibited his genitals, walking around the house in boxer shorts and swimming in the nude. In contrast, the mother had been very modest. Extending M. Sperling's (1978) finding that the anorexic woman sees father as a rival for mother's love, my research shows that the anorexic woman envies and desires father's body and magical phallus in order to gain mother's love. In the female unconscious, fat equals feminine and thin equals masculine, so the wish to be thin and the fear of being fat mask conflicts about penis envy.

CASE 12   Body-Phallus Fantasies

Preoedipal and oedipal fantasies about the penis were condensed in the dream of Laura, a married anorexic woman: in the dream, a great snake slithered down a flight of stairs. That night, Laura had had intercourse with her husband on top. She preferred the superior position as it gave her control. She was at a stage in her analysis where her anorexic symptoms had been resolved but she was still amenorrheic. Her associations were to her husband being a beast; men, including her father and analyst, had everything and got away with everything while women had to stay in the home. She thought of how proud she was of her new figure; she could do all sorts of tricks with her body in intercourse. For example, when she was on top, she could writhe her body and drive her husband wild. She recalled a pet snake she had had as a child.

The night of the dream, Laura had not been orgastic and had not communicated with her husband during intercourse. The dream had been precipitated by the fact that her husband was on top in intercourse, which allowed him to be the snake. This had aroused castration fear and provoked preoedipal and oedipal penis envy and body-phallus fantasies about being the snake herself.

Laura had studied and loved ballet as a child, as was the case with many of the anorexics I analyzed. One anorexic whose therapy I supervised was a professional ballerina. All anorexics are very conscious of their figures and constantly exercise, work out at health clubs, and engage in strenuous athletics. These pseudosublimations reflect their body-phallus conflicts. Similar, but less intensely cathected, preoccupations with the figure, weight, and exercise are the obsessive concern of women in our culture who fear being fat.

Dr. Ira Mintz provides confirmation of my hypothesis about the female's displacement of conflict onto the fear of being fat with the case he presents in Chapter 17.

DISCUSSION

Conflicts Displaced onto the Fear of Being Fat

In the neurotic cases presented above, sexual conflicts, fears of oral and anal impulses, fears of regression, and a superego prohibition against facing these conflicts were displaced onto the fear of being fat. Similar, but more intense, preoedipal and oedipal conflicts were displaced onto the fear of being fat in the anorexic cases. Conflicts from every developmental phase can be repressed and displaced onto the fear of being fat.

In discussing this chapter, Dr. Stanley Friedman (1978) cited a novel, *Final Payments* (1978), by Mary Gordon, where a woman has incestuous conflicts about exhibiting her breasts to her father; in self-punishment, she destroys the beauty of her breasts by overeating, eventually becoming depressed and bulimic. Friedman's confirmatory case material included a woman who, at age nine, had fellated a 12-year-old boy who ejaculated in her mouth. She fantasized that the seeds remained inside her and, in adolescence, awaited every period with the anxiety that she might be pregnant. Her weight shifted radically. Her fear of being fat concealed a wish to become pregnant by her brother, and she made herself sexually unattractive by excess body fat. Another patient was convinced that a weight of 129 lbs. meant being female, while 131 lbs. meant being male, the extra fat concealing a fantasied penis. The masturbation fantasy of another woman analysand was that she was in a Nazi brothel where the soldiers only liked fat women so that all sorts of tempting foods were made available. To eat and become fat meant to be sexually out of control, a prostitute.

Mintz (personal communication, 1978) noted an anorexic for whom the folds of fatty flesh in the inner aspect of her thighs symbolized a penis. She starved herself to get rid of her conflict. M. Sperling (1978) and Goitein (1942) noted that anorexia nervosa can defend against prostitute fantasies and wishes. One anorexic whose therapy I supervised worked as a prostitute when she was bulimic; when fasting, she withdrew from people (men) in a self-imposed punishment. Likewise, in nonanorexic women, sexual fantasies and conflicts can be avoided or gratified depending on the amount of weight the patient wants to gain.

As the clinical cases show, the fear of being fat masks fears of loss of impulse control. Control is a central symptom in anorexia, as M. Sperling (1978) and Bruch (1978a) have also noted. Diagnostically, anorexia nervosa is a symptom complex that is found in a wide variety of pregenitally fixated character disorders (M. Sperling 1978). Since the fear-of-being-fat syndrome has been found in normal, neurotic, and anorexic women, from one point of view there is a continuum of cases. However, along with Mintz (Chapter 4) and Sours (1980), I feel that although some patients present a mixed clinical picture, abstaining anorexics usually can be differentiated from bulimics. For example, the bulimics have a perfectionistic, but less strict, superego structure than the abstainers. Furthermore, the bulimic ego is deficient in impulse control so that it is periodically overwhelmed by impulses to binge, purge, use drugs, alcohol, and cigarettes addictively, and act out. There many other difficulties associated with impulse control, e.g., thumb-sucking, phases of obesity, head-banging, nail-biting, nose-picking, and enuresis. The persistent use of dangerously large amounts of laxatives occurs in certain patients. Others have a history of neurotic childhood vomiting, encopresis, anal masturbation, and hair-pulling and hair-eating. In certain cases, in lieu of such habits, there is excessive good behavior interrupted by isolated episodes of loss of impulse control. As with other psychosomatic disorders (M. Sperling 1968a, Wilson 1968b), when anorexic symptoms subside in treatment, acting out becomes a problem as fears of acting out are displaced onto the fear of being fat.

As illustrated in Case 3, the fear of being fat covers anal-phase conflicts. Kaplan (1976) feels that, in latency, there is a greater tendency toward oral and tactile contact in girls than in boys. Ritvo (1976b) attributes the probably universal feminine attitude of concealment of menarche and all sexual feelings and fantasies to the more powerful repression of the pregenital, and particularly anal, strivings in the girl than in the boy. An unconscious purpose of anorexic self-starvation is the repression of any manifestation of anal impulses. Sours (1974) noted the analization of the ego (Sandler and Joffe 1965) in seriously disturbed anorexia nervosa patients. In my experience, such patients try to stop having bowel movements by their anorexic constipation; when they become thin enough, they stop perspiring, which they equate with smelling. Their amenorrhea eliminates the menses that they unconsciously confuse with excretory anal processes.

The fear of being fat hides a fear of regression in the female. Anorexics in particular are stoically proud. Although their emaciation is an appeal for sympathy, pity, and feeding, they vehemently deny any such emotions and wishes. It is an advance in analysis when they can admit to these feelings. In contrast, neurotics openly say, "I am guilty; half the time I behave like a baby." The fear of being fat is a denial of neurotic and normal dependency needs.

Male Collusion with the Anorexic Female

Certain fathers, husbands, and boyfriends of anorexic females are strongly attracted to the pathological personality and body image of the anorexic female, whom they unconsciously confuse with the idealized, spiritual mother. These compulsive, anally fixated men have intense latent homosexual conflicts. For example, an analysand knew intellectually that his girlfriend was anorexic, but shared her fear of being fat. They dieted and exercised together, and he criticized her frequently if she was less than perfect in her behavior or diet.

In the past, he had been attracted to two types of women: voluptuous, sexy females, whom he saw as exciting but low class; and thin, spiritual women, whom he idealized but with whom he was sexually and emotionally inhibited. In his analysis, prior to a holiday separation, he reported a nightmarish dream in which he chased a female ghost. There was a bad smell. His associations were to his mother, who had been emaciated and cadaverous when she was dying of cancer. He had been horrified at her smell when he visited her in the hospital. Talking of smells reminded him that he was repulsed by female smells, particularly menstrual smells. He had arranged it so that he and his girlfriend used the bathroom at specified, separate times and he insisted that she be very neat and clean. Her anorexic symptoms had developed after they had lived together for a year, and it was evident that his neurotic, compulsive fear of being fat had helped to precipitate them. In his transference, separation from the analyst aroused fears that, like his mother, his analyst would die and desert him. However, the dream ghost he was chasing represented the idealized mother-analyst who had no body, flesh, or smells.

Two fathers of anorexic girls told me that their first serious love affairs were with young women who became anorexic in the course of the relationship. Neither of these fathers could face the developing sexuality of their adolescent daughters; unconsciously, they wanted their daughters to be thin and spiritual. The fear of being fat can mask unresolved incestuous conflicts that interfere with subsequent interfamilial and heterosexual object relationships.

Superego and Ego Ideal

I am in agreement with Blum (1976) that the female ego and superego are different from, but not inferior to, those of the male. Analysis of the fear of being fat shows that one important difference is caused by the demands of the woman's maternal ego ideal, which confronts the feminine ego with a longer and more complex maturational process than is the case in males. I would extend Blum's conclusion that "conflicts between the maternal ego ideal and infanticidal impulses are ubiquitous" (p. 189) to include conflicts about homicidal impulses toward all objects. Freud's observation (1932) that the female has the more difficult task of changing her object choice from mother to father to lover is also borne out by this research.

Anorexics have a harsh, punitive superego. As Ritvo (1976a) and I (1978) have emphasized, the anorexic's rage with the mother, which was initially rooted in repressed, sadomasochistic oral conflicts, has been externalized and displaced onto food. Because the parents of anorexics are overconscientious people with strict superegos, they legislate against the expression of emotion in their children (Bruch 1978a, Minuchin et al. 1978, M. Sperling 1978, Wilson 1977). Thus, anorexics fail to internalize a good object representation of the mother and of the self. It is the introjected bad mother (Wilson 1978)—and, by extension, other objects—whom the anorexic tries to starve by fasting or incorporate by gorging. One anorexic expressed it graphically in a parapraxis. She intended to say that when she visited her polio-crippled older sister, she ate a normal meal; instead she said that she "ate her sister." In her association, she said that when she gorges, she gets rid of her sister (and other objects, including the analyst).

The reason that the most frequent time of onset of anorexia is adolescence is because this phase demands final separation and individuation. The anorexia-prone girl develops too strict a superego. As M. Sperling (1978) points out, there is a shift from a positive to a negative Oedipus complex, along with a regression, in the girl. This regression is not only to preoedipal, but also to preadolescent latency, levels of functioning and fantasy.

Twenty-five years of experience in the analysis of anorexic patients and the parents of anorexics has shown me that the predisposition to develop anorexia is established in the mother-child relationship in the earliest years of life (Wilson 1971, 1980a; M. Sperling 1978). The mother uses food to control the child and may control feeding so much that her children never learn to cook.

The Metapsychology of the Fear-of-Being-Fat Complex*

In psychodynamic terms, the metapsychology of this complex is rooted in unresolved sadomasochistic oral-phase conflicts that result in an ambivalent

---

*I am indebted to Dr. Howard Schwartz (1980) who restated my findings in a meta-psychological framework which I have elaborated on in these formulations.

relationship with the mother. Fixation to this phase of development, with its accompanying fears of object loss, is caused by maternal and/or paternal overcontrol and overemphasis on food and eating functions as symbols of love. This unresolved conflict influences each subsequent maturational phase so that anal, oedipal, and later developmental conflicts also are unresolved.

The genetic influences on this complex are parental conflicts about weight and food specifically, and about aggressive and libidinal expression generally. In addition, the parents tend to be compulsive, moralistic, and perfectionistic, significantly denying the impact on the developing child of their exhibitionistic toilet, bedroom, and other behavior. Other genetic factors are cultural, societal, and general medical influences, as well as secondary identifications with women and/or men who share the fear-of-being-fat complex.

From an economic point of view, the unremitting pressure of repressed, unsublimated aggressive and libidinal drives, conflicts, and fantasies is a central issue for these inhibited patients. The terror of loss of control (i.e., of becoming fat) comprises the conscious fear of overeating and the unconscious fear of incorporating body parts, smearing or eating feces, bleeding to death, mutilating or being mutilated, or masturbating and/or becoming nymphomaniacal, which could result in orgastic pleasure. All these feared drive eruptions are masked by the fear-of-being-fat complex and held in check by the terror of retaliatory punishment from the archaic, sadistic superego.

From a structural point of view, ego considerations are central. In the preoedipal years, the ego of the anorexia-prone (fat-phobic) child becomes split. One part develops in a pseudonormal fashion: cognitive functions, the self-observing part of the ego, adaptive capacities, and other ego functions appear to operate normally. These children are often described as "perfect" and have excellent records in school. The ego represses, denies, displaces, externalizes, and projects conflicts onto the fear-of-being-fat complex. In many cases, conflicts are displaced onto habits such as thumb-sucking, enuresis, encopresis, nail-biting, head-banging, and hair-pulling. In other cases, there is a concomitant displacement and projection of conflict onto actual phobic objects. In some patients, anorexia alternates with other psychosomatic disease syndromes, such as ulcerative colitis. This split in the ego manifests itself in the intense, psychotic-like denial of the displaced wishes, conflicts, and fantasies. In other words, the split-off neurotic part of the personality is denied in the fear-of-being-fat complex.

From an adaptive point of view, conflicts at each maturational and libidinal phase are denied, displaced, and projected onto the fear of being fat. Conflicts in separation-individuation (Mushatt 1975, 1980, 1982) are paramount and are denied by the parents and developing child. Normal adaptive conflict is avoided and denied. Many parents of anorexics raise them in an unreal, overprotected world. Perfectionistic parents impair the ego's decision-making functions with their infantilizing intrusions into every aspect of their child's life. Age-appropriate activities are not fostered and encouraged by these parents. There is an effort completely to deny any psychological conflict in the obsessive fear of being fat and wish to be thin.

Figure 1 is a simplified outline of the application of the fear-of-being-fat complex to anorexia nervosa.

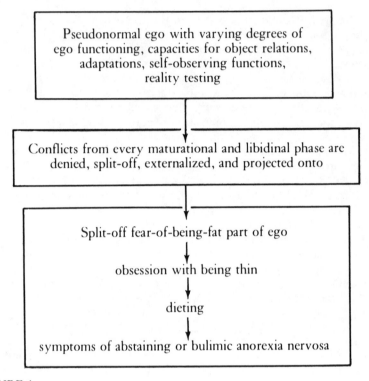

FIGURE 1.

Body Image

The fear of being fat is a conscious manifestation of unconscious body-image conflicts. Freud (1923) stated that the ego is first and foremost a body ego, the projection of a surface. The surface of the mother's breast—and, by extension, her figure—is projected in the anorexic's body image. The fear of being fat reflects the terror of oral sadistic incorporation of the breast, mother, and, later, other objects. The average expectable environment of a female in our culture offers the fear of being fat as a normative value that reinforces the developing girl's body-image conflicts. The intensity and irrationality of the fear of being fat points to its primitive ontogenetic source; analysis reveals its primary process roots. A graphic example is the anorexic's ambivalent all-or-nothing fear of being totally fat or totally thin, which can result in psychosomatic suicide by starvation.

As Freud (1923) emphasized, the perception of pain is important for the development of a normal body image. Because of parental psychopathology, the anorexia-prone child is overindulged and the ego does not develop sufficient capacity to delay impulse gratification. Parental oral conflicts disturb the important role of the mouth and hand (Hoffer 1950) in differentiating the self from the nonself. Preoedipal and oedipal primal-scene experiences, and other overstimulating parent-child sensory interactions whose significance is completely denied, severely distort the significant role of visual perception of the face and genitals (Greenacre 1958) in the development of a normal body image. The strict superego of the mother and/or father limits and warps the normal autoerotic and playful body investigations that build up early self- and object representations (Jacobson 1964) and aid in differentiation of self and nonself (Fenichel 1945b). The parents' need to control and retain the child as an infantile object prevents normal separation-individuation. Their intolerance of aggressive and libidinal drive manifestations also prevents normal separation-individuation in the anal phase. The histories of my cases correlate with and confirm Sours's (1974) observations that the details of the child's development from 16 to 25 months, Mahler's rapprochement phase (1972), are entirely lacking. The oppositional behavior and negativism so commonly seen from 24 to 36 months (Mahler and Furer 1968) are likewise absent.

The preoedipal component of the body-phallus identification is foremost; overt homosexuality is infrequent among female anorexics. For nonanorexic women, parallel, but less intensely cathected, developmental body-image conflicts underlie the fear of being fat. Preoedipal penis envy and pregnancy fears, as well as the maternal ego ideal, are particularly important in the fear-of-being-fat body-image disturbance.

The denial of time and aging in anorexia is startling, but there are comparable conflicts in most women. For instance, because of her narcissistic investment in looking young and beautiful, a woman executive avoided pointing out to subordinates, when necessary, that she had 20 years of business experience.

The female body-image conflicts manifested in the fear of being fat are particularly heightened during adolescence, which recapitulates earlier developmental conflicts with the added libidinal and aggressive manifestations of puberty. Parental intolerance of the latter makes adolescence the prime time for the emergence of anorexia. In comparison to males, females must undergo more complicated physical and emotional changes (Freud 1932, Blum 1976); they are subject to the combined pressures of the maternal ego ideal, greater dependency needs, and oedipal and preoedipal penis envy, all of which contribute to the universal female fear of being fat.

Anorexics often are admired and envied by their female friends, who unconsciously have a similar, but less intensely cathected, body-image conflict. Most developing females share aspects of this body image and the fantasy of being thin. Thus, at all maturational phases, the developing girl has potential secondary identifications with women who fear being fat. This fear is part of the average expectable female environment.

Social and Cultural Factors

Another factor in the apparent increase in the fear of being fat and anorexia nervosa in our culture is the breakdown of established societal institutions and attitudes that have afforded the female definite paths for identity formation, impulse control, and sublimation. Faced with complete freedom to leave home, go away to college, etc., the anorexia-prone girl has no choice but to regress and starve herself. This social anomie is a precipitating, but not a root, cause of anorexia. These cultural and societal changes have resulted in much earlier puberty for the female, with ensuing conflict.

In recent decades, there have been cultural factors pressuring women to overvalue thinness and weight loss. Cultural attitudes about female pulchritude in 18th-century France were expressed by Jean-Anthelme Brillat-Savarin (1825, pp. 228-229), a diet specialist of the era, in *The Philosopher in the Kitchen*: "Every thin woman wishes to put on weight; this is an ambition that has been confided to us a thousand times." He clearly stated that society expected women to have full figures and that thin figures could not be disguised by fashionable dresses. He recommended fattening diets.

Otto Sperling (1978b) suggests that Victorian women, particularly young pregnant women, were encouraged to eat because of the fear of tuberculosis, for which there was no cure; this may have contributed to the cultural acceptance of a full, voluptuous female figure. Recent medical research, which has emphasized the dangers of obesity in relation to diseases such as hypertension and coronary artery pathology, has resulted in the proliferation of reducing diets. The greater participation of women in athletics also sets a premium on a thin figure. In its extreme, this has even led to attempts to masculinize the female figure by hormone treatment for superior athletic performance. Another cultural force is female fashion trends. Women's fashion magazines emphasize the thin figure; some models actually have anorexic figures. A pertinent comment was made by a doctor who resigned his job at a Florida resort health spa. He said there was no point in his work because the women were in two groups: the obese females who weighed 250 lbs. and lost 10 lbs. only to put it on again; and those who weighed 100-110 lbs. and came to lose 5 lbs. He said this latter group was obsessed with the fear of being fat and actually did not have to lose weight at all.

Another important cultural factor is the changing value that society gives to motherhood. As Ritvo (1976a) points out, "when a woman's fertility and childbearing functions had high economic value, her prestige and worth depended very much on her fertility . . . instead children are an economical burden" (pp. 135-137). Ritvo (1976b) emphasizes that the ages of menarche and of beginning sexual relations for girls have become progressively lower. Jawetz (1976) notes that this change has given girls less and less time to resolve earlier conflicts before having to deal with problems of emotional and sexual intimacy, a situation to which she attributes the current increase in bulimic and anorexic eating disturbances. She (1976) feels that the marked preponderance of eating disturbances in adolescent girls, rather than boys, points to a difference in their psychosexual development, which for the girls involves a genital (vaginal) incorporation that may revive an earlier unresolved oral conflict. Jawetz (1976) also feels that females' greater need of mothering, society's encouragement of female-male competition, various environmental changes such as the loss of objective standards of conduct, and the opening up of many different life choices confront adolescent girls with difficult maturational problems from which many retreat by way of eating disorder symptoms. It may be that the fear of being fat in our culture masks a basic conflict in women between their biological drive toward motherhood and its diminished societal value.

Henry and Yela Lowenfeld (1972) observe that when the environment becomes more permissive, the symptoms of hysteria are replaced by a multitude of character neuroses and psychosomatic manifestations. The increased incidence of anorexia nervosa confirms their hypothesis, as it is most often when the adolescent girl leaves the safety of home for the liberated atmosphere of camp or college that she becomes anorexic.

We have no accurate statistics on the incidence of anorexia in other cultures. Psychoanalytic anthropologists L. Bryce and Ruth Boyer (personal communication, 1980) note that in 24 years with the Apaches and during various periods with Northern Athabascan Indians and Eskimos in Alaska, they have never seen a case of anorexia nervosa or anything even tending in that direction. Whether these Indians' and Eskimos' preference for well-padded women is in any way contributory, they could not say. Bernal Y Del Rio and his colleagues at the Puerto Rican Institute of Psychiatry (personal communication, 1979) note that anorexia is rare in Puerto Rico, where a rounded, "zoftig" female figure is culturally accepted and admired. Cultural institutions and social and religious organizations offer the developing adolescent stable models for identification.

As regards healthy feminine self-assertion: in spite of the gains achieved by the women's liberation movement a double standard still prevails. The father who manifests intense aggressive or sexual behavior may be referred to as a "bastard" or a "son of a bitch" with grudging admiration. There is often a more critical attitude toward comparable female behavior. The fear of being fat masks a fear of identifying with healthy aggressive sexual aspects of the mother's behavior which are pejoratively referred to as "being bitchy." This conflict is reflected in the anorexic's dream of her mother-in-law as a pig in Case 8.*

Displaced onto and hidden by the fear of being fat are the female's normal and neurotic fantasies of being spiritually and morally beautiful, as well as sexually exciting and physically beautiful. In anorexics, these fantasies are vehemently denied. This was highlighted by the anorexic's dream of being ethereal in Case 7. In the postoedipal behavior of anorexia-prone girls, we can see the manifestation of these fantasies. Similar, but less intensely cathected, fantasies underlie the fear of being fat in women in general.

Successful analysis results in a basic change in the female's fear of being fat and body image. Bruch (1973b), although utilizing a different technique of treatment, does emphasize that "a realistic body image concept is a precondition for recovery in anorexia nervosa" (p. 90). This change is most dramatic in anorexics. Dreams of being fat or thin do not usually appear until the later stages of analysis. The self-observing function of the ego is markedly strengthened in analysis. Nonanorexic women show a remarkably rigid and persistent need to have a thin figure even when they have a husband or lover who likes them just the way they are and with whom they are orgastic. In fact, it appears that the body-image conflict expressed in the fear of being fat cannot be changed in women in our culture except by analysis. The change in the body image of anorexics in analysis is a gradual process. The most crucial factor is the transference neurosis, where the analyst modifies the superego and strengthens the ego, particularly its self-observing functions.

---

*See Chapter 2 for an in-depth discussion of the mother-child relationship in families of anorexics.

"Fat Phobia" as a Diagnostic Term

My research indicates that "phobic fear of being fat" or "fat phobia" should replace "anorexia nervosa" as a diagnostic term. These patients do not suffer from lack of hunger, but from the opposite—insatiable hunger (Sours 1980, M. Sperling 1978, Thomä 1967). Names have powerful unconscious meanings; to use a word that implies a lack of appetite when the true state of affairs is the opposite is unscientific and misleading. The defenses of the ego in these patients—denial, displacement, externalization, and projection—are the same as in the traditional phobias and, indeed, many are phobic.

The major difference is in the nature of the phobic object, which in the usual phobia is not ingested (incorporated). However, the psychodynamics of acute anorexia, in which there is total terror of eating and an avoidance of food, are similar to those of phobias. Common to both are suicidal conflicts when patients are forced to face and master the phobia. Of course, in the phobic refusal to eat, the anorexic is starving herself (the internalized object) to death, whereas the patient with a traditional phobia is not bringing about total self-destruction. Recent research (Sarnoff 1970) concludes that it is only in the first half of the third year that symbols with unconscious meanings appear and that the child becomes capable of producing true phobias. Wurmser (1980), an authority on addictions, emphasizes the phobic core of addictions with claustrophobia seen as the primary phobia. He sees the use of drugs as counterphobic and he notes that another impersonal agent, food, can be used as a problem solver. Wurmser's formulations confirm my hypothesis that anorexia nervosa is a food phobia. In anorexic families the mother and/or father's fear-of-being-fat syndrome from the earliest years causes a continuous displacement and projection of conflicts onto food and the eating process which profoundly warps and distorts this aspect of the child's reality. In fat-phobic patients, conflict in the oral phase results in a displacement and projection of conflicts with the mother (breast) onto food and the eating process. Traditional phobias develop at later maturational phases when the ego is more mature, there is a choice of phobic objects, and the object relationships with parents are more advanced. However, in both types of phobia, aggressive and libidinal drives, fantasies, and conflicts are split off and projected onto the phobic object.

The retention of "anorexia nervosa" as a diagnostic term seems likely at present, but its gradual replacement by "phobic fear of being fat" or "fat phobia" seems inevitable. Howard L. Schwartz (1980) uses the term "fat phobia" in his confirmatory discussion of my research. For the purposes of this book, readers will gain a deeper psychodynamic understanding of these patients if they substitute "phobic fear of being fat" or "fat phobia" for "anorexia nervosa."

SUMMARY

Analytic work with anorexic female patients focuses on their intense fear-of-being-fat body-image disturbance. Comparable, but less intensely cathected, psychodynamics are found in neurotic female analysands. These findings, coupled with nonanalytic therapy with women, lead to the conclusion that most women in our culture have a fear of being fat.

The universal prevalence of this fear in our culture among women, but not men, is caused by gender-based developmental differences in the superego and maternal ego ideal. The markedly greater incidence of anorexia nervosa in women is caused primarily by the female's unique superego structure.

The body-image disturbance reflected in the fear of being fat in women is greatly overdetermined. Illustrative dreams and clinical material have been presented to show the drives, fantasies, conflicts, and defensive structures that are masked by the fear. Important determinants are fears of: (1) loss of impulse control; (2) regression; and (3) undoing the ego's defenses of denial, repression, and displacement, with the danger of the emergence of oral, anal, and oedipal conflicts.

The predisposition to develop anorexia is established in the mother-infant relationship. Mothers of anorexics have an intense fear of being fat and use food to control their children. A secondary reinforcement of anorexia comes from women in the environment who have less intensely cathected fear-of-being-fat body-image conflicts. The fear-of-being-fat concept demonstrates that there is a continuum of anorexic cases. However, the abstainers should be differentiated from the bulimics because of their different ego structures.

Various societal and cultural factors promoting thinness—e.g., the medical danger of obesity, increased athletics for women, and the female fashion industry's emphasis on a slender figure—appear to play a significant role in the fear of being fat among women in our culture.

Anorexia nervosa is misleading as a diagnostic term, as patients with this syndrome suffer from fears of being overwhelmed by unconscious impulses, including hunger. "Phobic fear of being fat" or "fat phobia" should replace "anorexia nervosa" as a diagnostic term. A psychodynamic understanding of the fear of being fat brings anorexia nervosa into connection with normal and pathological female psychology and is crucial for the analysis of this life-threatening disease.

2
The Family Psychological Profile and Its Therapeutic Implications

C. PHILIP WILSON, M.D.

Psychoanalytic research with the families of 50 anorexia nervosa patients[*] revealed a parental psychological profile that appears to be etiologic in establishing a personality disorder in the children which later manifests itself as anorexia nervosa. Melitta Sperling's analysis (1978) of anorexic children and their mothers laid the groundwork for this research with her finding that the predisposition for anorexia nervosa is established in early childhood by a disturbance in the mother-child symbiosis. Four of the six features of the psychological profile correlate with parental attitudes and behavior described by Bruch (1978a) in 50 cases and by Minuchin et al. (1978) in 53 cases. Sours (1980) confirms these features in his family research. The two features of the profile not described by these authors are usually only uncovered by psychoanalysis, a modality of treatment they do not utilize.

THE PSYCHOLOGICAL PROFILE
OF THE ANOREXIC FAMILY

Although the psychiatric diagnosis in anorexia nervosa cases ranges from neurosis to psychosis and the symptoms offer dramatic evidence of conflict, usually anorexic girls vehemently deny their conflicts. Most often the unhappy

---

[*]The patients researched in this project were treated by members of the Psychosomatic Workshop of the Psychoanalytic Association of New York, Inc., which comprises 15 child, adolescent, and adult psychoanalysts. I am particularly indebted to Drs. Otto Sperling, Ira Mintz, Cecilia Karol, Charles Hogan, and Gerald Freiman for their contributions. The profile was originally studied in 30 families (Wilson 1981) and has since been confirmed in 20 more families.

parents bring them in for consultation. These parents are usually highly motivated, well-meaning people who will do everything they can for their sick child. It is healthy for a child to grow up in a home where there are rules, limits, and a parental example of impulse control, responsibility, and ethical behavior; however, in their *overconscientiousness*, the parents of anorexics *over-control* their child. The adolescent anorexic girl is in a situation of realistic and neurotic dependence on her family, so that changes in the parents' behavior and attitudes toward her can be crucial for therapeutic success. Parents may try to withdraw their daughter from treatment prematurely because they cannot tolerate the rebelliousness and antisocial behavior that surfaces when the anorexic symptoms are resolved. They may need therapy themselves in order to accept the emotional changes in their daughter and to understand certain pathological interactions they have with her. Research on the 50 anorexic families yielded the following six-part anorexic family psychological profile:

1. Parental overconcern with fears of being fat and dieting was apparent in every case. In two families, the mothers dieted and were afraid of being fat; in one of these families, the father was also afraid of being fat and dieted because of colitis.

My research (Chapter 1, this volume) has confirmed M. Sperling's observations (1978) that specific conflicts and attitudes of the mother and/or father predispose a child for the development of psychosomatic symptoms (e.g., a mother's overconcern with bowel functions may predispose a child for ulcerative colitis). The specific etiological factor in anorexia is the parental preoccupation with dieting and the fear of being fat, which is transmitted to the daughter by identification. The other features of this profile are also found in the parents of patients suffering from psychosomatic symptoms such as asthma, migraine, headaches, and colitis.

2. All the families showed perfectionism. The parents were overconscientious and emphasized good behavior and social conformity in their children. Most were successful people who gave time to civic, religious, and charitable activities. Many were physicians, educators, business executives, or religious leaders, i.e., pillars of society.

Parental overconscientiousness was reflected in the exemplary childhood behavior and performance of the anorexic children. Divorce was rare, occurring in only two of the families studied. In these families, the parents were conscientious, religious people who lived near each other and continued to be caring, concerned parents after the divorce.

Two mothers were addicts (one to alcohol, the other to morphine), but their addictions were family secrets and both women were compulsive, perfectionistic college professors who tried to be perfect mothers. Their addictions expressed a rebellion against their hypermoral character structure. Both these addicted mothers had bulimarexic daughters. My research and that of Sours (1980) show that the compulsively perfectionistic parents of bulimarexics have more personal and marital conflict than do the parents of abstaining anorexics.

3. Repression of emotions was found in every family group; it was caused by the hypermorality of the parents. In several cases, parents kept such strict control over their emotions that they never quarreled in front of the children.

Aggressive behavior in the children was not permitted, and aggression in general was denied (e.g., one father's volunteer military service was disdained by his family). Most families laughed at the father's assertive male behavior and saw him as the "spoiler" in the sexual relation; the mother was the superior moral figure. The father's authority was diminished further by his busy schedule, which left him little time for his children.

4. The overconscientious perfectionism of the parents in these families resulted in infantilizing decision-making and overcontrol of the children. In some of the families, fun for fun's sake was not allowed. Everything had to have a noble purpose; the major parental home activity was intellectual discussion and scholarly reading. It was no surprise that the anorexic daughters hated the long hours of study they felt compelled to do. In therapy, it was difficult for them to become independent and mature and to get rid of the humiliating feeling that they were puppets whose strings were pulled by mother and father.

The last two features of the profile are usually uncovered only by psychoanalysis.

5. Exhibitionistic parental sexual and toilet behavior, whose significance was completely denied, was found in every family. Doors in these homes were not locked, and bedroom and toilet doors often were left open, which facilitated the curious child's viewing of sexual relations and toilet functions. The children frequently witnessed parental sexual intercourse. Such experiences, coupled with parental hypermorality and prudishness, caused an inhibition in normal psychosexual development in the anorexic daughters. Many were virginal, sexually repressed girls who feared boys.

Sours (1980) does not observe as much exhibitionistic behavior in families of self-starving young anorexics. However, he notes exhibitionistic parental behavior in families of gorging, vomiting anorexics, including frequent, seductive sexual behavior by the fathers.

6. In these families, there was an emotional selection of one child by the parents for the development of anorexia. This child was treated differently than the other children. Such a choice may result from (a) the carryover of an unresolved emotional conflict from the parents' childhood (e.g., the infant may represent a hated parent or brother or sister); (b) an intense need to control the child, so that the child is treated almost as a part of the body of one parent; (c) a particular psychological situation and emotional state of the parent(s) at the time of the child's birth which seriously damaged the parent-child relationship (e.g., the child may be infantilized because he or she is the last baby or may be overcathected by a parent who has suffered a recent loss).

CONSULTATION WITH THE ANOREXIC FAMILY

The therapist should be well acquainted with the symptoms and clinical picture of anorexia nervosa. Ample time should be set aside to see the parents and the anorexic child. Most often, the parents are frightened and bring the child for consultation. Usually the anorexic is seen first, then the two parents are seen together, and, finally, if it seems advisable, they are seen separately. It can be useful prior to consultation to ask the parents to write up and send a history of their daughter's psychological development and medical treatment and any relevant family problems. It is crucial to explain to the parents both the serious, possibly fatal nature of the disease and the treatment aims—to clear up the anorexic symptoms and resolve the underlying personality disorder. Parents must be prepared for aggression, hostility, and criticism from their daughter; they can be reminded that, to a considerable extent, these attitudes are normal adolescent manifestations. The therapist should explain that rebellious acting out, as well as suicidal preoccupations or gestures, may occur.

While explaining these probable developments, the therapist also assesses the parents' capacity for psychological understanding, their knowledge of people, and the nature of their transference. This assessment helps the therapist to decide whether the parents need psychotherapy concurrently with their child. No matter what degree of psychopathology the parents may exhibit, they should be asked to do psychotherapy themselves only for the sake of their sick child. Otherwise, because they are perfectionistic and deny conflict, they may become angry, refuse therapy, and obstruct their daughter's treatment. A talk with the attending pediatrician or other specialist, with the family's permission, is important. It is not advisable to criticize the parents; suggestions as to ways they should change their relationship with their daughter should be carefully explained. A frequent parental question is "Should we encourage eating?" The rationale for leaving this issue up to their daughter should be explained. It is most important to tell the parents that if they and the daughter cooperate in a treatment program, the prognosis is favorable.

If the patient has been in previous therapy, the parents should be forewarned that she may soon be hostile and critical of the therapist and want to stop, and that the parents will have to back up the treatment. The therapist should take emergency calls from anxious parents and quiet their anxieties by interpretation. In some cases, the therapist needs to explain carefully how and why his or her treatment method differs from the patient's previous one.

In the initial interview with the anorexic adolescent, a developmental history is taken. It is very useful to ask the girl what kind of conscience she thinks she has. Questions about the family's religion, ethical and moral values, rules, regulations, and attitudes about social issues may reveal cogent information. Although the ego structure, diagnosis, and motivation for treatment vary from one patient to another, all anorexics are very guilty people who deny conflict and control emotions. They withhold information and lie about their habits (e.g., fasting, gorging, vomiting, and taking laxatives). The therapist may be aware that a patient is not giving a straight answer, but should not pressure her with more questions. Anorexics also withhold and lie about their object relationships and sex life. Many have had no boyfriends and are virgins, and they usually will state this. Others will say they have no sexual conflicts and are orgastic. They must be allowed to tell their story, as it is only after months, or even years, of analysis that they will level with themselves and the therapist about their sexual conflicts.

It is best to begin by asking the least conflict-laden questions. It is helpful to inquire about the past first: "Did you have boyfriends in adolescence?; How intense were the relationships?; Did you go steady?; Were you engaged?"

The therapist then can ask about the patient's sexual experiences. Next, the therapist should concentrate on current experiences, such as fears of pregnancy, which can be intense in these patients, and the use of contraceptives (many anorexics do not use contraception of any kind, as they deny pregnancy). Another important line of questions involves the birth of siblings. Particularly important is whether the patient was prepared by the parents for the coming birth of a younger brother or sister. Likewise, the therapist should ask whether the patient was given information about puberty and menstruation. For adolescent patients, all these areas should be explored with the parents as well.

Masturbation and sexual fantasies should be brought up. However, the therapist has to realize that the superego of the fasting anorexic can be so strict that she may never have masturbated or permitted sexual fantasies. The gorging, vomiting anorexic usually has had sexual experience with masturbation, sexual fantasies, necking, and intercourse. The fasting anorexic is frequently afraid of thoughts and fantasies and only wants to talk about dieting and food. Questions about homosexuality should be asked, although the latter is rare among anorexics. One of the 50 cases studied had had homosexual experiences. She was a bisexual gorger-vomiter whose much-older homosexual lover was a maternal object.

Amnesia for childhood events is frequent. Often the anorexic girl is silent and negativistic. The best approach is to interpret her need to control emotions and deny conflict. The therapist may decide, based on knowledge of the girl's history, to detail her real problems to her. It is not wise to accept an anorexic patient for therapy shortly before a vacation because there is a serious risk that she will express her unconscious anger at the separation by extreme fasting or even suicide. The adolescent anorexic is told that she will be informed of any conversations and communications with the parents.

The psychological profile of the anorexic family should guide the therapist's interviews with the family. A useful acronym for the profile is PRIDES. P = perfectionism, R = repression of emotions, I = infantilizing decision-making for the anorexia-prone child, D = parental overconcern with dieting and fears of being fat, E = sexual and toilet exhibitionism, S = the selection of one child for the development of anorexia. Another psychological situation that should be kept in mind in consultations with anorexics is the split in their ego. One suicidal, gorging and vomiting anorexic told me very rationally about a book she was writing and her interesting editorial job and the next minute talked of how she should die because she was such an awful person. At the end of my first interview with a 17-year-old anorexic, I told her the time was up and we would continue the following day. She covered her face with her hair as if to hide from me and made no sign of leaving or hearing me. I sensed that she wanted to provoke a fight and knew from her history that she had often provoked her father into losing his temper and sometimes hitting her. I hazarded the interpretation that she seemed to have a princess in her who wanted all my time and that we would find out about this princess in therapy. She responded by getting up and leaving. I had hit the target with my educated guess, as later in treatment she revealed layered narcissistic fantasies that she really had been the child of a wealthy, aristocratic, noble family.

These patients' wishes for immediate gratification should be interpreted early in analysis. Since they deny their illness and the danger of their self-starvation, they are brought to consultation by their parents, husband, lover, concerned friends, or family physician. Because of the anorexic's extreme denial and weak ego, *whoever brings or influences the patient to come for consultation should be viewed by the therapist as the patient's auxiliary ego*.

For example, I saw the parents of a 15-year-old anorexic girl in consultation. After several interviews, I arranged for analysis of the daughter, suggesting that the parents see me for a few sessions to learn to cope better with their daughter. It became evident in our meetings that the mother, who had initiated the therapy, had a remarkable capacity for psychological insight, whereas the husband, a severe obsessive-compulsive, was almost "psychologically blind." The mother went into psychotherapy with me; the father went to a colleague for treatment. Throughout the daughter's analysis, the mother maintained a positive therapeutic alliance, effecting basic healthy changes in the way she and her husband related to their child.

On the other hand, a 25-year-old anorexic businesswoman was driven to my office for a consultation by her husband, who waited for her. My interview session with this woman seemed to be excellent, clarifying, and productive. The patient had been brought up in an Orthodox Jewish home, the youngest of two girls. The father was a conscientious, hard-working mechanic who owned and operated a gasoline station; the mother, who was overweight and always dieting, took care of the home and did her husband's bookkeeping. It was clear that, with her "slender, lovely figure," the patient was the apple of her parents' eye. Her history was typical. She had been a good child and an excellent, hard-working student, but had few close friends outside the family. Her anorexic symptoms developed when she became engaged. The consultation ended by my arranging for therapy with an analyst in her suburban town. Two weeks later, I received a hostile, critical letter, and the patient did not go into therapy as suggested. Reviewing the case, I realized that my error had been that I had not seen the patient's husband. It was he who had forced the patient to come for consultation when he became alarmed by her loss of weight. Even though this woman was 25, she should have been viewed as an adolescent. In this respect, depending on the circumstances, the therapist should consider seeing the concerned relatives or friends of an anorexic regardless of the patient's age.

While with adult patients the therapy of the parents is not as essential as in working with children, it can be of value. A 30-year-old anorexic had a long history of psychotherapy with no improvement. With the patient's permission, I saw her 65-year-old mother, whom I placed in therapy with a colleague. This patient had an unresolved symbiotic relation with her mother similar to that of an adolescent, and the mother's therapy was of assistance in helping the patient to analyze her dependency conflicts.

A 25-year-old anorexic lawyer came for consultation, ostensibly of her own accord. Her anorexic fasting, gorging, and vomiting dated back ten years. Actually it was the husband's anger about his wife's habits, their marital conflicts, and the extraordinary financial burden of her food addiction that triggered the consultation. She would secretly "eat up a storm," adding as much as $80 to their monthly food bill. At the husband's request, and with the wife's consent, I saw him once in consultation. I explained that there were emotional conflicts behind anorexic symptoms and that analysis was indicated. I did not urge him to enter therapy himself as I did not feel it was necessary. However, I warned that the acting-out phase of his wife's treatment, which would replace her anorexic symptoms, might test his patience. The husband was an educated, insightful man who loved his wife; he paid for and supported her during her eventually successful analysis.

SITUATIONS INVOLVING SEPARATION-INDIVIDUATION

In taking a history from both the anorexic patient and the parents, the therapist should focus on situations that involve separation-individuation. The first major separation is birth. Breast-feeding and weaning should be asked about in detail. Because of their overconscientiousness, many anorexic mothers have trouble dividing up their time. One mother, who worked as her general practitioner husband's secretary and bookkeeper, could not relax for breast-feeding. The daughter was bottle-fed, and mother's feedings were compulsive and pressured. In the daughter's later anorexic behavior, she took revenge on her parents by keeping them at the table endlessly watching her cut up food that she did not eat.

Bladder and bowel control, walking, and talking all involve separation-individuation. The birth and death of siblings and relatives, particularly the death of grandparents, involve profound separation conflicts. One anorexic recalled in her analysis that her grandmother's death had been denied by the parents. She was not taken to her beloved grandmother's funeral when she was four years old, but was told that "grandmother went to sleep."

The first school experience is also very important; frequently there is a history of school phobia in nursery school, kindergarten, or first grade. Any geographical moves of the family provoke separation-individuation conflicts. Because their egos are immature, anorexia-prone girls usually do not adjust well to new surroundings, new schools, and new friends. Each school graduation involves conflict. Frequently, anorexics do well in high school, but procrastinate on the major maturational step of graduating from college. It is important to inquire about all situations that involve separation from the family, such as sleepovers, camp, and college. Questions should be asked about whether the girl could handle things on her own or telephoned home often. Also, how did the parents handle the separation? Daily phone calls to and from daughters away at college are common in families of anorexics.

The first job and marriage involve other separations. The first love affair can provide very useful information, but the nature of all the patient's object relations are important. Frequently, the anorexic girl's best friend is her mother and she is not close to her peers. Another conflict-laden event is illness in either the patient or her parents. Later in life, the loss of a mate or a parent may be significant in precipitating the separation conflicts, which may manifest them-selves in anorexic symptomatology. Anorexic symptoms mask and defend against depression and most anorexics are dry eyed; it is a sign of therapeutic progress when they become depressed and cry.

METHOD OF TREATMENT

The technique of therapy advocated here is intensive psychotherapy or analysis of the anorexic, with concurrent psychotherapy of parents, if necessary, with a different therapist. If the same therapist treats both the anorexic and the parents, the anorexic will tend to mistrust the therapist, who becomes identified too closely with the judging parents. In some cases, the mother and/or father need intensive therapy in order to change their unhealthy relationship with their child. In many cases where the anorexic patient refuses or resists treatment, preliminary therapy of the parent(s) can lead to a healthy treatment motivation. The technique of psychotherapy differs from one case to another. Modified classical or traditional psychoanalytic treatment methods are often used. For example, in certain cases, even though the patient may be seen three to four times a week, the couch may not be used until late in therapy. If the only practical arrangement is psychotherapy, much can be accomplished at two times a week, although three sessions are better. It is useful therapeutically for the adolescent patient to pay some part of the fee herself if possible.

Clinical Material

CASE 1   Perfectionism

The R.'s came for consultation about their 17-year-old daughter, Sally, who six months earlier had started a diet that she then rigidly followed until she lost 30 lbs. and became anorexic. A hyperactive, overconscientious girl who got up at 5:00 A.M. to recheck her homework, Sally gave a history typical of anorexic adolescents. She always had been a good girl, obsessed with proper behavior, studying, and social achievement. The father, a 50-year-old successful business executive, grew up in Boston. Mr. R. was very idealistic. He disapproved of the business world and always wished he could have become a physician. The care of the children was relegated to his wife. Mrs. R., a 45-year-old social worker, divided her time between a full-time career and her family. She was very ladylike and overconcerned with manners and proper behavior for her daughter. When faced with emotional situations or fights, she frequently developed skin rashes and hives. She was very afraid of being fat and nagged her husband, who was a few pounds overweight, to join her in dieting.

Sally's brother Robert, two years her senior, was an easygoing adolescent boy who had a succession of girlfriends, smoked, drank, and enjoyed parties, dancing, and rock music. Although the mother weakly argued with Robert and chided him for his poor school performance, most of her attention was focused on her daughter. She did everything she could for Sally, helping her with her studies, reviewing her homework, and barraging her with advice and criticism.

The R.'s followed a strict regime: meals were always on time, television was rationed at one hour a day, and the major parental relaxation was intellectual discussion and serious reading. The parents never quarreled in front of their children and in general shared the same ethical, social, and political views.

Primal-scene memories of witnessing parental intercourse emerged in Sally's analysis. At three years of age, when she woke up screaming with nightmares, her mother, to quiet her, had her sleep the rest of the night in the parental bed, where Sally overheard the heavy breathing of intercourse. She fantasied that it was an attack by her father on her mother. She also witnessed parental intercourse at four and six years of age. There were no operable locks on the doors in the R.'s home, and parental nudity and toilet behavior were also frequently observed by Sally, who became inhibited and afraid of boys.

THERAPY.   As with all anorexics, many different conflicts were displaced onto and masked by Sally's anorexic symptoms. Therapy focused on showing Sally the nature of her overstrict conscience, which demanded perfect behavior in herself and others. She was also hypercritical of her analyst. Memories and dreams revealed that she had developed this attitude by identifying with her mother's perfectionist attitudes.

Both Mr. and Mrs. R. were referred for psychotherapy. Mrs. R. came to understand that she was treating Sally very differently than Robert and that she had been pressuring her daughter to carry out certain of her own unfulfilled aspirations in life. The R.'s moderated their overconcern with dieting and weight loss, and learned to tolerate and understand the emerging rebellious, critical adolescent behavior that Sally manifested as her anorexic symptoms subsided. Mrs. R. changed her intrusive, controlling attitude toward her daughter. The parents also took some vacations together (alone) for the first time and began to permit themselves to quarrel in front of their children. Operable bedroom and bathroom locks were installed, and Sally was given a degree of privacy appropriate to her age.

CASE 2   Fears of Growing Up

The parents of Alice came from an educated, middle-class, Italian Catholic background. The mother, Mrs. T., was a polite, conscientious housewife who was an excellent, almost a gourmet, cook. A buxom woman, she had been overweight before marriage, was afraid of being fat, and dieted. She clung to her daughter, telephoned her daily, and showered her with gifts. She never criticized her and made no demands on her. Her husband, a very successful computer-company executive, worked long hours and was frequently away from home. He doted on his wife, who made most of the decisions for their children. Mrs. T. guiltily smoked cigarettes, but Mr. T. neither smoked nor drank. He suffered from bouts of intestinal distress and colitis (not ulcerative colitis) that forced him to take time off from his busy schedule. He was always on a special diet. His one hobby was stamp collecting. The T.'s lived a restricted social life that centered on their family. Although financially successful, they did not belong to any clubs or participate in athletics. Both parents controlled their emotions, never argued in front of their children, and shared the same moral, social, and political views.

Alice's analysis revealed many dreams and fantasies that had been caused by repeated witnessing of parental sexual relations. The parents always had left their bedroom door ajar. As a young child, when Alice was awakened by nightmares, she went in to sleep with them. Family nudity and toilet exhibitionism, which were completely denied, continued into Alice's adolescent years.

When sexual dreams and fantasies about her analyst emerged, Alice manifested behavior that reflected secret wishes to spy on and surprise him. She would come very early or very late for sessions and would turn around on the analytic couch to "catch" her analyst. She had no conscious memory of the birth of her two brothers (one when she was two, the other when she was six). Nor did she recall her mother being pregnant. Although outside the home she was very well behaved and a model child and student, she was very jealous of and hostile toward her younger brothers, sadistically picking fights with them. She had been given no information about sexual matters, pregnancy, or birth by her inhibited, hypermoral parents. Alice's mother was modest and inhibited in dress and manner, whereas her father never used a bathrobe and walked around the house in loose-fitting boxer shorts that revealed his genitals. Alice frequently witnessed him urinating in the bathroom, the door of which was always open. This parental behavior provoked incestuous fantasies whose repression caused sexual inhibition and intense fears of boys.

Alice's childlike attachment to her mother was a major analytic problem. Alice had trouble sleeping alone and left the light on. In the transference, she was afraid that the analyst would leave her or that something would happen to him. A crucial turning point in treatment occurred when she gained enough confidence in herself to move out of the parental home. The denial of aggression in the family was an important subject for analysis. The fact that the father had volunteered for the Air Force and had bombed the enemy in Korea was never mentioned in the home and was a source of anxiety, alarm, and fear when it came up in treatment. All of Alice's boyfriends were passive and inhibited, which was her conscious impression of her father. This attitude was fostered by her mother, who referred to her husband as a "sweet, kind gentleman."

THERAPY.   In her analysis, Alice came to understand that her overstrict conscience made her give up and resort to anorexic symptoms when she felt she could not be perfect. Many conflicts that had been displaced onto her symptoms were uncovered; among them were fears of growing up, menstruating and becoming pregnant, having a voluptuous figure and exciting boys, and losing control of emotions, particularly anger.

As a result of psychotherapy, Mrs. T. stopped infantilizing her daughter; the daily maternal phone calls ceased. Mr. T. began to take time off from business and go on vacations with his wife. The T.'s allowed themselves to express differences of opinion in front of their children and no longer were overconcerned with Alice's diet. They even could accept their daughter's postanorexic, voluptuous figure. The parents became normally modest in their personal behavior and began to close and/or lock doors appropriately.

CASE 3   *Separation-Individuation*

Mr. and Mrs. B. came for consultation when their daughter Ruth developed anorexia at college. The mother, a slender, 45-year-old, college-educated house-wife, was shocked by her daughter's illness. Ruth had been a "perfect" child, had had many friends, and had been an excellent student active in school projects and social activities. The mother had been raised on a farm and described her own mother as a "good soldier" who dominated her husband and daughter.

She said she had been spoiled as a child; her parents had sacrificed everything for her. In late adolescence, Mrs. B. had fallen in love with a college sopho-more, an aggressive, "sexy guy" of whom her family had disapproved. Her mother had broken up the relationship. Several years later, Mrs. B. had met and married Mr. B., a hard-working engineer whom her parents liked very much. After Mrs. B.'s father died in a car accident, her mother moved in with the newlyweds, taking over all the cooking and housework.

Mrs. B. realized in retrospect that she had been depressed when Ruth was born, but had kept her feelings to herself. Secretly, Mrs. B. was unhappy and angry with her husband and mother and tried to give all her love and attention to her daughter whom she clung to and spoiled. Mrs. B. was very conscien-tious, did not smoke or drink, and was "submissive" in her relations with her mother and husband. There were no fights or quarrels. Mrs. B. was very afraid of being fat and dieted and exercised to keep her weight down. She realized that it had been a mistake to have her mother live with her.

The father, a 48-year-old man, said he realized he was a workaholic and did not have much time for his daughter. His repressed, hard-working parents had been strict with him as a child. His father, an automobile salesman, would beat him if he misbehaved. Mr. B. was compulsive and punctual. He had no hobbies and did not like sports. Until adolescence, he had been seriously overweight. At 12 years of age, he had begun to diet and had continued ever since. He was very afraid of being fat and realized that he communicated this fear to his daughter.

THERAPY.   Both parents were referred for psychotherapy with the goal of preparing them to face the rebellion and acting out that would emerge when their daughter's anorexic symptoms cleared up in analysis. The mother had great difficulty in stopping daily phone calls to her daughter at college. She began to assert herself with her own mother, who moved out of the home. Mrs. B.'s struggle to separate from her daughter precipitated a severe depression, and she went into analysis. Two dreams reported by her analyst typified her conflicts. In one, she was Moses leading the enslaved Jews out of Egypt. She felt the enslaved Jews represented herself and her daughter, who were being freed. In another dream, she and a friend went to the city to try to find her daughter, who was lost. This dream was precipitated by Mrs. B.'s decision to stop phoning her daughter every day and she said she knew it reflected her anxious wish to baby her daughter.

The husband's therapy helped him to stop trying to control his daughter and wife, for whom he previously had made every major decision. He began to take vacations with his wife and cut down on his long work hours. Prior to therapy, the B.'s never had locked any doors and the daughter had been permitted no real privacy. Mrs. B. recalled that there had been no locks in her parental home and that this pattern had continued when she married. She had severe conflicts about locking her bedroom door and putting an operable lock on the daughter's bedroom door. The parents also stopped inquiring into every aspect of their daughter's life and turned over age-appropriate tasks and responsibilities to her.

CASE 4   Archaic Superego

Mrs. K., the mother of Polly, a 15-year-old anorexic, was a compulsive woman who suffered from spastic colitis. She never lost her temper and was always cheerful and optimistic. She was an excellent cook who used food to pacify or quiet people. In addition to her role as mother and housewife, she had a full-time job as an editor of scientific books. Outwardly very friendly and sweet, she could be very stubborn and controlling, particularly with respect to infantilizing her daughter. She was the dominant parent to whom Polly brought her problems. Polly was very dependent on her mother, phoned her frequently when away at college, and inappropriately let the mother make decisions for her. The mother was very careful of her weight, dieted, and had an intense fear of being fat. For breakfast, mother and daughter each had a cup of coffee and a piece of rye toast. The mother "spoiled" Polly at home and also intervened to get her out of difficulties at school. The mother was very idealistic, did not smoke or drink, and supported many liberal social causes and charities. She was very conservative about sexual matters, did not prepare her daughter for menstruation, and told her that she should not have sexual relations before marriage.

The father looked down on the business that was his life work and felt he should have been an artist. He left the upbringing of his children to his wife. He did everything with her and had no friends. When repeatedly provoked by Polly, he would lose his temper and shout at her. He and his wife never quarrelled in front of their children. Mr. K. was immodest at home, often dressing and undressing in front of his family and leaving the bathroom door open when he urinated.

Polly was pretty, narcissistic, and hypermoral. She had no friends outside the family. A healthy baby, she had sucked her thumb until five years of age, at which time she began to bite her nails. She worked long hours on her studies, was compulsively worried about time, and was always ahead of time. She had great trouble making decisions and often created crises that mother had to solve for her. Her friendships with girls did not last because she was so critical of their behavior. She was afraid of and shy with boys.

THERAPY.   Mr. and Mrs. K. were both resistant to initial attempts to get them to change their controlling behavior with their daughter. Both were referred to colleagues for psychotherapy. The daughter was referred for analysis. Her anorexic fasting had developed at summer camp, her first separation from her parents. She had felt very lonely and homesick there. Her anorexic symptoms cleared within the first month of treatment, which focused primarily on the modification of her strict, archaic superego. Eventually, Mrs. K. was able to give her daughter more autonomy and Mr. K. began to spend some time with his daughter and assert himself more in the home. He also became normally modest. The K.'s stopped concealing their quarrels and disagreements from Polly.

CASE 5   *Hypnotic Subjugation*

Is there anything to be learned about the etiology of anorexia from a family where all three daughters developed the disease? In this family constellation, both parents had fears of being fat and dieted religiously. The father, a former choreographer, made his living in the theatre. He subjected his daughters to a constant barrage of warnings about their figure, weight, diet, and health. He and his wife worried about their daughters' every activity. He disapproved of smoking, drinking, and sexual freedom, and constantly lectured them. The mother, who had studied ballet and was overconcerned with food and dieting, had a degree in psychology. She did research in hypnosis and, whenever her daughters became emotionally upset, she hypnotized them. Even after their marriage ended in divorce, both parents devoted excessive time to their children, whom they infantilized.

The development of anorexia in all three daughters seemed to be caused by: (1) their identification with the parents' extreme fear of being fat and preoccupation with dieting; and (2) the extreme control exercised by both parents, but particularly the mother, who literally had her daughters in hypnotic subjugation. In analysis, the third daughter resolved her anorexic symptoms and the major conflicts masked by her fear-of-being-fat complex. Particularly important was the analysis and resolution of her separation-individuation conflicts, which enabled her to go to an out-of-state college. The two untreated sisters became chronic bulimic anorexics and had to be supported by the parents.

THE SUPEREGO STRUCTURE
OF THE FAMILY

Although there is a great variety of parental character structure, in anorexic families both parents are typically perfectionistic compulsives. Many are formally religious; their archaic superego structure drives them to be dogmatic. White lies, antisocial behavior, nonconformist ideas, iconoclastic or sarcastic wit and humor are ego alien. Another group of parents rebels against overly moralistic, religious parents and manifests modern liberal attitudes toward behavior. Their hypertolerant ego attitudes are reaction formations against an internalized strict superego. Unconsciously they are as controlling and intolerant as the overtly hypermoral group. In all these homes, the basic inflexible parental hypermorality is enforced by disciplinary measures that range from the threat of total loss of approval and love to explosive physical punishment, such as slapping the child in the face.

One anorexic social work student came for therapy at the urging of her teachers, who told her that she was too rigid and hypermoral. They referred to her attitude as extreme perfectionism. Her father was a professor of religion and her mother was a latent anorexic, a thin, nervous woman who devoted herself to her family and charitable activities. She was amenorrheic and had had her periods induced by hormonal injections each time she decided to get pregnant. The daughter's anorexia was rooted in her identification with her mother.

A hospitalized male anorexic, who grew up in an orthodox religious home, developed his symptoms when his wife divorced him because he was so cold and hypermoral, and he lost his teaching position because he was too critical and asocial. The early hospital consultations consisted of his politely bringing a chair, pad of paper, and pencil for the analyst, and then sitting silently, refusing to reply to any questions. Using his voluminous case history, which detailed years of ineffective treatment that included behavior modification and electric shock, his analyst explained his overconscientiousness to him and emphasized that he was trying to starve himself to death because he could not be perfect. For six such sessions, the analyst interpreted his masochism to him while he silently listened. At the end of each session, he thanked the analyst and opened the door for him to leave. In the seventh session, he spontaneously said that he had dreamt of a religious figure who had burned himself to death. The analyst connected this material to his masochistic perfectionism. From that session on, he worked well in therapy. He developed a strong positive transference and within two weeks began eating and putting on weight.

Several anorexics grew up in traditionally religious families where the parents totally controlled their children, preventing any contact with the "licentious modern world" until their children left home for college. Many of the fathers, although remarkably successful in their work, were openly conscientious, obedient, "good boys." They usually hid the aggressive aspects of their behavior and personality from their children.

The United Moral Front of the Parents

The anorexic child is often confronted with the united moral front of the parents and cannot play one parent off against the other or turn to one parent for love and support when working through problems with the other. I suspect that the dramatic clearing of anorexic symptoms by family therapists (Minuchin et al. 1978) is caused less by their family-systems manipulations than by the anorexic child's sense that the parents have lost their controlling position and authority.

Smugness in the Family

Many mothers and fathers of anorexics evidence smugness, and anorexic analysands frequently accuse their analysts of being smug and complacent like their parents. During the working-through phase of their analyses, anorexics may become smug and hypercritical for a time. For example, one married woman, who for ten years of marriage had secretly gorged and vomited, worked through her fears of being fat and no longer experienced her gorging and vomiting impulses. Her weight became normal and her body image healthy. However, she became very smug with her husband, criticizing him for his "disgusting" oral pleasures, such as his gorging of food at parties and his drinking. It was as if her whole anorexic period had been forgotten.

Arlow (1957) notes that smugness represents "oral satiety with incorporation of the good object, which is ultimately identified with the penis-breast and milk. Smugness implies a temporary diminution of tension between ego and superego, plus a relatively large and transitory withdrawal of the cathexis invested in objects" (p. 8). These psychodynamics are certainly confirmed in the analysis of anorexic smugness. The terror of being fat includes a fear of becoming a "fat cat," i.e., smug like the parents.

Some parents of anorexics are so smugly hypermoral that they will not cooperate in any treatment program for their anorexic child. One such parent was a woman dentist who from the earliest years did all her daughter's dental work. This mother was obsessed with oral hygiene and the prevention of caries. Through the medium of dentistry she conveyed to her daughter all her attitudes toward cleanliness, beauty, and emotional control. The daughter's anorexic symptoms developed after a short rebellious phase that the mother described as "her opening her dirty mouth to me." This mother and her husband, a passive businessman, refused treatment for their daughter. They viewed her behavior and symptoms as evidence of "moral weakness."

Anorexia and Bulimia

While Wilson and Mintz (1982) have demonstrated that anorexia nervosa and bulimia are two sides of the same coin, Savitt (1977) questions the interrelatedness of obesity and anorexia. He notes the same unconscious conflicts in obesity as in anorexia, including hypothalmic amenorrhea. I was able, in six cases of obesity, to resolve the underlying characterologic disorder so that the patients achieved normal weight levels. In each case there were different attitudes of the parents toward eating and dieting, as well as a different quality to the parent-child relationship. The parental superego structures in the obese were not as rigid and perfectionistic as in anorexic bulimic families. One analyst, Sours (personal communication, 1981), concurs with my formulations, noting that "the anorexic superego is punitive, cruel, and perfectionistic; the obese individual's superego is punishing but uncontrolling; it does not know perfection."

Affluence and Anorexia

Most anorexics seen in treatment come from well-to-do families. They usually do not come for consultation of their own accord, but are brought to therapy by educated relatives or friends. Perhaps anorexics from families of lower socioeconomic levels are not brought to treatment because of an educational deficit in the family and friends. However, in my opinion, psychodynamic factors give the impression that the families of anorexics are affluent or rich. All these parents are caring, conscientious people who work hard and are good providers. In most families, both the father and mother work. Frequently, one or both are "workaholics." Because of their strict superegos, they take few vacations and do not spend money on hobbies, entertaining, clubs, or recreational activities such as sports. Everything is work and family. They therefore succeed in their fields of work by dint of long hours and diligence. For example, in two of the cases studied, both the father and mother were physicians. In another case, both parents were lawyers. In a third, the father was a famous internist and the mother, the headmistress of a private girls' school. Most of the parents were socially and culturally upwardly mobile.

Another dynamic factor contributing to the impression of the affluent home is the reaction formation in the parents, particularly in the mother, which results in their giving in to their daughter and "spoiling" her. These parents give their children gifts, vacations, and clothes that they cannot give to themselves because of their masochism. The mother who masochistically does everything for her daughter conveys the impression of wealth in the background. A graphic example was one mother who was a college professor; in addition to her college lectures and other duties, she took care of the home and cooked three separate dinners every day—one at 5:30 P.M. for her professor husband, who had evening classes; one at 6:30 P.M. for her anorexic adolescent daughter; and another at 8:00 P.M. for her 25-year-old son, who worked late. The daughter had never learned to cook because the mother took care of everything.

THE NARCISSISM OF THE PATIENT

Anorexic patients are extremely narcissistic. In spite of conflicts and behavior that are obviously neurotic to their friends and family, they themselves deny any conflict. Their narcissistic denial of reality has two major psychodynamic components. The first is moral pride; having identified with the strict superegos of their parents, they are extremely proud of their asceticism. When they are starving themselves to death, they frequently volunteer to serve the food trays on the ward in the hospital. One anorexic came late to many analytic sessions because she spent endless hours "being a mother to her friends." She tried to write a vegetarian cookbook that she could not finish and that publishers had told her had no market. She was extremely critical of the analyst and of his interpretations because he "did not appreciate her good works and kind deeds." Another anorexic said that her girlfriend who was in analysis called her "my superego."

The second major cause of their narcissism is the experience of having been "unconsciously chosen" by the mother and/or the father; in family after family, regardless of their socioeconomic situation, the anorexic child has been spoiled. The mother and/or father does everything for this child. Frequently, the mother does all the cooking and the daughter does not know how to make a meal. In therapy, the mother of an anorexic girl mentioned with slight irritation that her daughter brought too much dirty laundry home from college. Questions revealed that the mother had always done the daughter's laundry and that she had never asked her daughter to take care of herself. When this and other infantilizing behavior of the mother were interpreted, the daughter stopped coming home so often and evidenced other maturational advances. The conscious and unconscious feeling and experience of being treated in a special way increases anorexics' narcissism.

THE "LADY BOUNTIFUL" EGO IDEAL

The extreme ego ideal of the anorexic who has to feed and take care of others while she deprives herself expresses a "lady bountiful" ego attitude that can be observed in women in our culture in general.

A neurotic, married professional woman in analysis for severe depressions reported a dream in which she was breast-feeding many babies who had milk all over their faces. Her associations were to being extremely depressed the night before—her husband had been away on business, none of her friends had called, and she had missed her "children." She corrected herself, saying that her two sons were grown men in their midtwenties. She thought of how much she had enjoyed them when they were babies and needed her. She thought of her younger son, a successful designer, whose apartment is a total mess. He does not make his bed or wash the dishes. His girlfriend comes in and cleans up for him.

She thought of what a "slob" she had been as a child and how much her mother had done for her. She laughed ruefully and said to her analyst, "I guess I still want my son to be at the breast again and to totally need me, and I must be depressed that you and my husband don't mother me." The valid insight of this patient was the result of a long series of interpretations of her unresolved oral conflicts. Her behavior and character were replete with manifestations of her "lady bountiful" ego ideal. She worked full-time as a clinical psychiatrist in a family therapy center and, in her private life, she was driven to be everyone's advisor and friend. She gave to innumerable charities and could not say "no" to anyone.

In the transference neurosis, she wanted to take care of her analyst. On the other hand, she became very angry when people did not appreciate her kindness or do comparable things for her. However, although she had a fear-of-being-fat complex, her ego was stronger and healthier than the anorexic's ego because of the quality of her relationship to her mother. Her mother had spoiled her as a young child but, after the oedipal period, she had made many realistic demands on her and had not infantilized her as the mothers of anorexics do with their daughters.

In the anorexic female, we find an extreme of the "lady bountiful" ego ideal. For example, early in analysis, a 19-year-old bulimic reported a dream she had had prior to the development of her anorexia. The dream was of a breast that could be molded into anything. At the time she reported it, she was amenorrheic and fasting, gorging, and vomiting—a bulimic anorexic. Her associations to the dream led to the "Arabian Nights," genies, and the miraculous rug on which people could travel. An interpretation was made at the time of belief in magic. The interpretation was responded to by an increase in her symptoms of fasting, gorging, and vomiting. It was only several years later that she could accept and understand the many meanings of this plastic breast dream, particularly that she wanted the analyst to be the all-providing breast in the transference while she would be the breast-mother, a "lady bountiful." Like other anorexics, she split off and denied her oral conflicts, acting them out in her anorexic symptoms and behavior. All mothers of anorexics evidence this "lady bountiful" ego ideal, which their husbands aid and encourage because of their latent homosexual conflicts.

RESEARCH

In 1970, Anthony and Benedek coedited an important book, *Parenthood: Its Psychology and Psychopathology*, which offers a comprehensive overview of parent-child interactions. Particularly relevant to anorexic research are the chapters by Spitz on "The Effect of Personality Disturbances in the Mother on the Well-Being of Her Infant," and by M. Sperling on "The Clinical Effects of Parental Neurosis on the Child." Elsewhere, M. Sperling (1978) describes the treatment of anorexics and their parents, and, in young children, the simultaneous treatment of the anorexic child and parent. Sperling reports a case of a 2-year-old anorexic girl whose mother's analysis revealed that she had rejected her daughter because of her sex and her personality, considering her "a weak crybaby." The essential goal of the mother's treatment was to help her to accept her daughter and herself as female.

I analyzed the compulsive husband of a married anorexic woman who was in analysis with a colleague. This man unconsciously wanted his wife to be a man, and promoted this latent homosexual goal by making his wife diet and exercise to pathological extremes. When this man was able to accept his wife as a woman with a woman's figure, she regained her sexual desire and stopped her extreme dieting.

As noted earlier, Bruch's (1978a) observations of 50 anorexic families correlate closely with our profile. She notes aspects of the overconscientious parents: polite behavior is emphasized and nonexpression of feelings is the rule. She notes the infrequency of divorce and the absence of parental arguing in front of children. She describes the parents of anorexics as taking it for granted that they make all plans and decisions and direct the child in every respect. Minuchin et al.'s (1978) findings in 53 anorexic families also substantiate our hypothesis. They note that anorexic families see themselves as loyal, protective, responsible, and responsive, which correlates with our analytic finding of the families' strict perfectionist conscience. They note that their pathological overconcern curtails normal growth and autonomy. The meanings of Minuchin's global term "enmeshment" are similar to the psychoanalytic developmental concepts such as unresolved symbiotic attachment to the parents and conflicts in separation-individuation. Minuchin's treatment is aimed at altering the pathological parent-child interactions, but does not go on to the analysis of the personality disorder that underlies anorexia, which we have found to be necessary for lasting results in these patients.

SUMMARY

Psychoanalytic research with 50 anorexic families revealed a parental psychological profile that appears to be etiologic in establishing a personality disorder in the children which later manifests itself as anorexia nervosa. Four components of this profile correlate with the findings of Bruch (1978) and Minuchin et al. (1978): (1) overconcern with dieting and fears of being fat; (2) overconscientious perfectionism; (3) repression of emotions; and (4) infantilizing decision-making. The last two features of the profile were un-covered by psychoanalysis in six cases: (5) sexual and toilet exhibitionism, whose significance is denied; and (6) the unconscious selection of a child to develop anorexia because of parental conflicts. This chapter shows how a psychodynamic understanding of this pathological psychological profile can be crucial for the treatment of anorexia nervosa.

PART II

Psychodynamic Structure

3
A Reevaluation of Classification, Concepts, and Treatment

MELITTA SPERLING, M.D.

(Reprinted from *Psychosomatic Disorders in Childhood* (1978) with additional case material from Melitta Sperling's files (pp. 66–71) which was provided by Dr. Otto Sperling.)

The term "anorexia nervosa" was coined nearly 100 years ago by Gull (1873a, 1888) to describe a condition in young girls which consisted of a refusal to eat "due to a morbid mental state," weight loss, and amenorrhea. Since then, this condition has become widely known and has received considerable psychiatric and some psychoanalytic attention. For a detailed survey of historical and other data on anorexia nervosa, the reader is referred to Blitzer et al. (1961), Kaufman and Heiman (1964), and Thomä (1967).

Numerous reports on this subject during the last 15 years have greatly enhanced our understanding of this syndrome, but have also raised more questions and some controversy. Does anorexia nervosa occur only in adolescent girls and should this term be reserved for this specific eating disorder in this age group? Does it afflict only females? Is it associated with a specific type of personality? If so, what are the characteristics of such a personality? What is the exact etiology and what are the significant dynamics? Can we identify the factors that determine the severity and final outcome of this illness? Is it a purely psychological disorder or do emotional factors play only a precipitating and contributing role in an otherwise physiologically predisposed patient? Most of all, what treatment is effective for this often serious, and sometimes even fatal, condition?

Because a valid assessment of the existing knowledge and additional insight and understanding can come only from thorough clinical studies and experiences, clinical data will be presented first and used as a basis for meaningful discussion and constructive suggestions.

Feeding and eating disturbances are the earliest and most frequent disorders in children. These disturbances are the first indications of something amiss in the mother-child relationship, but they seldom come to the attention of an analyst or child psychiatrist. The work of Spitz, especially on hospitalism (1945)*, and

---

*Hospitalism is a severe eating disorder which leads to starvation and sometimes death in infants.

research in child development by psychoanalytic investigators such as Benedek (1938), Brody (1956), Escalona (1954), Rank (1948), and Ribble (1943) are of importance in this connection. In addition to the fact that infants and very young children are not brought to psychoanalysts for treatment of an eating disturbance, it is not possible to study such young patients directly by the psychoanalytic method. Therefore, the work of the investigators referred to above consisted of observations and conclusions derived from them.

My association with the pediatric department of a general hospital* provided me with the opportunity to see a large number of child patients. I devised a method that enabled me to study and treat young children psychoanalytically. The main feature of this method was the inclusion of the mother in the treatment. Children of preverbal age were treated indirectly by treating the mother (Sperling 1949, 1950a). For children of verbal age, the approach was simultaneous treatment of mother and child (in separate sessions, but by the same analyst) or successive treatment (mother treated first and the child later, if necessary) (Sperling 1949). Even in cases where direct psychoanalytic treatment was possible, a positive relationship involving occasional contact with the mother was necessary to support her and to insure her willingness to allow her child to resolve the pathological relationship existing between them. I (1959) have demonstrated clinically that some eating disturbances leading to starvation and illness are the consequences of a disturbed mother-child relationship and represent the equivalents of depression in children.

CLINICAL RESEARCH

I would like to summarize briefly some relevant findings from my clinical research, particularly those involving the genetic aspects of anorexia nervosa. The analytic exploration of the mother in cases of severe eating disturbances in infants invariably revealed highly ambivalent feelings and, in some cases, unconscious rejection of the child by the mother (Sperling 1970). Making the mother aware of her feelings and at least of some of their unconscious sources in a brief "analytic first aid" approach was strikingly successful in many cases. These feelings frequently stemmed from unresolved ambivalence conflicts from the mother's own childhood, which she had transferred to her child, or from an unconscious identification of the child with repressed and rejected aspects of the mother's own personality (Sperling 1949, 1950a, 1959). Follow-up studies revealed that, in many cases, the changes in the feelings of the mother effected by this brief technique were sustained during the important developmental stages of the child (Sperling 1970).

In prelatency children, whose personality had already been molded according to the unconscious expectations of the mother and whose eating disturbance had become a focal point of conflict between them, simultaneous treatment yielded the quickest and best therapeutic results. At the same time, this method

---

* I established and was in charge of the child psychiatric clinic of the Jewish Hospital of Brooklyn, New York, for 15 years.

proved to be the most rewarding approach for a fuller understanding of the dynamics of the mother-child relationship and their role in the child's psychopathology. The following clinical vignettes from the psychoanalytic treatment of young children, adolescent girls, and adults suffering from anorexia nervosa illustrate this point and the dynamics that I consider essential in anorexia nervosa.

Simultaneous Mother-and-Child Treatment of a 2-Year-Old Anorexic

In young children, the basic dynamics characteristic of the pernicious type of anorexia are already clearly discernible. Fortunately, however, at this early stage the pathology can be reversed by simultaneous treatment of mother and child. One brief clinical vignette taken from a case report published in 1952 may serve as an illustration. Linda developed a severe eating disturbance at age two. At 22 months of age, she had been referred for play therapy by the hospital where she had been treated twice for nocturnal attacks of paroxysmal tachycardia. Among other symptoms indicative of a disturbed mother-child relationship were states of withdrawal, excessive sucking of her tongue and lips, and disturbed sleep. Linda had suffered from eating difficulties since infancy, with an intensification following a tonsillectomy at 19 months of age and an acute exacerbation after the birth of a brother when she was two years old.

Linda had reacted to these traumatic events with feelings of abandonment and loss. These feelings were aggravated by the fact that the birth of the brother occurred during her therapist's summer vacation, which had interrupted her play therapy of two months' duration. The repression of oral and anal sadistic impulses initiated earlier by the premature weaning and toilet training intensified. The use of primitive mechanisms of defense against a breakthrough of the repressed impulses—in particular, externalization, projection, and displacement—led to the formation of phobic symptoms, with a disturbance in the sense of reality that had a slight, but definite, paranoid taint.

The depressive and paranoid features and the disturbance in the sense of reality, which make the treatment of anorexia nervosa in adolescents more difficult and which cloud the prognosis, were clearly observable in Linda's case. If not for the referral of paroxysmal tachycardia, Linda's anorexia nervosa would certainly not have come to the attention of a child analyst. Her play therapy enabled her to bring to the fore and resolve her repressions, as well as her oral greed and envy and the depressive and paranoid feelings associated with them.

The concomitant treatment of the mother revealed that Linda's feelings, though distorted and exaggerated, were founded on reality, i.e., her mother's psychic reality. The mother had rejected Linda because of her sex and her personality. She considered her "a weak crybaby." This rejection was based on the mother's feelings about herself and her own mother. She had repressed these feelings and displaced them onto Linda. The essential achievement in the treatment of the mother was her improved relationship with Linda, which was the result of coming to terms with her own mother and accepting herself and her daughter as female.

Psychoanalytic Treatment of a
Latency-Age Anorexic Child

Seven-year-old Karla was referred for therapy because of a severe eating disturbance that had not responded to medical treatment. It included all the classical symptoms of anorexia nervosa except amenorrhea. Since the onset of the anorexia nervosa a year earlier, she had lost 10 lbs. and, in addition to a general refusal to eat, she had marked aversions to certain foods. She would frequently force herself to vomit after eating, and her attitude toward food and her mother had a paranoid quality. The acute onset of the anorexia nervosa had followed the birth of a brother when Karla was six years old. At that time, she also developed a fear of cats and a suspicious attitude toward her mother. In her treatment, she expressed ideas that her mother was not giving her the right food, did not care for her, disliked girls, and was too preoccupied with the baby brother. As was the case with Linda, the birth of the brother was particularly traumatic for Karla because of the highly ambivalent mother-daughter relationship. She experienced the birth as a rejection by mother on various levels. She had competed with mother for father's attention before and became more possessive and demanding of her father after the baby's birth.

Oral impregnation and anal birth fantasies dominated her fantasy life. Because Karla had also become very constipated, the mother gave her frequent enemas. This was an added stimulation to her already strongly developed anality and became a factor in the distortion of her psychosexual development, which remained bisexual with definite leanings toward a homosexual orientation. This manifested itself in her somewhat paranoid attitude toward her mother, in her cat phobia, and in her hypercathexis of the anal zone. Karla's analysis provided an opportunity to study the oral, anal, and phallic roots of food symbolism and its role in her anorexia nervosa. She had strong cannibalistic impulses that had to be repressed, leading to an inhibition of biting and chewing. She had wishes to eat something "alive." These wishes expressed her fantasy of the baby getting into mother's belly by being swallowed alive. These repressed impulses were in part externalized and projected onto cats in the cat phobia. Her coprophagic impulses played a part in her paranoid attitude toward food; at times, she treated it as if it were a dangerous poison, which in her mind equaled feces-breast-penis and baby. Karla worked well in her treatment, which was brought to a successful conclusion after one and a half years, with a follow-up into late adolescence. The mother was able to avail herself of the guidance offered, and her understanding and cooperation aided the success of the treatment and sustained the therapeutic results.

Karla's attitude toward food is so characteristic of patients with anorexia nervosa that it deserves closer investigation. A few comments about some of the similarities and differences between anorexic food aversion and phobias and nonanorexic, neurotic eating difficulties seem to be indicated.

Nonanorexic, Neurotic Food Idiosyncrasies

Usually, food idiosyncrasies in nonanorexic children also develop in response to maternal attitudes; however, in these cases, the mother passes on her own feelings concerning certain foods to the child. The usual complaint is that the child is very selective and limited in choice of food. This is not a refusal of food because of a need to starve oneself, although this selectivity may lead to undernourishment secondarily. Such food idiosyncrasies occur with equal frequency in both sexes, while true anorexia nervosa is predominantly an affliction of females.

The case of 7-year-old Ted illustrates how such idiosyncrasies can be determined by the mother's own food predilections. Ted did not eat red meat, liver, eggs, butter, most vegetables (especially those with bright colors), anything that contained chocolate, fish and seafood, or anything that smelled. While giving me the history, his mother said, "If you can get him to eat these things, you are a wizard. I can't eat them, so I can't make him eat them." In this case, the mother was fully aware of her own idiosyncrasies, but not of their origin in her own unresolved anality or of the part this had played in her handling of her son's anal phase development.

In some cases, the mother has an unconscious ambivalence about food and about feeding stemming from unresolved conflicts in her own childhood. This is frequently covered up by an overtly indulgent attitude and by offering a great variety of choices to the child. Such an attitude is confusing, and the child senses the mother's ambivalence and responds with finicky eating. This situation can be corrected by making the mother aware of her ambivalence and its role in feeding her child. Once this is overcome, the child usually will eat any food the mother prepares without objections.

The mother may use food as a sadistic weapon against a particular child. Although this may not be apparent to others, the child invariably senses it and responds to it, usually with behavioral and characterological difficulties rather than anorexia nervosa or food idiosyncrasies. The case of Paul, an 8-year-old anorexic, illustrates this point. In the consultation, his mother told the therapist that she was actually aware that she did not want her son to eat in the morning and that, by rattling off a list of foods, she was confusing him—"hitting him with my tongue." He finally would leave for school without breakfast. For dinner, she often would prepare food she knew he did not like and would not eat. The ensuing arguments ended with Paul being sent to his room without dinner. Paul would take money from his mother's purse, stay away from school, and make up stories. He also was a bed-wetter and liked to make fires. In this case, it was necessary to work with the mother first to induce her not to discharge her resentment of her husband on her son and to help her to resolve her hatred of men, which stemmed from her relationships with her brother and father.

Food Phobias and Aversions
in Anorexia Nervosa

Food phobias are common in anorexics; they usually appear during the anal and phallic phases of development when oral and anal impulses are repressed and the symbolic expression of pregenital and phallic impulses (e.g., via food and anal excretion) becomes possible. The specific unconscious meanings of such food phobias can be established only through psychoanalytic investigation that separates the unconscious meaning of the food from the food itself. Pronounced food phobias and aversions in anorexia nervosa are usually an indication of a coexisting strong anal fixation (Sperling 1953, 1970). This can be observed clearly in the psychoanalytic treatment of patients with ulcerative colitis, who have very marked anal fixations (Sperling 1946, 1960, 1969).

Patients with ulcerative colitis frequently also suffer from severe anorexia, which usually is considered a consequence and secondary symptom of the ulcerative colitis. While there can be no doubt that anorexia is a frequent secondary symptom in severe somatic illness, the similarities between adolescent girls with ulcerative colitis and those with true anorexia nervosa regarding behavior toward food, amenorrhea, and bouts of hyperactivity are striking. Like anorexia nervosa, ulcerative colitis frequently afflicts adolescent girls. The combination of ulcerative colitis and anorexia nervosa in some adolescents raises the question of whether these are two different coexisting syndromes that serve different pathological needs or are interdependent and fulfill similar needs through a disturbance of different organ systems and functions (Sperling 1961).

Usually, by the time a patient with ulcerative colitis is referred for psychoanalytic treatment, the ulcerative colitis has existed for a considerable period of time, and anorexia and weight loss are readily accepted as symptoms belonging to the clinical picture of ulcerative colitis. Experience in the treatment of adolescent girls suffering from ulcerative colitis and severe anorexia has made me question the validity of this assumption and prompted me to investigate such cases with this view in mind.

A correct assessment of the dynamics and economic function of each of these two syndromes in the psychopathology of the patient is important both for adequate treatment and for prognosis. The presence of anorexia nervosa points to a predominantly oral fixation and a disturbance in the mother-child relationship at this early (oral) level. Such a fixation may predispose the child to severe (psychotic) depressive reactions with disturbances in the sense of reality in situations of separation and object loss (real or imagined). In contrast, a predominantly anal fixation, especially on the second anal phase, makes for a better prognosis. Some of these points are illustrated in the following case example of the analysis of ulcerative colitis and anorexia nervosa in an adolescent girl with many food phobias and aversions.

CASE 1   Analysis of Anorexia Nervosa and Ulcerative Colitis in an Adolescent Girl

Carol was 16 years old when she was referred for treatment of ulcerative colitis, which she had developed two months earlier while away from home on a summer vacation. She had the typical symptoms: abdominal cramps, bloody diarrhea, anorexia, and weight loss. In the course of analysis, it was found that Carol had suffered from attacks of severe anorexia nervosa several years earlier. Carol's anorexia had set in during puberty when she was about 12 years old. She had always been very close to her mother and up to age 12 had never been separated from her. She felt that her mother had wanted her to be a boy and would love her more if she were one. She had always tried to be boyish in her appearance, interests, and behavior. She had also been very close to her grandfather, with whom she shared many interests and hobbies. She complained that her father was rather distant and frequently absent because of his work.

When she was 12 years old, her grandfather got sick and her mother sent Carol to camp that summer while she took care of him. Several factors made this a particularly traumatic experience for Carol: (1) it was her first separation from her mother; (2) she was disturbed about the pubertal changes she was experiencing; and (3) unconsciously she felt guilty about her grandfather's illness. Her grandfather, who had been a widower for two years, had remarried shortly before he took sick. Analysis revealed that Carol had experienced his remarriage as a rejection and had harbored unconscious death wishes toward him. Her grandfather died while she was in camp. Her unresolved oedipal conflict, which had been displaced onto her grandparents, was reactivated by her grandmother's death and her grandfather's remarriage, illness, and death.

When Carol was three years old, a sister was born. She experienced this as a disappointment and rejection by both parents and responded with a marked change in personality. She became overly submissive and exaggeratedly clinging and dependent on her mother, and her eating difficulties (she had been a finicky eater from infancy) became more pronounced. She also developed cramps and occasional diarrhea, which had recurred since then at times of tension or excitement. She had been told that she had inherited her "weak belly" from her maternal grandmother. Carol's strong identification with her grandmother played a significant part in her ulcerative colitis and, in particular, in her wish to have "all her insides" taken out, as had happened to her grandmother.

During her stay in camp, she starved herself and lost 15 lbs. during the first three weeks. As she put it, "I cut off my appetite." She also neglected her appearance and would not dress, bathe, or wash herself properly. When her mother came to take her home, she looked like a skeleton. This was her first attack of anorexia nervosa. The anorexia nervosa never fully subsided, and it became more intense in certain situations. Her psychoanalysis, which was undertaken for the treatment of her ulcerative colitis, provided an opportunity to study the genesis and dynamics of her anorexia, as well as the relation between the two syndromes.

THERAPY.   The following fragments from her analysis occurred when her ulcerative colitis had greatly improved and she was overcoming a severe, 9-month attack of anorexia nervosa. She was 18 years old and had had two years of analysis.

She had thought about what she was doing to herself. She said that it felt just like it had at puberty when she had been afraid of growing up and developing definite sex characteristics. Now she was getting herself back to that stage of no breasts, no roundings, no menstrual periods. The attack of anorexia had followed the breakup of her relationship with her boyfriend and her renunciation of all sexual interest and activity. It also had coincided with her sister's pregnancy; as her sister got fuller and fuller, Carol got skinnier by the day. She felt that she had gotten herself back to prepuberty and said that she even had the same sensations that she used to have then, in particular, the sensation of being "all bones and the skin off." When she touched her skin, she felt as if she were touching a toad.

She suddenly realized when and how the feeling of being just bones had originated. When she was in nursery school, she had to take a nap, but she didn't want to sleep, so she would lie there and fantasize about witches tying her up and torturing her, especially by tickling her feet. She would lie on her stomach with her legs pulled up and her arms under her legs. The arms and legs would fall asleep, and she would have the sensation of being just bone until the feeling came back. She also remembered a (cannibalistic) witches' game she used to play in kindergarten (age 4–5). In this make-believe game, the child playing the victim would be symbolically sprinkled with salt and pepper, roasted in the oven, and then eaten by the group.

These memories provided access to her infantile sexual fantasy life, with oral sadistic impregnation and anal sadistic birth fantasies. Genital sexuality, especially masturbation, was dangerous because of its murderous implications, which resulted from her intense, unresolved oedipal conflict. This sexuality was displaced from the front (genitals) to the rear (anus) and from below upward (mouth). Her heterosexual and homosexual wishes also were dealt with on this regressed level and found symbolic expression in the symptoms of her anorexia nervosa and ulcerative colitis. Because of the incestuous and destructive nature of her fantasies and impulses, pleasure was turned into pain. Instead of experiencing sexual excitement and masturbatory temptations, she would awaken during the night with bellyaches and a need to run to the toilet or with nausea and a need to vomit. She also had strong coprophagic and phallic wishes.

Sometimes she would have the sensation that her legs were stiff and enlarged, and this sensation could spread over her whole body. Her body would feel huge, like a giant's body. She was afraid of injections; it was the sticking in of the needle, rather than the pain, that upset her.

It was of the utmost importance to her that her abdomen be absolutely flat, preferably nonexistent, and for this reason alone rigid starvation was necessary. This obsessional need for a "flat abdomen" is a frequent feature in adolescent girls with anorexia nervosa. Carol was frigid and fearful in intercourse, to which she had submitted in order "to keep" her boyfriend and get a feeling of "bodily closeness." She was very possessive and controlling in all her relationships and, at times, her suspiciousness had a paranoid quality.

In the course of the analysis, her numerous food aversions and the cannibalistic and coprophagic impulses underlying them were brought to the fore. To her, feces were poison. Even if there were only a slight stain on her finger and she "accidently" brought her hand to her mouth, it could poison her. A hamburger was diarrhea; cheeseburgers were even worse. Sometimes she could eat them voraciously and sometimes not at all. Her grandfather and father liked to eat Camembert, and they used to give her little pieces when she was a very small child. She would eat them very slowly. During the period of anorexia, it could take her an hour to eat one cracker with a little piece of Camembert. She would eat it baby-fashion, in tiny pieces. At times, she only wanted to eat "light" food—that is, food that was light in color and consistency, such as milk, ice cream, and chicken soup. Then she felt like a baby. At other times, she could eat "dark" food, which represented feces, poison, sperm, babies, and people. It therefore had to be gotten out before it could do her harm—that is, poison or impregnate her. At such times, she had nausea, vomiting, and diarrhea, and looked for blood in her stools.

When she was constipated, she felt good on the toilet, as if she were giving birth to a baby. Formed stools meant a full-term baby. Diarrhea was a miscarriage—a baby cut up into pieces (Sperling 1960). She talked about the colitis as her "way of miscarrying." As a child, especially when her mother told her about the amniotic sac bursting, she wondered how the baby could be prevented from falling into the toilet. After relating such fantasies, she would ask, "Do you hate me?" She felt angry that she had talked about her fantasies and projected her anger onto me. She felt as if she had cement in her mouth and expressed the idea that diarrhea was soft cement that hardened in the mouth.

She loved vegetables and salads because they are grown in manure. She also loved cheese, especially Camembert, because it smelled like feces. Her father was a food ritualist who ate the same things all the time. For Carol, eating meant carrying out a ritual for mystical reasons. Food was not food, and eating was not for the pleasure of eating or to satisfy hunger. She was never hungry, she said. Eating was devouring feces or something forbidden. She would eat the same breakfast all the time: oatmeal or hard-boiled eggs. She could not stand the soft, loose egg white: this was mucus, snot. She never ate mayonnaise: this was snot, too, because of its color and consistency. She would get a craving for a certain food and would eat it continually and exclusively for a short time—and then stop as abruptly as she had started. Recently, she had a craving for frankfurters, and ate them. It felt good to get the warm frankfurter inside; it felt as if she had "a fetish" inside. She made sure to add that, to her, a fetish was not a sexual symbol, but represented feces and "other things." As in conversion hysteria, there was a displacement from the genital to the pregenital level, but with a conscious deemphasis of sexuality. She liked drinking milk because it made her feel like a baby with her mother. She liked to mash up her food so that she could not tell what was in it.

During this period of analysis, she was eating and gaining weight. She noticed that her skirts did not fit. She had not even been aware that she had put on that much weight—10 lbs. She just ate; it was not like before, when she was so self-conscious and it was such an effort to eat. Before, she would actually stop herself from eating. She complained that now she looked like a girl and had her period, whereas before she had had no period, had been emaciated, and had not looked like a girl at all.

She was a compulsive tooth-brusher and mouth-washer. She brushed her teeth innumerable times every day and at times washed her mouth out with soap. She carefully examined her teeth for (fecal) stains. She always had to brush her teeth before leaving her house or she would be forced to return. Now she frequently "forgot" to brush her teeth, just as she "forgot" to stop eating after a few bites and instead finished everything on her plate. Likewise, she often "forgot" to go to the toilet as soon as she took a bite or felt a little cramp. It became quite evident that an important mechanism in her anorexia nervosa was her compulsive need to control her appetite and food intake. The decision to eat and the appeal and repulsion of certain foods were clearly based on psychological, rather than physiological, factors.

The Interrelated Dynamics of Anorexia Nervosa
and Ulcerative Colitis

In my initial studies of ulcerative colitis in children (Sperling 1946), I gained the impression that the severe eating inhibition in these cases was not a secondary symptom and consequence of the ulcerative colitis. Rather, I saw it as a primary symptom that served a dynamic function on the oral level, just as the cramps and diarrhea served such a function on the anal level. I considered severe ulcerative colitis to be the somatic dramatization of the same conflicts that caused overt melancholic depression in other patients. I saw the severe eating inhibition in these patients as a defense against the oral sadistic (cannibalistic) incorporation of the need-object, and the diarrhea as a mechanism of instant (anal) discharge of the sadistically incorporated object(s). The degree of destructiveness and libidinization (sexualization) determined the psychodynamics of the underlying depression, which ranged from psychotic to neurotic (Sperling 1946, 1955a, 1957, 1960, 1967).

In continued work with such patients, I found that the depression underlying the ulcerative colitis was often of the manic-depressive type. The depression was expressed mainly in the eating inhibition, disturbed sleep, and bodily suffering, and the manic tendencies were most evident in massive denial and visceral hyperactivity (Sperling 1968a). I have found very similar dynamics to be operative in anorexia nervosa. Here, too, the depressive tendencies are manifested in the eating inhibition, and the manic tendencies are manifested in excessive denial and general hyperactivity. The phenomenon of alternating episodes of anorexia nervosa and bulimia in some patients is also of interest in this connection. Here, the depression is expressed in the anorexia, and the manic tendencies, in the bulimia (Wulff 1932). Many anorexic patients fear that giving up the anorexia will result in loss of control—that they will not be able to stop eating or other activities when they want to. For them, the anorexia is equated with impulse control. Anorexia as a mechanism of control—or rather, "overcontrol"—will be dealt with more extensively in the discussion of the clinical material.

The Coexistence of Anorexia Nervosa
with Other Psychoneurotic or Psychosomatic Disorders

Anorexia nervosa may coexist with other psychoneurotic or psychosomatic disorders. The case of an adolescent girl referred for treatment because of cyclic vomiting comes to mind in this connection. Her attacks of vomiting were limited to the time of her menstrual period; the anorexia nervosa, however, was a permanent symptom that became aggravated during menstruation. Analysis revealed that both symptoms represented specific modes of dealing with unconscious conflicts, fears, and fantasies concerning impregnation, pregnancy, and childbirth. This patient also suffered from severe cat and insect phobias. She was especially fearful of swallowing flying insects. She was also a hair-puller and hair-eater (Sperling 1968b). Like many patients with anorexia nervosa, she could "turn off" her appetite by completely denying her hunger.

Since this patient retained her menstrual periods, it may be questioned whether this was a true anorexia nervosa.

Other investigators have observed the association of anorexia nervosa with various psychosomatic disorders and have remarked on the frequency of surgical intervention in these cases. Tucker (1952) reports on two patients who suffered from ulcerative colitis and anorexia nervosa. The female patient had had many hospitalizations, several courses of ECT and insulin shock treatment, and various surgical interventions, including an ileostomy. According to Tucker, a bimedial prefrontal lobotomy resulted in a cure of all her symptoms. There was a 6-month follow-up at which time the cure persisted. The male patient suffered from severe anorexia, constipation, and gastrointestinal symptoms. Like the woman patient, he had not responded to psychotherapy or medical treatment, and so a bimedial frontal lobotomy was performed. At the 4-month follow-up, the patient had doubled his weight and still had a "definite tendency to overeat." The follow-up periods are short; the personality changes subsequent to these lobotomies are glossed over; and the two patients are used to advocate the efficiency of psychosurgery in such cases.

Ferrara and Fontana (1966) report on the coexistence of anorexia nervosa and celiac disease in an 11-year-old girl. They found that the severe weight loss and eating inhibition of this patient were due to anorexia nervosa and were not secondary symptoms and sequelae of the celiac disease. Because of this girl's history of similar episodes and withdrawn behavior during her hospitalization, a psychiatrist was consulted. His diagnosis was nonspecific psychiatric disorder with extreme dejection and blunted affect. During hypnosis, it was brought out that disgust and fear of bowel movements appeared to be associated with ingestion of food. Her father had put great emphasis on defecating and eating. Hypnosis also revealed that strong aggressive feelings were directed against the father; the hypnotist felt that the anorexia was a powerful weapon and rebellion against him. This patient's illness had set in shortly after her twin sister's menarche. The patient herself remained amenorrheic during the several months of her hospitalization.

The Father-Daughter Relationship

The emphasis in this chapter has been on the role of the mother-child relationship in anorexia nervosa. A few remarks about the father-daughter relationship and the dynamic role it plays in this condition seem indicated. My therapeutic work with the parents of anorexics has shown that frequently the onset of anorexia nervosa symptoms was preceded by, or coincided with, a change in the overt behavior of the patient toward her parents. In the analytic treatment, it was found that the change in the overt behavior reflected a change from a positive to a negative oedipal constellation in these patients. Instead of competing with mother for the attention of the father, as before, these patients now exhibited a competitive rivalry with the father for the affection of the mother with a possessive-controlling (homosexual) attitude toward her. This regression from the oedipal to the preoedipal (oral-anal) relationship with the mother was often associated with a negation of genital sexuality and heterosexuality. The anorexia nervosa also served to defeminize the girl and to make her unattractive to her father and to men.

These changes in feelings and behavior, as well as the onset of the anorexia nervosa, often follow a real or imagined disappointment and rejection by the father. For example, one 12-year-old girl started a rigid diet that later developed into anorexia nervosa following a remark of her father's concerning her weight and her preference for fattening foods. She had interpreted this remark as a rejection of her developing femininity. Of course, this is only one link in the chain of pathological developments and traumatic experiences that precipitates the manifest symptoms of anorexia nervosa in these girls. In the case of the patient just mentioned, she had correctly interpreted her father's remark. He had a decided preference for slim, boyish-looking women, but, even more important, as long as she still looked infantile, he could be close to her without guilt. Again, it must be stressed that this was only one of many contributing factors.

When the patient devalues or denies the father's influence, she is employing a defensive maneuver against her powerful positive oedipal strivings. The following case material from the analyses of an anorexic adolescent and her mother illustrate this point.

CASE 2   *The Psychoanalytic Treatment*
of an Adolescent Girl and Her Mother

Helen was referred for treatment when she was 15 years old, following a 9-month period of illness during which she had been hospitalized three times in different hospitals because of severe anorexia, vomiting, and a low-grade fever for which no organic basis was found. In the hospital, her condition improved, but the cycle repeated itself as soon as she returned home. After three sessions, it was clear that she would not accept treatment because of her relationship with her mother. The latter's overeagerness for Helen to start therapy concealed opposing unconscious wishes, and it was to these that Helen was reacting. Helen was not pressured when she indicated her unwillingness for therapy. She and her analyst agreed that she should return to school in spite of her mother's apprehensions; she would contact the analyst if she experienced any difficulty.

THE MOTHER'S THERAPY.   Without Helen's knowledge, the analyst arranged psychoanalytic therapy for the mother because this seemed the best way to help Helen at that time and also, perhaps, to render her more amenable to psychoanalytic treatment in the future. The mother revealed very strong guilt feelings regarding her daughter's illness. She felt intuitively that her child's condition was in some way related to her, although she did not know how. She had expressed this feeling to the attending physicians and had actually prompted Helen's referral. She was very aware that Helen could eat much better away from home and that she stopped eating and began vomiting when she returned home.

Helen was her only child and she had always given her much attention and care. Until Helen was about 13, they had been very close. At that time, Helen began to detach herself from her mother and became very close to a girlfriend. At her mother's instigation, she broke off this friendship shortly before her 14th birthday. The mother now blamed herself for having destroyed this relationship and connected this event with the onset of Helen's illness. She tried to rationalize that the friend was not a good influence on Helen, but came to realize that she had actually resented the friend for taking her daughter away from her.

Later, in Helen's analysis, it was found that in her attempts to separate herself from her mother in early adolescence, she had transferred her pathological relationship from mother to friend, becoming as dependent on the friend as she had been on her mother. For some time preceding the onset of the acute anorexia and vomiting, Helen's mother, who previously had been overindulgent with Helen (reward for dependence), had been very critical and disapproving of her (rejection of strivings for independence). During her analysis, the mother was able to understand that she had been unable to differentiate herself from Helen and to accept her as a separate being with an individuality of her own. The relationship with Helen made up for an unsatisfactory marriage, and she could not bear to lose her to the girlfriend. She was even more distressed by Helen's interest in boys, which she considered premature and blamed on the influence of the girlfriend. She managed to bring about the social isolation of her daughter who, instead of having a party (she had no one to invite), got sick on her 14th birthday.

Helen improved remarkably during the first few months of her mother's treatment. She lost her symptoms, gained 20 lbs., and her menses returned. At the analyst's suggestion, the mother did not coax Helen to eat, but permitted her to take her food herself and to eat her lunches in school. Helen made up with the girlfriend and made a number of other friends at school. She spent very little time at home.

THE DAUGHTER'S THERAPY.   Helen came for psychoanalytic treatment at the age of 16 1/2, after her mother had terminated. The precipitating event was a disappointment in a boyfriend, to which Helen had reacted with a sore throat and persistent fever that resisted medication. Organic bases for her condition had been ruled out. She readily accepted her doctor's suggestion (he knew of her past history) to see her ex-analyst. She told the analyst that she had been seeing a young man and that, shortly before she had become ill, they had had a quarrel. She had expected him to call her and had stayed home for two days guarding the telephone, constantly expecting his call. Because they had had an argument she was not certain that he wanted to see her again. It was on the second day of her anxious waiting that she fell ill.

Helen was able to understand and overcome her psychosomatic mode of reacting to disappointment, separation, and loss. She learned to tolerate consciously painful feelings without getting sick physically. In the course of her analysis, it was possible to explore the deeper dynamics of her earlier anorexia. She stated that as a child she had been aware that her parents were not happily married and that her mother monopolized her by excluding her father. Her mother had always belittled her father and portrayed him as inconsiderate and interested only in sexual exploitation. She felt that her mother had a low opinion of men in general. The mother seemed to have conveyed to Helen a masochistic concept of the female role. This attitude toward the husband and men in general is a prevalent feature among mothers of anorexic adolescent girls. Her father's attempts to get closer to her were experienced by Helen as seductive attempts that she both enjoyed and feared. Up to about 14 years of age, she had been overweight and had masturbated excessively, with only barely concealed incestuous rape fantasies. At that time, boys were beginning to make passes at her and her father frequently would remark that she was developing into a real woman. She was preoccupied with sexual fantasies and temptations, and the close friendship with her girlfriend served to protect her from these heterosexual dangers. At the same time, it made it possible for her to continue in a more acceptable form the type of relationship she had had with her mother. She had been her mother's confidante, favored at the expense of her father.

Her menses had been irregular since her menarche at 13 1/2. Shortly after her 14th birthday, she had decided to stop masturbating and had gone on a reducing diet and lost weight rapidly. She had vomited whenever she transgressed her self-imposed dietary restrictions. She also had developed amenorrhea. Her amenorrhea had preceded the weight loss and had lasted for exactly nine months. Analysis revealed that she had displaced her masturbatory conflicts and her pregnancy wishes and fears from the genital (overtly sexual) to the oral sphere. Instead of being preoccupied with sexual thoughts and temptations, she had become preoccupied with controlling or, rather, "overcontrolling" her food intake. This mechanism is characteristic of anorexic patients.

Another typical feature of anorexic patients is the feeling of "either-or," which is particularly threatening in regard to sexuality. This tendency, too, Helen had displaced to the oral sphere. She was afraid that unless she stopped certain urges or activities completely, she would be unable to control them at all and would be totally at the mercy of all her (dangerous) impulses. This latter tendency to lose control and to act out her impulses became more apparent after she gave up the anorexia. She made innumerable friends (all very superficial relationships), spent little time at home, let herself be picked up by strange boys (playing with the very danger she feared most), and had periods of overeating.

Helen could be diagnosed as a cyclothymic personality, with a tendency toward alternating depressive and mild hypomanic states. In her psychosomatic pattern of response, the depressive aspects manifested themselves in the somatic symptoms, physical pain, and forced inactivity; the hypomanic tendencies were expressed in her acting-out behavior. In her anorexia nervosa, the depressive aspects were expressed in the refusal to eat or enjoy pleasure (cutting off all sexual fantasies and activity), while the hypomanic tendencies were evident in the vomiting and general hyperactivity.

When Helen got engaged at age 19, her mother had a recurrence of the insomnia with depressive feelings. She returned for more treatment. Her daughter's analysis had been successfully terminated (Sperling 1970).

CASE 3   *Analysis of an Adolescent Girl with a Psychotic Mother*

This case shows that successful treatment is possible in some cases where the mother is too sick to be involved in her daughter's treatment.

Anita was 14 years old when she was referred for treatment by the hospital where she had been admitted because of severe anorexia nervosa. Anita was unhappy and uncooperative in the hospital and the consulting physician suggested psychiatric exploration. Anita accepted the referral readily.

Following menarche at age 13½, Anita put herself on a diet "because she didn't like the way her breasts began to look" and, in less than six months, her weight dropped from 98 to 62 lbs. She also suffered from constipation and amenorrhea. She refused to eat with her family and would throw food that her mother made for her into the garbage pail. Sometimes she would retrieve and eat some of this food. After eating, she would go to the toilet, lock the door, and force herself to vomit. She would remain there for an inordinate length of time, knowing that this upset and frightened her parents.

Anita's mother suffered from a physical handicap that made communication with her rather difficult. In addition, she appeared quite paranoid. Anita's maternal grandmother, who lived with the family, was overtly psychotic. The father appeared to be comparatively healthy and genuinely interested in Anita's welfare. Anita also had a brother five years younger than she, of whom she was intensely jealous. Following the birth of the brother there had been a manifest change in her feelings; in her words, "the house became cold." She would often state that she felt cold at home, even on hot summer days.

Anita had always suffered from constipation. She claimed that she never had had a "natural" bowel movement and always had needed laxatives and enemas. With the onset of the anorexia, the constipation became even more severe and Anita would tell her mother that she had not moved her bowels for two to three weeks at a time. She had been receiving frequent enemas from her mother, but her analysis was interfering with this habit. She was in a constant struggle with this "habit," especially after she convinced herself on several occasions that she could have a natural bowel movement.

This struggle became even more intense after her anorexia improved. She would make promises to herself and swear on a Bible that she would not ask her mother for enemas anymore. Toward the end of her first year of analysis, the following incident occurred. One evening, Anita had taken a laxative but could not move her bowels. She felt that she had to get "it" out or she would explode. She went into the kitchen and took a knife and started to cut herself near the pubic region. Her mother came in and took the knife away and offered to give her an enema. She was so panicky that she broke her oath. For some time following this incident, Anita again became dependent on her mother for enemas. Anita seemed to have sensed and responded to her mother's need to regain anally, through the "enema relationship," the control she had lost on the oral level.

Since Anita's mother was neither available nor amenable to therapy herself, it was Anita's task to understand and renounce the gratification she derived from this pathological relationship with her mother. Fortunately, Anita showed a remarkable degree of determination to overcome her illness and use her innate abilities constructively.

Another favorable circumstance was her positive relationship with the referring physician. He had taken her out of the hospital and she felt that she could not disappoint him. Besides, if her treatment failed, the alternative was rehospitalization. Finally, she seemed to believe that her analyst understood her and could be trusted. In view of the fact that she was quite suspicious generally, this was a favorable indication.

During the first few years of her life, when she was the only child and grandchild in the family, Anita was indulged by both her mother and her grandmother. From early childhood on, Anita had been very fond of her father, expressing wishes to marry him. Her strong positive oedipal relationship indicated normal psychosexual female development. However, her mother would accuse her of being in love with her father and interested in older men; these accusations continued up to the time of Anita's treatment. With the birth of her brother, her relationship with her mother changed manifestly, while the resentment against her father was kept under repression and, overtly, she retained the positive relationship with him. Anita felt displaced by the baby. She developed some eating difficulties and became constipated, apparently competing for mother's attention. Her analysis revealed that there had been deeper motives and meanings behind her early eating difficulties and constipation. Stimulated by her mother's pregnancy and the birth of the brother, Anita had been expressing unconscious infantile pregnancy and birth fantasies (Sylvester 1945).

Anita became resentful of her father during puberty, when he began to favor her brother, who was becoming a big boy. Anita had been a tomboy, which both of her parents seemed to have encouraged. She had to face the fact that she could not outdo her brother in this way, but she did not consider herself successful as a girl. Also, a boy in whom she had been interested began to pay attention to her girlfriend. She felt rejected as a female. She suddenly stopped masturbating and went on a diet. Her masturbatory struggle was now displaced from the overtly sexual, genital sphere to a struggle over food intake. She regressed to oral and anal levels and dealt with her oedipal and sexual conflicts on these levels. There was also a regression from heterosexuality to the preoedipal relationship with her mother. This became apparent in Anita's attitude toward her mother and her two girlfriends.

With the onset of the anorexia nervosa, her constipation increased and she became preoccupied not only with controlling her intake of food but also with her output of feces (instead of with sexual fantasies and masturbation). She renounced her femininity: she did not want to have breasts and a menstrual period; she would make herself unattractive to boys. She was competing with boys for the attention of her girlfriends, with whom she had a controlling relationship similar to the one with her mother. She hated her grandmother for monopolizing her mother (grandmother and mother had never been separated). She had conscious murderous impulses toward her grandmother. The grandmother controlled the entire household and had become particularly demanding and critical of Anita. In part, these impulses stemmed from her unresolved positive oedipal conflict and were deflected from her mother to her grandmother. Femininity and sexuality were dangerous. They were associated with injury and murder. Her frequent nightmares usually dealt with murder, stabbing, and bleeding. In one recurrent nightmare, a girl was killed and Anita was suspected of the murder. Analysis of these dreams revealed that one meaning of her anorexia nervosa was to kill the female in herself because she identified it with mother, grandmother, and insanity.

The meaning of the enemas was also overdetermined. In giving her the enemas, the mother became the seducer and attacker. In this way, Anita relieved herself of some of her guilt feelings about her own murderous impulses and her perverse relationship with her mother, which she instigated and needed, and from which she derived gratification. Obviously, her mother's own need played a part in this, but it was not possible to explore this aspect. When Anita held back her stools for long periods of time and then urgently needed an enema, it meant that her mother was delivering her of the baby (brother), whom she had wanted to take from mother. Analysis revealed that the cutting with the knife had represented a Caesarean operation. In the transference, the cutting was aimed to intimidate the analyst so that she would be agreeable to the continuation of the enemas.

Anita was not seriously suicidal, although she permitted herself to go to the "brink" in her self-starvation. Like many anorexic patients, she felt omnipotent and invulnerable. She took pleasure in sadistic teasing, a typical anorexic characteristic, and liked to frighten, upset, and punish her mother. Once her mother found a rope in Anita's bed and, suspecting a suicide attempt, accused her of being crazy. Anita's reaction was, "If she had found a rope in my brother's bed, she would have thought nothing of it. Everything he does is right, everything I do is wrong." She actually had placed the rope there in order to provoke such a reaction from her mother. Anita was also cruel with herself; not only did she deprive herself of food and pleasure, but she also hurt herself in her most sensitive area—her appearance. She was very sensitive when people called her skinny; yet she made herself look like a walking skeleton. She had the idea that if a boy touched her, he would hurt himself because she was so bony. She thought that boys would never ask her out because of her appearance.

In the second year of analysis, when these dynamics were brought to the fore and worked through, Anita began to show interest in boys and started dating. She had given up the anorexia nervosa and self-destructive hyperactivity earlier in her analysis. She had regained the lost weight, and her menses had returned during the first year of analysis. She rarely needed any laxatives. Her analysis was terminated after two years.

An episode some two years after termination indicated that she had achieved a real change in personality. She contracted a gastrointestinal infection that usually causes vomiting and lack of appetite, but she neither vomited nor lost her appetite during this illness. Her internist was the same one who had referred her for treatment; he was so impressed with this behavior that he informed the analyst.

Eight years after termination, Anita remained well; she was preparing for a professional career and had been happily married for two years.

CASE 4 *Analysis of a Middle-Aged Woman*

This is the first report in the literature of successfully treated anorexia nervosa in a patient of middle age.

Rose, a married woman, began her analysis in her early fifties. She had lost 30 lbs. during the three months preceding the start of analysis. She had been so weakened by this weight loss that she had collapsed at home and had been rushed to a hospital, where a diagnosis of anorexia nervosa was made. She had not wished to remain in the hospital and had been referred for analysis.

She appeared depressed and did not speak much. For the first few months, in a monotone, she reiterated how she had sacrificed herself to her family. Her mother had suffered from paranoia before Rose was born, and she had become schizophrenic when Rose was three. There was a two-year-older brother, and a three-year-younger sister, and a much younger brother born during Rose's adolescence. She had a very close relationship with her older brother, but hated her sister so much that she could not be in the same room with her. She would start to scream and run away whenever her sister appeared. Nevertheless, she had found her sister a husband and had arranged the wedding for her. She also had bought her furniture and had given her a sizable amount of money. She had set up her older brother in business and had cared for her younger brother as if he were her own baby. She had put him through school, including college and graduate training. Quite clearly, she felt that she had successfully replaced both parents. She had been able to do this because she had worked for a wealthy man who became interested and extended his generosity to her family.

At age three or four, she had been aware of her mother's illness and incompetence and, as a young child, had taken over many chores for her mother. Later in her analysis, when speaking of this period of her life, she would refer to herself as the "little old lady." She visualized herself as a tiny creature who rushed around doing things like a big person. She once drew a sketch of herself as a dwarf carrying bundles bigger than herself. She considered herself the pillar of her family and thought of her father as an unreliable man and provider. She had been a very bright child and had entered high school when she was 11 years old. Yet, because of her other interests, she had barely managed to finish high school and had not gone on to college.

She had educated herself fairly well and was very proud that she had accomplished this on her own. Although pale and emaciated, she was still a handsome woman. Later in her analysis, she spoke in a flat voice with little affect, but obvious pride, of her appeal to men. In childhood, she had entertained a wish to marry a rich man. At age 18, in order to get away from home, she had married a young man who was neither rich nor intelligent; he had agreed to make no difficulties for her should she want a divorce. After one year of marriage, she had divorced him, although she thought that they were well-matched sexually. This had been her first and only satisfactory sexual experience.

After her divorce, she had met the man who became the benefactor of her family. She had worked at his office for several years and then had left her family and hometown. She had married her present husband after a short courtship and appeared to repeat with him the life pattern of her family. For many years, she had earned more money than he and had supported his hobbies and "extravagant needs." After the first two years of marriage, she had stopped sexual relations with her husband. The marriage was childless. She did not want to have any children and rationalized this with a concern that her offspring might inherit the insanity of her mother.

In the course of her analysis, it was found that precursors of her anorexia nervosa went back to childhood. During puberty and early adolescence she had had several episodes of acute withdrawal, depression, and refusal to eat. During these episodes, she would neglect herself, not washing, dressing sloppily, and staying out of school. She would snap out of these states and resume her activities as if nothing happened—in fact, with excessive vigor. She had had increasingly severe recurrences of such episodes all through her life. At her husband's suggestion, she had gone for analytic treatment early in her marriage. She was aware that she had not really made use of that opportunity and had gained little from her treatment.

She was aware that she really did not want to eat and ate just enough for survival. She had great difficulty in associating freely, and there were long silences and no dreams. She maintained that she very seldom dreamed. She recalled that during her first analysis she also had had very few dreams.

Her first reported dream, at the beginning of the third month of analysis, was clearly a transference dream. She was in the waiting room of a sanitarium similar to the one where her mother had been a patient. Her analyst appeared both as herself and as the physician in charge. The analyst had "this look" in her eyes and Rose knew that the analyst was crazy. When she awoke, she felt hopeless, that her analyst was crazy and could not help her. Associating further, she said that previously she had felt very secure with the analyst. In fact, she had felt that if anybody could help her, it was the analyst. But this had completely changed now. The day before the dream she and her analyst had discussed her suspicion of the analyst and her irrational treatment behavior. Her analyst had indicated to Rose that she was giving in to the irrational part of herself instead of listening to her. The interpretation was made that she was punishing herself by denying herself the pleasures of eating, sleeping (she suffered from severe insomnia), and a sex life.

The analyst pointed out that while Rose impressed herself, the analyst, and others with what she had done for her family, it appeared that she treated herself as if she had committed a crime. She responded by telling the analyst that she had figured out what the crime was: "Maybe I was pushing my mother aside and taking her place." Actually, as an adolescent, she had arranged for her mother to be committed to a mental hospital. The situation at home had become very bad; her mother had not been feeding Rose's baby brother because she claimed that the milk was poisoned. On occasion, she had picked up a knife in anger and had threatened her children with it. Nobody had wanted to accept the seriousness of the mother's condition, so Rose had taken the initiative. She had visited her several times in the sanitarium, but then had stopped because it was too much of a strain. She felt guilty for not visiting her mother and for taking the baby away, although consciously she felt that she had done the right thing.

Later in her analysis, after she recovered her dream memory, she not only remembered many dreams, but her dreams seemed to be more vivid and colorful. This was also true of her feelings in the waking state; she became more aware of colors and light, whereas previously everything had been grayish. She had many dreams about her father and about moving. Wherever she moved, her father was there. He seemed to follow her. She understood that he did not actually follow her, but that she could not let go of him. She would often ask, "How do I get a divorce from him?" Her anorexia had developed shortly after she had moved from one apartment to another. She had felt overwhelmed, unable to get the place in order and take care of the necessary repairs. She could not shop for the things she needed and finally became so fatigued that she could not even prepare a meal.

This condition persisted during her analysis. She felt as if she had lead in her legs and had to "grit my teeth" to get up. It was a tremendous effort to wash, to dress, or even to brush her teeth. She spent many hours of the day resting in a prone position. At night, she could not sleep, but would smoke incessantly and walk around the apartment. After she moved, she felt it had been a big mistake. This was her general attitude toward any change, and it manifested itself as resistance in her analysis. In the past, these periods of fatigue had alternated with episodes of hyperactivity in which she would dance to exhaustion and work long hours without interruption.

She was overpunctual—always on time, most often early—and never missed an appointment. If she missed once, there was a danger that she might not come at all. If she started to eat, she might not stop. She had to exercise this rigid overcontrol as a defense against the impulse to lose control, particularly in the sexual area. She was extremely constipated and very secretive about her bowel habits. She often had to remove pieces of stool from her rectum manually. Every improvement provoked renewed resistance. She had to be frigid on all levels—sexually, with food, with pleasure, with life in general. She permitted herself no enjoyment and was very envious of her husband's ability to enjoy himself. These dynamics were evident in a dream about a drunken bum who came into Rose's apartment. She could not speak, so her husband called the police. A male detective and a policewoman walked in. By this time, the bum was lying on the floor and Rose had her foot next to his head, ready to kick him if he moved. The policewoman showed her a leash on which to put the bum.

In light of previous discussions about her fear of her repressed impulses (the "bum in her") breaking out, she wondered why she had thought of the intruder as a bum, rather than a burglar or someone threatening, and why she had been so terrified of a mere bum in the dream. After the analysis of this dream, she felt freer to talk about her past and her impulses. She was surprised that she had managed to leave her past behind. She thought that the way she had carried on, she easily could have ended up as a drunken bum.

She really did not like to drink and would pretend to be drunk when she had had one drink; it was like "putting on an act." She connected her frozen feeling and inability to speak in the dream with her overcaution in analysis; she was afraid to open up because something might slip out that she did not want to reveal. In the dream, her husband had called the police because she was unable to speak; in reality, her husband had played an active part in her referral to the analyst (the policewoman). She knew she was suspicious and overcautious. She was very rigid and had to plan and think everything over in advance to prevent becoming upset and losing control. It was later brought out that this attitude concealed an intense fear of being psychotic and ending up in an institution like her mother. This fear was apparent in the first dream she reported, but she projected it onto the analyst, making her the crazy one. This fear explained her intense resistance to analysis. Once it had been partly worked through, her fear of losing control, of feeling, and of recognizing her impulses was brought out more openly. Denial, overcompensation, and reaction formation were the main mechanisms that protected her from her feelings and impulses; to her, being aware of them meant releasing them instantly.

Her narcissism was so intense that it could be protected only by continued masochistic behavior. In her second year of marriage, she had felt hurt and rejected by her husband. Instead of discussing her feelings with him, she had stopped their sexual relations and actually had coaxed him into behavior that was hurtful to her. She became the martyr (her earlier family role) and was indispensable to her husband. He confided in her as her father and older brother had, and she was helpful and "suffered," accumulating a store of justifications for her hatred and for the emotional deprivations she imposed on him. His dependence on her gratified her fantasy of omnipotent control and counteracted her fear that he might leave her. Further analysis revealed that, to her, her marriage had the meaning of continuing to live with her father. After her mother's death, her sister's and brother's marriages, and her divorce, she had returned to live with her father and her younger brother. The working through of her relationship with her father, her brothers, her husband, and men took considerable time. She had been unable to form any genuine relationships with men. Her relationships were of a mutually exploitative nature, but she always had felt that her husband got more than he gave. She also had had this feeling from childhood in relation to her father and older brother. Her father did not remarry, and her older brother confided that he had an "asexual marriage." The younger brother, who was very young when his mother died and supposedly did not know about her illness, was the only one who had children. She regarded him as her child (in punishment for "taking him away from mother," she could not have a child of her own) and had genuine grandmotherly feelings for his children.

Her analysis terminated after three and a half years by mutual agreement. Rose no longer had anorexia nervosa and no longer had to atone for her "crimes" by depriving herself of all enjoyment and instinctual gratification, i.e., food, sex, sleep, and excretory functions. She could enjoy her home life, work, and social life.

Positive factors that contributed to the successful outcome were Rose's relatively happy infancy and early childhood (before age three, when her mother became ill), and her well-developed ego and superego. Analysis helped her to modify her rigid, obsessive-compulsive defenses, to relax her fears of a breakthrough of impulses, and to utilize the energies freed from her symptoms and "overcontrol" for the pursuit of more appropriate and constructive activities in real life. She had maintained these gains in a 6-year follow-up.

Anorexia Nervosa in Males

Like most investigators, my experience with male anorexic patients is limited. Of the three anorexic male patients I have analyzed, one had ulcerative colitis and the other two had spastic colitis and hemorrhoids. All three were adolescents and none came for analysis because of the anorexia, although it was severe in each case. An unconscious identification with the mother was a prominent feature (see Falstein et al. 1956). In addition, in two patients, an identification with an envied and hated sister was an important dynamic factor. It was my impression, however, that the feminine identification was primarily a defense against intense castration anxiety that stemmed from an unresolved positive oedipal conflict with hate and fear of the father. All three patients had marked bisexuality, with feminine wishes and pregnancy fantasies symbolically expressed in pregenital conversion (and somatic) symptoms (i.e., constipation, diarrhea, abdominal cramps, hemorrhoids, and rectal bleeding) (Sperling 1957, 1961). Like female patients, male patients may use anorexia as a means of controlling sexual impulses and activities via displacement onto food.

However, certain qualities characteristic of true anorexia nervosa in females are missing. While, in the female, refusal of food is a declaration of independence from mother and often expresses a reversal of roles, in the male, it may increase dependence and be a means of getting special food—i.e., special attention and love—from mother. Also, the other cardinal symptom of true anorexia nervosa in girls, amenorrhea, is missing. Finally, the female with anorexia nervosa consciously wants to be thin. She does not want any roundings and exhibits her thinness. The male anorexics I have treated were concerned about their thinness and were making conscious efforts to gain weight (see Blitzer et al. 1961, Falstein et al. 1956, Waller et al. 1940).

DISCUSSION

The understanding of anorexia nervosa is still limited and there is controversy regarding classification. Different investigators have labeled it a psychosomatic disease, a special type of psychosis, and an obsessive-compulsive neurosis. Let us see what psychoanalytic understanding can contribute to the solution of the classification problem.

In psychosomatic disease, it is assumed that psychological factors, such as unconscious affects, conflicts, and fantasies, are expressed through various organic systems, whose functions and tissues are demonstrably affected and altered (Sperling 1955a). In conversion hysteria, according to the classical concept, the function of the affected organ is altered and usually inhibited, but there are no demonstrable tissue changes or damage. In anorexia nervosa in adolescent girls, the organ and function affected are the uterus and menstruation, respectively. There is an inhibition of menstruation without demonstrable tissue changes in the uterus. The amenorrhea is a neurotic inhibition of a physiological function acting through the hypothalamic structure. The weight loss and the bodily changes are sequelae of the starvation, but not of the amenorrhea. Amenorrhea is an essential criterion in the diagnosis of anorexia nervosa and sometimes precedes the onset of the anorexia nervosa itself.

Another organic system affected by anorexia is the gastrointestinal tract; here, too, the function is usually inhibited, leading to constipation and a preoccupation with the processes of evacuation. The latter was most evident in the cases of Anita and Rose. Such patients frequently use vomiting and the refusal of food to torture the parents. In many instances, vomiting that appears spontaneous is induced psychologically or even manually.

The cardinal symptom from which the term "anorexia" is derived, however, is the refusal of food intake, which actually affects no organ or function. The anorexic patient is fully capable of eating and does so under her own very special conditions. The refusal of food is not related to a disturbance of appetite. It is a conscious hunger strike in which the patient turns hunger on and off at will. It is a conscious rationing of food intake that may involve nausea and vomiting. There are no physiological impediments to eating. Food intake is inhibited consciously, with rationalizations, since the true reasons are unconscious and are not known to the patient. This is typical neurotic behavior. For example, the phobic patient consciously avoids phobic situations and objects, using a variety of rationalizations, but is not conscious of the true reasons for this behavior. Unlike the patient with globus hystericus and fears of choking (Sperling 1953), the patient with anorexia nervosa does not refuse food because of fear of choking on it. Some patients with anorexia nervosa also have aversions to certain food items. These aversions relate to the symbolic meaning attributed to foods by the patient.

A very important dynamic factor operative in the anorexic patient's behavior is a disturbance in object relationship. This disturbance is significantly different in quality from that found in psychosomatic patients (Sperling 1955a). In the latter, the actual dependence on mother is increased by the illness. To psychosomatic patients, being sick and dependent on mother means being a good and obedient child who is rewarded by mother's special care and attention. The psychosomatic patient's mother does not tolerate overt expressions of aggression or strivings for independence. Therefore, the rebellion and aggression are not expressed overtly, but are converted into somatic symptoms and discharged bodily without conscious awareness. In anorexia nervosa, the rebellion against mother and the attempts to establish independence from her are expressed more openly in the rejection of food, especially that prepared by mother, and in accusations that mother does not give the proper food, that the food is bad or poisoned, etc. Anorexia nervosa patients want to handle, prepare, and ration their food themselves. They prefer to eat alone instead of with the family—a rejection of mother. Anorexic patients usually are hyperactive, even when emaciated, and prefer to feed others rather than to be fed.

While anorexia nervosa is not a psychosomatic syndrome, it can occur in patients with psychosomatic symptoms. Usually, the anorexia nervosa and other more manifestly neurotic behavior precede the psychosomatic symptoms. The anorexia nervosa seems to have the economic function of protecting the patient from developing psychosomatic symptoms; the onset of the psychosomatic symptoms signifies a failure of this defensive function and a further regression in object relationship.

I am in agreement with those (Palmer 1939, Sours 1969, Thomä 1967, and others) who consider anorexia nervosa a neurotic symptom complex. It can occur in patients with a variety of pregenitally fixated character disorders, including borderline, depressive, obsessional, and hysterical psychopathology.

An unresolved, ambivalent relationship with mother is an important dynamic and genetic factor in anorexic psychopathology. The anorexic patient generally has been conditioned since early childhood to regard food as a means of controlling life. Peculiarities toward food in parents of the anorexic patient are common and often are subtler variations of the patient's feelings about food. There is usually great emphasis on food in general, as well as specific concerns, e.g., about the "safety" of food prepared by anyone other than mother. The dangers of overeating and of eating the wrong food are stressed, and the skipping of meals, especially after having eaten "too much," is recommended. Some mothers are latent anorexics who act out their psychopathology through another member of the family. A good example is the mother who went on a diet and began to look anorexic herself when her anorexic daughter began to eat. On several occasions at this time, she did not prepare dinner for her daughter as she had for the rest of the family, rationalizing that her daughter would not eat a particular food. The daughter (rightly!) accused her mother of not wanting her to eat. The anorexic patient unconsciously equates food with the life-controlling, omnipotent mother. The term "mother" as used here includes the father and other members of the family. In these cases, the mother assumes the leadership and gives the cues as far as food and eating are concerned.

Some investigators underestimate the seriousness of the psychopathology underlying anorexia in adolescents; they maintain that these patients will "outgrow" their disease. For example, Dally (1969) believes that anorexia nervosa is but an "exaggerated" adolescence. Unfortunately, this is not the case in neurosis. Instead, the manifest symptomatology changes; the anorexia nervosa may be replaced by severe character or personality disorders. Anorexia nervosa is the culmination of a specific pathological psychosexual development that starts with a specific pathological relationship with the mother in early childhood. It can only be influenced and resolved satisfactorily by psychological intervention.

There are some dynamic similarities between anorexia nervosa and addiction. In addition, the life-controlling, destructive mother is symbolically represented by dangerous substances (drugs, alcohol, etc.) that the patient cannot resist incorporating. In contrast, anorexic patients maintain the inhibition against incorporation through their more advanced defense mechanisms. If the anorexia —the means of achieving control over food intake—is removed before sufficient modification in the object relationship and personality structure of the patient has occurred, the defensive structure breaks down and the patient may resort to dangerous acting out not only in the area of control over food intake, but in the area of impulse control in general.

This is a point to be kept in mind in the therapeutic management of anorexic patients, especially when considering force-feeding or other coercive procedures. A case in point is an adolescent girl whose anorexia had improved considerably after a few months of analysis, but who had not yet achieved any significant changes in personality structure. At the time of an anticipated separation from her therapist, for which she was not ready, she began to ingest large quantities of aspirin, resorted to wrist-cutting, and had a psychotic episode. She thus dramatically demonstrated that, to her, giving up control over food intake equaled loss of impulse control.

King (1971) reports on an adolescent girl hospitalized for severe anorexia nervosa who would starve herself rigidly most of the time but, on occasion, would consume a 5-pound bag of sugar within a short time. This change from excessive control (noneating) to loss of control (binges of overeating) can be seen in cases where episodes of anorexia nervosa and bulimia alternate in the same patient (Berlin et al. 1951, Dally 1969, Sylvester 1945, Wulff 1932). My material indicates that the anorexic's strongest fear is of losing control altogether, i.e., gratifying impulses without restraint. This pertains particularly to sexuality, since these patients deal with their sexual impulses by displacement from the genital to the oral level. In this connection, Rose's dream about the bum (her repressed impulses) is particularly instructive.

Anorexics use food to reverse the early childhood situation when mother was in control of food and, by extension, the patient's life. By assuming control over food intake, the patient puts herself in the place of the mother and assumes control over her own and her mother's life. Some of these patients like to feed or overfeed others, especially their mothers, while not eating themselves. This makes the patient a better mother than her own mother. As with every neurotic behavior, the behavior of the anorexic patient is overdetermined and serves the gratification of needs from various levels of development. This was particularly clear in the case of Anita, whose self-starvation was her way of killing her grandmother-mother-hated female aspects of herself.

To be able to go without food is also to prove that life is possible without mother. It proves the opposite if carried to the extreme. The patient's compromise is to reduce food intake to a minimum and to renounce the pleasures of eating, excreting, sleeping properly (many of these patients suffer from sleep disturbances), and having a sex life—the essential instinctual gratifications. By doing this, the patient rebels against, and declares her independence from, mother while expiating her guilt for the hatred and murderous impulses toward mother.

Anorexic patients have a deep-rooted feeling of being rejected by mother, which in part is due to a projection of their own hatred, and in part is founded on reality, at least on the unconscious feelings (psychic reality) of the mother. Their mothers are ambivalent toward them and usually identify them with some rejected parts of their own personality. These mothers also suffer from unresolved infantile conflicts, particularly in regard to their sexual identities and impulse control. Such feelings are reinforced in the daughter, who may develop anorexia nervosa later under certain precipitating conditions. One adolescent girl said that she "closed up her throat" so that she could not swallow her food. She would do this when foods she liked were served, knowing that otherwise she would eat everything on the table. With a burst of anger she cried,"My mother never wanted me to eat food I liked. She never wanted me to do things I wanted to do. She controlled my life." The pervasive feeling was "my mother never wanted me." Later in her analysis it was uncovered that she had felt rejected because of her female sex. As in the case of Anita, the mother and grandmother lived together and dominated the father and the entire household.

In addition to the struggle against eating, there is a struggle against accepting the female role and identification in the anorexic girl. Because of the hatred and murderous impulses toward mother, the female role and genital sexuality are dangerous and are shunned by the anorexic patient. I found (1950b) that the anorexic's penis envy and competition with men are not prompted primarily by the wish to please mother as a male, as some investigators have assumed (Leonard 1944, Masserman 1941), but rather, by the wish to possess and control mother sexually, as father does. Father's sexual power and control over mother are attributed by the patient to his having a penis. In all other areas, the father and other males are usually devalued by the family of the anorexic patient. In the patient's mind, possession of a penis becomes the symbol for ultimate control over mother (Sperling 1950b).

The *essential* dynamic factor in the genesis of anorexia nervosa in adolescent girls is the revival or persistence of an intense, positive oedipal conflict during puberty and adolescence. Puberty and adolescence are critical developmental stages and are also the preferred time of onset of anorexia nervosa in girls. Unresolved oedipal conflicts are a frequent finding in a variety of neurotic and character-disordered patients. The difference is in the specific way an individual patient deals with these conflicts. This, in turn, depends on the patient's early premorbid dispositions involving specific fixations and object relationships. The ego and superego determine the choice of defense mechanisms and both structures contain the incorporated parental attitudes toward instinctual demands.

From the psychoanalytic point of view, anorexia nervosa can be considered a *specific pathological* outcome of unresolved oedipal conflicts in a female whose preoedipal relationship with her mother has predisposed her to this particular reaction under certain precipitating circumstances. Masserman (1941) and Leonard (1944) stress the role of the inverted oedipal conflict; the anorexia nervosa is viewed as a defense against growing up and assuming the adult female role.

The unresolved preoedipal fixation on the mother contributes to the difficulties in psychosexual development and the intensity of the oedipal conflict in these girls. These difficulties become particularly apparent during puberty and adolescence, when the reliability of a proper sexual identification, the ability to separate from the love (need) objects, and the ability to make peer and heterosexual relationships are tested. Anorexia nervosa is initiated by a regression from the genital to the oral level and is associated with a deemphasis of manifest sexuality and instinctual pleasures in general. Sexual and masturbation conflicts are displaced from the genitals to the mouth, and food and eating become equated with forbidden sexual objects and sexual activities. Depending on the degree of libidinization, the picture of the anorexia nervosa is more hysterical, obsessive, depressive, or psychotic.

The amenorrhea in anorexia nervosa is a primary, rather than secondary, symptom. Thomä (1967) and others believe that amenorrhea in anorexia nervosa is primarily psychological rather than endocrinological. During World War II, 60%–70% of women capable of menstruation developed amenorrhea immediately after they were captured and interned in Hong Kong (Sydenham 1946). This psychological amenorrhea was then reinforced secondarily by weight loss. In most cases, the amenorrhea precedes or occurs simultaneously with the anorexia. Amenorrhea is highly overdetermined. It supports both the patient's unconscious pregnancy fantasies and her wish to regress to an infantile level preceding sex-role definition (Berlin et al. 1951, Lorand 1943, Sylvester 1945, Waller 1942). These dynamics were particularly clear in the case of Carol, who wanted to be a baby, a boy, and pregnant like her sister and her mother had been, all at the same time. When she decided to be a girl (of her age), she started to eat and to menstruate.

Vaginal bleeding is unconsciously associated by these girls with internal injury, castration, and birth, all of which are dangerous and have to be avoided. Menses and anything else that is manifestly an indication of femininity must be avoided. One of the aims in the pursuit of thinness is the avoidance of feminine roundings such as breasts, buttocks, and belly. The constipation is as important a symptom to these patients as the amenorrhea. It is psychologically motivated and maintained. Some patients are more preoccupied and concerned with the constipation than with the amenorrhea because, on the infantile level, impregnation, pregnancy, and birth are associated with the digestive system and with excretory functions. This was particularly clear in the cases of Anita and Carol; to both, impregnation was an oral process and birth was an anal process. It has long been observed that anorexia nervosa and its accompanying constipation are particularly well suited for the expression of infantile oral impregnation and birth fantasies (Leonard 1944, Lorand 1943, Masserman 1941, Sylvester 1945).

In some patients with anorexia nervosa, the admixture of anality may show in overt obsessive-compulsive, phobic, and paranoid features. In the latter case, paranoid feelings manifest themselves in patients' attitudes toward certain foods, which may be equated with poison, and in their relationships with people.

REVIEW OF THE LITERATURE

During the past 15 years, most of the literature on anorexia nervosa has been phenomenologically, rather than dynamically, oriented. Some investigators (Bruch 1962, 1973b; Crisp 1969; Dally 1969) hold the view that a psychoanalytic approach should be avoided. For example, Bruch (1962) advises that "motivational analysis and insight should be avoided" (p. 192) and states that anorexia nervosa patients do not associate freely, do not bring material, and do not report dreams.

My experience with anorexia nervosa patients, as well as that of other psychoanalytic investigators (e.g., Blitzer et al. 1961, Jessner and Abse 1960, Lorand 1943, Margolis and Jenberg 1960, Thomä 1967, Waller 1942), most certainly disproves the validity of such a position. A preconceived attitude on the part of the investigator is neither therapeutic nor rewarding in terms of gaining insight into the dynamics of the illness and personality of the patient. Fenichel (1945a) has shown the wealth of information and insight one can gain in only two psychoanalytic interviews with an anorexic patient. In one case, he recognized the role of the mother-daughter relationship and the role of food in her family. He also recognized the basic differences in the dynamics between male and female in anorexia nervosa—the female starts off by not wanting to eat on a conscious level.

In his treatment recommendations, Dally (1969) emphasizes weight gain (2 lbs. per week) by any means necessary, i.e., by confining patients to bed under a strict hospital regime. Chlorpromazine treatment is given routinely to such anorexia nervosa patients. He reports that many of these patients shed the enforced weight gain as soon as they leave the hospital and that this hospital regime may be repeated several times. A number of the patients he reported on turned into compulsive overeaters, one committed suicide, and several others made suicide attempts. Only careful psychoanalytic study permits a full understanding of the importance of these patients' intense, very vulnerable narcissism. All their lives they have felt manipulated by their mothers and they are extremely sensitive to any manipulation, especially by the therapist.

Hospitalization is also recommended as a means of separating the patient from the family. The emphasis is on physical, rather than emotional, separation. Those who remove the patient from the family without providing psychoanalytic therapy for the patient do not understand that the patient's struggle with the internalized mother will go on no matter where the patient is. Unless this internalized, unconscious struggle can be made conscious, there is no possibility of achieving a more realistic solution. If the patient gives up the anorexia nervosa, other neurotic, psychosomatic, or psychotic symptoms will replace it. Numerous reports about the outcome of untreated or inadequately treated anorexic patients confirm this statement. Russell (1975) estimates that the mortality of anorexia nervosa on long-term observation is not more than 5%. Kay and Shapiro (1965) found a 15% mortality rate at a follow-up of anorexics treated physically in a hospital for at least three months; the remaining 85% had protracted anorexic symptoms, and more or less permanent undernourishment and impaired sexual adjustment. Crisp (1969) gives a poor prognosis when there is rejection, overprotection, or ambivalence on the part of parents. In his opinion, the best prognosis is when the attitudes of the parents are "normal." He seems to overlook the fact that the children of parents with "normal" attitudes do not develop anorexia nervosa. In addition, a superficially appropriate attitude often conceals the unconscious pathological rapport between the anorexic patient and her parents.

As far as psychotherapy is concerned, Dally (1969) recommends anaclitic treatment in which the therapist acts as a substitute parent. Some years ago, such treatment was attempted with psychosomatic patients; it was supposed to be followed by psychoanalytic therapy. The anaclitic treatment produced such severe states of regression that the patients not only became unsuitable subjects for psychoanalysis, but also suffered severe aggravation of their symptoms, psychotic breaks, and other unmanageable behavior (Sperling 1957, 1960, 1967).

Tolstrup (1965) recommends isolation from home and considers hospital treatment essential in anorexia nervosa. He practices a superficial supportive therapy that emphasizes eating and discussion of daily problems. In simply encouraging the patient to eat, Tolstrup overlooks the fact that the noneating has an important unconscious dynamic function for the anorexic patient. As mentioned in the case material, it is the main pathological defense against loss of control. Groen and Feldman-Toledano (1966) recommend education of the family for the purpose of allowing the children more expression of aggression and more freedom. However, they ignore the role of sexual identifications and the displacement of genital sexuality to the oral zone.

Many who report on anorexic "cures" following hospitalization have no long-term follow-ups and do not consider subsequent personality changes (e.g., the breakdown of obsessive-compulsive defenses and the transformation of compulsive noneating into acting-out behavior and compulsive overeating) to be psychiatric sequelae of the hospital treatment. The nonanalytic interference with the mechanisms of defense by untrained or inadequately trained personnel can have the most deleterious consequences on the emotional equilibrium of patients.

Bruch (1973b) stresses that the disturbance of body image is of delusional proportions in these patients. She maintains that there is a *lack* of sexuality based on a deficiency of perception. While repression can be lifted with psychoanalytic treatment, deficiency is not corrigible analytically. Bruch's explanation for anorexic behavior is faulty learning, but she leaves out the role of the unconscious and the drives, as well as the vicissitudes of pathological development of aggression and sexuality, in the genesis of anorexia nervosa. She falls back on neurophysiology and behavioral concepts.

Thomä (1967) reported on his analytic treatment of anorexic patients. Most were treated in the hospital, at least in the initial stages. Of 19 patients who accepted psychotherapy, two did not improve, eight showed improvement, and nine improved after a period of psychotherapy and therefore "mostly spontaneously" (apparently in a flight into health). He was aware that anorexic patients lie or refuse to talk about anything that could disturb their precarious equilibrium and that the analyst has to take a more active stance. The hospitalized patients were also treated by other medical personnel, which, in my opinion, makes the application of the true psychoanalytic method rather difficult because of split transferences and contamination of the transference with the analyst when the latter is compelled to intervene actively in hospital and other real-life situations of the patient. These real-life interventions lend reality to the patient's transference feelings (every patient wants to make a parent of the analyst) and add to the time needed to work through the transference (Sperling 1967).

Selvini Palazzoli (1965) stresses the anorexic patient's struggle against hunger and the experience of the nourished body as a threatening, indestructible force. This is her explanation of why the patient's food intake is reduced to an absurdity. She does not consider anorexia nervosa a defense against oral sadistic impulses, but points out that, at puberty, anorexia nervosa is a defense against depression and schizophrenia. She takes the position that the body represents the mother and therefore must be kept in check. She greatly minimizes the role of instincts and states that impregnation fantasies cover more primitive fantasies of being invaded by the mother. She hardly mentions sexual conflicts, masturbation, or sexual identifications. Like Bruch, Selvini Palazzoli considers anorexia nervosa a special psychosis that lies midway between schizoid paranoid psychosis and depression; she, too, is against using interpretations and insight-oriented treatment.

In my opinion, anorexic patients must keep the body in check because all the dangerous impulses, especially sexuality, emanate from it. If there is no body, there are no sexual feelings. These patients make a negative exhibitionistic display of themselves that has a shock effect. The nourished body, especially the fat body, represents the pregnant mother. Food equals different objects on different levels: on the oral level, it is various part-objects or breast-penis-mother; on the anal level, it is feces or devalued part-objects (e.g., poison, sperm, urine, feces-penis, feces-baby); and, on the phallic level, it represents pregnancy (i.e., identification with mother as a female), which the anorexic patient cannot accept because of her hostility toward mother. In comparison to depressives and schizophrenics, the anorexic patient has more object libido available for cathexis because she actually has received gratification from the mother and others.

SUMMARY

In this chapter, case material on anorexic patients was presented and discussed. A brief survey of the literature was offered. Some problems surrounding classification were clarified; it was suggested that anorexia nervosa is a neurotic symptom complex that can occur in a variety of character disorders ranging from borderline to hysterical psychopathology. It is not a psychosomatic syndrome. It occurs in females who have been predisposed to it by their early relationship with mother and other early experiences. It usually occurs in adolescence and is an indication that these patients have not reached true genitality, but have remained fixated at earlier levels of development and are therefore unable to establish proper sexual identification and heterosexual relationships. There is no specific anorexia nervosa personality, although these patients do show some common features. Depending on the level of fixation and the degree of regression, the pregenital characteristics of narcissism, omnipotence, ambivalence, some bisexuality, and low frustration tolerance will be more or less evident, but they are present to a pathological degree in all patients with anorexia nervosa. While control over food intake, which represents impulse control in general, is important in anorexia, it is not the primary dynamic. Anorexia nervosa is a specific outcome of an unsuccessful attempt at solution of an unconscious sexual conflict concerning sexual identity.

In the male patient with anorexic symptoms, feminine tendencies and feminine identifications are a major dynamic. However, the situation in the male is different: the nature of their oedipal conflict is different, and they do not possess female genitals and the capacity for procreation. Unconscious pregnancy wishes and fantasies do not necessarily need to be worked out through anorexia. In my opinion, anorexic symptoms in males are an indication of a pathological relationship with the mother and belong to a neurotic, or even psychotic, eating disturbance rather than to true anorexia nervosa.

There are infantile forms of anorexia nervosa that should be differentiated from other eating disturbances. True anorexia nervosa, even in children, indicates the primary difficulty of the child in accepting her femaleness. While children do not have to make a decision about functioning sexually as a female, they can indicate their unwillingness to accept the female role. Such behavior is an indication of the pathological relationship with mother. A manifest eating disturbance in childhood does not necessarily precede the onset of anorexia nervosa in adolescence. As in any neurosis, the infantile neurosis may remain latent until a trauma in later life mobilizes it and revives it in a manifest form. This manifest form is predetermined by the earlier relationship with mother and early experiences. Childhood anorexia nervosa does not have to continue or be revived later unless there are specific traumatic life situations at work.

There is considerable controversy concerning etiology. Some believe that anorexia nervosa is a psychosis, or deficiency, and therefore hold to a constitutional etiology. This outlook affects their attitude toward treatment. In my opinion, the early mother-child relationship acts like an early acquired constitution. The emphasis on food and deemphasis of sexuality also play a part in determining the choice of symptoms. The severity and outcome of the anorexia are determined in part by the level of fixation: the more orally fixated a patient, the poorer the prognosis.

The dynamics of anorexia nervosa are very complex. Nonanalytic investigators who do not work with the concept of overdetermination in illness and symptom formation and who need to simplify everything reduce the dynamics to one formula (e.g., oral fantasies, aggression, or pregnancy fantasies). They assess only the manifest behavior without considering the underlying unconscious motivations and take verbalizations and rationalizations of the patient at face value. For instance, the fact that the affect of depression is missing consciously is taken as an indication that there is no depression operative in the patient (Crisp 1969). Actually, anorexic patients do not feel capable of tolerating consciously painful affects, such as depression, sexual feelings, or even hunger, because of a fear of succumbing to and acting out these feelings (e.g., becoming depressed, going insane, committing suicide, becoming prostitutes) (Goitein 1942). The symptoms of anorexia have to be considered depressive equivalents (Sperling 1959) that protect the patient from experiencing her true feelings.

A survey of the literature discloses that the methods presently used and recommended for anorexic patients are grossly inadequate. Many still consider these patients unsuitable for psychoanalytic treatment. As my work and that of others show, psychoanalytic methods are applicable to a variety of patients who would have been excluded previously. One has to realize, though, that the establishment and maintenance of a workable (i.e., uncontaminated) transference is no easy task with anorexic patients. It can be achieved only by persistently analyzing and frustrating the patient's need to turn the analyst into the mother. If the patient succeeds at the latter, the analyst will be treated with the same ambivalence and distrust as the mother. It is only in the transference that the patient can gain some insight and learn to separate the analyst and others from the mother. True emotional separation based on analytic insight and changes in the ego structure of the patient must be distinguished from transference "cures" that merely shift the patient's dependence to the therapist or medication, or change the patient's manifest psychopathology. In the analytic treatment of anorexic patients, it is best to begin by analyzing superficial defenses and resistances, and to avoid content interpretations, especially in the area of sexuality, until a reliable transference has been fully established.

The physical separation of the anorexic patient from her parents also misses the point because the patient will always find someone with whom she can act out the mother transfer. Only psychoanalysis or psychoanalytically oriented therapy can bring about the personality changes and growth that enable the anorexic patient to cope with instinctual drives and conflicts in a more appropriate way. Psychoanalytic treatment enables the patient to separate from the mother while superficial psychotherapy and anaclitic treatment encourage the patient to maintain the pathological tie to the mother by transferring it to the therapist.

4
Psychoanalytic Description: The Clinical Picture of Anorexia Nervosa and Bulimia

IRA L. MINTZ, M.D.

ANOREXIA NERVOSA

History of Syndrome

The term "anorexia nervosa" was coined by Gull in a series of three papers read before the English Medical Society beginning in 1868. The earliest description of the illness, however, is ascribed to a Genovese physician, Simone Porta O. Portio, in 1500. A clear and easily recognizable clinical syndrome was presented by Morton in 1689 in England. Thomä (1967) quotes from Morton's account:

> Mr. Duke's Daughter in the year 1684, and in the eighteenth Year of her Age in the month of July, fell into a total suppression of her Monthly Courses from a multitude of Cares and Passions of her Mind . . . from which time her Appetite began to abate, and her Digestion to be bad; her flesh also began to be flacid and loose, and her looks pale. . . . She was wont by her studying at Night, and continual poring upon Books, to expose herself . . . to the injuries of the air. . . . Loathing all sorts of Medicaments, she wholly neglected the care of herself for two full years, till at last being brought to the last degree of a Marasmus, or Consumption, and thereupon subject to Frequent fainting Fits, she apply'd herself to me for Advice.
> I do not remember that I did ever in all my Practice see one that was conversant with the Living, so much wasted with the greatest degree of a Consumption (like a skeleton only clad with skin); yet there was no Fever, but on the contrary a coldness of the whole body; no cough, or difficulty of breathing, . . . or of any other Entrail. . . . Only her appetite was diminished, and her Digestion uneasie, with Fainting Fits, which did frequently return upon her. . . . Being quickly tired of Medicines, she beg'd that the whole Affair might be committed again to Nature, whereupon consuming everyday more and more, she was after 3 months taken with a Fainting Fit and dyed. (p. 4)

Thomä gives Morton credit for his acuity in recognizing the patient's amenorrhea, loss of appetite, weight loss, constipation, and indifference to her severe cachexia. The inappropriate preoccupation with studying is also characteristic of the illness, as I shall discuss later. Strikingly, Morton seemed to link the onset of the illness to a "multitude of Cares and Passions of her Mind." Self-destructiveness and an unwillingness to cooperate with treatment, both of which are so characteristic of the illness, also seemed to be present in the patient's indifference to her progressive deterioration and in her refusal of medication and medical care from the good doctor. Finally, this patient seemed to have convulsed repeatedly from potassium deficiency. The clinical syndrome remains essentially unchanged from that described by Morton almost 300 years ago.

Almost 200 years later, Lasegue (1873) provided a more penetrating psychological view of the illness, which he saw as a type of hysteria.

> A young girl, between 15 and 20 years of age, suffers from some emotion which she avows or conceals. . . . It relates to some real or imaginary marriage project, to a violence done to some sympathy, or to some . . . desire.
>
> At first she feels uneasy about food, vague sensations about fullness, suffering, and gastralgia post prandium. . . . The patient thinks to herself that the best remedy . . . will be to diminish her food. . . . Gradually she reduces her food, furnishing pretexts, sometimes a headache . . . and sometimes a fear of a recurrence of pain after eating. At the end of some weeks there is . . . a refusal of food that may be indefinitely prolonged. The disease is now declared, and so surely will it pursue its course that it becomes easy to prognosticate the future. Woe to the physician who, misunderstanding the peril, treats as a fancy without object or duration an obstinacy which he hopes to vanquish by medicines, friendly advice, or by the still more defective resource, intimidation. With hysterical subjects, a first medical fault is never repairable. Ever on the watch for the judgments concerning themselves, especially such as are approved by the family, they never pardon. (p. 9)

Like Morton, Lasegue gave evidence of considerable clinical acumen. He recognized the nature and course of the clinical syndrome. He saw important elements of emotional conflict—problems surrounding marriage, growing up, and ambivalent desires. He noted the many excuses found for not eating, including the common postprandial abdominal pains. Of considerable interest are his awareness of some of the technical difficulties in treating these patients and his remarks about what we would feel today is the crucial importance of the primitive, hypercritical superego. He warned against misunderstanding the nature and the severity of the disease, noting the obstinacy with which the patient holds on to the illness. He knew that treatment ranging from friendly advice to intimidation was of little help. Finally, he described a primitive superego whose critical fault-finding was applied to the patient and others with equal and appalling vehemence: "they never pardon."

A further analytic perspective was provided by Freud (1887–1902) in his letters to Fliess, where he associated anorexia with melancholia; in 1905, he made the same comment in the Dora case.

Additional psychoanalytic data emerged in the 1940s. Eissler (1943) noted the importance of the anorexic's dependency relationship with the mother, and

Sylvester (1945) reported on anorexia in a 4-year-old girl, emphasizing the sadistic oral conflicts. Masserman (1941) and Leonard (1944) emphasized the anorexic's fear of growing up and becoming a mature woman. Fenichel (1945b) also commented on the importance of the parent-child relationship.

Sperling (1949, 1970, 1978) emphasized the importance of the mother-child relationship in the origin, maintenance, and resolution of severe feeding disorders of childhood, psychosomatic diseases, and anorexia nervosa. She stressed the need to treat the mother and the need for the mother to recognize her ambivalent, often rejecting, attitude toward the child. She felt that the "feelings frequently stemmed from unresolved ambivalent conflicts from the mother's own childhood which she had transferred to her child or from unconscious identification of the child with repressed and rejected aspects of the mother's own personality" (Sperling 1978, p. 140).

Falstein et al. (1956) described the conflict in anorexic boys who attempt to deal with female identifications by becoming thin. Bruch (1965, 1970, 1978a), Selvini Palazzoli (1963, 1978), Sours (1974, 1979), Sperling (1970, 1978), and Thomä (1967) have expanded and further described the nature of the defenses, identifications, object relations, drives, and essential conflicts of anorexia nervosa.

Signs and Symptoms

Anorexia can be defined as a conscious refusal to eat, or self-starvation, which can be so severe that it results in death. It is a deliberate pursuit of thinness, tenaciously adhered to in spite of warnings of danger by family and physicians. It is most common in adolescent girls, although it is also present in older women and has become increasingly evident in adolescent boys. Recently, I treated a 40-year-old man with classical symptoms of anorexia.

The rationale given by the patient for the self-starvation is that the patient feels too fat and needs to be a little thinner. This attitude can be held even when the patient reaches the stage of severe malnutrition and emaciation. All attempts to confront the patient with the emaciation and critical medical condition are met with a bland denial and a vigorous pursuit of the starvation. Many patients cite previous periods of childhood obesity and teasing as reasons for initiating a diet. Others ostensibly respond to a family member's comment about their excess weight.

The diet of anorexic patients shows qualitative as well as quantitative changes. Usually all fattening foods, which often were previously enjoyed, are renounced. They tend to pick at their food, to eat a bite here and there, and to spread the food about on the plate to give it the appearance of having been eaten. They deal with the meal in an ostentatious, provocative manner, invariably under the watchful gaze of the frustrated and apprehensive parents.

In addition to decreasing caloric intake, the patients make prodigious attempts to burn up calories and further decrease their weight. This may take the form of an endless series of exercises presumably designed to keep in shape but actually undertaken to promote the state of emaciation. Characteristically, there is hyperactive, energetic-appearing behavior that is in marked contrast to the patients' sick cachectic appearance and that serves to deny their helpless state.

These patients rarely complain that they feel hungry or miss eating the foods that they once enjoyed. Bruch (1978a) makes the somewhat puzzling statement that none of her anorexic patients began dieting with the intent to starve; rather, their dieting became starvation because they never experienced the sensation of hunger. "It seems that the *way* hunger is experienced accounts for the decisive difference, whether the dieting remains what it was intended to be, a means of losing a few extra pounds, or whether it becomes a compulsive force that dominates their whole life" (p. 19). She concludes that hunger sensations are absent, rather than merely repressed, in anorexic patients. This does not hold up when one considers the periodic return of an insatiable appetite, with resultant gorging, in these patients. This phenomenon is explicable as a momentary failure of repression. In anorexia, there is a denial of hunger and of the longing for certain foods. During the starvation, anorexics report being fearful of eating because they will put on too much weight and get fat. The incongruity of the starved, emaciated skeleton who complains of a fear of eating and getting fat is difficult to reconcile unless one recognizes that the starvation covers up a strong unconscious impulse to gorge. It is this impulse that the patient unconsciously recognizes and fears.

In some patients, the clinical syndrome involves alternating bouts of starving and gorging. Typically, sustained periods of starvation with weight loss and emaciation alternate with momentary bouts of bulimia in which tremendous amounts of food are ingested and then vomited up, with no net weight gain. This behavior can enter a chronic phase that persists for years. It may be characterized by an acute exacerbation of starvation, with emaciation, electrolyte imbalance, and convulsions that require hospitalization, followed by remission and return to the community until the next exacerbation. At other times, the original, prolonged starvation and emaciation may be replaced by overeating and eventual obesity. Although the external picture changes from too thin to too fat, and denying the impulse to eat is replaced by acceding to the impulse to eat, the unconscious problems may remain unchanged.

BULIMIA

In contrast to the starving, emaciated anorexics who unconsciously deny their impulses to eat, their appetite, and their enjoyment of food, bulimic patients may acknowledge an enjoyment of eating, a voracious appetite, a fear of not being able to stop eating, and a terror of becoming fat. Like the starving anorexics, the bulimics usually have a family history of excessive interest in food and dieting, parental weight problems, and an earlier history of obesity. In these patients, the desire to be slender disguises the fear of being fat, which stems from the inability to contain their overwhelming impulses to gorge. When gorging does occur, the patient becomes so frightened of a tremendous weight gain that vomiting becomes a necessary, if frightening, expedient. Some patients may gorge and vomit for years with minimal anxiety until they attempt to stop and recognize that they cannot. Not infrequently, the gorging and vomiting is done in secret; on occasion, it may be done with another bulimic.

Being thin provides these patients with a safety valve; the uncontrollable gorging and weight gain will not immediately propel them into a state of obesity. Many of these patients attempt to establish controls over what is eaten by making the food portions complete in themselves, often packing each meal in a little container. Frequently, bulimics will not eat what the family eats in an attempt to stay thin by exercising total control over their own food. The food is all theirs, to be bought, packaged, and dispensed in a manner totally under their control. If their meals were a part of the family's food, their complete control would be compromised. To put the uneaten portions of the family meal back into the refrigerator would open these patients up to the all-consuming impulse to gorge.

Whereas the starving anorexic represses the impulse to eat and attempts to get a sibling or a parent to gorge and eat her food, the bulimic patient has an insatiable appetite and often eats the other family members' food in addition to her own. This often takes place when she eats the same food as the rest of the family. In an attempt to avoid gorging, the bulimic patient may minimize eating all day in order to eat the major meal at night. Some bulimic patients have acknowledged that, after eating at night, they have the opportunity to fall asleep, which curtails the temptation to gorge further. Thus, sleep serves as a defense against eating.

Clinical and Psychodynamic Relevance of Gorging

Bulimic patients are terribly fearful of their impulse to gorge. It is rightfully viewed by them as a sudden, complete loss of control over the impulse to eat. These patients can eat tremendous amounts of food. One patient described eating an entire chocolate cake, a quart of ice cream, four sandwiches, and a bowl of fruit. The gorging of food is analogous to the gorging of laxatives. Strika (personal communication, 1979) described a patient who was accustomed to taking 200 Ex-Lax tablets a day, with resulting weight gain and a cholesterol blood level of 400. The gorging of food and laxatives reflects a loss of impulse control and is related to unsatisfied infantile yearnings for food, closeness, and security, as well as to aggressive discharge.

The anorexic patient who starves and does not gorge has unconscious impulses to gorge which are repressed and kept in check by a punitive superego and intact ego controls. Wilson (1982) pointed out that the gorging patient's deficient ego controls and strict but ineffective superego result in an inability to adhere consistently to the demands for starvation and the denial of infantile cravings; these demands are overwhelmed from time to time with bursts of bulimia. This deficiency in ego controls is so threatening to the patient that the slightest weight gain often produces a sense of loss of control and panic, and a frantic return to exercising, laxatives, and starving. The internal destabilizing effect of the repetitive gorging complicates the treatment process, as the patient fights the slightest weight gain.

Bulimic patients are much more prone to act out impulsively, especially during adolescence, than are starving anorexics. They become sexually promiscuous and/or delinquent, often steal, and characteristically lie and deceive. One gorging patient suddenly began to steal at a point in treatment when her conflicts were not resolved but the understanding of her anorexia precluded a discharge of her conflict through anorexic behavior.* The impulse to quit the treatment in response to anxiety-producing conflict is also greater in these patients.

It should be clear that if the impulse to eat and gorge is unconsciously defended against by the need to starve, then the underlying conflicts are the same whether the patient is starving or gorging, too thin or too heavy. The conflicts are merely responded to with different sets of defenses. Those modalities of treatment whose sole goal is the restoration of normal body weight without normal psychological functioning provide a less than complete therapeutic achievement.

THE PSYCHIATRIC PICTURE
IN ANOREXIA NERVOSA AND BULIMIA

Even a superficial psychiatric evaluation provides an astonishing degree of conformity in these clinical syndromes. These patients are insecure, dependent, and immature. They are extremely attached to the parents, although this attachment may be masked by pseudoindependence and hostility. The parents, in turn, reveal an equally remarkable degree of uniformity. They are rigid, controlling, demanding, infantilizing, and very attached to their children. One or both parents are very much involved in the child's life, to the point of intrusiveness and interference with the child's maturation and independence. At the same time, the parents are concerned about the well-being of the child and attempt to cooperate with the child's recovery. A great deal of control is exercised by the parents over the life of the child. Most of the time, the child passively accedes to this domination.

With the onset of the anorexic syndrome, a subtle but intensely powerful defiance becomes increasingly evident in the patient's stubborn refusal to eat. The decision to starve is maintained in spite of very strong parental pressures and threats. A battle ensues over who is to eat what, and when. The battle expands into all areas of food and eating. What the child is not able to accomplish by open defiance and self-assertion in other areas of her life, she achieves in the very circumscribed area of food. As one patient commented, "Not eating is all I've got." I am in agreement with Sperling (1978), who emphasizes the importance of the starving in the patient's intrapsychic equilibrium and sees it as a main pathological defense against a total loss of control. Through the mechanism of illness, the patient is able to be defiant and assertive without being fearful of direct parental disapproval and punishment. In essence, the patient proclaims, "I do not eat because I am sick, not because I choose to be rebellious and to challenge your authority." The need to be rebellious and defiant without being exposed to fears of parental attack adds to the patient's tenacious adherence to the illness and endless preoccupation with food and weight.

---

*See Chapter 9.

Kramer (1974) feels that the "domineering mother" concept has been over-emphasized as an etiologic factor in anorexia. Although Mahler's descriptions of the infant's early separation and individuation phases (Mahler and Furer 1968; Mahler et al. 1970, 1975) offer a new and vital perspective on the child's intrapsychic development, one still cannot minimize the powerful and overwhelming effect of the parents on these children. Accounts of parental behavior given by patients, their siblings, and the parents themselves provide clear-cut evidence to support the thesis that early domination and control exercised by the powerful mother play a major role in the evolution of anorexia and bulimia. The battle for control is intensified during treatment, and the therapist has more than adequate opportunity to view its vehemence, tenacity, and repercussive forces. Increased assertiveness on the part of one patient, in spite of the mother's attempts to prevent it, almost resulted in the mother's decompensation. Sperling (1978) also notes intensification of unconscious parental conflicts as the patient improves and the mother begins to starve.

Avoidance of Real-Life Problems

Overdetermined and multidetermined factors in all psychic events, however, require that adequate consideration be given to genetic factors and the child's role in the entire complex constellation of events. These patients do not wish to deal with or discuss the true problems that exist in their lives, but rather, to speak continually about eating, dieting, and weight loss. Once they begin to recognize and accept that the preoccupation with eating and dieting in part is used to avoid dealing with real-life problems, the anorexia may begin to abate. Indeed, once these patients decide to abandon the anorexia, they frequently feel considerable anxiety about how to deal with the problems their anorexic preoccupations had masked.

These patients acknowledge that very often all their waking hours are monopolized by food, dieting, and weight loss. They think about what foods to eat and what foods not to eat. They are conversant with dietary facts, knowing the number of calories and the amounts of carbohydrates, fats, proteins, minerals, vitamins, and trace elements present in every portion of food. They think about their meals long in advance. Their illness facilitates their ability to dictate what food is served at home and what restaurants the family visits. The assertiveness that begins with the starving spreads into other areas of eating and dining. Just as these patients initially deny having any problems in their lives, they also deny feelings of hunger and interest in eating foods that they previously enjoyed. Sperling (1978) points out that a preoccupation with eating patterns and food is frequently present in the early life history of these patients and in their families.

Problems around passivity, dependency, and needs to be taken care of are frequent in these patients. The preoccupation with not eating can represent both the need for the dependency care (achieved through the parental concern over the possible starvation) and the denial of this need (not eating). The preoccupation with feeding is certainly linked to problems of nurturing.

Anorexic patients frequently report that they have nothing to talk about and that there is nothing that troubles them. This results from their conscious withholding of all vital thoughts and feelings because they do not trust the therapist. In addition, not eating tends to bind the patients' conflicts defensively. Once patients begin to eat, they often report feeling flooded by all kinds of upsetting ideas—which can be so frightening that the patient returns to her starvation. After beginning to eat, one patient reported being so upset by the emerging ideas that he could not sleep. Another commented that she was afraid of going crazy.

The involvement with weight is equally consuming. The slightest increase in weight can set off feelings of panic in some patients.

Disturbance in Body Image

The majority of the more serious cases reveal disturbances in body image. Patients look at themselves in the mirror and see themselves as fat, when in truth they appear like concentration-camp victims. Only during the period of recovery will they acknowledge that they are still very thin, so they must have been quite emaciated indeed earlier in the disease. This disturbance in the body image is often present in the parents as well. In a number of cases where the patient had quite recovered from the physical illness and had gained 20–25 lbs., the mother still saw the patient as skeletal because she had difficulty seeing and acknowledging the improvement.

Some anorexic patients whose illness is less severe do not suffer from body-image distortion; they recognize and admit that they appear thin, and they acknowledge being troubled by it. I do not agree with Bruch (1970, 1973b) that a disturbance in the body image is essential to establish the diagnosis of anorexia, since I have seen a number of patients who are less severely ill, who clearly recognize that they are too thin, and who would like to be heavier. They are unable to put on weight in spite of their conscious wishes to do so because self-starvation is their characteristic (unconscious) means of coping with conflict.

These patients' persistent claim that they are obese almost has the ring of the amputee's perception of a phantom limb. Anorexic patients feel fat long after every trace of fat is gone.

Control

What emerges most clearly in the majority of these patients is the problem of control. They have grown up never feeling that they had an appropriate degree of control over the vital issues of their lives. When they are repeatedly frustrated in dealing with important experiences and cannot control what is happening, they displace their need for control from the external events to their eating habits, choice of food, and weight. In essence, they shift the inability to control the external object to control over the functions of their own body—just as psychosomatic patients who feel they cannot control external events shift the conflict and control a part of their own body instead. The importance attached to controlling the external situation also becomes displaced onto the eating, which in part accounts for the tenacious quality seen in anorexic patients' need to control the eating. Every aspect of food choice, the actual methods of eating, and the weight loss are associatively linked to, and stand for, aspects of external events that are out of control. When patients cannot achieve what they wish with their friends and family, and with their hopes and aspirations, they act out with food. A frustration in the external world, such as an argument with a parent, often results in an exacerbation of the self-starvation.

Another method of controlling others is feeding and stuffing them. Bruch (1978a) reports a number of anorexic patients who prepared meals that their younger siblings had to consume prior to going to school; one patient forced her mother to eat to the point of obesity. The parents of another patient felt obliged to give in to her whim to force food on her younger sister. Terrible fighting would ensue whenever the younger child refused to acquiesce to the older sister's stuffing. It was clear that the anorexic patient was behaving in a sadistic fashion, identifying with what she felt was the overcontrolling mother, and doing to the sister what she felt had been done to her.

Occasionally, the need to exercise control over food can reach almost bizarre proportions. One 18-year-old girl described in exquisite detail an eating and vomiting ritual in which she would gorge certain colorful foods in sequence and then attempt to vomit them up in reverse order, each food separate from the other, before they had been mixed in the digestive process. It was also important to stop the vomiting before she brought up the gastric acidity from the emptied stomach.

A 17-year-old girl exercised, masturbated, took laxatives, smoked, and ate garlic, all with the goal of facilitating control over her bowel products. One can easily envision the desperate quality and the intensity of the driving forces behind such a need for control. They should not be tampered with lightly.

Anorexic patients gravitate toward excellence in school and work very hard to become the best student. The need for achievement in school—to control the academic material—is similar to the need to control the eating and is striven for with the same intensity. This may account for the inordinately large number of scholastically outstanding anorexic patients. At the same time, the need to do well in school can also represent growth, independence, and mastery consonant with the adolescent phase of development. Perfectionistic performance in school can also represent a form of defiance for which the patient does not fear excessive punishment. The markedly driven patient who studies constantly and voices dissatisfaction with anything but perfect grades often distresses the parents, who recognize the drivenness and helplessly attempt to persuade the patient to work a little less and to enjoy herself more. The more the parents encourage the child to ease up, the more perfectionistic the child becomes, thus defying the parent, achieving control, and punishing herself by the fatiguing drivenness.

The persistent, almost frantic, quality attached to the studying is similar to the attitude toward eating and exercising. Anorexic patients exercise feverishly to lose weight, even in the stage of emaciation, where the presence of fatigue is typically denied. The other goals of exercise are the same as those of starvation and studying: discharge of aggression through motor activity, sadistic defiance of the parents, avoidance of retaliation by parents, gratification of dependency needs through the worry and concern of the parents, and self-punishment by exhaustion.

Dependency and Separation

Dependency problems and separation anxieties play a major role in these patients' lives. They are ambivalent about the defiance, assertiveness, and independence toward which they aspire. Their illness, which contains the seeds of their rebellion and subtle assertiveness, also permits them to be further fussed over, controlled, and dominated in the name of their parents' concern for them. The patient may stay at home more frequently, fighting with her mother about the food while using the argument as an opportunity to remain in her company and away from her friends. One patient commented plaintively that when she had been anorexic, everybody had fussed over her, paid attention to her, and tried to do things for her. She didn't have to say a thing. Now that she had gained weight, people no longer did that and she felt quite neglected. Loss of close friends and threatened loss of parental affection can contribute to the crystallization of the anorexia syndrome.

As young children, these patients received an inordinate amount of attention; they were fussed over excessively and never learned to do things for themselves and to achieve gratification and confidence from the accomplishment. Thus, they feel helpless and dependent, deprived of the experiences on which self-esteem, separation-individuation, mastery, and elements of identity are developed. They remain in constant need of attention.

One anorexic patient (Robins, personal communication, 1978) reported that when she was a little girl, her sister got hit by a car, and then everyone catered to her. The patient remembered standing in the center of the street waiting to get hit by a car, so that she could share in the attention. At the last minute, she "chickened out." The realities of serious injury had overpowered her impulses to get attention by self-destructive behavior and by being ill. At age 11, she developed anorexia and was hospitalized. In treatment at age 17, after alternating bouts of starving and gorging, she became obese. The self-destructive behavior and the need for attention persisted. She became involved with a delinquent girl whom everyone paid attention to because of her daring.

Sexual Conflicts

Overdetermination and multidetermination of self-starvation and weight loss reveal considerable sexual preoccupation and conflict. In adolescent girls, these psychological difficulties are almost invariably accompanied by disturbances in menses, i.e., amenorrhea. The amenorrhea often precedes the weight loss and is not thought to result from malnutrition or the hormonal changes associated with the starvation.

It is generally accepted that great anxiety over adolescent sexual changes—development of curves of the hips, legs, and breasts—contributes to the frequency of the disease at this point in time. Starvation and weight loss diminish these changes and give the patient the appearance of a preadolescent child.

At an unconscious level, the loss of bodily tissue can represent the manifestations of a conflict over psychosexual identity. Many of these girls unconsciously would prefer to be a boy, and their ambivalence about their sexual identity takes the form of the desire to lose body tissue that unconsciously represents the displaced penis.

One very emaciated patient would get panicky any time she felt she was putting on the slightest amount of weight; she would squeeze the muscle mass on her legs and arms, wanting to get rid of it. She was especially distressed by the tissue on her inner thighs and would squeeze it, complaining that she "can't stand it hanging there between her legs and has to get rid of it." The same problem was symbolized and displaced from the genitals onto muscle tissue in other parts of her body.

The accompanying amenorrhea reflects a part of the same picture: the need to be premenstrual, i.e., to be a little child not yet ready for sexuality. At the same time, ambivalent feelings about the conflict take the form of pregnancy fantasies, with the amenorrhea representing the pregnant state, and the slightest evidence of an abdominal protuberance symbolizing the early pregnancy. Thus, the patient unconsciously flees from sexuality and pregnancy, develops a childlike physical state, and reverts to premenstrual sexual functioning; yet she also has wishes for the forbidden pregnancy and is preoccupied with abdominal bulges and amenorrhea. This unconscious preoccupation with pregnancy provides some understanding about the panicky response of these patients to the slightest evidence of a belly in their emaciated state, and the accompanying zealous attempts to starve it away.[*]

Premorbid Personality

The developmental history of anorexics reveals a surprising degree of uniformity in the family environment, in the parents, and in the patients' behavior. The powerful, overcontrolling mother (and, at times, father) requires and elicits obedience, conformity, submission, and perfection from an early age. The children are described as quiet, accepting, healthy, happy, and responsive. They never give the parents any trouble. The parents do not remember any eating difficulties. Yet, the older brother of one boy whose early life was described in those idyllic terms vividly remembered the traumatic force-feeding, the vomiting, and the refeeding of the vomitus. Often the conflicts of the parents are such that they need to force the child into an oversubmissive role, and yet are not aware of it at the time or later. The mother views the child as an extension of herself and requires the behavior and functioning that she feels is consonant with her own attitudes; she does not recognize the separateness and individuality of the child. Normal phases of separation-individuation, especially negativism, aggression, and exploration, suffer the most interference. To use Sours's words (1974), the attachment to the mother "promotes fusion rather than nurturance" (p. 571).

---

[*]For further discussion of the unconscious meaning of the amenorrhea and its relationship to the acceptance of a feminine identification, see Chapter 17.

Oedipal and latency periods are described as calm and tranquil. Performance in nursery and grade school is encouraged and usually achieved. Separation anxieties are often noted in regard to parental vacations and the entry into kindergarten or nursery school. Excessive clinging as a toddler is commonly remembered. Later in life, the separation anxiety aroused by the entry into high school or college is manifested in anorexic symptoms.

As the child reaches adolescence, the organized, relatively quiescent, obedient, responsive stage of latency is replaced by adolescent turmoil (A. Freud 1958). Physical, psychological, and sexual growth are accompanied by increased aggressive and sexual impulses, as well as the defenses against them. The consistent, thoughtful, responsive child of latency is replaced by the rebellious, unruly, assertive, and provocative adolescent. Sexual impulses, fantasies, and (often) behavior become overpowering and preoccupying, and alternate with feelings of asceticism, mysticism, and sexual abstinence. The need for increasing independence, distance, and separation from the parents oscillates with impulses to be close, cared for, and dependent. These drives exist in all adolescents, but are handled in different ways.

The preanorexic child is unable to absorb the usual changes of adolescence. The external controls are too strict, too firm, and too punitive. At the same time, the impulses for increased assertiveness, rebelliousness, and aggressiveness impinge on the child's ego controls. The child faces increasing conflict as the powerful aggressive and sexual drives reverberate against the child's own strict superego and the strict parental controls, with their threats of rejection and punishment for assertivenesss and misbehavior. The result can take the form of a compromise: a regressive pull to the anorexic syndrome.

The anorexic channels the emergence of the independence, assertiveness, and aggression into not eating, and does not incur the wrath of the parents because this subtle, indirect defiance takes the form of an illness, rather than open rebellion. At the same time, the increased independence, defiance, and sexuality, which frighten the patient, are muted through the illness, as it provides the patient with an excuse for dependency gratification.

The patient's guilt over unconscious feelings of aggression and sexuality is assuaged by a strict punishing conscience that dictates starvation, illness and the possibility of death, and the deprivation of all pleasurable foods. Regression causes the infantile ties to the mother, which never have been severed, to reemerge with an archaic, omnipotent ego that strives for megalomanic control over food, the patient's body, and, through them, the external world.

The use of the mouth in gorging and vomiting has passive and active symbolic aggressive and sexual connotations. To gorge is to use the mouth and teeth actively to destroy. To eat passively is to introject and keep mother inside forever, never to separate, to retain childhood images and never grow up, to suck at the breast forever for security and nurture. To shove the food down the throat forcibly is to be violated repeatedly with unconscious sexual fantasies of rape and bodily damage displaced upward from the vagina. The starving patients who refuse to eat or to give in to their impulses to gorge have the same conflict, but deal with it in a different fashion. Both starving and gorging patients have unconscious pregnancy fantasies, fears of oral and genital damage, and a preoccupation with a flat abdomen.

Patients who vomit act out unconscious fantasies of undoing and losing control of what is inside. The gorger who vomits is actively attempting to relive, as well as undo, the rape, to eject the semen, the baby, the passive yearnings for perpetual infancy without responsibility, and the symbiotic attachment to the mother. The violent thrusting of the finger into the throat to induce vomiting symbolically reproduces the rape fantasy. At times, patients use their fingers so violently that they get cut and scarred. The vomiting is a symbolic outpouring of rage (disguised as a symptom and therefore not vulnerable to retaliation). The fear of what will pour out frequently accounts for the anorexic's inability to talk both outside and within the treatment sessions.

The bulimic's loss of control with aggressive and sexual acting out can be compared to the starving anorexic's aggressive acting out after the latter gains some insight and ceases to displace repressed aggressive feelings onto anorexic symptoms and behavior. The starving anorexic's acting out includes increasing defiance of the parents, overt hostility to siblings, and indirect forms of aggression that elicit minimal retaliation. This usually includes a changing attitude toward school. The previous perfect attendance, excellent grades, and responsive social behavior begin to deteriorate. The patient gets to school late, cuts classes, does not pay attention, fails to complete homework, and gets poorer grades. Parents call up very distressed about the "terrible changes." This parental concern in part reflects genuine worry over the consequences of a poorer academic performance on college entrance opportunities, but it also reflects an inner awareness that the behavior represents defiance of their, and the school's, authority. The parents should be encouraged to consider the possibility of healthier children at the expense of poorer grades. The conflict remains, but the expression of aggressive and sexual drives has shifted. This enables the patient to begin to renounce self-destructive starving and to start to consider the underlying conflicts masked by the anorexia. In cases of severe starvation, the shift in the expression of the conflict can be crucial, for it permits the patient to start eating.

Some patients become depressed after they begin to eat. The self-destructive conscience that dictated suffering by starvation shifts to an alternative form of criticism, suffering by feeling worthless and depressed. The conflict is not resolved, but merely shifts to a form that can be dealt with more advantageously in analytic treatment. Ultimately, with successful treatment, patients will be able to channel their sexual and aggressive drives into healthier forms of expression. Bulimic patients have more difficulty controlling this type of behavior because ego and superego controls are less rigidly applied.

The defensive displacement of unbearable conflict onto preoccupations with food takes place with both the starving anorexic and the gorging bulimic. The main difference is that the starving anorexic, who represses the desire to eat, thinks of diet foods while the bulimic, who does not deny the impulse to eat, thinks of high-calorie foods. This displacement of the conflict often appears during treatment sessions. For example, a 17-year-old female patient of mine had great difficulty keeping friends. As we discussed the situation in great detail, she began to get more and more upset and stopped speaking. After a considerable pause during which she seemed to regain her composure, I wondered about what she was thinking. With some embarrassment, she replied that she was thinking about what flavor ice cream she should buy at the local supermarket after she left the session. It was apparent to her that she had replaced the problem of friends with the problem of eating. Like starving anorexics, many bulimics displace their inability to control people onto compulsive control over food. The patient described above was extremely fussy about the way she ate her food. The food had to be prepared in a very specific manner and eaten only at a certain time. If mealtime was delayed, she was furious. This was one of the very few times that she allowed herself to be angry with her mother. She loved fruit and would eat a great deal of it, but it had to be in perfect condition. If it didn't taste just right, or if there was a minor imperfection, she would throw it out and take another. In this manner, she could go through a tremendous amount of fruit. She readily acknowledged that she would like to control her friends the way she controlled her food, but knew that that was not possible. It became increasingly clear to her that she lacked friends in part because she avoided them.

This patient was particularly fond of cornbread and, when gorging, would eat an entire loaf. On one occasion, her sister ate some of the cornbread that she had purchased for herself. She became infuriated, yelling and screaming at the stunned sister, and finally hit her across the face. It took her a long time to calm down. The patient could not understand the cause of her outburst; in her associations, she commented that the slices of bread were like little children. The cannibalistic conflict in this bulimic patient was quite similar to that found in starving anorexics. With this patient, gorging and "blowing up" were obviously related to aggression, with the feared weight increase symbolizing explosive loss of control.

Clinical Variants

The clinical picture may take any of the following forms, each of which is dominated by one feature; sometimes one form merges with another.

1. Acute, transient, mild anorexia with episodes of dieting and preoccupation with food, but only minimal weight loss; often accompanied by amenorrheic episodes and the psychodynamics of anorexia. This variant usually is not recognized or brought to the attention of a physician.

2. Acute anorexia of moderate intensity with weight loss and amenorrhea, no body-image distortion, and little or no gorging.

3. Acute, severe anorexia with marked weight loss, amenorrhea, body-image distortion, and bouts of gorging and vomiting.

4. Acute anorexia followed by a chronic, subclinical anorexia with thinness, but minimal evidence of starving or gorging; accompanied by the characteristic psychological picture of anorexia.

5. Chronic, severe anorexia with starving, gorging and vomiting, amenorrhea, and body-image distortion; periodic hospitalization.

6. Acute or chronic anorexia with bulimic gorging and vomiting a principal symptom; may or may not involve weight loss and amenorrhea.

THE PARENT-CHILD RELATIONSHIP: WHO CONTROLS WHOM

The parents' need to control the anorexic child is remarkably strong and tenaciously adhered to; it arises from parents' anxiety over loss of control over the environment, of which the child is an integral part. It does not necessarily arise from dislike for the child, but may result from the parents' attempt to cope with threatening aspects of their own personality, or from a childhood relationship displaced onto the current child.

When the anorexic child is in treatment, it is quite desirable, and often necessary, for the parents to see another therapist to be able to understand the nature of the illness in general and to learn what to do to facilitate the child's progress. When parents are able to recognize their need to control the child and then relinquish this control in a positive fashion, the effect on the child can be helpful and, occasionally, quite remarkable. When they are unable to relinquish control, progress can be markedly impaired. If the child makes progress in self-assertion and independence in the face of marked parental resistance, the parents' psychological stability can become impaired to the point of decompensation.

In general, it is feasible to see the parents together for about 6-10 consultations. During that time, one obtains a history of the anorexic syndrome and the developmental background that preceded it, along with an evaluation of the parents' problems, attitudes toward one another, and behavior toward the patient from birth onward.

The parents are told that the anorexia covers up major problems of independence, helplessness, aggression, and sexuality. It is indicated that the patient's endless preoccupation with food and eating in part is an attempt to control eating because the patient feels unable to control much else, and that the patient must learn to deal with the other aspects of life. Toward this end, the parents are encouraged to avoid all discussions of food. The more attention the parent pays to eating and food, the more the patient is encouraged to maintain the preoccupation with food, instead of dealing with the other major problems that have been avoided. At the same time, when the parents push the patient to eat, the patient derives a sense of sadistic satisfaction from not eating and from irritating the parents. The greater the sadistic gratification, the less willing the patient is to renounce it. Getting the parents to give up the concern over eating and food is a very difficult task, especially when they are confronted by a starving, emaciated, and provocative child.

The parents are warned that as the anorexia begins to subside, it may well be replaced by different behavior—depression, aggressive acting out, or other forms of aggression—which must be tolerated so as not to force the patient back into the anorexia.

A DYNAMIC APPROACH TO THERAPY

In the transference, anorexic patients become demanding, manipulative, and hostile in an attempt to control and coerce the therapist into backing down, just as they have felt forced to behave over the years by the controlling parent. Concomitantly, however, in identifying with the weak, helpless aspects of their own personality, they are fearful of retaliation by the therapist for their assertiveness, thus anticipating a response similar to that of the parent. These attitudes must be revealed and discussed carefully as transference manifestations.

Sometimes patients act helpless, weak, ineffective, unassertive, and frightened; they feel unable to deal with the exigencies of life and frantically hold on to anorexic symptoms in order to avoid inner conflicts and perpetuate unconscious infantile gratifications. This behavior also predominates in the treatment and requires careful and repeated transference interpretation. These character traits must be analyzed if patients are to establish satisfying, mature relationships with people.

In the early phase of treatment, it is very important that the therapist be dissociated from authority figures and convince patients that his or her sole interest is to understand their problems, rather than to make them eat or to control them. Patients who are in danger of dying require hospitalization and treatment by the pediatrician or internist to help them recover from this emergency, but once they are out of medical danger, treatment should focus primarily on problems and conflicts, not eating. Anorexic patients are experts in dealing with coercion, and there are few therapists that have the ability to outdo them. Forcing patients to eat on Sunday frequently is followed by their starvation or vomiting on Monday. Treatment methods that coerce patients to eat are often temporarily successful. While they are in the hospital and under considerable pressure from a very controlled and controlling environment, they may eat. Once discharged, however, they starve themselves and lose all the weight they have gained.

While patients should not be coerced into eating, this does not mean that food and eating habits are not discussed. The discussions are directed toward understanding patients' eating and starving behavior. The one major contribution that parents can make toward anorexic patients' well-being is to refrain from discussing food and from attempting to get the patient to eat.

The therapist should indicate from the very beginning that food, eating, and starvation are not the primary problems of the anorexia. In essence, they are a smokescreen for the true conflicts. The therapist must help patients to realize that it is much more fruitful to consider and discuss what they feel are the major difficulties in their lives. The advantages of focusing on these issues, rather than coercing patients to eat, are manifold. Family, friends, physicians, and, in some cases, other therapists have attempted to force these patients to eat without recognizing the inordinate inner pressures that prevent them from eating. As a consequence, they feel misunderstood and need to fight against the therapist. The therapist becomes one of "them."

The case of a 22-year-old anorexic woman graphically illustrates how an autonomous ego function became transformed into conflict and was permeated by doing things for "them." After telling her parents that she would be home for dinner after work, this patient went out for the evening with friends instead. When she came home at 11:00 P.M. that evening, she was startled to find her mother sitting out on the porch in the rain, waiting for her with the statement, "You promised that you would be home at 8:00 P.M. and eat for me." The patient was so overwhelmed with guilt at the sight of her drenched mother that she could not cope with this desperately manipulative behavior and felt like a worthless failure. Significantly, the mother expected the patient to eat for "her." This patient's inner view of herself as a thin, sticklike puppet with someone else pulling the strings was demonstrated by her anatomical appearance, as well as by her robotlike obedience.

A therapeutic alliance gradually emerges as the reasons behind the starvation are explored and the anorexic behavior becomes more comprehensible. Most anorexics initially are not cognizant of the true reasons for their self-starvation and expecting them to renounce it at once is akin to demanding that phobic patients simply "go into the elevator." A dynamic approach supports patients' need for understanding, clarifies the reasons for their illness, and provides a methodological approach for its resolution. This attitude should foster trust and a willingness to work with the therapist.

RELATIONSHIPS WITH PEERS

Many anorexic girls have major difficulties in developing healthy relationships with their peers. Attempts to reach out and establish stable peer relations usually are aborted during the acute stage of the anorexia. Prior to the overt illness, beginning manifestations of adolescent separation from the parents often are evident, although the deep and excessive attachment to the parents usually impairs any substantial separation. Lifelong dependency and attachment problems preclude achieving a separation from the parents and a subsequent emotional attachment to friends. During the acute stage, patients frequently renounce tenuous peer relations and return to hanging about the house, remaining close to the parents under the guise of being ill. One 13-year-old anorexic girl followed her mother all over the house complaining that she had nothing to do, but she would not leave the house except to go to school. A 12-year-old boy who had been a good athlete gave up all sports and spent his time watching television and looking in the refrigerator but not eating anything. Anorexic girls who continue to see their girlfriends often see them on a less frequent basis because of the revived attachment to the mother. In some cases, the relationship with a girlfriend becomes a manipulative, bossy one in which the patient treats the girlfriend the way she feels she has been treated by mother.

Where boyfriends are involved, often the girl will put the boyfriend off and discourage any amorous interest. One 18-year-old girl complained bitterly about being abandoned by her boyfriend, although it was clear that her behavior had unwittingly caused the event. Unrecognized sexual anxiety had prevented any developing relationship. Frequently, when a relationship does develop, the patient has unconsciously selected a boyfriend who treats her just as her mother has treated her, i.e., he is domineering, overprotective, and demanding, and wants to be with the patient all the time. The patient initially accepts the relationship, but gradually becomes more and more upset by it, finally recognizing that she feels trapped, has no free time, and feels controlled, without recognizing that she engineered the situation. She has difficulty asserting herself to change or terminate the relationship because it is an unconscious replay of the early mother-daughter attachment.

The relationships with same-sex and opposite-sex peers reproduce the earlier wished-for or acted-out relationship with the parents. Patients are unable to assert themselves quietly and effectively or to protect their well-being in a realistic fashion. Instead, a regressive infantile attitude emerges; either patients aggressively manipulate parents and/or peers in a perceived identification with a parent, or they are manipulated and controlled by a friend who represents a symbolic mother. Sometimes they act out both sides of this conflict.

One 19-year-old girl admitted that she was so attached to her boyfriend that she could not drop him, although she disliked almost every aspect of his behavior. She felt the same way about her girlfriend. She described the two in such vitriolic terms that her father could not understand why she maintained the relationships. Initially, she was unable to explain it herself. She would make the most outrageous demands of them, knowing that her behavior was inappropriate, and would fly into a rage if they did not accede to her wishes. She would tease her boyfriend seductively whenever there was no chance of privacy, and then become very cold and disinterested when they were alone. At other times, she would insist that everything be done her way without regard for his feelings or interests. When identifying with the helpless child in her, she would permit her friends to take advantage of her in the most self-destructive fashion so that she would end up feeling exploited, worthless, and depressed. Healthier relationships where she could be treated as an equal were avoided.

CLINICAL MATERIAL

The following case examples illustrate the range of clinical variants discussed earlier.

CASE 1   *Acute, Moderate-Intensity Anorexia without Vomiting or Gorging*

Sheila, an 18-year-old woman, developed anorexia during her freshman year in college. During that year, her father almost died from a bleeding gastric ulcer. She was concerned about doing poorly in examinations. She and her boyfriend broke up and, for a brief time, she was fearful that she might be pregnant. Although her brother attended the same university, she was unable to confide in him about any of her worrisome preoccupations. She weighed 127 lbs. and was 5'7". A gradual disinterest in food developed and was compounded by her need to study constantly. Her weight began to drop rapidly; in two months, she lost 18 lbs.

As she lost interest in food, she became fussier about what, when, and how much she ate. She renounced starchy foods, candy, and "unhealthy junk food."

She ate mostly vegetables and consumed very small amounts of meat. She noted that if she did not eat protein, she felt weak.

There was no gorging, vomiting, constipation, or use of laxatives or diuretics. Her periods, which had begun at age 14, were regular until the beginning of her anorexia. In contrast to many other anorexics, this patient did not have a body-image disturbance. She was fully aware that she was somewhat emaciated, and it troubled her. She felt that she did not look well and that the thinness detracted from her appearance. She noted how thin her neck, shoulders, ribs, and hips were and wanted to increase her weight to 120 lbs. She was also acutely conscious of and disturbed by the bony prominences of her sternum and clavicles, and attempted to obscure them by wearing high-necked clothing that covered the area.

Exercise was important to her and was performed regularly. She ran and also did exercises in her room. She acknowledged that she exercised to increase weight loss and to discharge aggression. In the first interview, she commented, "I exercise when I begin to get upset. I suppress my feelings, and instead of screaming or throwing things, I exercise." She was also aware that her appetite fluctuated with her aggressive impulses. In discussing how her parents pressured her, and how much it bothered and upset her, she added, "I could be hungry, but after a fight with my mother or father, I lose my appetite. When you are upset, you don't feel like eating."

While there was no body-image distortion, her weight loss, choice of foods, and method of eating were typically anorexic. Her starvation was a means of self-assertion, discharge of aggression, self-punishing retribution for her hostility, and dependency gratification through illness. Arguments with her parents were followed by conscious impulses to defy by not eating and by exercising to further her weight loss.

Sheila was born and raised in a small Southern town; she had four older brothers. The father was poorly educated and farmed the small family homestead with his three brothers. Shortly after the grandfather died, oil was discovered on the property, enabling the father and brothers to sell their land and go into business. Increased fighting among the brothers resulted in the patient's father selling his share of the company and going into business for himself. The father's drinking affected his ability to run the business, with the threat of bankruptcy a frequent problem. The mother was somewhat better educated than the father, and she fought with him frequently over his drinking and his constant need to have his brothers bail him out. At the time the patient entered treatment, the family lived in the North. Two of the patient's older brothers were alcoholics.

Sheila described in great detail a typical pattern of interaction between herself and her parents. It took the form of a lifelong relationship in which the parents controlled and dominated her and she passively acquiesed. Sheila never felt that she could make a decision about anything. Her mother always told her what to do, how to do it, and when to do it. Whenever she attempted to do something her way, the mother got so upset and so angry that the patient became frightened and withdrew. "I felt that I never could assert myself, and if I tried, it didn't make a dent. I ended up keeping it in until I couldn't swallow it anymore." At that point, she recognized the relationship between defiance and starving. She continued, "Then as I kept it all in, I began to realize that talking didn't work, so I began to use food. Even now, when I assert myself, I feel guilty about it, even when I know intellectually that I'm right."

Sheila complained that while the mother treated her like an infant and constantly told her what to do, she also seemed to reverse roles and complain to the patient about the father and the marital discord. The mother phoned the patient weekly when she was away at school, complaining constantly and weeping bitterly about the father's alcoholism and derogatory behavior. The patient dreaded the calls, and felt hopeless to cope with them. Sheila told her mother that the marriage seemed impossible and that the mother should consider a separation. The mother refused to consider extricating herself, but continued to complain. On rare occasions, when Sheila suggested that these conversations upset her and seemed to serve no purpose, the mother violently attacked her, accused her of lacking interest and compassion, and made her feel guilty. Thus, any attempt at self-assertion was countered by mother's anger and evocation of guilt in the patient.

The patient reported an episode in which the mother asked her to phone the father and give him instructions about picking up the car. When Sheila attempted to do so, the father got angry and hung up. When the patient reported this incident to the mother, the mother chastised her for not doing what she was told and for being unreliable and irresponsible. The patient's attempts to defend herself by pointing out that the father did not listen were to no avail. Sheila's initial reaction, aside from becoming upset, was to think that the mother was very unreasonable and that she (Sheila) could in no way be responsible for what had transpired. As the mother continued her criticism, however, Sheila felt less sure of her position and thought that perhaps she was in some way to blame. She felt guilty and distressed. The mother's behavior served to undermine Sheila's self-confidence and to impair her ability to assess reality clearly. At the same time, when the patient performed well in school, the mother's response was quite perfunctory. Instead of praising Sheila, she would bring up the brothers' accomplishments.

Over and over, Sheila stressed how difficult it was to get her parents to listen to her. At one point, she added, "Now that I'm sick, she listens to me, . . . treats me like I'm fragile."

It was clear that both parents were unduly preoccupied with food and eating. Sheila recalled the father both depriving her of food and force-feeding her. To punish misbehavior, he withheld food that she liked. He also forced her to eat food that she disliked. Food became an instrument of punishment and coercion early in Sheila's life, and this contributed to the later symptom choice.

The mother also had an intense preoccupation with food and would complain that the patient ate too much of this or that food. At times, the mother would make a big fuss over Sheila's choice of food when, in fact, it was a matter of indifference to her. When Sheila began to recover from her anorexia and eat more normally, the mother failed to recognize the improvement and still discussed food as a problem; she even complained when Sheila gave up eating grapefruit in favor of bacon and eggs. It was almost as if there were a complementary involvement with food. As Sheila gave up her almost constant preoccupation with food, her mother became increasingly interested in food and attempted to get Sheila reinvolved with it.

Sheila described her father as a businessman whose drinking interfered with the running of his company. The early sessions were filled with an outpouring of resentment toward this man, whom she saw as a provocative, selfish, critical, and self-indulgent person. The father's flagrantly controlling and domineering behavior was recounted by the patient in a multitude of experiences. Sheila felt that he was critical of everything she did and unpredictable in his behavior. Occasionally, he hit Sheila or her brothers when they openly disapproved of his wishes. Attempts at reasonable self-assertion were countered by his "Get out of the house and don't come back!" He also threatened to lock her up because she was crazy.

This patient revealed an all-consuming investment in her schoolwork. Even though she was an excellent student who received high grades, she was continually apprehensive about not doing well and felt forced to study long hours for examinations. The copious time she allotted to prepare for tests and to write papers reflected her doubts about her own capacity and ability. These doubts were a consequence of the crippling criticism from the parents and of her own acquiescence to passive experience (which replaced active mastery).

The preoccupations with food and studies in part were displacements from her involvement with people and tasks in the external world. She wanted omnipotent and perfectionistic control over every aspect of her food and studies—in lieu of the same control over her relationships with people, which she could not achieve.

As is typical of anorexic patients, Sheila revealed a great deal about the turmoil with her parents very early in treatment, but did not discuss her sexual conflicts. With these patients, sexual conflict should not be dealt with in the opening phase of treatment. Sheila described her parents in a rather florid and harsh light. While the intensity of a patient's repressed feelings may tend to overdramatize parental behavior and the patient's plight, the domination, control, infantilization, and preoccupation with food are usually integral aspects of the parent-child relationship.

A number of times when Sheila got caught up in the conflicts with the parents, and began to feel helpless and trapped, she was surprised to recognize the emergence of thoughts and feelings about not wanting to eat. During an argument with her mother the thought "I'm not going into the kitchen to eat" occurred to her with such suddenness that she remembered being startled by the idea. But the thought of revenging herself on the mother was countered by the realization that the starving was self-destructive.

Sheila's anorexia was less severe than most cases, but the dynamic motivations for her self-starvation, as well as the family constellation, are typical of anorexia. Because she was less ill, she may have been more readily able to reveal the purpose of her anorexic behavior. Those with severe anorexia tend to adhere more tenaciously to discussions of food, starvation, and other symptomatology in order to preserve the defensive aspects of the illness, the discharge of aggression, and the infantile gratifications.

In Sheila's case, as in many others, there was distress over appearance and a desire to eat and gain weight. However, not eating preserved the route of self-destructive discharge. Conversely, eating would block this discharge and the patient would have to find an alternative means of coping with the aggressive thoughts and feelings. Inner awareness of this problem frequently results in the patient "needing the anorexia" and holding on to the starving in the face of consciously wanting to eat and put on weight. If the patient gives up the self-starvation without understanding its aggressive aspects, a depression often develops. Some patients who sense this and are unwilling to deal with the emerging sadness return to self-starvation without telling the therapist. Only on careful questioning will the patient reveal the fear of the depression and the return to the anorexia to avoid it. The crucial role that the aggresive conflict plays and the importance of analyzing it must be underscored.

CASE 2   Chronic, "Nonsymptomatic" Anorexia

Aline was a 15-year-old girl whose anorexia developed at age 12. Her parents had separated when she was three years of age. The father, an engineer, lived in California and had remarried. While he never returned to the East Coast, where Aline lived, she visited with him every Christmas and for one month every summer. These visits were usually disappointing and frustrating. She was not able to accept her two young half-sisters from the second marriage. As a consequence, the father's second wife was cold and rejecting.

The mother, a singer, was the main support of the family. Mother, Aline, and her two-year-older brother lived alone, but in close proximity to the mother's mother. The grandmother had played a major and domineering role in the upbringing of the mother and in the life of the children. The grandmother was an overcontrolling, domineering, and manipulative person who totally controlled her daughter's life. The mother stated that she had felt completely dominated by her mother all through childhood and adolescence. At the age of 20, early in her career, she had felt helpless, insecure, depressed, frightened, and ill at ease in the company of men. She had entered psychotherapy at that time, but had abruptly terminated after three months. A number of years later, she had met and married her husband. The marriage had lasted four years. After its breakup, mother had returned to live in close proximity to, and under the domination of, her own mother. Under the guise of needing to share in the raising of the grandchildren, the grandmother had continued to control and dominate both the daughter and the grandchildren.

The maternal grandfather was an easy-going, affectionate, unassertive physician who was also dominated by his wife. The patient established an understanding and comfortable relationship with her grandfather, although she resented his inability to protect her from the mother's and grandmother's domination. He died when Aline was 12 years old and, one month later, she developed anorexia. The patient was 5'3" and weighed 120 lbs. at that time. Within two months, she lost 20 lbs. Her slightly overweight condition was more than corrected, but when the patient was brought to her pediatrician, the mother was told that nothing was wrong. Two months later, she weighed 78 lbs. and was hospitalized. During the 12-week hospitalization, she began to eat and was discharged at a weight of 100 lbs.

The acute stage of her anorexia was typical. She renounced all fattening foods and remained on a high-protein diet. She exercised constantly and never seemed to sit still. She ran and swam a great deal. Any attempts to encourage her to eat were futile. She complained of constipation, cramps, and diarrhea, and used these symptoms as justification for not eating.

When seen in consultation at the age of 15, she had never menstruated. Her height was 5′4″ and her weight was 104. She was not acutely symptomatic in that she was not starving herself, was not markedly underweight, and was not physically ill. Her physical symptoms were minimal, except for the absence of menstruation. The most obvious and clear-cut manifestation of her illness lay in her character structure, which was typical of anorexics with more overt symptomatology.

In attempting to classify these patients, Sours (1974, 1979) makes a point of defining primary and secondary symptoms. He sees the primary symptoms as willful food restriction, pursuit of thinness, control over the body, fear of fatness, hyperactivity, and amenorrhea. He describes as secondary symptoms the manipulative dieting behavior, the avoidance of food, the all-consuming preoccupation with eating, and the distrustful behavior toward the nurturing parents. In addition, he mentions the presence of sadness and guilt, but not true depression.

These so-called secondary character traits were quite evident in Aline, but my experience indicates that they are integral, pervasive, and central elements of the disease, rather than by-products of it. These characteristics constitute crucial aspects of the ego's functioning, were crystallized in the early mother-child relationship, and require considerable analytic work even after the disappearance of the anorexia in order for true growth and development to resume. The controlling and manipulative behavior with food extends into all aspects of these patients' lives. The behavior is in part a defensive identification with the aggressor, but it also is indicative of the emergence of a regressed, infantile, and omnipotent ego that is incapable of maintaining mature object relationships. These patients are out to control objects, not to relate to them. Their distrust of authority further interferes with the establishment of deep and meaningful relationships.

One of Aline's major conflicts was her inability to achieve a reasonable degree of independence and autonomy through direct assertiveness, separation from parental figures, and peer-group involvement. Since direct assertiveness was not possible, Aline asserted herself indirectly through the illness. After Aline returned from the hospital, the mother's fear that she would get sick again resulted in her acquiescing to her daughter's demands.

The mother stated that after her hospitalization, Aline became the "cook" in the house. She did all the food shopping and all the cooking. She decided what and when the family would eat. She brought no salt or sugar into the house and bought a great deal in health food stores. She insisted that the family eat at 7:30 P.M. each evening and became furious when circumstances occasionally prevented it. She would not allow her mother to watch her eat or comment on her eating. She became a tyrant with food. As the mother said, "I couldn't even go into the kitchen anymore, and sometimes I felt that I was not living in my own house. When she went shopping, she didn't even want me to walk down the aisles with her in the supermarket. She had to do it all herself."

The independence and decision-making activities absent in the rest of Aline's life were clearly manifested and carried out through her interest in food. She accepted domination and control by others in all areas but food, where she reigned supreme. Rather than maintain the identification with the victim, she identified with the aggressor and victimized others. Passivity was replaced by activity. Because she could not control reasonable elements in the external world, she miniaturized her world and exercised complete control over it.

When Aline finally was seen by a therapist she stated that she never had had any treatment other than the hospitalization and didn't want any now. She was hostile, provocative, and defiant. Her unhappiness burst through in a few minutes, and the early sessions were filled with tales of sadness and anguish. She spoke about always having suffered as a scapegoat from the beginning of her school days. The children were mean at the parochial school. They made fun of her. The boys punched her and, even though the nuns saw it, they did nothing to protect her. She never had any friends that could protect her. There was no one in school with whom she could talk.

In subsequent sessions, she spoke about how the grandmother controlled and bossed around both her and her mother. She couldn't stand it, but whenever she got angry, she felt very guilty. As a child, she used to have dreams of being burned by fire and was always afraid of dying. She used to dream of her mother and her grandmother dying; then she would be all alone. As she commented, "I have to get along with my mother. I have no one else."

While the self-starvation had abated, the need to control, manipulate, and engage in self-destructive behavior continued unchecked. The patient achieved a degree of control over the environment by the threat of starving and by controlling circumstances related to food. Since she could not control the rest of her life, but needed to be in control of something, this behavior was perpetuated.

This patient illustrates the course and psychological consequences of eliminating the symptoms (i.e., self-starvation, fanatic exercise, and other means of inducing weight loss) of anorexia without resolving the major underlying conflicts. Aline was still markedly disturbed, but the disturbance was manifested as a character disorder. She was infantile, controlling, demanding, manipulative, bitter, and hostile. She had few friends and was masochistic in her relationship with them. Her sadistic attitude toward her mother was primarily in reference to food. However, as the sadistic qualities in her personality never had been analyzed, they would persist and might be displaced onto other activities. She was still afraid to grow up, was excessively attached to her mother, needed to alienate friends in order to avoid dealing with maturing in the world, and disliked and blamed her mother for her helplessness and immaturity. Treatment modalities that concentrate solely on the recovery of body weight at the expense of psychological recovery and maturity reap very modest gains indeed.

If one diagnoses the anorexic syndrome purely by its clinical manifestations—self-starvation, weight loss, the pursuit of thinness, body-image distortion, amenorrhea, vomiting, excessive exercising, and the use of laxatives—then it is reasonable to conclude that this patient was no longer anorexic. However, the patient was not well: her illness merely had shifted. Symptom shift is not uncommon during the course of psychiatric and psychosomatic illness. Phobias can be replaced by depression or self-destructive acting-out behavior. In children, enuresis can be replaced by asthma, and asthma, by ulcerative colitis or other illnesses. During the course of treatment for anorexia, emerging depression is very common. To replace the anorexia with depression or a severe character disorder is a dubious clinical triumph.

CASE 3   Chronic, Severe Anorexia with Psychological Decompensation

Dolores, a 23-year-old woman, had an 11-year history of severe anorexia, including five hospitalizations during the past 18 months. She was 5'2" and weighed 80 lbs.

In addition to self-starvation, the patient was markedly depressed and had made a number of suicide attempts by cutting her wrists. She had also overdosed on Valium, Thorazine, Doriden, and phenobarbital. She was in the habit of taking 50–60 laxatives at a time, along with an unknown number of diuretic pills, all in the service of "losing weight." At times, her electrolyte imbalance had produced grand mal seizures that required hospitalization. The combination of emaciation, tranquilizers, diuretics, laxatives, and sleep medication had precipitated a coma on more than one occasion.

At the time of consultation, the patient was living at home after an abortive attempt to attend a university away from home. She spent most of her time in her room, watching TV or arguing with her mother. She had no interests and no friends. Her parents were constantly apprehensive because of her wrist-cutting episodes, her previous overdosing on medications prescribed by physicians, her obtaining diuretics from which she convulsed, and the severe anorexic condition itself. Their concern about her illness provided her with the justification for accepting the infantile gratifications from the illness. The patient had one sibling, a married brother who was two years older and healthy.

According to the parents, the patient had been well until age 12, when her engineer father was promoted and sent on an overseas assignment. He had planned to get established and send for his family in three to four months. The mother had not noticed any insecurity shown by Dolores over the father's leaving, but, in the ensuing month, she became aware that Dolores had lost her appetite and had lost about 9 lbs. The weight loss had continued even after the reunion with the father, creating such concern that the father cut short his work and the family returned to the United States. The patient had been hospitalized and then treated by a psychiatrist; she seemed to improve a little. The patient had had her first menstrual period in Europe at age 12 and had had only two scant periods since.

Salient features in the patient's early history related to separation problems. The parents recalled that when Dolores was two years old, they had gone away for a weekend without her and her brother and she had been so upset that she had followed the mother all over the house for a month and would not let her mother out of her sight.

The separation anxiety persisted into nursery school. Dolores had been unable to tolerate the separation from the mother and had remained at home. All through her preadolescence, when her friends were enjoying sleeping over at their friends' homes, Dolores had been unable to do so. She could have friends sleep at her home, but she was unable to stay overnight at their homes.

The mother added that, as a child, Dolores had not fallen asleep easily and that she still slept with her door open and the hall light on. The father added that she had been very close to his father, who died when she was nine years old. She had been very distressed by it. The parents had attempted to minimize the difficulty by not telling the patient about the funeral.

When seen in consultation, the patient was a thin, emaciated-looking woman who appeared chronically ill. Her clothes hung on her in spite of her wearing small sizes in an attempt to minimize her starved state. Her face was thin, with prominent zygomatic bones and a hollowness beneath them. Her nose was peaked and her skin was pale and thin. Her hair was short and brittle and lacked a healthy lustre. She appeared wound up, tense, and in constant motion even while sitting in the chair.

She began by stating that she had been in and out of treatment since the seventh grade and it had not helped. She had been on all kinds of drugs, had been hospitalized five times recently, and had been cutting her wrists since the eighth grade. She felt that she had been having nervous breakdowns for which she had an amnesia. She had overdosed on all kinds of medication.

She spoke a good deal in the initial consultation. She volunteered that

> the scale determines my mood and whether I'm suicidal. As I put on weight, I get more depressed. At 85 lbs., I'm a fat horse, but I still can do things. At 90 lbs., I get more depressed and I begin thinking of cutting my wrists and taking pills. . . . I feel so fat and ugly that I won't go out of the house and I wear pregnant-type outfits. . . . I can't stop eating now. In the hospital, I couldn't eat at all, . . . but they did save my life. I couldn't walk without passing out.

Clearly, an inverse relationship existed between the severity of the patient's anorexia and the severity of her depressive, suicidal behavior. When she was very emaciated, she was less depressed and had fewer suicidal impulses. As her weight increased, she became more and more depressed and her self-destructive acting out escalated. I have found that anorexic starving behavior is a specific manifestation of self-destructive acting out and, as such, drains off destructive drives. When the destructiveness is not discharged via the anorexic behavior, it seeks discharge through other avenues. This can take the form of increasing depression and suicide attempts. Some feel that aggression plays a minimal role in anorexia, but I feel that it is of paramount importance in the evolution, maintenance, and resolution of the illness. It plays an important role in the patient's characteristic resistance to entering treatment, in the nature of the transference, and in the technical handling of the treatment.

Dolores described her relationships with people. She did not trust anyone, including therapists. She had few friends. She had not had a date for over a year. She never had dated anyone more than two times. She would break it off because she felt so ugly.

She remembered when her anorexia started. She used to exercise all day long, and her weight dropped to 66 lbs. They all thought she might die. She was still afraid that she would get too fat. She would gorge and try to vomit, but often could not. At times, she would take 60 laxatives at a time, twice a day. She still took 3-4 water pills a day when she could get them.

She stated that she never had had a normal menstrual period, even though doctors had given her hormone shots. In the consultation with the mother, she stated that Dolores had had her first period when the family arrived in Europe for the reunion with the father, and only two scant periods since.

This patient's chronic anorexia alternated with or was accompanied by other forms of severe self-destructive behavior. In this case, the treatment of the anorexic symptoms necessitated dealing with other symptoms and behaviors that were inextricably intertwined with them. Unfortunately, Dolores's parents were not psychologically supportive, and she refused to remain in treatment.

CASE 4   *Acute, Transient Anorexia*

Transient, self-limiting attacks of anorexia may be recognized in retrospect during the evaluation of other psychological problems. Many such episodes may go undetected.

Nan, a college junior at a competitive university, was seen in consultation during her summer vacation. During her sophomore year, she had suffered from intermittent depressions brought on by what she felt were manifestations of inadequate performance, lack of dedication to her work, and doubts about her ability and self-worth. She described alternating between bouts of frenetic activity in which she threw herself into her work and felt exhilarated and gratified, and bouts of lassitude, indifference, and slowed productivity. This behavior had been present to a lesser degree during her freshman year. Nevertheless, she still had achieved almost a straight-A average. This year, however, while her grades had faltered only slightly and could be perceived as disappointing only by a perfectionistic standard, the patient still had been distressed by them. Her intermittent indifference to performance had set off anxiety that she might stop working entirely.

During the year, Nan had gone on strict diets and lost weight, but the diets always were followed by bouts of overeating and weight gain. The dieting did not approach that practiced by a severe anorexic, nor was the preoccupation with food all consuming. Likewise, the bouts of overeating were not as rapacious as typical bulimic episodes. However, an eight-month amenorrhea in the beginning phase of the dieting and a transient disturbance in body-image perception at the peak of the weight loss provided clues to the true nature of the syndrome. The patient had lost 18 lbs. and was delighted by it. Questions were raised in her mind, however, when friends began to comment on her gaunt, excessively thin appearance. Then she realized how thin she was and put on a little weight. At that time, she was 5'3" and weighed 98 lbs.

Experiences of this kind are rarely brought to the attention of a psychiatrist as a primary cause for referral. It is reasonable to assume that these "mini attacks" of anorexia accompanied by momentary psychological decompensation are common during periods of excessive stress, much as transient phobias and similar phenomena occur in periods of growth and development. Nan's impulses to stop driving herself perfectionistically and thereby to punish herself were similar to her impulses to stop starving and then to gorge.

While the anorexic episode was transient, the character disturbance was not, and the patient went into treatment.

CASE 5   *Bulimia*

Thelma, a 16-year-old girl, was referred by her uncle. His daughter had been treated for anorexia a number of years earlier. Thelma was a bright, attractive girl who was quite verbal and quite unhappy. She stated that she had been gorging and vomiting for almost three years. She was 5'4" and weighed 110 lbs., the correct weight for her height, but previously she had weighed 150 lbs. Overweight since childhood, she frequently had been mocked and had few friends. In the seventh grade, she and her mother had gone to Weight Watchers, where Thelma lost 35 lbs. She had felt marvelous, but eventually began to gain weight again.

In the beginning of high school, her friend had taught her how to vomit, and she had been eating and vomiting ever since. She could gorge and vomit up to 12 times a day. Sometimes the vomiting resulted in a sore throat, but she couldn't stop. Sometimes when she overate, she felt so full that she couldn't go to sleep. After vomiting, she felt like a new person. "When I don't throw up, I get frightened and I'm afraid that I'll get fat again. Why do I punish myself that way, as if I'm a terrible person? I always think that I could do a better job at whatever I'm doing, but all I ever do is vomit. I eat food the way an alcoholic drinks." The patient described eating as her way of avoiding things. Whenever she had schoolwork to do and didn't feel like doing it, she went into the kitchen and ate.

Thelma was on a perpetual diet of salads, vegetables, cottage cheese, jello, and tea. During her binging episodes, she would consume prodigious quantities of rich food—ice cream, soda, cereals, bread, cake, spaghetti, chocolate—until she felt that she would burst. Then she felt terrible, vomited, and felt guilty. The mother guessed that the patient's gorging cost the family $50 a week more than the cost of her regular eating. The patient said that during a bout of gorging, she would eat everything in sight, including any part of a dinner that was prepared for the evening. On one occasion, when her father and three brothers returned late from a ball game, the patient sneaked into the kitchen and nibbled away at their dinners until nothing was left. They all scolded her and she felt terrible. At other times, she would surreptitiously nibble away at their meals without getting caught. Gorging anorexics often eat the food of the individual toward whom they have aggressive feelings; eating the other person's food represents an attempt to identify with him or her. In contrast, the starving anorexic attempts to stuff the hated sibling or parent while continuing to starve herself. In this manner she expresses hostility toward the person, attempts to control him or her, and identifies with the aggressor.

Surprisingly, Thelma was very voluble in the first session. She spontaneously described the setting in which the vomiting began. Her father, an executive in a paper company, was transferred to a distant state just before the patient graduated from grammar school. He moved and found a home, and, after the June graduation, Thelma and the rest of the family joined him. Thelma was terribly distressed at the loss of all her friends and felt empty, lonely, and depressed. Her friend at the new high school was the one who suggested that she vomit when she felt full.

The productivity of the patient in the first session, which continued during treatment, was of special interest because of her two previous unsuccessful attempts at treatment. At 13, she had seen a therapist who attempted to stop her gorging and vomiting and encouraged her to eat normally. When this did not work, the therapist became angry with her and threatened and scolded her, reminding her of her mother. After one month, the patient refused to continue. She stated that her second psychiatrist, also a man, stared at her and never said a word. He did tell her that she had problems that she would have to solve, but she felt that he was not helping her. Long periods of silence left the patient feeling increasingly uncomfortable. After three months, the patient refused to continue, and the therapist acknowledged to the parents that he could not help her because she would not cooperate.

Technically, it is advisable to be more active, talkative, and open with teenage patients than with adult patients. With anorexic patients specifically, it is often helpful to interpret resistances and conflict earlier, especially when patients are on a rapid downhill course. With Thelma, active listening was sufficient to encourage her productions.

The parents, who were seen in the second visit, described Thelma as a very bright, sensitive child who easily felt rejected and had great difficulty reaching out to friends. Both parents were born and raised in the South and felt that it was important to be socially adept and to have friends, even though the father clearly indicated that the mother was socially ill at ease with people and quite isolated. Both acknowledged that Thelma had been an insecure, clinging child from the time she was able to walk. As a toddler, she had followed the mother all over the house, pulling at her dress. The youngest brother had been born when the patient was three, and after that, she became even more clinging and demanding. The mother had been hospitalized for two weeks for severe depression when Thelma was six. Both parents agreed that the patient had been very close to her mother and confided in her all the time up until high school. Then a dramatic change occurred and mother and Thelma seemed to be at each other's throats all the time. The father said that the screaming was impossible, and he and the boys would clear out of the room when the arguments began to escalate. With some bitterness, the mother interjected that the father also knew how to scream and that he would not tolerate any independence on the part of the two older boys. The fighting between father and the oldest son became especially violent when father drank excessively, which he often did.

The initial interview with the parents quickly revealed that, although these parents loved their children and were obviously prepared to do whatever they could to help them, there was considerable turmoil in the household, including screaming, drinking, and physical punishment of the children.

The parents of gorgers seem to have lacunae in their own ego and superego functioning; their acting out via a chaotic life style, intense arguing, drinking, and violence permits the child to identify with the same type of ego structure. In comparison to the starver, the gorger is much more apt to act out with fighting, stealing, lying, promiscuity, alcoholism, and drug usage, as the inelastic ego defense system is incapable of containing the battering impulses arising out of increased adolescent drives and psychic instability.

The parents of anorexics who starve with minimal gorging have more ego and superego controls. Their rigidity is consistent, and their loss of control is minimal. These parents are rigid, but well-contained. In their identification with the parents, the children achieve the same degree of rigidity in their ego structures. They establish viselike controls over their functioning. Both the starvers and the gorgers have a primitive, punitive conscience that punishes them, but the starver is punished more consistently.

In the third session, Thelma continued to describe her symptoms and behavior. She acknowledged an occasional loss of her menstrual period, but this was irregular rather than sustained. She had suffered from headaches in the back of her head, with occasional dizziness, for the past five years. She usually suffered in silence and rarely took medication for it. She clearly recognized that when she fought with her mother or father, it was often followed by a headache that would last for hours. Her inability to face her mounting resentment was somatized into the headaches or displaced onto eating preoccupations.

While she was very angry at both parents' behavior, she was more furious with her mother. She felt that the mother was especially critical of her and would attack and belittle her every accomplishment. Thelma was an excellent science student and hoped to become a physician or get a Ph.D. in scientific research. Nevertheless, the mother would often tease her, telling her that she would not want to be her patient or that no university would ever hire her. The patient was especially incensed at the thought that the mother criticized her eating patterns but seemed to want her to be fat. She always bought her fattening foods. When Thelma weighed 110 lbs., the mother criticized her for being too fat. It seems that the mothers of gorging patients who have trouble with obesity may complain that they are too fat when they are normal, while the mothers of emaciated patients may complain that they are too thin when they are normal. Both sets of parents often have body-image disturbances.

Thelma typically felt that she was both fat and ugly. When she ate, she felt fat in her stomach and thighs. Most anorexics are particularly concerned with the belly and thighs. Thelma also stated that her face, arms, wrists, fingers, back, and toes were fat. All these body parts have symbolic meanings.*

In discussing the gorging in detail, the patient acknowledged that it seemed to happen when she was upset and that the upset feeling disappeared during the bulimic attack. It was pointed out that if she could think about what upset her, she might not have to gorge. One month later, Thelma reported that she had gone for three weeks without gorging, until the previous night, when she had binged and vomited. Her mother had yelled and screamed at her and hit her across the face when she had defended her older brother's choice of a college. The mother had become enraged, had called her stupid, and had told her to get out of the house. She had run upstairs sobbing, overwhelmed by the feeling that no one cared for her. Later that night, she had eaten all the food in the ice box, had felt stuffed, had vomited, and then had eaten again and felt sick. The dorsum of her hand had bled from the violent thrust into her throat. She admitted that the gorging episode had eliminated the previous depression and sense of panic.

---

*See Chapter 17.

Instead, she hated herself for her eating and vomiting. She had hated her mother and then felt guilty, but after the vomiting, she had felt "purged" and relieved. The vomiting seemed to serve both as a somatic eruption of anger and as a punishment.

Thelma remained in treatment and eventually was able to work out her problems.

SUMMARY

This chapter presents a psychoanalytic point of view about anorexia nervosa. The illness is becoming increasingly common, but it has a long history and was accurately chronicled over 300 years ago. Its flagrant symptomatology has changed little in that time. Morton's early case died, and we still face a significant mortality rate.

A historical review of the literature is provided, with a description of the predominating views of the major clinicians.

The clinical syndrome and the underlying unconscious reasons that perpetuate the behavior are described. The patient's "need" for the illness is clarified. A suggestion is made for a rational treatment plan that emphasizes understanding of the illness and that enables the patient to renounce the disease and attempt to get well.

The early developmental history of anorexic patients is described. It demonstrates an inordinately close relationship between the developing child and the parents. The parents unwittingly relate to the child in ways that encourage dependency and helplessness, and interfere with self-reliance and independence. The overcontrolling parents contribute to the development of a passive, "perfect," obedient child. With adolescence, emerging psychic turbulence, characterized by increased aggressiveness, sexuality, and independence, destabilizes the previous equilibrium and produces strivings for independence that conflict with the parents. The inability to confront the parents directly is reflected in an indirect defiance that takes the form of "an inability to eat," rather than more overt forms of rebellion, which would produce a critical attack on the patient's ego. The anorexia syndrome can be seen as a compromise in which the patient can defy through illness without receiving the rejection that more flagrant rebellion would cause.

Sexual conflicts, separation anxieties, problems with aggression, difficulties in accepting the female role, pregnancy fears, and anxieties over motherhood are all additional major sources of conflict that are intertwined and acted out in the illness. Careful psychiatric treatment by an experienced clinician provides the best opportunity for the resolution of the anorexia and the underlying conflicts. Without resolution of these conflicts, they will remain as major personality difficulties or become channeled into a different illness.

5
Psychodynamics

CHARLES C. HOGAN, M.D., D. MED. SC.

Much has been written about the psychodynamics of anorexia nervosa. It generally has been observed by analytic authors that there is a flight from adult sexuality accompanied by a regression to more primitive defenses (e.g., Fenichel 1945a; Gero 1953; Lorand 1943; Masserman 1941; Moulton 1942; Selvini Palazzoli 1963, 1978; Sperling 1953, 1968b, 1978; Thomä 1967; Waller et al. 1940; Wilson and others in this volume). This regression involves conflict around primitive sadistic and cannibalistic oral fantasies (Selvini Palazzoli 1963, 1978; Sperling 1953, 1968b, 1978). Typical pregenital defense mechanisms are at work (Fenichel 1945a; Masterson 1977; Sperling 1953, 1968b, 1978; Volkan 1965, 1976).

Thomä (1967) and Sperling (1978) stress the etiologic role of the unresolved ambivalent mother-child relationship. Sperling notes that, from early childhood, the anorexic patient is conditioned to regard food as a means of controlling life. Thomä states that the anorexic patient abandons the genital-sexual stage of development both subjectively and objectively, and becomes almost completely independent of food and of the environment through negativism and unawareness of illness. He notes that the patient's manifest behavior contradicts the unconscious yearning for mother and that, gradually, the patient's object choice becomes an identification. Thomä discusses the clinical manifestations of the regression, and the conflicts with the maternal figure and the maternal object representation.

Sperling (1978) notes that unresolved preoedipal fixations to the mother contribute to difficulties in psychosexual development. She feels that anorexic girls displace sexual and masturbatory conflicts from the genitals to the mouth, thus equating food and eating with forbidden sexual objects and activities.

Most analytic authors agree that the regression of anorexic patients is a flight from their own insatiable instinctual needs, which are defended against with primitive defenses of equal force. Sperling (1978) has labeled anorexia nervosa "an impulse disorder."

The role of unconscious pregnancy fantasies in the genesis of this illness is almost universally recognized by psychoanalytic authors. The anorexic patient fears and denies these fantasies.

Sperling (1978) notes that the "dynamic factor . . . essential in the genesis of anorexia nervosa in adolescent girls is the revival or persistence of an intense positive oedipal conflict during puberty and adolescence" (p. 165); the patient's specific way of dealing with this conflict depends on the patient's early acquired premorbid disposition involving specific fixations and object relationships. She also notes conflicts over accepting the female role and feminine identification because of hatred and murderous impulses toward the mother.

We see from this brief discussion that most analytic authors recognize an emotional disturbance that emerges around puberty in the form of a retreat from developing adult sexuality via a regression to the prepubescent relationship with the parents. This prepubescent emotional adjustment is accompanied by amenorrhea, weight loss, and anorexia with or without bulimia.

Palmer and Jones (1939), Lorand (1943), Fenichel (1945a), Sperling 1953, 1978), Thomä (1967), and the other members of our group consider anorexia nervosa primarily a neurotic symptom, but also tend to agree that it can occur in a variety of pregenitally fixated character disorders such as borderline, depressive or hysterical types.

I have seen one case in consultation that was overtly psychotic and have observed that many anorexics will regress to temporarily disorganized behavior, particularly in analysis or analytic therapy. There seems to be no indication that these patients are primarily schizophrenic or psychotic in their character structures. Masterson (1977) places them in the borderline category into which, if one likes this diagnosis, some of them would probably fit. However, I, along with Sperling (1978), do not agree with Bruch (1962, 1965, 1970, 1978a), Crisp (1965, 1967, 1969), Dally (1969), and Selvini Palazzoli (1978) that a psychoanalytic approach to these patients should be avoided. The experience of our group agrees with Blitzer et al. (1961), Jessner and Abse (1960), Lorand (1943), Margolis and Jernberg (1960), Masserman (1941), Sperling (1953, 1968b, 1978), Thomä (1967), Waller et al. (1940), and with others, that psychoanalytic investigation is of the utmost importance in understanding this illness, as well as the treatment of choice in most cases.

CLINICAL MATERIAL

The clinical material utilized in this discussion is drawn primarily from the five patients briefly described below.

These cases all fall into the classical category of anorexia. All are female. They varied in age at the time treatment began from Debora, who was in her middle teens, to Ellen, who was in her early forties. Both Debora and Ellen had been mildly overweight during their prepubescent years and had started using vomiting as a control measure at about age 11. Ellen had menarche at 13, but after irregular menses lost her periods at 18. Her weight had been in the seventies and her height was 5'5". Debora had had only one period at 13 and no further periods until in treatment at the age of 15. Her weight had been in the eighties and her height was 5'4".

Anna entered treatment in her early thirties and had been anorexic since the age of 17. Earlier problems with weight dated to age 11. Menarche was at 13 and amenorrhea had developed at 16. Her weight was in the low seventies and her height was 5′ 4″.

Betty was in her midtwenties when she came into treatment. She had been anorexic since the age of 16, with weight problems since the age of 11. Menarche was at 13. Periods had ceased four years before entering treatment, but had been irregular since 16 years of age. Her weight was in the low seventies and her height was 5′ 5″.

Claudia was in her late teens when she began treatment. She had had weight problems all through childhood, but began losing weight at age 11, after menarche. Her weight had dropped to 90 lbs. and her height was 5′4″. Amenorrhea had developed at 15 after an irregular menstrual history. Her weight had returned to normal temporarily when the amenorrhea appeared.

The personality structures of these patients varied from hysterical to obsessional and depressed. Anna's and Betty's early analyses were characterized by a multitude of dreams and a rich fantasy life that frequently was used defensively. Claudia, Debora, and Ellen, with their more obsessional natures, reported few fantasies or dreams early in treatment.

As is characteristic of anorexics, all five were good, conscientious students with outstanding academic histories.

As children, they had been conforming, "good" girls on the surface, displaying little overt oppositional behavior. However, Betty and Anna had displayed overt rebellious behavior during their adolescent years. Sours (1974) notes this characteristic lack of oppositional behavior in anorexic patients, and Kramer (1974) speculates that these patients lack aggression.

My own findings entirely contradict Kramer's speculations. The superficial conformity of these patients is patently a reaction formation to repressed and denied hostility. The superego is clearly and consciously identified with the maternal object representation, who consciously is seen as a powerful, controlling figure. Aggression is displaced and makes its appearance through psychosomatic symptoms, amenorrhea, anorexia, bulimia, and withholding behavior. Anna, Betty, and Claudia all had shown overt sadism in childhood toward siblings, other children, and animals. It seldom had been displayed toward, or in the presence of, the mother. As treatment progressed, it was found that all three had had overt sadistic fantasies toward the maternal figure in childhood, but subsequently had denied or repressed them. Betty had tortured her sister and birds. At ages eight to nine, Claudia had fantasied being a voluptuous woman who was captured and tortured as a prologue to displacing and inadvertently dismembering the "queen." She occasionally had indulged in overt sadism toward younger siblings. Debora, whose behavior had been that of a model child, had experienced grandiose fantasies of world applause in response to her self-sacrifice. As treatment progressed, such grandiose elated fantasies and dreams were replaced by fantasies and fears of omnipotent power that she reacted to with aggressive acting out or panic. Ellen, the oldest of the patients, had conscious castrative wishes toward men and repeated dreams of violence at the hands of males. Early in treatment she remembered and reveled in her anger at her mother, whom she saw as a "sadist who wished that I had not been born."

In all of these women, the displaced primitive aggressive fantasies toward the maternal object were amalgamated with more classical oedipal concerns. For example, Claudia's childhood fantasies of dismembering the "queen" were recalled in connection with a dream of fondling her father's genitals. At another time, she was surprised by one autocunnilingual fantasy of "eating" herself, with the physical sensation of crunching pubic bones between her jaws.

From a dynamic point of view, these brief case descriptions illustrate overwhelming reaction formations in the submissiveness and compliance of anorexic patients. Such reaction formations have to be accompanied by identifications with object representations and by displacement of aggression onto self-perceptions and object representations.*

FANTASIES OF SUPERIORITY AND OMNIPOTENCE

The anorexic patient's submission and compliance always seem to be accompanied by a grandiose sense of superiority. The superiority appears universally in areas of morality and control. It also frequently involves the intellect, although here there is more conscious uncertainty. For example, Claudia consciously felt morally superior to other members of her family. Between the ages of six and eight, she had been intensely religious. When something would go wrong and other members of the family would get angry, she would quietly but triumphantly state, "It is God's will!" Anna saw herself as a physical superwoman as a result of her strict physical conditioning. She looked with contempt on those who allowed their bodies to fall into "flabbiness." Betty was inordinately proud of her intellectual superiority and beauty, although this narcissistic pride covered intense fears on both scores. She felt technically and morally superior to her analyst. She noted real and fantasied errors in the analyst's technique and gave him rather sharp, severe lectures on his imperfections. Debora pictured the world worshiping her because of her self-sacrifice. Ellen, in a demure and ingratiating way, saw her solutions to the world's problems as the only answers worth considering.

Many authors have noted such characteristics and have recognized the underlying hostility and negation. Volkan (1965, 1976) has called attention to omnipotent fantasies similar to those observed in Betty.** This omnipotent negativism serves to deny outside reality, psychic reality, and instinctual needs.

---

*I use the terms "self-*perception*" and "object *perception*" to indicate any person's conscious, subjective experience of the contemporary external self and object, respectively. These perceptions are affected by projections, projective identifications, introjective identifications, scotomata imposed by previous experience and conflict, etc. In contrast, self- and object *representations* are for the most part unconscious and only their derivatives—in the form of self- and object perceptions—become available for analysis.
**See Chapter 6 for a more detailed description.

FRAGMENTATION

Primitive individual identifications with omnipotent object representations (primarily of the maternal figure) give rise to a rather characteristic fragmentation in the thought processes of anorexic patients. There is a clear isolation of individual affective states that gives rise to a certain lability, especially early in treatment. Such lability is characterized by interference with associations and thought processes. Inordinate concentration on one or another detail separates associative material from free spontaneity and any recognition of the larger context. Such a dissection may stop and lead to a contradictory association, with resultant anger and confusion. In general, the individual contradictory "trees" obscure the "forest." Although there is not a complete breakdown in thinking, the fragmentary quality of thought is clearly recognizable.

A characteristic, conscious behavior pattern seems to be related to fragmentation and to earlier, isolated affective states. During latency or puberty, these patients often become involved in "self-improvement" activities, repudiating and changing one part of their personality or self-perception. For example, Betty did not like that "stick of a girl" who was such a study grub, so she made herself more successful socially. At age nine, Claudia gave up conscious fantasying and dreaming and devoted all of her energies to studies, athletics, and socializing. These examples are representative of numerous changes self-induced by these two young women. Others give similar histories of control, change, and developmental pressures consciously applied to the self-image and corresponding self-representation by their rather severe superegos. Two patients abruptly gave up crying during their latency years.

Such splits in the self-image, which represent splits in the self-representation, sometimes give rise to rather chaotic disorganizations in treatment. These self-limited and reversible episodes dramatically demonstrate the fragmentation of associative processes.

Bruch (1978a) calls attention to the frequency of disturbances in the sense of time in patients with anorexia nervosa. I have also noted such disturbances and feel they are directly related to the splitting off of partial self-representations with isolated affective and ideational states. For patients with evening bulimia and vomiting, there is no tomorrow. As these patients fasten their attention on one facet of the present, they lose the context of their experience.

All anorexia nervosa patients demonstrate ego splitting with totally contradictory ideation. It is obvious in feelings and ideation surrounding self-starvation, body imagery, and the relationship with mother. It is part of the continuum of fragmentary states.*

The rather primitive pregenital defense mechanisms of denial, isolation, and projection, as well as reaction formation and displacement, play important roles in character formation. Incorporative and projective internalization fantasies are prominent defenses against underlying aggressive and sexual impulses. As one analyzes such thought processes, the erotically tinged sadistic fantasies emerge.

---

*See Chapter 6.

SYMPTOMS

Hyperactivity

This characteristic is almost universal, at least during some period in the development of anorexia. Anna's capacity for physical exercise and exertion was phenomenal. Betty's capacity to work, play, and avoid sleep seemed impossible. She could survive for long periods on three to four hours of sleep per night. To a less dramatic extent, Debora could also get by with little sleep. Claudia was able to study daily until 2:00 A.M. or 3:00 A.M. after a full school day and an afternoon filled with athletic activity. When she was not working, Ellen occupied herself with athletics, bulimia, and vomiting.

Such hyperactivity is an aggressive way of handling anxiety and maintaining a fantasy of power and control. It is often accompanied by a mild elation and a conscious fear of the depression that will ensue if the patient relaxes. For Anna and Betty, it involved rather continual sexual acting out without much conscious sexual satisfaction. In other cases, it aided in avoiding sexual contact and involvement.

As is usual with such symptomatology, the impulses giving rise to the hyperactivity were also manifested in acting out in the transference—particularly in aggressive, outgoing bulimic patients. Sperling (1978) has called attention to this danger of acting out.

Such hyperactivity and acting out are manifestations of primitive omnipotent or "manic" defenses (Fenichel 1945a, 1954; A. Freud 1968a; Lewin 1950; Riviere 1936a; Thomä 1967) against equally primitive sadistic and sexual impulses. They accompany specific omnipotent fantasies, which usually are not consciously available early in treatment. This situation gives rise to the erroneous concept of "alexithymia," which assumes that there is little fantasy life in psychosomatic patients. The fantasies accompanying the impulse, action, and defense are available with careful analytic work. Beneath their omnipotent qualities, they have a very primitive and sadistic content. This infantile sadism is amalgamated with later oedipal fantasies of a sexual nature. Claudia's fantasies of dismembering the queen and her anxiety dreams of a huge penis shooting at her, which replaced certain of her pathological masochistic activities, are examples. Betty replaced her sexual acting out of transference fantasies with remembrance of her rage at her teasing, often-absent father and with fantasies of controlling, torturing, and teasing her analyst and other men.

Of course, such hyperactivity and acting out also demonstrate a low frustration tolerance. These patients need immediate gratification of impulses as soon as the latter become consicous. Frustration leads to rage that must be diverted toward the self or others.

Suicidal and Self-Destructive Behavior

The self-destructive nature of this illness is evident in the masochistic self-starvation and vomiting and in the suppression of menstruation and secondary sexual characteristics. Suicide fantasies appear as primitive pregenital activities are given up and the depression connected with ambivalence toward the maternal figure is faced. Patients attempt to maintain a conscious sense of euphoria and superiority while they systematically walk a tightrope of self-destruction. They present suicide fantasies consciously in one form or another and act them out unconsciously via self-injury, etc. There is a real danger of consciously motivated suicide in patients inadequately treated, deserted, or manipulated by behavioral modification.

From a structural point of view, one can observe that portions of the patient's ego are at the mercy of a chaotic, primitive superego system. This primitive superego will allow certain types of gratification with all of their attendant complications. The nature of the acting out and symptom formation insures that such gratifications will be followed by punishment. Any real satisfaction of the patient's needs must be amended or denied. The patient's body and impulses are the enemies and constant attempts are made to bring them under conscious control. The patient denies guilt about such impulses and fantasies but continues to displace them and act them out in self-damaging impulsive or suppressive ways.

Vomiting

Vomiting is a typical compromise between a symptom and a defense. It is a conscious acting out motivated by a number of unconscious impulses and defenses. It is a pregenital defense insofar as it is consciously motivated and the nature and implications of the activity are denied. It is overdetermined and, at the most primitive level, represents a rejection and ejection of the maternal figure, food, and the breast. It is a negation (Freud 1923, 1925b; Thomä 1967) of the most primitive sort. Patients sometimes show their displeasure with treatment and the analyst by regressing to this behavior and associating to deprivation by the world, the analyst, and the mother. Vomiting is always carried on in secret and is felt to be shameful and dirty. In my patients, as the aggression was admitted, it brought forth guilt-laden fantasies and dreams. The defenses against cannibalistic fantasies were quite clear and, in some cases, became conscious.

Some patients are quite conscious of the fantasy of ridding themselves of painful images of frustrating objects in their immediate environment—often the mother or analyst. At times, there is some euphoric delight as the image is spit out. The activity seems to aid in the suppression of a conscious awareness of the upsetting conflict with the internalized object representation.

Insofar as vomiting is a conscious adaptational attempt to maintain the prepubertal, starved, sticklike figure, it is also a less conscious defense against sexuality and pregnancy wishes. Vomiting anorexic patients (but not non-anorexic bulimic patients) frequently lament that they appear pregnant after eating. Very early in treatment, Ellen admitted to vomiting whenever she felt something in her stomach might be causing a protuberance. She immediately associated this to her overweight mother and pregnancy. Later, she more directly associated it to the vomiting of pregnancy and pregnancy wishes.

Anna, Betty, and Ellen associated vomiting to incorporation of the penis and abdominal pregnancy. For Claudia, whose vomiting played a relatively minor role in the illness, the little vomiting that did occur was clearly related to her impulses to devour the penis, castrate the tempting father, and become pregnant by him. Claudia acted out such pregnancy fantasies during her first amenorrhea, when she became certain she was pregnant and developed morning vomiting without consciously inducing the activity. She experienced a pseudocyesis. Her motivation for vomiting was completely unconscious. The vomiting was given up when she discovered she was not pregnant. Anna, Betty, and Ellen eventually associated vomiting with primitive envy and aggression against the maternal figure, whom they wished to destroy, devour, and eject. Such fantasies were available as they recognized their denial of a need for mother. It negated their frantic bulimia. In some patients, vomiting also represents an acting out of anal conflicts. Two patients reveled in the disgusting mess they made of their own bodies and the bathroom during their projectile orgies. Such exploits were followed by periods of shame and depression.

Constipation and Laxative Use

We know that some anorexic dietary habits contribute to the constipation in these patients and that the use of laxatives is rationalized on this basis. However, the huge doses often involved have nothing to do with any rational consideration of the problem. The intermittent constipation is as much related to personal conflicts as it is to dietary considerations.

Because of the nature of the illness, one is inclined to direct attention to the primitive oral sadism and to neglect the anal hostility and withholding. Anorexic patients show clear anal-oriented conflicts with the world which involve unconscious withholding and attempts at discrete conscious control. Patients with obsessional personality structures manifest typical obsessional anal concerns. For example, one patient showed her defiance of parental obsessive cleanliness by wearing the same underclothes for weeks at a time. This behavior was admitted in analysis only after an interpretation of the anal sadism in connection with a dream and was accompanied by an intense sense of humiliation. The patient's associations were to equally embarrassing sadistic and masochistic impulses and activities. Two other patients displayed symptomatic derivatives of anal conflicts in their absolute phobic avoidance of defecation or urination in public restrooms when anyone was within hearing distance. Defecation and urination were associated with an intense sense of humiliation when exposed to anyone else.

Anorexic patients manifest conflict between the fantasied internalization and retention of part-object representations and the expulsion of such fantasied introjects. The latter often are perceived and verbalized as "foreign bodies" and experienced in the abdominal region as sensations of "fullness" (which lead to laxative use). These perceptions then are associated to the fantasied introjects.

One such chain of associations was demonstrated by Betty. After much complaining about "a woman's lot" and the fantasied terrible pain of childbirth, there was a period of colitis. During this interval, there was a dream of her cat giving birth by anus to bloody, tamponlike kittens. Other associations confirmed fantasies of her once-hated sister in various internalized forms, as well as bloody anal and oedipal concerns.

One patient referred to her laxatives as "little parents." Another likened her "turds" to her mother and to fetuses. In treatment, the negativism and with-holding frequently were associated with and to constipation.

As one might expect in any patient with pregenital regressions, conflicts over oral and anal impulses are invariably mixed and the sadistic wishes are always linked to both phases of development. The almost universal constipation and laxative use in anorexia nervosa are intimately associated with such conflicts.

Amenorrhea

Amenorrhea is the classic symptom that differentiates anorexia nervosa from other functional anorexia in females. I should like to call attention again to Thomä's observations (1967) that it usually antedates the weight loss and is not simply an endocrine reaction to cachexia. In Sperling's patients (1978), the amenorrhea also preceded or occurred simultaneously with the weight loss. I found some variation among my twelve treated cases: seven patients developed amenorrhea when at normal weight or before the onset of their weight loss, while five had a relatively prolonged history of anorexia before the amenorrhea developed. I am in agreement with Sperling (1978) that the symptom is overdetermined and supports both the patient's unconscious pregnancy fantasies and her wish to regress to an infantile level that preceded sex-role definition.

It should be noted that amenorrhea does not always preclude pregnancy. One patient, while in a previous therapy, had been amenorrheic for over a year and had been assured by her physician that she could not conceive. She avoided contraception and became pregnant.

While pregnancy fantasies of anorexic patients are apparent in their fears and are frequently acted out (in attempts to become pregnant) as the menses return, they are also rather violently repudiated. Repudiation of adult femininity also occurs. In Claudia and Ellen, it had been conscious since latency. Both had been consciously disgusted with their breast development and their menstrual periods. Claudia's repudiation had followed earlier fantasies of a voluptuous figure. She had indulged in conscious fantasies of controlling her menses after her menarche at age 11. Ellen hated sex, males, and any suggestion that her stick-like figure be changed in any way. Two other patients had had similar conscious wishes. Typically, anorexic patients reject the ideal of the female figure.

SEXUAL ACTIVITY

None of my anorexic patients were orgastic in intercourse. Anna and Betty, although vaginally anesthetic when they began treatment, feigned interest in sexual activity and regularly acted it out. Each had a history of continuous manual masturbation with clitoral orgasm during latency. Claudia did not indulge in clitoral masturbation during latency, but would fantasize voluptuous images of herself with sexual excitement in early latency. Debora, who was a virgin, could not remember ever achieving an orgastic response from her frequent masturbatory activity. Ellen had engaged in sex only when necessary to accommodate a partner. She took no pleasure in the activity itself and was often conscious of intense hatred toward her partner.

One common thread ran through the sexual behavior of these women before their analyses. The splits, introjections, and projections in their self- and object representations were never clearer than in their love relationships and sexual activities. All, except Ellen, were intensely self-aware and, at times, painfully self-conscious. All but Debora and Ellen had a partial, mild dissociative reaction to sexual intercourse; their self-image, a reflection of their self-representation, was intensely flavored with either humiliating or grandiose affect states. Anna either felt she was manipulating the male with her sexual abilities or felt out of control and anticipated total rejection. Betty was extremely self-conscious. When she saw herself as a performer she felt shameful and awkward. When she saw herself as the observer she felt superior and contemptuous. In treatment, she talked of the difficulties in getting all those discordant arms and legs into co-operating positions. Genital foreplay was often accompanied by dissociative states and elated fantasies, but early in treatment these patients reported little or no physical pleasure from genital contact or stimulation.

Although some authors compare anorexic symptomatology to hysterical symptomatology, and the oedipal and sexual conflicts in both might appear superficially similar, anorexic patients are utilizing more primitive defenses. Unlike patients with milder transference neuroses, the anorexic patient often is consciously aware of her intense attachment to and sexual interest in her father even before treatment begins. This is often disguised by projection, which allows the patient to deny her own guilt-ridden, incestuous wishes.

OEDIPAL CONCERNS

Family Constellation

My experience with anorexic patients replicates in part the observations of Sperling (1978). All my patients defended themselves against intense adolescent oedipal attachments to the father that seemed to be the outgrowth of equally intense infantile attachments. In order to understand the context in which oedipal problems develop, it is helpful to be aware of the family constellations of these patients.

Bruch (1965, 1978a) and Sperling (1978) have noted that the fathers of anorexic patients generally are depreciated by the mother and sometimes by other females in the family. I have noted a somewhat masochistic behavior pattern among these fathers. The father of Claudia is a prime example. A successful professional man, he had tried to be both father and mother to his three daughters. He would get into fights with his complaining wife, who always saw herself as a martyred, misunderstood woman who had sacrificed everything for her family. However, he always would give in and sympathize with his wife's predicament. When he was not at work, he was trying to hold the family together. He would side with his wife in any confrontations with the daughters, but would seductively discuss his wife's "condition" with them: she was "a disturbed woman."

Sours (1974) notes the large number of absent fathers among these girls. Betty's father filled both Bruch's and Sours's criteria. He seemed dominated by a depressed wife and an aggressive sister, who both felt that life had deprived them of their just due. His profession gave him the relief of prolonged absences from home. When he was present, he was intensely involved with his daughter, whom he taught, counseled, and teased provocatively.

The mothers of anorexic daughters are often professional or working women who have given up their careers to raise families. Resentment toward the father and children for this "sacrifice" is frequent. All the mothers I saw displayed overt symptoms and signs of depression and went through periods of temporary, but marked, emotional withdrawal from family responsibilities. One was obviously seriously disturbed; another had recurrent depressions and episodes of psychosomatic illness. In all but one case, when the father was present, he was intimately involved with and caring toward the daughter. The fathers seemed to accept the guilt imposed by the "deprived" mothers, which led to a rather submissive, masochistic relationship and somewhat depreciated position in the family (Bruch 1965, Sperling 1978).

In addition, something seemed to be missing in the relationship of the parents and the fathers looked to their daughters for the satisfaction that they could not obtain from their depressed wives. This may have contributed to the intense oedipal attachments against which all of the patients defended themselves.

Case Examples: Father-Daughter Relationship

CASE 1   Provocative Teasing

Betty's highly ambivalent, intense involvement with her family included an intermittent, teasing, provocative relationship with her father well into adolescence. As a child, she consciously had fantasied romantic images of her parents as "king" and "queen." She treasured the closeness with her father and vigorously defended their relationship against the intrusions of her younger sister. She both hated and enjoyed her father's provocative teasing and she resented his frequent absences. She consciously felt she understood her father better than her mother did and she pitied his "lonely, misunderstood" existence.

The material was rather violently acted out early in the transference when Betty took a lover who was roughly her father's (and her analyst's) age. She alternately treated him as the exalted father and as the disparaged, inferior younger sister whom she could best intellectually and physically. This corresponded with defensive masculine self-images in which she openly envied her lover, her father, and the analyst. The pregenital nature of the availability of this material should be noted; the latter had to be acted out, rather than worked with, early in the analysis. Even the pregnancy wishes and fears had to be acted out as she tried to maintain a variety of omnipotent controls over the material, the conflicts, and the analyst.

Later, in a less chaotic way, rather classical oedipal interests and fantasies were brought to light and worked through. It was clear, however, that in adolescence Betty had been almost consciously afraid of a union with a seductive father or surrogate. Early in treatment, she was quite certain of the analyst's active interest in her and consciously feared humiliation at his hands. The intensity and immediacy of her expectations and demands, as well as the "reality" she attributed to her fantasies and expectations, reflected the disturbed relationship with her mother and the fragmentation of her self- and object representations. She soon became consciously aware that her intense conscious affection could readily dissolve into equally intense envy and competitive wishes toward the transference object or a contemporary loved object. Dreams and fantasies of losing extremities, babies, and penises indicated concerns with her own "castrated" state, which she blamed on her mother. She compensated with rather grandiose fantasies about her phallic body and superior brain. Such fantasies were amalgamated with more primitive representations of herself as an omnipotent, all-giving, all-controlling, and all-destroying mother. Eventually, her more tender affectionate needs were tolerated consciously, and the accompanying repressed sexual interests and excitement became available for enjoyment.

CASE 2   Taking Mother's Place

Claudia always had enjoyed the conversations with her father about her mother's "disturbed condition." She could remember prepubertal fantasies of taking father away from mother, and more disguised fantasies of being the voluptuous captive who replaced and dismembered the queen. Open dreams of fondling her father's genitals frightened her early in treatment.

In a less conscious vein, she was frightened of big penis and breast images that kept reappearing in dreams and fantasies. She expected rape, humiliation, and impregnation, all of which consciously scared her. However, through her masochistic acting out, she repeatedly placed herself in compromising positions where she was in danger of all three. Like Betty, during adolescence, she had been involved in a continual mutual flirtation with the father, which she both enjoyed and resented. The recognition of this led to her more repressed classical oedipal concerns and fears. Her transference neurosis began to emerge, with fantasies of the analyst's interest in her body and her resultant control over him. Later, with some humiliation and chagrin, dreams revealed her interest in the analyst. Curiosity about his genitals was interrupted by regressions to cannibalistic dreams and fantasies of incorporating his penis for both impregnation and identification.

CASE DISCUSSION

Both Betty and Claudia verbalized the typical anorexic fantasy (and probable fact) that they could relate to their fathers more directly in the prepubertal period than after adolescence. They felt that their fathers had been more comfortable with a "little girl." However, there was a great deal of adolescent flirting. Both recalled and were excited by the idealized visions they had had of their fathers in infancy.

Like all my anorexic patients, Betty and Claudia had defensive fantasies about being a boy, a reflection of earlier concerns with penis envy.* These

---

*See Chapter 4.

phallic concerns were amalgamated with more primitive omnipotent fantasies. In part, the wish to be a boy reflected the wish to control mother just as the powerful father of infancy had done.

Betty, Claudia, and my other anorexic patients were all partially aware of their fears of becoming pregnant and of their disgust for the appearance of the pregnant female. On a less conscious level, fears of pregnancy were associated with fears of internal explosions, internal dissolution, internal contamination, or being eaten. Such fears seemed to be the reciprocal side of their sadistic "masculine" or "cannibalistic" fantasies—usually directed unconsciously at the depriving, envied, and competitive maternal representation. Also, each had a conscious repugnance for displaying to the world the "flabbiness" of their middle-aged mothers. They all had contempt for the visual evidence of indulgences such as pregnancy, eating, or even relaxed partnerships. They defended themselves against evidence of any such bodily impulses and then covered their concern with elaborate social rationalizations.

There were fears of being like mother and of literally taking over her position with father. These patients were well aware of the sexual connotations of a soft, rounded female body and wished to deny any implied seductive impulses. This dynamic material was elucidated only after the pregnancy fears and seductive wishes toward the father had been discussed. When, as a result of treatment, the patients' bodies matured, they were slow to accept the implications and their own genital seductive wishes.

The content of these patients' oedipal fantasies and conflicts is reasonably typical of that observed in the usual "neurotic" or "normal" female. Nevertheless, it displays a special quality in that the infantile and adolescent attachments to the father seem to be unusually intense and threatening, particularly with reference to genital concerns. Also, it is specifically characterized and disguised early in treatment by its amalgamation with pregenital defenses and sadistic impulses that are directly traceable to conflicts with, and attempts to, control the maternal figure and her internalized representations.

Analysis of the more primitive defenses of these anorexic patients allowed for a traditional analysis of the ubiquitous oedipal concerns.

SUMMARY

The "final common pathway" of symptomatology in anorexia nervosa represents certain preoedipal conflicts which have been detailed here. These conflicts represent and result from specific defensive maneuvers utilized to deny and avoid typical, but intense, oedipal conflicts. The daughters' oedipal attachments to the fathers seem to be unusually close and threatening as these patients pass through puberty. This contributes to the specific regressive maneuvers characteristic of anorexic women at this time of their lives.

In the patients described in this chapter, as the pregenital activities, guilt, and hostility were brought to the surface, they became aware of the intensity of their impulses and their fears of such impulses. This allowed them to deal more directly with previously repressed, suppressed, and displaced oedipal concerns.

It became clear that early and continuing conflicts with the mother contributed heavily to these patients' interest in their fathers.

In general, my psychoanalytic treatment of anorexic patients replicates that of most psychoanalytic clinicians. It seems partially to contradict psychoanalytic investigators such as Bruch, who feels that psychoanalysis is not the treatment of choice for these patients. In my opinion, therapeutic approaches involving behavior modification or drugs are deleterious to such patients.

The underlying psychological conflicts of anorexia nervosa are relatively severe and require extended, intense attention. This is particularly important to bear in mind in cases where the central symptomatology clears rather early in treatment. For example, Minuchin et al. (1978) claimed remarkable results from family therapy, which they stated could last only six months, and that the anorexic symptomatology disappeared two to eight weeks after the beginning of treatment. One must question their classification of a "satisfactory adjustment" when dealing with the residual neuroses. From my own and my colleagues' experiences with anorexic patients, I conclude that, in the vast majority of cases, psychoanalysis is the treatment method of choice.

6
Object Relations

CHARLES C. HOGAN, M.D., D.MED.SC.

"I was with him. He complimented me on my intelligence and I was delighted. Then I was in a garden where I was joyfully leading around an elephant and giraffe."

Such was the manifest content of a rather typical early dream of Betty, a 25-year-old anorexic analysand.* Her associations to elephants and giraffes included: the idealized male figure presented in the dream, lovers, phalluses, childhood presleep fantasies of such large animals, and the analyst.

This wistful fantasy of playful control contrasted dramatically with her frantic masochistic efforts to manipulate her lover and the analyst in the ensuing months of treatment. She would accept the lover's verbal and physical abuse and then agree with his harsh judgments of her character, her intentions, her intelligence, her health, and her sanity. She consciously attempted to see the relationship from "his side of the fence" and lived in terror of abandonment.

As she acknowledged the transference significance of the lover and began to see that he was replacing the analyst, she told her analyst, "I have to turn you into someone I can look up to and respect. I have been able to construct your image in my mind and I like it. There can be no surprises. When you challenge this picture, I feel afraid. I don't care to look too closely at you or my feelings about you. I keep you completely under my control."

Anna, a 32-year-old hyperactive anorexic analysand displayed her need for control in a different way.** Although vaginally anesthetic, she was a masochistic sexual acrobat for each of her successive lovers. She felt that none had any interest in her as a person, but fantasied that each was enthralled by her sexual abilities, her submission, and her flattery. However, at the first hint of restraint on the part of her partner, she would move on to another idealized lover whom she could fantasy as a slave under her control. She temporarily controlled the analyst and the analysis with her "acting out."

These brief case descriptions illustrate the pregenital nature of the anorexic's relationships with important objects. There is a constant effort to pressure and control the external perceptions and internal representations of those objects at

---

* See Chapter 5 for further discussion of Betty.
** See Chapter 5 for further discussion of Anna.

any cost. Case material from the analyses of these and other anorexic patients will be presented later in an attempt to demonstrate the importance of the primary object in the analysis, the life, and the transference of the anorexic patient.

REVIEW OF THE LITERATURE

This brief review of the literature will remain within the general object-relations framework of this chapter, with the following qualification. Clinical material seems to gain clarity when presented in terms of object representations and self-representations associated with drive derivatives and their accompanying affects. There also seems to be therapeutic and interpretative value in conceptualizing pregenital constellations, particularly those involving splits in ideation and affect, in such terms. An examination of the common content and affects associated with characteristic anorexic fantasies, i.e., those motivating and perpetuating the split-off segments of the mental apparatus, should clarify the integrative process by which anorexic patients acknowledge, accept, and understand the impulses associated with their self- and object representations and perceptions (drive derivatives).

Melitta Sperling has contributed immeasurably to our knowledge of the regressed nature of all psychosomatic illnesses. She has noted the need of such patients to control and use their objects as fetishes (1953, 1961, 1967, 1968a,b, 1978). She has indicated that anorexia is related to other disabilities with pregenital regressions and is closely allied with other psychosomatic illnesses. She has repeatedly directed our attention to the omnipotent, defensive, controlling maneuvers that anorexic patients use to defend against intense pubertal and postpubertal oedipal problems (1968b, 1970, 1978). She has noted (1978) that the anorexic female's unresolved preoedipal fixation to the mother contributes to psychosexual problems, including severe oedipal conflicts. In addition, "depending on the degree of regression, the pregenital characteristics of narcissism, ambivalence, some degree of bisexuality and a low frustration tolerance will be more or less evident" (p. 171).

In Sperling's view (1978), anorexic patients' disturbance in object relationships is significantly different from that in psychosomatic patients. In the latter, since the mother does not tolerate overt expressions of aggression or strivings for independence, rebellion and aggression are converted and discharged bodily without conscious awareness. In anorexia nervosa, aggression is expressed more openly in the rejection of food. Sperling has compared anorexia nervosa to the phobias, and feels that it is an "impulse disorder" that occurs in certain pregenitally fixated patients. She has noted that it can occur in conjunction with psychosomatic symptoms. In such cases, "the onset of psychosomatic symptoms . . . signifies a failure of the defensive function of the anorexia and indicates a further regression in object relationships" (1978, p. 161).

My clinical material points to a closer alliance between anorexia nervosa and psychosomatic illnesses, in that I have never seen a case of anorexia nervosa that was not accompanied by psychosomatic symptoms such as hives, headaches (simple or migraine), siallorhea, vasomotor phenomena, or colitis. Such symptoms always cleared during analysis and usually their specific etiology was apparent, but the regression to a more primitive adaptation that Sperling posits was not evident.

Volkan (1965, 1976) has described a "little man" phenomenon in an 18-year-old anorexic patient whose early object and self-representations were concretized in omnipotent fantasies accompanying identifications that were projected onto other figures in her contemporary environment. Her sense of omnipotence had been preserved because this ego segment never had been integrated with the rest of her ego. Similar phenomena had been described previously by Niederland (1956, 1965) with reference to other narcissistic conditions.

Thomä (1967) has focused on the psychogenesis and psychosomatics of anorexia nervosa. His discussion of ambivalence, object relations, and identification emphasizes the primitive identifications with the maternal imagoes. He also has emphasized the all-important aggressive and sadistic impulses of these patients, noting that they condemn themselves in a depressive manner and deny the danger of death in a hypomanic way. Their self-accusations are really accusations against the object that the ego has assimilated. Thomä has related the aggressive and destructive oral impulses of these patients to their negativism, acting out, vomiting, and amenorrhea. His description of the regressive material of these patients is as complete an exposition as any in the literature to date.

Selvini Palazzoli (1961, 1970, 1978), whose approach to anorexia nervosa has evolved from individual psychotherapy into family therapy, feels that these patients have regressed to, or are fixated at, a very primitive stage of development. In her opinion (1978) these patients hover between schizophrenia and depression. She feels that the postpubertal body is identified with the "negative, overpowering aspects" of the maternal object and thus is "a threatening force" that must be held in check. Despite such observations, she has played down the importance of oral aggression and oral frustration. She has compared her stance on anorexia nervosa to that of Bibring (1953) on depression. Sperling (1978) has noted that Selvini Palazzoli had described the content of the anorexic's psyche only in the most regressed state and hardly has mentioned sexual conflicts, masturbation, or sexual identifications.

However, Selvini Palazzoli (1978) has stated her preference for outpatient treatment of anorexic patients and has noted that, "while hospitalization may benefit the patient physically, it can ruin the interhuman relationship that is likely to have a much more decisive and curative effect" (p. 117). In short, "it is advisable to avoid hospitalization if there is any alternative" (p. 116).

Masterson (1977) has dealt with the specific regressive intrapsychic organization of anorexia nervosa. He has classified these patients as "borderline" cases and has described the "borderline split-object-relations unit" that contributes to the "split ego" in such patients. He has contrasted and compared his object-relations theory with Bruch's interpersonal theory. From a clinical standpoint, the two have much in common. It should be noted that Masterson has reported on patients in psychotherapy, rather than psychoanalysis.

While Bruch has shown some interest in the work of Fairbairn (1941) and Guntrip (1961) and an object relations approach to the problem, she rejects a psychoanalytic approach. She has pointed out that a "disturbed interaction between an organism and its environment results in distorted functioning of conceptual thinking and body awareness. . . . The variety of motivational defense mechanisms with which analysts usually concern themselves must be considered secondary to this basic deficiency" (1961, p. 479). Furthermore, she feels that "traditional analysis has been conspicuously ineffective in anorexia nervosa" because these patients are unable to know what they feel—it is mother who "knows" what they feel (1965, p. 565). She has observed that conventional analytic interpretation of unconscious feelings has no meaning to them, but my observations would indicate that a thorough psychoanalytic understanding of the vicissitudes of aggression toward the mother and the resultant identificatory defenses evolving from such ambivalence allow both patient and analyst a comprehension of such an identificatory state.

More recently, Bruch (1973a) has indicated that she might agree with more sophisticated psychoanalytic approaches that she feels are of recent discovery, inferring that such modifications were anticipated by her. However, M. Sperling had been publishing her experience with the psychoanalysis of psychosomatic disorders for 30 years and there is no serious discussion of Sperling's work in any of Bruch's papers. Twenty years ago Sperling was discussing the pregenital defenses of these patients, their needs for omnipotent control (how they use their objects as fetishes), and the need to analyze this material before the symptoms are given up and the underlying psychoneurosis reveals itself.

It is puzzling that Bruch has played down the importance of aggression and sexual conflict in the genesis of this illness. She feels that pregnancy fantasies also play a minor role in anorexia nervosa (1978a), but the very clinical material she presents to support this assertion seems to contradict it. She (1973b) has provided careful clinical descriptions and superb family studies based on casework with 70 patients, but has presented little that is helpful in understanding the object relations of these patients.

My experience also has indicated that the primary symptomatology frequently responds quite rapidly. However, the significant psychopathology underlying the primary symptomatology requires intensive treatment even after the latter has been given up. One must question what Minuchin et al. (1978) classify as a "satisfactory adjustment" when they are dealing with the residual neuroses.

Many authors (e.g., Berlin et al. 1951, Fenichel 1945a, Gero 1953, Goodsitt 1969, Jessner and Abse 1960, Lorand 1943, Masserman 1941, Meyer and Weinroth 1957, Moulton 1942, Palmer and Jones 1939, Waller et al. 1940) have discussed the regressive patterns in anorexia nervosa and most agree on the importance of early conflicts with the mother, oral frustration, ambivalence with resultant aggression, and sadism.

DISCUSSION OF OBJECT RELATIONS IN FIVE CASES

The five anorexic young women whose analyses are used to illustrate the following discussion on anorexic object relations were defending themselves against an intense oedipal attachment that had to be denied at puberty or adolescence. This conflict was intensified by severe conflicts with the maternal figure during early development and at the time of the onset of the illness. The conflict seemed to be intensified in adolescence by the seductiveness of their fathers, whose interest in their daughters increased as that toward their wives diminished.

The regressive symptomatology in these patients (i.e., anorexia, bulimia, vomiting, weight loss, amenorrhea, and hyperactivity) was derivative of oedipal and preoedipal fantasies. For example, the amenorrhea condensed the unconscious fantasy of being the sexless latency child with the unconscious fantasy of pregnancy.

In treating such patients, one should not expect much content to be verbalized early in analysis. These patients are unable to free-associate in conventional terms for quite some time. It is of help to divide the material artificially and approach it in terms of: (1) its dynamic content, which includes oedipal and preoedipal fantasies that are disguised, merged, and confused; and (2) the formal manner and means of its presentation.

By focusing on this latter aspect of the material, one can open up the dynamics of the patient's character structure and self- and object perceptions and representations. This usually allows the patient greater spontaneity in free associations and should bring to light underlying preoedipal dyadic fantasies, with their primitive impulses, conflicts, and defenses. The "style" of presentation hides the content of the material from the patient and the analyst.

The aim of this discussion is to demonstrate the nature of the regression from, and the defenses against, oedipal conflicts and to illustrate the quality of the relationships these patients maintain with their important objects. The following elements of anorexia nervosa will be explored: (1) the conscious and unconscious attempts to control internal object representations, external object perceptions, and impulses; (2) the varieties of omnipotent fantasies and activities that cloak the various self- and object representations; (3) the fragmentation and isolation of part-self- and part-object representations, which result in splitting, as well as disturbances and detachments in thought processes; and (4) the way these defensive maneuvers aid in the denial and repression of primitive aggressive impulses and fantasies, with accompanying guilt and shame. Naturally, these categories all overlap and each of these defensive organizations is overdetermined.

With regard to the first point, the cases of Betty and Anna, briefly described at the beginning of this chapter, illustrate the need for an illusion of control over both object perceptions and internalized object representations, with accompanying denial of impulses toward such object and self-representations. The three other female patients with classical anorexia nervosa showed needs and predispositions similar to those shown by Betty and Anna.

A vignette from the therapy of Joe, an anorexic man in his early twenties who did not have classical anorexia nervosa, is pertinent here. The case was notable because of the early conscious accessibility of certain thought content. In his preanalytic sessions, Joe obsessively described conscious mental manipulations directed toward control of his mother and his own impulses. He elaborated on a consciously recognized internal representation of mother and on how he utilized this image to instruct himself, direct his activities, and help suppress his wishes and desires. At the same time, he insisted that he did not "need" his "real" mother. He was not "dependent" on her. His greatest hope was that he could "cure" himself and not be so "weak" that he would have to depend on analysis. This patient did obtain a rapid transference cure insofar as his appetite and weight were concerned, and he put off serious analytic treatment until some time in the future. His omnipotent fantasies were temporarily successful. He maintained the illusion of control.

Claudia, a teenager when she entered analysis, evidenced the illusion of control over her family and analyst more passively, by her complete submission to all.* She was aware that in her projective identification she fantasied controlling mother's thoughts. Debora, in her early teens, outmothered her controlling mother, and Ellen, in her forties, went into narcissistic rages at the analyst when her transference wishes were not met.

In general, anorexic patients control mother (perception and representation) by abject submission and fantasied identifications. It is here that Bruch's idea (1965) that these patients do not know how they feel—that only mother knows—originates. It is true that such fantasies and activities of control are usually in response to an insensitive, possessive, demanding, and controlling mother who freely utilizes guilt to obtain compliance. Nevertheless, the patient's submission represents unconscious fantasies about, and attempts to gain, control over the object perceptions and internal object representations of mother.

Herein evolves the anorexic "symptom" of academic excellence. All five patients with classical anorexia nervosa labored untiringly to maintain their remarkable academic standings, but in the beginning of treatment none had any particular interest in any particular subject. They felt lost when choices had to be made. It was all done to impress and control mother and surrogate objects.

Transference Manipulations

Anorexic patients use a variety of means to gain control of self-perceptions, self-representations, object perceptions, object representations, and accompanying impulses. The symptoms themselves unconsciously delight the patient in their provocative, controlling effects on patients' perceptions of mother, the rest of the family, friends, and psychoanalyst. Betty's preoccupation with her lover was used provocatively against the analyst as she avoided important analytic material. Examples of this type are endless.

Such a wish to control the object is probably universal in the unconscious and makes its appearance in every analysis. However, when one observes pregenital regressions in analysis, one sees the wish and the attempt to fulfill it used continuously as a defensive measure. Sperling (1961, 1967, 1968a,b, 1978) has thoroughly discussed how psychosomatic patients use their object as a fetish.

In anorexia nervosa, fantasies of, and attempts to, control gratify unconscious sadistic fantasies of omnipotent control (e.g., Betty discovered that she fantasied total physical control of her lover to the point of torture and murder; Claudia uncovered fantasies of dismembering mother to get her to quiet down).

---

* See Chapter 5 for further discussion of Claudia.

They also act to avoid a confrontation that might bring such fantasies into consciousness.

In the transference, these fantasies of, and attempts to, control may be: (1) illusory, essentially passive, ideation of what is happening in the analyst's mind and how his or her thoughts are under the patient's control; (2) active projective identifications (or even fusion fantasies) with attempts to manipulate verbal analytic material to produce the fantasied, expected results in the analyst; (3) active attempts forcefully to intimidate the analyst with narcissistic rage, overt and obvious withholding, masochistic activity, etc.; and (4) intimidation by appeals to outside authority (i.e., friends and acquaintances, parents, other clinicians).

Attempts to control the analyst in the transference situation are ubiquitous. However, in anorexic patients, as in other patients with pregenital problems, the intensity of the attachment to the primary object, the ambivalence toward that object, and the resulting projective identifications lead to a sense of truth and validity in their mental constructions that sometimes approaches the delusional in its certainty. It escapes the definition of a delusion because it is readily interpretable.

Anna was convinced in many ways of her analyst's need for her and would fantasy her future control over him. For years, Betty would not speak of some of her sexual activities and fantasies for fear of seducing her analyst, yet she obviously relished the power that she felt she had over him. Claudia was certain that her sexual fantasies would disgust and overwhelm her analyst as she felt that they had overwhelmed her father, but she also enjoyed speculating about this power. Ellen enjoyed using her bulimia and vomiting in unconscious attempts to provoke the analyst; she was certain that he would be as disgusted as she was.

Masochistic control is a universal, constant preoccupation among anorexic patients. Threats of dying, suicide, etc., always play an important role. One patient indulged in self-mutilation (carving herself with a razor blade) as a means of obtaining anxious concern.

The proclivity of anorexic patients to lie early in treatment has been observed repeatedly in the literature. This lying is an attempt to manipulate the analyst's thoughts and behavior, and is a response to the patient's projections. It is utilized to deny guilt and to avoid anticipated narcissistic injuries. These patients consciously try to manipulate the analyst with their fabrications. They feel that if such constructions are accepted as "true" by the analyst, they will be "true." This certainly is a regression to omnipotent magical thinking, but also reflects the family pattern of interchange and thinking.* The magical thinking process is engaged in by both patient and family and is indicative of the lack of personal separation and individuation achieved by them.

Temper tantrums and severe bouts of narcissistic rage are not uncommon ways of attempting direct intimidation. In my experience this is more common in aggressive patients inclined toward bulimia and vomiting. Anna, Betty, and Ellen all engaged frequently in such noisy indignation when their wants were not met.

---

* See Chapter 9.

With omnipotent certainty, Betty would often revert to the role of professional critic and teacher. Whenever she caught the analyst in a real or fantasied error, she seriously and conscientiously warned him about the possible disastrous consequences of his ineptitude. When attempts to interpret her need to control were made, she would frequently turn the analysis around and lecture the analyst on his attempts to control her.

The tendency of anorexic patients to control their parents by playing one off against the other is reflected in treatment by their appeal to authority. As others have mentioned, parents of anorexics allow their children little privacy and are quite exhibitionistic about their own problems. This sometimes lends itself to unusual needs to "share" analytic experiences. Gregarious patients such as Betty act out and "share" analytic problems and material with lovers, colleagues, friends, acquaintances, or anyone else who will listen. After such sharing, Betty would bring back a variety of other opinions about herself and her treatment to fill the hours or to confront the analyst. Other patients with greater fear of their exhibitionistic impulses play off analyst against parent, rather than analyst against acquaintances. For example, Claudia was an expert at starting battles with mother that she knew would cause mother to want her to leave analysis. Similar masochistic exhibitionistic activities were part and parcel of the transference behavior of the other three anorexic patients as well.

At times, when acting out, appealing to friends, and other such transference manipulations have been exhausted, anorexic patients make more direct appeals to outside authority. One patient used the analyst's mild impatience with her repetitive acting out as justification to question his competence and engage in a series of consultations with another psychoanalyst. When in narcissistic rages, Ellen frequently threatened such a strategy in the early days of treatment. Debora, when frustrated, would miss sessions quite deliberately and then complain to her parents.

These attempts to control external perceptions and internal representations of the object are based on early internalizations of particular aspects of the primary object, usually the maternal figure. These internalizations maintain their primitive, split-off part representations. They may be idealized or depreciated. However, such self- and object images are later projected onto others, and often there are complex dyadic relationships in which the male and his penis are seen as the potential controlling figure and/or object. The need to defeat and control the male is seen as a male self-representation. Here is the substrata for the amalgamated fantasies that superimpose phallic and oedipal strivings on earlier ambivalent conflicts with the primary object.

Betty's acting-out relationship with her lover demonstrates this with remarkable clarity. On the surface, she at first idealized his intelligence, character, and power. She soon became involved in attempts to compete with all of these idealized (in her mind, phallic) virtues to prove that she was better than he was and to obtain his acquiescence to her own moral and intellectual superiority. This led to a sadomasochistic struggle over supposedly phallic attributes, with brutally explicit sadistic fantasies and dreams of castrating and castration. Later, as she came to recognize the acting-out nature of the relationship, the maternal-breast qualities of the lover came into prominence, and the primitive ambivalence toward him and the analyst was clarified. These displaced transference phenomena replicated her family history. Early conflicts with a depressed and controlling mother had been complicated by colic problems during the first months of life. Such conflicts had been expressed in rage and, later, after the birth of her sister, when Betty was two and a half years old, in vomiting. These symptoms had been replaced by Betty's sadistic control and sexual manipulations of the sister, whom she always had bested intellectually and physically. This controlling superiority, with its attendant sadistic sexual fantasies, had been in stark contrast to her abject submission to mother, teachers, and other environmental forces. The frequently absent father had served as a displacement for the early idealization of the mother. She had found it necessary to act out each of these roles. Another variant of her identification with the male and the penis was based on the fantasy that the idealized father was able to control mother.

Claudia had a similar history of real and fantasied sadistic manipulations of a younger sibling concomitant with abject submission to an unstable, controlling mother and an older sister.

In a similar vein, Anna had used a younger sister as an outlet for her sadism and fantasies of absolute control.

It should be apparent that this need to control object perceptions, object representations, and the impulses associated with self- and object representations is a means of both gratifying unconscious sadistic needs and suppressing any conscious recognition of such impulses.

Omnipotent Defensive Posture

These attempts to control, particularly with acting out, lead directly to a discussion of the omnipotent nature of such fantasies and activities. Above and beyond specific omnipotent and grandiose affects and fantasies associated with isolated ego states, anorexia nervosa patients universally seem to have an organized omnipotent system of defense. With all of their abject helplessness and appeals for love and sympathy, they have an unbending, tough sense of superiority and certainty about their "rightness." J. Palmer et al. (1952) administered a variety of psychological tests to five hospitalized anorexic patients and noted that, despite having very different personalities, the young patients all were "overintellectual and overidealized" in their thinking and showed a defensive superiority.

Such a generalized, defensive posture puts one in mind of Riviere's classic 1936 article, "A Contribution to the Analysis of the Negative Therapeutic Reaction." While discussing Freud's and others' work on an unconscious sense of guilt, she called attention to omnipotent fantasy used as an "organized system of defense." In Kleinian terms, she saw it as a "manic" defense against the "depressive position." She clearly emphasized that it was a defense aimed at warding off depression and guilt over primitive destructive impulses. While I do not feel that the term "manic" should include the range of omnipotent fantasies involved, it does direct attention to the elated affect that sometimes accompanies the defense, particularly when the patient is acting out. There is no doubt that this generalized self-appraisal is utilized as a defense against depression and guilt.

Anna, amid her dodging and ducking, maintained a certainty of her physical superiority and sexual sophistication. She never questioned her excellence in these areas. Despite her self-depreciation, for months she also maintained a certain contemptuous superiority toward the analyst.

Although she felt "stupid," Betty was continually re-proving her intellectual excellence. Her judgments were final: "I know when I am right." She recalled deciding early in latency that she was really superior to her depressed, hypochondriacal, withdrawn mother; this decision had enabled her to suppress her painful guilt and identification. The acting out of her sadism toward animals and the sexual manipulations of her sister were associated with a sense of omnipotence, power, and excitement. During later latency, such feelings became associated with her masculine self-representations (e.g., tomboy behavior; intellectual superiority to her sister; conscious wishes to be, and fantasies of being, a man). When her omnipotence and sense of superiority were threatened in childhood or in adult life, she was inclined to indulge in private rages, tears, and temper tantrums.

The generalized defensive omnipotence in each of the five patients demonstrated certain specific omnipotent identifications. Needless to say, all five displayed a temporary, seemingly impervious, certainty as to their own "rightness." In Betty's case, such fantasies of power and superiority became associated with genital, exhibitionistic, masculine content. The internalization of, and identification with, a father and his phallus may become superimposed on the internalization of an idealized, all-powerful maternal object perception. Similarly, the power and idealization of this internalized maternal representation may appear as a grandiose self-perception in the oedipal sphere. Betty, Debora, Claudia, and Ellen all had conscious grandiose adolescent certainties of their triumph over mother with respect to father. The genital aspects of this conquest were repressed. Recognizing this amalgam of pregenital, phallic, and oedipal fantasies is important in the realm of technique. It is usually necessary to interpret the grandiose, aggressive, and identificatory defensive nature of such self-representations early and to ignore the phallic and oedipal content until both patient and analyst understand how such fantasies are used defensively.[*]

"MORAL" SUPERIORITY

One particular group of superego fantasies of omnipotent superiority seems to be especially characteristic of anorexia nervosa. Otto Sperling (personal communications) has called attention to the battle anorexic girls have with their mothers to attain a sense of "moral" superiority. This search for a sense of moral perfection is later involved in other close relationships and appears in the transference. For example, very early in latency, Claudia went through a period of intense religiosity when she felt superior to the rest of the family. When something would go wrong and other family members would get angry, she would triumphantly and quietly say, "It is God's will." In her fantasy life she would compare her own self-sacrificing submission with her mother's chaotic, angry, contradictory, emotional character.

---

[*] See Chapter 9.

In Betty's case, this fantasy was acted out in a rather dangerous sado-masochistic way with her lover. After she had begun to mobilize some of her anger and had given up her totally submissive relationship with this man, she would typically provoke an argument and try to best him intellectually. If he could not win, he would usually resort to physical violence. Betty would have triumphant fantasies of moral outrage, feel contempt for his lack of control, and, when things had quieted down, would quietly point out his moral deficiencies. This would often bring forth his gratifying apologies. In the transference, Betty would continually search for signs of weakness or error in the analyst. When any were found or imagined, a firm, quiet moral lecture would follow and the patient would experience a mild, but definite, self-righteous elation. Needless to say, she repeatedly would attempt to provoke confrontations in the transference with her omnipotent, absolute judgments.

All anorexic patients are inclined to use provocative negation in the transference. As this is analyzed and the underlying hostility is brought to light, they become aware of their search for unjust retaliation and a passive, triumphant superiority. This moral superiority is present in the pride they take in their starved, bony figures. Those who only diet have an intense ascetic pride in themselves. Two patients displayed transient identifications with Christ. Those involved in bulimia and vomiting have greater conscious conflict as they repeatedly attack themselves for their "shameful" gluttony and "disgusting" vomiting.

GRANDIOSE SENSE OF SELF

Such a displaced need for control leads us to another area of pride and omnipotent superiority. The control over the body carries with it a somewhat grandiose sense of self. Anna, Claudia, and Ellen all were very much involved in sports and physical exercise to the point of excessive hyperactivity. Each had a sense of elated superiority accompanying the continuous motion and their fantasies about such activities. Claudia treated her body as a subservient machine. When her hands got cold while skiing, she would scold them and fantasy that they would warm up, although at one time she suffered from potentially dangerous frostbite. When her body or mind was fatigued, she would scold her arms, legs, or brain and force herself to continue with her activities or her studies. While she had great pride in her own bodily control, she had only contempt for her parents' perceived sloppiness.

Similar fantasies of a "power" or "will" separate from the mind and body were present in all five patients and often gave rise to experiences of depersonalization, particularly in sexual or hostile circumstances. All of these women took an elated pride in their "wills" as they indulged in hyperactivity, prolonged working hours, intense academic concentration, etc.

In addition to the almost religious devotion to grandiose ideas of bodily control and moral superiority that is characteristic of anorexia nervosa, there are also individual areas of grandiosity and elation specific to each patient's personality. For example, Ellen had an unusual grandiose and elated sense of self in association with her presumed expertise in fashion, and Anna's pride in her physical endurance led to unbelievable and debilitating demonstrations of her skills.

Idealization and Splitting Off of Object Representations

This generalized superior omnipotent posture, with its specific fantasies of rather grandiose superiority, is based on early internalizations of partial perceptions of mother or surrogates. These internal representations of the object and their accompanying self-representations are often associated with elated affect and grandiose self- or object representations. (Or they may be associated with humiliating affects and demeaned self- or object representations that are consciously denied.) Jacobson (1964, p. 61) has observed that these early identifications "seem actually to serve the absorption and neutralization of aggression which can be vested increasingly in counter cathectic formations and be discharged in ego functions." Furthermore, "the pre-oedipal precursors of the superego still reflect in part the small child's own boundless cruelty."

Such experiences of elation naturally represent a certain splitting off of ego functions and states. They specifically deny painful, suppressed or repressed ego fragments that encompass depressed and humiliated self-representations and accompanying memories. One patient would repetitively intone, in a childish sing-song voice, her love for "mother, who knows all about me. She feels as I feel." These ritualized, playful recitations represented early internalized impressions of similar verbalizations by her "devoted" mother. They also condensed the playful, elated split-off memory state with a mocking, playful irony as the humiliating, depriving representation was punished with the patient's self-destruction. When in a different mood, this same patient would consciously fantasy vomiting up aspects of mother and mother's verbalizations during orgies of bulimia and vomiting.

While this omnipotent ideation surrounding certain self- and object representational images and states becomes quite clear as the analysis unfolds, it is important to remember that, consciously, a different picture is presented early in analysis. These patients present an abject, hopeless, and helpless image of themselves. They idealize their important objects and speak as though they idealized the analyst, projecting their early fantasied internalizations of omnipotent object perceptions. A situation similar to that noted by Freud (1923) in reference to the unconscious sense of guilt seems to exist: "One has an opportunity of influencing it when the sense of guilt is a borrowed one. . . . when it is the product of an identification with some other person who was once the subject of an erotic cathexis." In discussing the idealization of the analyst, he added that the success of treatment may depend "on whether the personality of the analyst allows for the patient putting him in the place of the ego ideal" (p. 50, n. 1).

Needless to say, in practice this intense, early defensive idealization of the analyst, which corresponds to the exalted image of the preferred or "good" internalized maternal representation, does not last. In order to maintain the denial and repression of aggression, along with the denial of guilt and depression, the patient will displace the idealization onto another outside object and act it out as Betty did. Anna and Claudia attempted such maneuvers, but were unable to sustain an image of the object as a "genius."

In all five women, as the idealization was tolerated and interpreted, the grandiosity made its appearance and the omnipotent stance became available for analysis. At this time, the depreciated and degraded object representation is projected and the analyst feels the sting of the patient's superior contempt. One patient was "hopelessly embarrassed" by the "naivete" of the analyst for quite a period of time. Another did not call when she intended to miss a session. A third was quite concerned about the analyst's intellectual abilities. He seemed too "thick" and "unable to comprehend or understand."

During this stage of the analysis, patients' genius for negation makes its appearance. No interpretation "tastes" good enough (Freud 1925b). Whatever the analyst says is immediately negated. If it is temporarily examined, it usually is not accepted (self-starvation) or is soon ejected (vomiting). For periods of time, these patients contradict themselves repeatedly in order to maintain their sense of superiority and their depreciated image of the analyst. As such material is analyzed, the underlying anger surfaces. Thomä (1967, pp. 266–270) has a good discussion of the aggression and negation in these regressive states.

Volkan's (1965, 1976) case history of an anorexic clearly demonstrates the omnipotent and fragmenting quality of a group of regressive fantasies. He specifically described an omnipotent defensive fantasy involving a "little man" phenomenon in an 18-year-old anorexic girl. She had concretized early self- and object representations in internalizations of perceptions of her dead grandfather. The denial of his death was facilitated by her identifications with fantasies of being a "little man," a "stick man," and a "little seed." Her own infantile omnipotence was associated with this split-off ego segment that had never been integrated with the rest of the ego. Such fantasied figures were projected onto the environment. This patient seemed to be quite regressed, and the defensive and disorganizing aspects of her identifications were quite apparent.

In the five cases discussed here, omnipotent fantasies led to elation and seemed to defend against recognition of painful, self-destructive inner forces, but there was not the personality disintegration obvious in Volkan's case.

Freud (1923) discussed such identifications and their potentially destructive consequences. He observed that in melancholia (another pregenital regression) "an object which was lost has been set up again inside the ego . . . an object cathexis has been replaced by an identification" (p. 28). He continued, "at the very beginning in the individual's primitive oral phase, object cathexis and identifications are no doubt undistinguishable from each other [which] makes [it] possible to suppose that the character of the ego is the precipitate of abandoned object cathexis and it contains the history of those object choices" (p. 29).

Freud went on to indicate the possibility of a pathological outcome if the ego's object identifications obtained the upper hand and became

too numerous, unduly powerful and incompatible in one way or another, . . . It may come to a disruption of the ego in consequence of the different identifications becoming cut off from one another by resistance . . . multiple personality . . . even when things do not go as far as this, there remains the question of conflicts between the various identifications into which the ego comes apart, conflicts which cannot, after all, be described as entirely pathological. (p. 30)

All five patients described here had a series of splits in self- and object representations and self-perceptions; their manifestations ranged from rather conscious attempts at restructuring certain self-images to less conscious, mild fragmentation of ideas and affect. The splits were clearly observable and definable in terms of self-perceptions, object perceptions, self-representations, and object representations. One could easily distinguish a continuum between those that were conscious and were perceived to be under the patient's control, and those that seemed more automatic and were denied or repressed and out of the patient's awareness. In addition to the splits manifested by these patients, other isolated ego states, ranging from momentary confusion to contradictory subjective states to major ego splits, also should be included on such a continuum.

Grotstein's position (1981, p. 10) seems similar to the one advanced here: "The act of splitting may be active or experienced as passive and we can speak of macroscopic or microscopic splitting." He notes that "splitting can be done (a) under the auspices of perceptual or cognitive thinking where discriminations are required; and (b) defensively, which involves counter cathexis against unwanted perceptions and feelings" (p. 78). He also notes that splits that are experienced as passive lead to a feeling of fragmentation.

"Rebirth" Fantasies and "Self-Improvement"

The most benign and conscious of such splits seem to be quite characteristic of anorexic patients, particularly during their latency and adolescence. They are experienced as "self-improvement" activities and, when successful, are accompanied by an elated "remaking" version of a "rebirth" fantasy. Similar fantasies are common at entrance into analysis: Patients want to be "remade" or "reborn" as different people in the psychoanalytic process.

All five patients demonstrated such successful "resolutions"; a certain superior, omnipotent quality was noticeable in the pride over their "self-improvement." The cases of Claudia and Betty were particularly illustrative.

At eight or nine, ostensibly to please her parents, Claudia consciously changed herself from an overweight, withdrawn child who loved a world of fantasy to an active, socially striving, athletic achiever. At about the same time, she suppressed her daytime fantasies and her nighttime dreams to appease her conscious perception of her father, whom she felt would disapprove of her sexual and aggressive conduct. In early adolescence, she suppressed all crying because of the weak self-image she associated with it and was unable to cry until she entered analysis. However, while she demanded a tougher self-image for her own "consumption," as it were, she was quite willing to parade the weak, helpless anorexic image for her family's "consumption."

Parenthetically, at about the time of her first "self-improvement," her activities took on a rather mechanical, isolated quality, with obsession about details to the detriment of the whole. She suffered from a feeling of fragmentation.

Betty's conscious splits led to separate large areas of self-perception which took on "role-playing" characteristics. When she went away to school at age 11, she felt lost and was unable to communicate with the other girls. She projected her own superior, contemptuous fantasies onto those other students and alternated between feeling scorned and disgusted with herself and feeling intellectually superior. Her credible academic work was frequently accomplished with a spiteful attitude toward superiors. She began to look with a certain disgust on her intellectuality and submission to authority, and called on two or more conscious internal representations of herself. Each was in competition with the other. That "stick of a girl," the good, submissive student, contrasted sharply with her view of herself as the glamorous, socially superior, aristocratic person. She would call forth one image of herself and indulge in contempt for the other. Like Claudia, at intervals during latency and adolescence, Betty consciously made several decisions to "change" her personality and appeared to be superficially successful in her endeavors.

A remarkable quality that separates anorexics from others is their apparent "success" with such "self-improvement" endeavors. Most of us have "good intentions" of improving ourselves at various times in our life experience, but we recognize the folly of such self-deceptions. Consciously, the anorexic patient feels "successful" and morally superior to other mere mortals, not recognizing that the remodeling is based on early infantile "splits" or isolated self-representations. In typical pregenital fashion, the splitting and appositional quality are conscious while the real, underlying conflicts and motives are repressed.

Fragmentation

With Betty, the apparent success had its painful corollaries. She associated the glamorous, socially superior, aristocratic person with her perception of herself in the mirror as a "beautiful woman." When confused or depressed, she would attempt to reassure herself by staring at and trying to reidentify with the beautiful woman, but she only experienced the image as though it were a separate person who had nothing to do with herself.

Such self-images are conscious manifestations of precipitates of earlier internalizations. They are replaced by conscious representations of other internalized figures from the past. While this occasionally leads to temporary chaos and confusion, it does not seem to cause the conscious pain and anxiety that occurs with less conscious manifestations of fragmentation.

The latter was dramatically demonstrated by Betty. At one point, she was having panicky anxieties about her colleagues at work. Her work became more and more affected by her preoccupation with minutia. Such insecurity gave rise to compensatory states of rather omnipotent, provocative superiority, with its attendant contemptuous acting out. This, in turn, led to further fears of her peers and superiors. At one point, she stated that her nerves felt like "a group of quarreling people." This led to a recognition of separate introjections of images of her various employers and coworkers, with projective identifications involving what she felt to be their omnipotent, superior, contemptuous feelings toward her. In her fantasies, such internalized representations fought with each other and she was fighting with all of them. These separate self-object images, which she both scorned and tried to appease, represented early internalizations of part-self- and part-object representations. Each particular condensed representation had its own affective charge, which changed when applied to a particular contemporary object perception. In her fantasies, as these representations became conscious, they battled with one another. Such a state of affairs reminds one of Freud's (1923) comments about "too numerous identifications." Heimann's (1942) patient, although probably more regressed than the patients presented here, demonstrated a similar phenomenon. Her "devils" represented separate, internalized part-object representations in fantasied form.

Debora's and Ellen's fantasied representations of themselves as "little devils" were quite similar to Volkan's (1965, 1976) "stick man" and Niederland's (1956, 1965) "little man" phenomena. Isolated fragmentation was apparent in all these self-perceptions.

All of these patients eventually saw the split between the sadistic part of themselves that enjoyed torturing others (the "monster" or "devil") and the submissive, idealized, "good girl" part of themselves. Early in analysis, one patient carried on a dialogue with "the dictator" who told her not to give in but to show her independence by starving, vomiting, or torturing herself.

The regressive defenses employed by anorexic patients give rise to the gross clinical picture described by Bruch (1962, 1965, 1970, 1978a) and Selvini Palazzoli (1961, 1978). Both were impressed by the pathetic helplessness of these patients and seemed to interpret this surface picture as indicative of weak ego or character structure. This interpretation is completely at odds with that of clinicians who use psychoanalytic treatment with these patients. The latter clinicians recognize both the power of the underlying ambivalence and aggression toward the primary object, which necessitates the defensive posture, and the impressive ability of these patients to analyze this process.

When the defensive maneuvers cover depression and guilt relating directly to intense sadistic and aggressive impulses in the defenses themselves, such aggression should be evident. In these patients' attempts to control, there is a defense against a confrontation with the perception of the object, which would bring the defended-against impulses into consciousness, but there is also a gratification of unconscious sadistic fantasies. The sense of omnipotence also enables these patients to avoid the threat of real confrontation through their illusion of superiority. Anorexic patients share with other pregenital regressions a fascinating defense. Once they make a judgment, they are unaware of the hostility involved, e.g., "My contempt for you is not a matter of aggression, it is merely a recognition of the fact of your inferiority" or "When I disagree and won't listen or consider your suggestion, it is not because I am hostile, it is only that I do not want to waste my time with something I am sure is not true." Such an omnipotent judgment both gratifies and denies aggressive, powerful fantasies. The aggression shows through brilliantly in the negation as well as the symptom.

The very process of fragmentation lucidly exposes the naked aggression trapped in the intrapsychic system. The hatred one self-representation, self-perception, or self-image displays toward another is truly remarkable and usually quite conscious in the "reforming" fantasies. Such battles between intrapsychic internalizations are equally clear in the analysis of more chaotic, unconscious separations between, and fragmentations of, self-images. Despite such clinical evidence, some investigators and therapists insist on overlooking, disparaging, or denying the importance of hostility in patients with anorexia nervosa.

Self-Destructive Behavior, Aggression, and Sadism

As one looks at the clinical picture, it seems fair to ask, What is the source of self-destructive behavior such as (1) the elimination of adult female sexuality; (2) the self-starvation to the point of cachexia; and (3) the panicky withdrawal from satisfaction in social relationships? Certainly such hostility toward the self indicates a lot of hatred somewhere.

The masochistic self-destructiveness is also evident in self-injury, occasional suicide attempts, and other self-destructive behavior. Even those who dispense with such behavior by labeling it "reactive" would have difficulty dismissing the underlying masochistic fantasies. Two patients had repeated, frightening fantasies of slicing their eyeballs with razor blades (in response to primitive, primal-scene fantasies and exposure to father's genitalia). One patient uncovered fantasies of tearing her face apart and for a while indulged in physically tearing the skin of her face in an attempt to destroy her spotless skin (in response to memories of torturing a pet in early childhood, which reflected earlier wishes to tear away an angry father's face, and probably still earlier needs to destroy mother's breast). Another patient had a fantasy of auto-cunnilingus, with the oral sensation of eating her pubis and crunching the bones (in response to fear of sexual interest and masturbatory fantasies about father, which involved eliminating mother).

The material underlying the self-destructive acting out becomes clear when patients are allowed to learn to free-associate. Patients become conscious of the need to deny aggression toward the object and divert it toward themselves at critical moments. The replacement of a hostile object perception (which itself has replaced a hostile object representation) with an idealized, martyred object perception (and presumable representation) inevitably becomes quite conscious, even before patients are able to change or modify their behavior. Conversely, the switch from a victimized perception of an internalized "good" representation changes to a perception of a sadistic "bad" self-perception, representing a splitting of the internal representation of the "bad" self.

The need for such primitive splitting, reversals, and denials rests on the unconscious need for immediate gratification. The impulse has not been modified, and represented in the free associations as a "wish" by a mature superego, but instead has remained as a denied need for immediate action and satisfaction.

In each of the five patients presented here, as the above defenses and impulses were reluctantly acknowledged and understood, there were temporary, rather severe depressions. These depressions frequently followed the relinquishment of the major anorexic symptomatology. The underlying violence, masochism, and sadism then became apparent. In her depression, Anna provoked a rather serious self-injury that necessitated hospitalization. Betty repeatedly provoked her lover to attack and injure her and once provoked such behavior from another male acquaintance. Claudia placed herself in potentially dangerous positions, but fortunately came through unscathed. Debora involved herself in potentially dangerous sexual experimentation with strangers. Ellen's depression and self-destructive provocativeness were always just below the surface and displayed themselves repeatedly. All suffered from "accidental" injuries during treatment.

Further aggression and sadism emerged as these depressive states and self-destructive behavior were interpreted in the context of the patients' hatred and self-punitive conscience, rejection by and loss of mother, humiliation at wanting and not getting, etc. As the patients became willing to examine and understand this aggression and sadism, a number of ego states became available for analysis. After recalling dismemberment fantasies of mother, Claudia recalled repeatedly feeling intense hatred toward her mother, accompanied by a sense of profound helplessness and humiliation. At such times, she would turn her face away from mother so as not to see her. She would "white out"—a white screen would blank out everything. Then she would develop a rather detached (and sometimes depersonalized) passivity in which she would sink into a state of profound submission and self-loathing. Further analysis led to the recognition and memory of lightninglike, transient fantasies of decapitation and obliteration of mother as Claudia turned her face away. As she remembered the details of the elaborate but instantaneous fantasy, she realized that, as an adult, this identical series of thoughts and fantasies was present in a momentary, condensed version every time she gave in and felt unable to stand up to mother. In three extreme situations this progression had led to migraine headaches. Claudia's "white out" may be related to the breast and the "dream screen" described by Lewin (1950).

Betty recalled similar detached and/or depersonalized moments in childhood, when she felt helpless and depressed as she identified with her depressed mother. Such states were followed by rather elated states of superiority and power. These minor elations covered fantasies of forcing mother into complete submission.

Anna recalled and relived in the analysis similar elated states that covered fantasies and bulimic orgies in which she devoured the world.

Ellen's bulimia was gradually replaced by states of helpless, "impotent," depressed rage at fate, the world, and, later, her mother. She realized that she was in a detached state of immobility at these moments, and this recalled similar states of depersonalization and derealization in childhood which had followed fantasies of elimination and obliteration of mother. As with Claudia, the fantasies were at times confined to elimination of mother's head or mouth.

These sadistic fantasies were frequently amalgamated with oedipal and phallic fantasies. For example, at times Claudia's detached ego states followed angry fantasies and thoughts of her potential superiority to mother as a wife for father.

In Betty's background, vomiting replaced anger and sadism shortly after the birth of her sister. At first, she kicked and pummeled the nurse taking care of her and then her rage attacks gave way to vomiting attacks that continued nightly for an indefinite period. In latency, she acted out such sadism directly in teasing, beating, and sexually provoking the sister directly, as well as by torturing and killing small animals that she equated with this sibling.

Claudia's anger and sadism included similar torturing and tickling of her younger sibling. At the age of six or seven, she threatened to "scissor" her older sibling and attacked him with the conscious intent of killing him. As with Betty, such acted-out aggression was never directed toward mother. Mother—

presumably was unaware of it, and it was repressed until the memories were recovered in analysis.

These patients felt guilty and ashamed of their needs for immediate satisfaction, which they perceived as selfish, greedy evidence of their "bad" self-images. As analysis progressed, they came to recognize their destructive impulses to act when their needs were not satisfied immediately. These impulses seemed to be derivative and representative of the pregenital denial and repression of aggression. The entire continuum of need → frustration → rage → action → destruction was denied by an identification with the frustrating object.

ANOREXIA VERSUS BULIMIA

It would be tempting to try to determine the exact pregenital determinants of the differences between the abstaining anorexic and the bulimic-vomiting patient.* The abstaining anorexic seems to present a more obsessional character structure with obsessional defenses. The gorger-vomiter is more likely to present an overideational hysterical character structure, with hysterical acting out and other hysterical defenses. However, both categories seem equally amenable to treatment. For example, both Betty and Claudia achieved clinical recovery—entirely new professional, social, and life adjustments, sexual responsiveness, and independence—in psychoanalyses of approximately the same duration.

Some recent nonpsychoanalytic articles on the two groups claim evidence for their separation and differential morbidity based on so-called "objective" evaluation of symptomatological differences, family environment, marital adjustment, parent-child relationships, stressful life experiences, etc. A recent study by Strober (1982) reviews some of that literature and presents his own statistical evidence, judgments, and speculations. As is typical of such studies, arbitrary scales with their own judgmental categories are used. Quantitative evaluation is attempted by computing percentages of patients in different categories arbitrarily assigned to such scales, and by numerical evaluation of character traits.

Such studies have little to do with a psychoanalytic approach to the problem. To categorize varieties in a group of similar patients on the basis of one facet of a symptom complex, when both the facet and the symptom complex are subject to multiple motivational determinants, is an unjustifiable oversimplification.

Studying statistical norms adds little to one's understanding of the individual case. For example, one abstaining anorexic analysand had a history of two alcoholic parents, one of whom was seriously disturbed. There had been serious physical abuse of the patient in her early years and a period of maternal abandonment. A statistical approach would look at this patient's personal, family, physical, and social history and place her in the "more serious" category leading to bulimia-vomiting and "greater resistance" to psychoanalysis.

---

* See Chapter 7.

However, she was neither a gorger nor unusually resistant to psychoanalytic treatment. The external evidence of difficulty had little to do with the subjective experience of this particular patient. Statistical classifications may gratify an obsessional need to feel in control of the material, but they are of little therapeutic use. The highly abstract process of determining judgments and categories yields general conclusions that may or may not be pertinent to individual cases.

To return to the issue of bulimics versus abstainers, of the five cases presented here, the bulimic patients seemed to have a somewhat less oppressive superego than the abstaining patients. They also had a history of more hyperactivity in childhood, and perhaps more overt (not more covert), provocative acting out. Certainly, copious alcohol use was more apparent in two adult bulimic patients, but it seemed to yield to psychoanalysis far more easily than alcoholism usually does. There was no other drug use by any of the bulimic patients, but two of the abstainers used LSD, cocaine, and marijuana. Neither was an addict, however.

The chronicity of the illness may play a part in the development of bulimia. For example, one older anorexic patient was an abstainer for the first few years of her illness and later discovered vomiting. A very seriously disturbed bulimic-vomiter had abstained for quite some time until she was hospitalized and learned the "advantages" of vomiting from other anorexic patients.

Bulimia and vomiting seem to be accepted as an appropriate way to maintain weight control by many young women of high school and college age who never become anorexic. Some patients with neurotic character structures and appropriate pregenital problems may discover and use this contemporary symptom to replace other neurotic or psychosomatic symptoms and to reinforce their defenses against unwanted oedipal pressures.

The bulimia comes to involve fusion with the maternal figure and the breast, and also represents orgiastic masturbatory activity. At the same time, it represents a sadistic devouring of the frustrating "bad" object and clearly replaces angry confrontations with that object perception.

Conversely, the vomiting represents the forceful expulsion of the "bad" object, the riddance of contamination, the erasure of the "stain," as well as the rejection of, and wish for pregnancy.

More research is necessary before one can make further generalizations about the choice of obsessional and hysterical defenses.

SUMMARY

This chapter offered an object-relations view of the dynamics of anorexia nervosa, concentrating on case material from five anorexic patients. A brief, selective review of the literature on regression and object relations in anorexia nervosa also was offered. Of the five cases presented, four women had completed or were well into psychoanalysis while the fifth was in psychoanalytic psychotherapy. The discussion of clinical material focused on the regressive defenses and object relations of these patients.

A description was given of the way these patients consciously and unconsciously attempted to control their internal object representations, external object perceptions, and impulses. The manifestations of this control in the transference to the analyst were illustrated. The need for such control was related to identifications with a controlling mother and unconscious sadistic impulses.

The varieties of omnipotent and grandiose fantasies used by these patients to deny their depression and guilt were described. The specific need of these patients to feel morally superior to mother, peers, and analyst was highlighted. It was noted that anorexic women also have an exalted idea of their omnipotent control over their bodies.

This discussion led into observations on the fragmentation and isolation of part-self- and part-object representations, which result in disturbances and detachments of thought processes. Included were splits in self-representations and self-perceptions ranging from conscious "self-improvement" rebirth fantasies to unconscious disorganization of thought processes with multiple identifications.

Evidence was presented to support the assertion that anorexic patients utilize the above defenses to deny guilt and depression. It was concluded that the guilt and depression are intimately related to intense sadistic and aggressive impulses directed toward the loved object. These sadistic wishes and fantasies are frequently amalgamated with phallic and oedipal concerns. Pregenital defenses are directed against intense oedipal conflict.

In this connection, it was noted that, like all patients with pregenital regression, anorexic patients have a low tolerance for frustration. They demand immediate gratification and, when it is not forthcoming, they become enraged and feel the impulse to act aggressively. Such patients attempt to deny and repress wishes that lead to such frustration and conflict.

It is abundantly clear that all of these defensive fantasies derive directly from regression to, and/or fixation at, the early relationship with a frustrating, controlling maternal figure. Internalization of various perceptions of this object and the accompanying self-perceptions and affects gives rise to the above defensive maneuvers and fantasies.

Finally, a brief discussion was offered regarding possible differences between the dynamics and object relations of the abstaining anorexic and those of the bulimic-vomiting anorexic. In the cases presented here, there seemed to be little difference in the morbidity or prognosis of the two "categories."

PART III

The Analytic Relationship

7
Transference

CHARLES C. HOGAN, M.D., D.MED.SC.

Anorexia nervosa patients present some specific problems to the analyst in understanding and interpreting their transference perceptions and behavior. Before turning to specific transference problems with anorexic patients, some general remarks on transference are in order.

GENERAL REMARKS

The idea of transference was introduced by Freud (1893–1895) in *Studies on Hysteria*. He also mentioned the subject in his letters to Fliess (1887–1902). His first real discussion of transference was in the "Dora" case (1905). This "Fragment of an Analysis of a Case of Hysteria" seems to be an appropriate and fascinating introduction to the problems facing analysts in the transference reactions of anorexic women. This patient of Freud's might well be classified as a psychosomatic case today, with her cough and migraines and self-destructive transference relationship so similar to that of many anorexic patients.

In Freud's discussion of Dora's negative transference, he asked,

If cruel impulses and revengeful motives, which have already been used in the patient's ordinary life for maintaining her symptoms, become transferred on the physician before he has time to detach them from himself . . . how could the patient take a more effective revenge than by demonstrating on her own person the helplessness and incapacity of the physician? (p. 120)

Freud was discussing the sadistic impulses and the self-destructive, masochistic utilization of their derivatives that we now associate with pregenital problems. He anticipated the inherent contradictions involved in handling specific impulses to harm the primary object or transference objects.*

Ubiquity of Transference

Freud (1925a) noted the ubiquity of transference (1909) and said that it arises "spontaneously in all human relationships." Today there seems to be

---

*See Sperling (1967) and Bird (1972) for discussions on the problems of handling specific denied and repressed impulses to do violence and harm to the object.

general agreement that transference is involved in every human relationship (Bird 1972; Brenner 1976; Freud 1909, 1925a; Gill and Muslin 1976; Greenacre 1954; and many others). However, there seem to be many who would like to limit its boundaries, who feel that it must be "maintained" or "developed," or who see it as only a product of the analytic relationship. Bird (1972) was so impressed with the universality of the phenomenon that he formulated an apt proposition: "transference would seem to me to assume characteristics of a major ego function" (p. 267).

Loewenstein (1969) discussed some of the attempts of authors (Greenson 1965, 1971; Greenson and Wexler 1969; Sterba 1934; Zetzel 1956) to narrow or widen the concept of transference. Sandler et al. (1973) also discuss this problem. My own feelings on the matter are in agreement with Gill and Muslin (1976).

> Freud accepted the existence of a personal relationship with the patient as a necessary and inevitable part of the analytic set up, in no sense inappropriate and not to be dealt with as a matter of technique. Though Freud called the relationship "the unobjectionable positive transference" or "rapport" many analysts seem to have forgotten that Freud referred to this aspect of the relation with a patient as part of the transference. It now goes by a number of other names—"basic transference" (Greenacre 1954), "mature transference" (Stone 1967), or else is subsumed by more complex concepts—"therapeutic alliance" (Zetzel 1956), "working alliance" (Greenson 1965), "real relationship" (Greenson 1971), and the "nontransference relationship" (Greenson and Wexler 1969). (p. 781)

Every aspect of these patients' cognition and feeling about their relationship with the analyst should be considered part of the transference and analyzable. In a self-destructive patient, what appears to be the most cooperative positive transference may turn out to represent masochistic submission and primitive identification. To classify a part of it as something other than transference and call it "working alliance" or "therapeutic alliance" unnecessarily limits the universality of transference. The working alliance, real relationship, etc., are all manifestations of positive transference and do not exist outside of it. It only confuses the conceptual model to contaminate Freud's "positive transference" with nonanalytic terms that suggest that an area of the analysand's personal experience is unavailable for potential analysis.

I am in agreement with Brenner (1979b) that "examination of the clinical evidence offered by proponents for the concepts of therapeutic and working alliance leads the author to conclude that neither concept is justifiable. Both refer to aspects of the transference that neither deserve a special name nor require special treatment" (p. 156). The concept is not only useless, it is positively damaging to the understanding of the psychopathology unless it is considered as but one facet of positive transference.

Hierarchy of Regressive Levels

The analytic literature is replete with discussions of what constitutes transference and what constitutes a transference neurosis. This is further complicated by the recognition of an occasional transference psychosis. In my view, it is a relative matter. It was well put by Giovacchini (1975b):

It is useful to view the object relationship qualities of transference from the viewpoint of an hierarchical continuum. Insofar as any transference is a recapitulation of an infantile state, the types of object relationships typical of such states would be similarly infantile. From the viewpoint of regression, narcissistically fixated patients would be characterized by primitive object relationships which are fragmented ones but in which contact with another person is still possible . . . absolute distinctions between narcissistic transference are no longer necessary. . . . Every transference, even those of highly structured psychoneurotics, has a narcissistic element, and the converse would also be true. (p. 11)

Such a continuum of regressive positions would seem to be consistent with the propositions of Arlow and Brenner (1964). However, such a relative approach will not satisfy a large number of analysts when it comes to the difference between the classical concepts of transference and transference neurosis. In anorexia nervosa and other psychosomatic illnesses, there are constant and repetitive fluctuations of the transference between the reconstitution of dyadic and triadic relationships from the past. Although this constant shifting is more toward primitive pregenital regressive defenses of a dyadic nature early in treatment and more toward the triadic oedipal struggle later, the transference continues to shift between narcissistic concerns and neurotic constellations. Giovacchini (1979) pointed out that "Freud did not state that the transference neurosis is derived exclusively from an oedipal conflict. Rather, he emphasized that a transference neurosis encompasses the patient's total psychopathology . . . he made the Oedipus complex the central conflictual core . . . he included other primitive psychic elements" (p. 457). Giovacchini described the essence of analytic transference as "the projection of relatively infantile elements into the mental representation of the therapist" and concluded that "the basic mechanism of all transference is primitive; its content may involve different levels of ego integration" (p. 468).

It is most important for the analyst to be aware of the patient's state of regression and the particular level of development of the self- and object representational projections (Blum 1977; Boyer 1979; Boyer and Giovacchini 1967, 1980; Giovacchini 1975b, 1979; Kernberg 1975, 1976). Blum (1977) pointed out that "in addition to conflict and defense, reconstruction now includes archaic ego states and object relations, reaction patterns and developmental consequences" (p. 758). Furthermore, "though an oedipal transference neurosis is central to analytic work, depending on the personality structure and the depth of regression, varying in duration and intensity of pre-oedipal transference may be discussed or inferred" (p. 781).

Extent of Transference Regression

The "final common pathway" of symptom formation in anorexia may occur in a variety of personality constellations, such as hysterical, obsessional, and narcissistic characters, character disorders, and even schizophrenic and psychotic disabilities. Despite the prognostic implications of such diagnostic labels, one finds that there is another dimension to the usual psychosomatic case and to the anorexic patient in particular. Once the anorexic symptomatology is relinquished, it is often astonishing to see the flexibility available in the analysis of the underlying neurotic structure. While time is required to analyze the various archaic pregenital defenses, these patients have greater flexibility than do many borderline narcissistic characters or neurotics with narcissistic features.

Giovacchini (1977) shed some light on this matter in his discussion of narcissistic character disorders. He pointed out that "this situation is different from a masochistic adjustment that is designed to effect a psychodynamic balance; the defensive constellation of my patient was vital to maintaining a total ego coherence instead of dealing with discrete conflicting disruptive impulses" (p. 10).

Anorexic patients have made a masochistic adjustment that has effected a psychodynamic balance similar to that discussed by Giovacchini. When this adjustment is analyzed and relinquished, the conflicting impulses represented by the masochistic and sadistic activity make their appearance and give rise to a "feel" and "clinical content" slightly different from those in "purer" borderline patients, narcissistic characters, and neurotics with narcissistic features. In some ways, the treatment of anorexics appears to proceed with more chaos, but a greater flexibility does exist. The framework of the neurosis seems to be shaken by the relinquishment of the psychosomatic symptoms.

Psychosomatic conditions in general, and anorexia nervosa in particular, involve the vicissitudes of primitive aggression, which become available and understood primarily in the transference (Cohler 1975; Flarsheim 1975; Giovacchini 1963; Jessner and Abse 1960; Masserman 1941; Savitt 1969, 1977; Selvini Palazzoli 1978; Sperling 1967, 1978; Thomä 1967; Waller et al. 1940). This aggression presents its derivatives in the form of self-destructive, masochistic activity, the psychic content of which becomes available as the symptom is understood.

In the context of regressive disturbances and their transference problems, Kohut (1971, 1977) contributes little toward our understanding of the pregenital (or narcissistic) manifestations of transference in anorexic or other psychosomatic patients. Stolorow and Lachman (1980), in their attempt to extend and reconcile aspects of Kohut and Kernberg, are likewise of little help.

ANOREXIC TRANSFERENCE

Anorexic patients bring with them a subjective world that is dominated and surrounded by a powerful, controlling, omniscient mother imago. They spend the greater part of their time subjugating themselves to this enveloping presence while also trying to provoke and control various fragmented part representations and perceptions of this primitive object.

When these patients enter psychoanalysis, their inner world is projected onto the analyst, who must interpret and demonstrate that world to them without being seduced by their masochism or overly provoked by their words and activities, as was the mother (and other objects in patients' perceptual world).

This subjective world of masochistic submission to, and omnipotent control of, such an enveloping maternal imago is represented in the transference of these patients and is available for analysis. The analyst must be tolerant of intense provocation, overt hostility, self-destructive intimidating manipulation, and contemptuous withholding of material, and yet must be able to maintain the traditional, somewhat detached psychoanalytic stance. This is a difficult task. For the most part, these patients' parents, parental surrogates, and peers have succumbed to the patients' particular brand of masochistic provocation and indulged their masochism. The psychoanalyst must use the transference to ferret out the hidden impulses and defenses motivating such behavior and must not be seduced from, or intimidated away from his job.*

Sperling (1978) noted that part of the anorexic's conflict is conscious, although the motivations are unconscious. I would add that many of these patients are well aware consciously of the demanding, infantile needs of the mother. One patient pointed out in an early session that her mother was a "bigger baby" than she was and would have "temper tantrums" when she didn't get what she wanted. Another patient observed that her mother was an "infant" who would withdraw into "depressions or nerves" when her needs were frustrated. A third patient was consciously aware of her mother's need for fusion, as the mother insisted that they knew each other "completely" and could "read each other's thoughts and feelings." While there is projective identification at work here, the descriptions of mother's activities and the quotations of mother's words indicate the validity of these patients' observations.

As is true with other psychosomatic illnesses, these patients' mothers want them to be ill, and show concern, anxiety, and love for them when they are ill (Sperling 1967). In anorexia in particular, the mothers seem to unconsciously want them to starve and die. Two mothers of anorexics told them when they were quite small, "I wish you were dead!" Another mother physically attacked and verbally disowned her anorexic daughter repeatedly. The wish to starve is often communicated by reaction formations (e.g., overfeeding or force-feeding). In a corresponding way, the anorexic child tries to provoke the mother's anxiety and concern, which the child equates with love. In the mother's desire to destroy her child is the unconscious impulse to destroy part of herself (many of these mothers have anorexic symptoms).

Early in the analysis of the anorexic's pregenital defenses, the transference is handled along the principles set forward by Kernberg (1975) and summarized by Boyer (1980) in regard to borderline cases:

(1) The predominantly negative transference is systematically elaborated only in the present without initial efforts directed toward full genetic interpretations; (2) The patient's typical defensive constellations are interpreted as they enter the transference [see discussion of particular defensive constellations below]; (3) Limits are set in order to block acting out in the transference insofar as this is necessary to protect the neutrality of the therapist [but with many limitations, see below]; (4) The less primitively determined aspects of the positive transference are not interpreted early since their presence enhances the development of the therapeutic and working alliances [only if we look at these alliances as part of the

---

*Wilson discusses such countertransference problems in Chapter 8. He notes that there is only one published article (Sperling 1967) on the subject of transference in psychosomatic patients.

positive transference—see discussion of limiting transference above], although the primitive idealizations that reflect the splitting of "all good" from "all bad" object relations are systematically interpreted as part of the effort to work through those primitive defenses; (5) Interpretations are formulated so that the patient's distortions of the therapist's interventions and of present reality, especially the patient's perceptions during the hour, can be systematically clarified; and (6) The highly distorted transference, at times psychotic in nature and reflecting fantastic internal object relations pertaining to early ego disturbances, is worked through first in order to reach the transferences related to actual childhood experiences. (p. 176)

Boyer adds, "I consider the understanding and pertinent interpretation of the unfolding transference to be of the utmost importance. I have come to contemplate each interview as though it might have been a dream and material from recent interviews as part of the day residue" (p. 176).

My general agreement with Boyer about the handling of the transference early in treatment is qualified somewhat by the differences in patient populations: Boyer addresses himself to borderline patients, and anorexic patients do not necessarily have borderline psychopathology. Usually, much less intervention in acting out (point 3) is indicated with anorexic patients. They have more flexibility than do borderline patients (Giovacchini 1977). Defended-against triadic oedipal material may erupt sporadically early in the analysis of anorexics and must be handled appropriately. In anorexic patients, the negative transference (point 1) and the participating defensive constellations (point 2) are so overtly masochistic that the self-destructive aggression and suicidal implications of fantasies and transference activities should be repeatedly interpreted. In this context and in the context of point 4, the anorexics' introjective and projective identifications are rather carefully worked out: when a patient is starving herself, it is fairly easy for her to see that she is punishing a bad self-representation —"I don't deserve to live"—and a bad maternal object representation— "Whatever she does she can't make me eat"—as well as attempting to provoke the analyst or to provoke the object perception of the analyst in fantasies—"I don't know what you think you can do for me. You can't make me eat. I am sorry that you are so helpless with me." In projective identifications, a patient also attempts to provoke and imagines such provocations in fantasy.

There is a special technical matter in interpreting the transference of the anorexia nervosa patient. The analyst should try to demonstrate the patient's need for immediate gratification early in treatment. This is not difficult with the bulimic-vomiting patient, but it does take a bit more time with the self-denying, self-starving patient. These patients feel they must have what they want immediately. If they do not get it, a destructive, killing rage ensues and usually is denied and turned on the self. Sperling (1967, 1968a) and others have emphasized the role of such aggression in psychosomatic symptoms. Bird (1972) wondered about the vicissitudes of destructive, killing impulses in the transference on a much wider scale:

> Negative destructive tendencies in contrast to libidinal drives . . . run into a good deal of trouble [in being experienced in the transference] ending up at best as wishes. . . . Those involving literal destructive acts seem to stand little chance of entering the transference at all. . . . When a patient behaves violently in

daily life and reports this to us . . . tell him to stop . . . [or] directly warn
him of the consequences. . . . . The patients' literal attempts to destroy the
analyst probably represent in the transference memories the patient's own attempts
to destroy certain aspects of himself and instead to destroy others. (pp. 287–289,
295)

In short, when the patient's frustration leads directly to the unconscious
impulse to destroy or mutilate the transference object perception and when the
patient proceeds to injure the unconscious object representation with self-
destructive behavior, one must do more than interpret a death wish toward the
analyst or parent. Often these self-destructive activities are represented in a
"split-off" fragment of the ego and they perpetuate themselves after their
genesis is ostensibly understood. One patient took an elated delight in her
ability to torture her mother and (sometimes in fantasy, occasionally in reality)
provoke the analyst with her suicidal drives and activities. This continued for
some time after she recognized that her bulimic–vomiting–self-starving behavior involved much more than the fear of being fat. After an almost orgiastic
night of bulimia and vomiting, she would say playfully, "You see, you
shouldn't frustrate me. You see what it does to me. When I die, it will be all
your fault."

The difficulty inherent in gratifying seemingly insatiable destructive and
sadistic impulses is the core problem in the early analysis of defenses in anorexia
nervosa. Once the material becomes available, the patients can be shown that
they don't just want to be thin, they want to destroy themselves. They don't
just want to control mother metaphorically, they sadistically want to immobil-
ize, torture, and destroy her. They don't just want to quit or prove the analyst
is unable to help them, they unconsciously want to destroy the relationship and
the analyst, even if they have to kill themselves to do it. The following clinical
material clearly illustrates the intensity of such impulses.

Clinical Material

The case histories of three young women with anorexia nervosa are offered.
Two of them presented seemingly different personalities and defenses in their
early analytic work. One began treatment with rather continual, provocative
acting out, bulimia, and vomiting. The other seemed completely cooperative,
interested, and analytically aware from the first interview. She even regained
her menstrual periods and began eating appropriately in the early months of
treatment. The third case illustrates how a mishandled countertransference may
aid and reinforce a patient's denial of important material and how a more
classical analytic stance in handling the transference can elucidate such material.

CASE 1   Acting Out, Bulimia, and Vomiting

Jill entered analysis in her mid-twenties after a prolonged period of unsuccessful treatment following hospitalization five years earlier. She went through
periods of self-starvation, but her primary means of weight reduction involved
vomiting following bulimic binges or drinking bouts. She suffered from sial-
orrhea and swollen salivary glands (as do many vomiting anorexics). These

symptoms appeared and disappeared frequently, often occurring the day after a severe bout of bulimia and vomiting.

There was a history of rather hectic, unsatisfactory social and sexual activity, which continued after entering treatment. Jill was somewhat disorganized and mildly fragmented in her thought processes, but was able to pursue an academically oriented career remarkably well. Her talents protected her from retaliation, despite her provocative tardiness and absenteeism.

Jill idealized analysis and the analyst in a fragmented and sporadic way, but was inclined toward contradictory negativism and petulant rages. She reminded one of Gedo's observations on narcissistic transferences (1977).

> If there is any agreement about anything concerning archaic character types, it is about ubiquitousness of another transference constellation, that of instant demands on the analyst for affirmation of the patient's exceptional worth, for delighted acceptance of his exhibitionism, and for self-abnegative renunciation of any acknowledgment of the patient's actual dependence on him. (p. 789)

Jill certainly demonstrated this "triad of vanity, exhibitionism, and arrogant ingratitude." With all anorexic patients, maximum tact is mandatory when responding to infantile claims. As Gedo (1977) noted, a failure in this regard leads to humiliation and outrage. However, one must not use the consideration or tact as an excuse for avoiding interpretation of available derivatives of primitive impulses and defenses.

In my experience, bulimic and vomiting anorexics like Jill are inclined to present a hysterical type of personality. They tend to be full of fantasies and dreams that are of little use early in treatment. There is such need for immediate satisfaction of the wishes involved that they are unwilling and unable to subject them to analytic work. Such fantasies and dreams are gratifying exhibitionistic gifts to the analyst, but remain untapped. These patients tend toward early, self-destructive acting out. One such patient burned herself with cigarettes, another carved herself with razor blades, and a third provoked a man to hit her in the jaw.

With all anorexic patients, it is important to allow the manifestations of the transference to emerge in as orderly and uncontaminated a manner as possible. It is wise to adhere to rather strict observance of traditional analytic rules (Sperling 1967). As Boyer stated (1980), "The best substitute parenting one can afford the patient is to hew closely to the classical analytic model" (p. 205). Certainly, it is dangerous to impose severe authoritarian or protective parameters on such patients.* Flarsheim (1975), Bettelheim (1975), and Cohler (1975) describe extreme countertransference reactions of a contrasting variety which causes one to question the handling of the transference in their cases. Cohler (1975) stated that "in the resolution of this symbiosis the therapist must be prepared to be placed in the helpless position of being controlled by the patient. The therapist's acceptance of this development helps the patient achieve individuation and a sense of autonomy" (p. 410). Needless to say, this method of handling transference is unnecessary and possibly destructive: such a stance may lend itself to severe ego and symptomatic regression. Flarsheim (1975) said of one patient, "I found myself compelled to relieve her pain . . . anything hopeful that I

---

*See Chapters 8 and 9.

tried to say made her worse" (p. 167). In this case, he recommended hospitalization to relieve his own anxiety and so informed the patient.

To succumb to these patients' self-destructive, controlling, sadistic manipulations and gratify their masochistic dependent needs is to make an interpretable
transference or transference neurosis almost an impossibility. Instead, one
merely contributes to and repeats the dyadic experience of infancy, with all of
its pathological implications.

Jill's transference was disguised by her acting out. However, her withholding and contempt were clearly demonstrated in her tardiness and contradictory
negativism. As she gave up her symptoms, her sadomasochistic acting out
increased. She would verbally provoke and tease others, frequently provoking
attacks on herself (some were serious). She would try to involve the analyst
and, despite knowing that the analyst would advise her to wait until the next
session, she would repeatedly call and tell him of her current state of distress.
These calls were always made in a state of intimidating desperation, with
demands for immediate reassurance and action. This was repeatedly interpreted
and discussed in the ensuing session.

Shortly after entering therapy, she started an affair with a much older
married man and acted out transference feelings with him. When her menstrual
periods returned toward the end of her first year in analysis, she did not inform
the analyst for a month and she credited her lover as the source of improvement.
The affair developed into a sadomasochistic relationship that continued for two
years.

Interpretations were directed at the self-destructive aggression. When the
material warranted, a particular piece of acting out was associated with fragments of self- and object representations. It was possible to demonstrate the
patient's simultaneous projection of sadistic maternal object representations
onto the lover and temporary idealization of the analyst as the good object.
She was able to see how this could abruptly reverse itself, making the analyst
the "dumb," discardable, controlling bad object. Rather typically, she would
provoke physical retaliation by the lover with her superior, contemptuous
challenges. Then she would feel morally superior and enjoy his abject apologies and pleas for reconciliation (and fusion). She attempted to provoke the
analyst with the same superior, contemptuous negativism. She was also able to
understand how her attachment to these primitive object and subject representations contributed to her fragmentation and splitting.

Jill's primitive fantasies of union with the analyst contributed to her continued projective identifications and assumptions. With her lover, she always
"knew" what he was feeling and thinking. The same certainties applied to the
analysis. Without any recognition of the subjectivity of her productions, she
could refer to and repeat dialogues with the internalized analyst as though they
had been reality, and then respond and act accordingly:

> Your feelings were hurt when I disagreed with you yesterday. Your insistence on
> my keeping Friday's appointment was a way of punishing me. After the hour, I
> could just see you gloating and I went down the street arguing with you. You
> know, you are just like D. [her lover]. You have the same arrogant, abusive
> attitude and tone of voice. I stopped at a bar and had two drinks. I thought to
> myself, "I will show him." You know, you are not fair.

When material of this type first presented itself, there was little use in pointing out the subjective nature of all of the associations. Such interpretations only lead to confusion and anger if they are made before the patient has sufficient awareness of the transference. At such an early stage, one can only comment in a general way (if one comments at all): "If you really feel that I was abusive and wanted to punish you for disagreeing with me, it is understandable that you should be angry." Initially, Jill would respond with something in the nature of, "Of course I am angry. I don't think analysts should retaliate toward patients. You should do something about that!" As time went on, she was able to tease out the projections and associate to them. If she was not too involved in isolated states of rage, she could associate to her need for a retaliating, punishing object and to her own morally superior self-perception.

One characteristic of anorexics is their propensity to fragment—to isolate a small segment of their subjective transference experience and devote all of their immediate attention to this split-off perception, with all of its less conscious, but affect-laden, associated representations. When such an isolated state involves rage, it is virtually impossible for the patient to see the moment in a larger psychoanalytic context. The analyst must suffer the rage and insult for the moment or session, but be ready to interpret the material when it surfaces at a later date. Such fragmentary experiences may also involve humiliation or elation. Each isolated state represents a particular perception of self and/or object onto which the patient has projected a past part-self and/or part-object representation.

In Jill's case, such states originated in her humiliation and rage at the birth of a younger sister. At that time, she had had a temper tantrum and vomited. Throughout her early life, she had strived and succeeded in proving her intellectual and physical superiority to this sibling. After early reprimands, she would not display such anger to her parents, but she would sadistically torture the little sister, as well as small animals that represented this unwanted family member. Whenever her adored and idealized father showed a preference for this "inferior" sibling, rage would arise within her and she would experience abdominal sensations representing the vomiting at the time of the sister's birth. Such reactions were isolated and overwhelming. The sense of unfairness and the fear of losing control of both herself and the perceptions of her father were seemingly more than she could bear.

When the analyst mildly questioned the devotion of Jill's idealized lover (an extension of her representation of herself in this case) and her rationalizing certainty that he would leave his wife and family, it was too much. It threatened to destroy the elated fantasies of identification and fusion with this idealized object. It also threatened to relegate her to the infantile position of being "second best," as she had been at the time of her sister's birth, a position that had been feared constantly during latency. A present-day representation of that early dyadic reaction to the mother at the birth of this unwanted intruder occurred. Jill wanted to control the analyst in the same way that she had omnipotently wanted to control mother forcibly, that she had humiliated and physically controlled her sister and small animals, and that she had fantasied controlling her adored father in her moments of rage with him. This latter control was continually acted out in her seductive, sadomasochistic relationship with her lover, which at this time was more dyadic than sexual. It replicated her relationship with her father, but was traceable to her earlier feelings toward mother.

At any rate, she reacted to the analyst's comments with quiet, determined withholding. Her face paled and she grabbed her abdomen as she reproduced the abdominal cramps of latency. She slowly lifted her head, turned toward the analyst, and let loose a torrential rage. She accused him of unfairly comparing her to her lover's wife, of preferring the virtuous but dull behavior of the lover's wife to her own, and of being motivated by jealousy of her lover. This continued throughout the hour and trailed off during the next three sessions.

The analyst managed to interrupt the stream of accusations briefly to call attention to the immensity of her reaction to the modesty of his speculative questions. Asking for a broader context of observation on her part was necessary, but useless at that moment. She was involved in a fragmented section of her life narrowing back to her representation of a powerful, unfair maternal figure who had contaminated the household with a hated, unwanted sibling. Probably this reaction began at an even earlier age, during the nursing period, when Jill had suffered from colic. The inverted pyramid of impulses and defenses had widened to include sister and father, and all of Jill's rage at these frustrating object representations was focused on the analyst. He was the target of the projections of all of these object and subject representations—the frustrating father, sister, and mother. The analyst was challenging her elated, omnipotent self-representation, which included the idealized lover as an extension of herself (as had her latency fantasies of her and father). He was challenging her self-image of superiority, conquest, and control over her lover's wife. It was perfectly understandable that all other considerations were temporarily of no interest.

That night, she acted out by drinking heavily, vomiting violently, precipitating a fight with her lover, and becoming so physically debilitated that she was unable to go to work the next day. While it was impossible to trace through all of these overdetermined threads of association at that time, by working carefully with other such rages and isolated fragmented experiences such reconstructions and memories were eventually possible.

One aspect of all patients with pregenital defenses, and anorexia nervosa in particular, is a tendency to dream of the analyst directly. In less regressed neurotic patients, dreams in which the analyst appears in an undisguised fashion are rare. However, in these patients, such dreams are reasonably frequent and undoubtedly reflect the primitive, intense attachment to the transference object. Such dreams do have a demonstrative value: When a patient brings in a dream with an undisguised representation of the analyst and angrily denies any need of or interest in the analyst, the contradiction is hard to explain away. After the rageful session described above, Jill had such a dream of the analyst, where he was unquestionably related to mother, father, and sister; it was of tremendous help. The associative material from this dream was recalled by the patient after later split-off rages preceded by abdominal cramps.

As Jill's analysis progressed, her life slowly settled down and she discovered a new constancy in herself. She became more able to understand and empathize with her chronically depressed mother. Her conscious perception of mother progressed from one of devoted idealization to that of a monstrous, controlling witch, and, finally, to a more realistic evaluation.

CASE 2   Self-Starvation

In contrast to Jill's rather frenetic early transference behavior and content, Lucy entered treatment with seemingly devoted enthusiasm. Although hyperactive in her work, studies, and outside life, she seemed to be the perfect analysand in the first year or so of analysis. She was a late adolescent with a history of self-starvation. Her only vomiting had occurred for a short period as part of a pseudocyesis when she first lost her menstrual period.

Patients who are primarily involved in self-starvation, with little or no vomiting, seem to be inclined toward obsessional behavior. Early in treatment, they have fewer dreams than bulimic-vomiters and are unaware of their fantasies. They are not overtly exhibitionistic and do not act out except for the neurotic actions and covert exhibitionism that are part of their symptomatology. This was certainly true of Lucy, who was the model of conformity. She idealized the analyst and analysis and devoted herself to treatment. However, there was an immediate overinvolvement that reminded one of Flarsheim's description of a patient (1975): "This was not a gradual developing transference but rather she brought it into the treatment situation fully formed and she just fitted me into it" (p. 156).

Although, or because, Lucy had suffered at the hands of a physically sadistic mother, she did not consciously feel such intense impulses to act as did Jill. The need for immediate gratification, the impulses to act, and the accompanying anger were there, but were completely repressed and denied. The very fact that her mother's behavior was so irrational seemed to be a help in the analysis. However ill Lucy was, it was not difficult for her to see that she was healthier than her mother.

She regained her menstrual periods and attained a normal weight in the first few months of treatment. This was obviously a transference reaction and not a meaningful response to understanding. The full-blown anorexia never returned, but on a number of occasions she missed periods and feared pregnancy. When disappointed in the analyst, she inclined toward involuntary anorexia (unconscious loss of appetite). Overtly, the analyst and analysis were idealized. Except for the early relative paucity of dreams and fantasy material, she appeared to be the ideal analysand who enjoys the introspective, observing role.

Parenthetically, some analysts assume such patients are ideal cases for psychoanalysis and proceed along conventional oedipal lines. They soon run into difficulty and give up in disgust, calling the patients unanalyzable. Anorexic young women all have had intense relationships with their fathers, who frequently have played a maternal role. These patients' primitive idealizations, in and out of the analytic transference, should not be mistaken for more mature libidinal interests.

Lucy evidenced the seemingly mature introspection characteristic of this type of anorexic. Such pseudointrospection is powered by the primitive, sadistic, somewhat fragmented superego and really is a sadistic self-dissection. In these patients, every self-observation is a self-judgment, just as every interpretation is a towering indictment. Early in treatment, the analyst interpreted that Lucy was using the analysis to excoriate herself as her mother had. It was easy for the analyst to demonstrate the fantasy that he would be transformed into an ideal mother-father who would give her everything she wanted if only she would conform. Such fantasies are the basis of my rejection of any outside limiting conceptualization of the analytic relationship. The idea of "working alliance" or "therapeutic alliance" is acceptable if it is seen as part of a positive transference, but it is unnecessary. If seen, as usually described, as separate from the transference, we will miss the potentially interpretable negative aspects of a seeming "alliance."

As the material evolved and she felt less constrained, violent memories and fantasies emerged. Lucy had inflicted violence on younger siblings in early latency. A multitude of oedipal-like fantasies that terminated with the mutilation or murder of mother or the "queen" were remembered and produced. She was surprised by an autocunnilingual fantasy that involved chewing and crushing her pubic bones. With the emergence of this and other fantasies, she panicked and feared that she would go crazy. She frequently saw herself as a monster or a maniac. Her associations would be interrupted by spontaneous fantasies of injuring the analyst or biting his penis. She would dream of self-tortures, of losing her breasts, and of slicing off the breasts of older women.

Memories of altered states of consciousness emerged. As a child, when pressed by her overwhelming anger at mother, she would "white out." A white screen would blank out everything in her consciousness. At times, this would be preceded by an instantaneous fantasy of decapitating her mother. At one point, this was reproduced as part of an Isakower phenomenon as she was going to sleep. Certain associations seemed to link the fantasy to both the breast and milk. It seemed related to the dream screen and probably represented the repaired and unmutilated breast.

As her superego constraints lifted, Lucy began to act out, but primarily with her family. She provoked battles with mother that on several occasions almost terminated the analysis. She verbally repeated the physical battles of infancy with her siblings. On three different occasions, she exposed herself to, and unconsciously tried to provoke, attack and rape. Like Jill, she would try to blame such acting out on the analyst.

Both patients constantly tried to manipulate and control analysis and analyst. Jill did so overtly, with her temper tantrums, withholding, and contemptuous judgments. At first, Lucy did so by conforming and being the "good" girl; then (still fairly early in analysis) she switched to pseudosexual seduction. This erotic negative transference was interpreted in the context of the controlling aggression involved. These manipulations involved both projections and projective identifications, and replicated the early relationship with mother.

Unlike most anorexic patients, Lucy did not experience a profound depression shortly before or after giving up her symptoms since that occurred so early in treatment. Her most depressed period occurred after about a year of analysis. Overt suicidal wishes appeared, as they invariably do in anorexic patients. Acting out of self-destructive impulses continued, but with much more conscious awareness of the intent. The desires to manipulate the analyst, to terminate or kill the analytic relationship, and to annihilate the analyst were repeatedly interpreted.

Both Jill and Lucy completed generally satisfactory psychoanalyses of their neuroses with their phallic and oedipal conflicts. The usual oedipal transference neuroses evolved and replaced the more primitive defensive postures. The violence of Lucy's activities and fantasies was emphasized as the "here-and-now" nature of the sadistic impulses was interpreted.

CASE 3   *Denial: Aided or Analyzed in the Transference?*

Twenty-three-year-old Flora had been in unsuccessful treatment for a number of years with an analyst who followed the general scheme of psychoanalytically oriented authoritarian and supportive psychotherapy. She had been in a hospital setting for a period of time, as her analyst and other therapists believed that analysis is unwarranted and that pregnancy fantasies have nothing to do with anorexia nervosa. For whatever reason, there had been extensive general discussions of these matters on the ward and later in treatment. Fun was poked at the very idea that pregnancy fantasies might be important in anorexia.

After only four months with a new analyst, Flora related spontaneously the onset of her preoccupation with weight to the birth of her brother. She commented that she could not remember the mother at the time. The analyst only commented, "or her weight?"

Flora utilized defensive, split-off states of consciousness that were not as loud and violent as Jill's, but were just as difficult to penetrate. She would use sarcasm with a particular sing-song voice that replicated certain of mother's conversations when she was an infant.

She fell into a temporarily impenetrable state at this moment. "Oh there you go. They told us that you big silly analysts believed in foolish things like pregnancy fantasies." After her long sarcastic lecture, the analyst pointed out that he had never mentioned "pregnancy fantasy" in her treatment and repeated the three words, "or her weight." This brought forth more sarcasm and further information about her earlier hospitalization and treatment.

That night she had a dream about being pregnant. It surprised her, but she refused to discuss it during the following hour. There was further sarcasm and absolute accusations that the analyst had planted the seed for the dream (impregnated her?).

A few weeks later, at a time when she was doing some creative work which she consciously associated with childbirth, she talked of feeling fat one day and thin the next—as though she had "lost something." She laughed and volunteered, "aborted." She allowed her associations to go back to the birth of her sibling, her concern over her mother's weight, the previous sessions, and the dream. She recalled feigned childhood illnesses which included fantasies of oral impregnation associated with disgust and vomiting.

It was impressive that the authoritarian attitudes of her previous analyst had not allowed for spontaneous expression of fantasies, but had willfully inhibited them in advance. However, when analysis allowed the fantasy life and the transference to unfold spontaneously, the defense against and the preoccupation with pregnancy emerged together.

It almost appeared as though the earlier denial involving ward conversations and her therapist had interpreted to her the idea which organized itself and emerged in the newly recognized transference. What countertransference material allowed the previous analyst to not only reject analysis but to bring up such fantasies to the patient and deny them categorically before the patient brought up the subject, is not known. Lest the reader assume that the entire construction is in the mind of the patient, it should be added that other sources confirm that the institution in question does adopt this attitude.

SUMMARY

A brief review of some of the literature on transference was offered here. Transference in general and transference in anorexia nervosa were delineated. It was concluded that transference is ubiquitous and exists in every human relationship. Analysis only demonstrates its extreme and uses it to reconstruct the past in treatment. Since it is ubiquitous, no limiting concepts such as extratransference "working alliance," "therapeutic alliance," etc., make any sense unless they are conceptualized as part of the positive transference. Most authors place them outside that realm. This conceptualization is of therapeutic importance, as the content of the positive transference of today (working alliance, etc.) may be part of the negative, hostile, or erotic transference of tomorrow.

There is a continuum of transference experience and fantasy from the most primitive, fragmented dyadic reactions to the most sophisticated, triadic oedipal constellations. There is not a qualitative jump from narcissistic transference to transference neurosis. This transference continuum corresponds to a similar continuum in object relations.

"The final common pathway" of anorexia nervosa symptomatology can occur in hysterical, obsessional, or depressive personality types. It can also occur in narcissistic characters, borderline characters, and people with transient psychotic states. However, in my experience, it seems that once the self-destructive symptomatology of anorexia nervosa has been worked through and given up, there is more flexibility and spontaneity in the psychoanalytic relationship than there is in that with patients who have transient psychoses or borderline or narcissistic characters.

Anorexia nervosa is a symptomatic representation of particular pregenital defenses and is a regression from an intense oedipal conflict. It involves a return to an ambivalent relationship with a maternal figure toward whom the patient maintains a masochistic, submissive, and controlling relationship. Part-self and part-object representations from this past are elements of the life, as well as the analytic transference reactions, of the anorexic patient. On the surface, control is achieved by submission and masochistic sacrifice. Unconsciously, it represents sadistic, immobilizing, and killing impulses.

Two case histories of patients with ostensibly contrasting personality configurations illustrated the nature of these repressed and denied impulses and wishes. One patient immediately displayed the narcissistic triad of "vanity, exhibitionism, and arrogant ingratitude" (Gedo 1977). The other initially displayed apparent submission and constrained, cooperative interest in analysis. Both had repressed and denied their primitive hostility and their wishes to control the primitive, primary object representation and its current representation, the analyst. Projections, projective identifications, and introjective identifications gave rise to isolations, fragmentations, and split-off ego states that had to be identified and understood. Attempts to control and provoke the analyst by acting out, temper tantrums, and contemptuous superiority represented the earlier relationship with mother, which had been preserved by internalized part-self and part-object representations. As such defensive postures were identified and worked through, symptoms were given up and the underlying masochistic and sadistic fantasies became available for analysis.

After the self-destructive and sadistic infantile conflicts with mother were analyzed and worked through in the transference, the phallic and oedipal concerns emerged. The typical triadic transference neurosis surfaced and analysis could proceed in the usual fashion.

A third case illustrated how a classically handled transference can uncover pregnancy concerns which had previously been denied. It was apparent that the denial had been reinforced by countertransference manipulations of the therapist and the treatment milieu.

8
Contrasts in the Analysis of Bulimic and Abstaining Anorexics

C. PHILIP WILSON, M.D.

Freudian psychoanalysts, Sperling (1978), Thomä (1967), and the contributors to this volume all include bulimia under the diagnostic category of anorexia nervosa. Boskind-Lodahl (1976) coined the useful term bulimarexia to indicate that bulimia and anorexia nervosa are manifestations of a basic syndrome. Various nonpsychoanalytic researchers have described bulimic behavior in anorexic patients. In a recent article reviewing bulimia research, Mitchell and Pyle (1982) note that bulimic behavior occurred in 16 to 47% of anorexic patients. They observe that the current DSM-III exclusion of bulimia from the diagnostic category of anorexia nervosa was published prior to current articles on the subject. However, neither such a recent article on bulimia nor the DSM-III diagnosis include the psychoanalytic studies of Thomä (1967) and Sperling (1978). Nonanalytic research on bulimia is of limited value because of the lying and withholding of bulimarexic patients (Chapter 9, this volume). Frequently in the initial history these patients report no conflict with their menses just as they deny conflict in other areas such as psychosexual functioning. In the course of analysis they report phases of amenorrhea, and they reveal that during their sexual relations they depersonalize and have little or no pleasurable feeling.

A recent study by Strober (1982) utilizes psychometric and interview techniques to compare two matched groups of adolescent female anorexics. He concludes that, relative to the abstaining anorexics, the bulimics evidence higher levels of core anorexic symptomatology and are more likely to show affective disturbance and alcohol use. They evidence more instability and behavioral deviance in childhood. There is more conflict in the family and less cohesion and structure in the family unit. The parents have histories of marital discord and a higher incidence of psychiatric problems. Strober hypothesizes that bulimia is rooted in early disturbances in ego functioning, personality development, and other maladaptive factors, and concludes that the pathological effects of psychological, genetic, and physiological factors on appetite-control mechanisms deserve further investigation. The findings of this research

169

on the differences between bulimics and abstainers correlate with our case material and that of Sours (1980). Bruch (1978b) notes that although treatment conditions and problems vary from one anorexic case to another, the most difficult cases are the bulimics, because they are the most "dishonest and deceitful" patients.

In my experience the most difficult and refractory anorexic patients are the chronic bulimarexics: those with a long-standing history of fasting, gorging, and self-induced vomiting. The abstaining anorexics do not gorge, vomit, or take laxatives. Their unconscious impulses are controlled by a strict, archaic superego. Their ego controls function to prevent aggressive or libidinal gratification. The bulimic patients have a less strict, although rigid, superego which is periodically upset by phases of gorging, impulsive acting out, and/or addiction to cigarettes, drugs, and alcohol.

I have analyzed four cases as well as seeing many more in consultation and supervision. One adolescent who alternately abstained, gorged, and vomited, resolved her conflicts in a year's analysis. She was neither amenorrheic nor dangerously underweight. The treatment prevented the development of phobic fear of being fat (anorexia nervosa). Both the second and third cases abstained, gorged, and vomited, but they did not use laxatives. Neither brought their weight down to dangerous levels. Diagnostically they suffered from mixed neuroses with severe preoedipal conflicts. Both patients, unlike the typical abstaining anorexic, had an abundant psychosexual fantasy life and had masturbated in childhood. Doubts have been expressed to me by experienced analysts about the possibility of analyzing any bulimic.* Cases I've analyzed and supervised have experienced a full resolution of their fear-of-being-fat body-image and their obsession with being thin. Long-term follow-up studies in certain cases showed that they were able to face and master the conflicts of self-fulfillment in a career, pregnancy, childbirth, and motherhood. In my experience, if the bulimic anorexic process can be analyzed *in statu nascendi* as in my first case, the prognosis is excellent. However, a longer and more complicated treatment is required for chronic adult bulimics, as I document in the fourth case. Of course, statements about prognosis must be qualified by the psychodynamic diagnosis of the individual case and by the presenting situation. Obviously if the addicted bulimic is seen when acutely alcoholic and/or under the influence of drugs, all the technical problems involved in the management and treatment of such cases confront the therapist.

CASE 1 *Chronic Anorexia with Bulimia and Vomiting*

The following case report highlights the transference and countertransference problems in the analysis of a bulimarexic who for many months kept her weight at near half normal, a level that many therapists (Bruch 1973, Thomä 1967) would insist requires mandatory hospitalization and emergency medical treatment.

Elaine, a 28-year-old woman, came for consultation after undergoing a long and expensive hospitalization with behavioral modification treatment that failed

---

* Aspects of the effective analysis of bulimic anorexic cases are presented in Chapters 1–9.

to resolve her anorexia. The history revealed chronic anorexia nervosa with symptoms of gorging, vomiting, and excessive use of laxatives dating back five years to the time of her father's death.

PATIENT'S HISTORY. Elaine's family was of Irish Catholic cultural background. The youngest of two girls, Elaine had been a model child, bright and precocious. As children, the daughters had differed markedly in appearance: Elaine's three-year-older sister had been blue-eyed, slender, and tall, whereas Elaine had been brown-eyed, chubby, and short. As an adult, Elaine thought of herself as "dumpy and fat," despite her awareness that men were very attracted to her. Photographs from her adolescence showed her to have been very attractive, with a sexy, almost voluptuous figure. Elaine, who was 5'2", always had envied her tall, slender sister. During her anorexia, she felt she looked beautiful at half her normal weight.

Elaine had been weaned from the breast at one and one-half years and bowel-trained before her second year. Throughout childhood, she had been so severely constipated that at times she had been given laxatives. Frequently, she would sit on the toilet and strain for up to half an hour. Walking, talking, and other motor functions had been normal. Severe nail-biting and cuticle-chewing dated back to Elaine's earliest years. She had phobias of heights and closed spaces. During adolescence, when agitated, Elaine would bite her toenails and toe cuticles, which caused serious local toe infections. In late adolescence, because of intense shame at the appearance of her hands, she had stopped nail-biting, but she then became a chain-smoker. As an adult, she was very proud of her long, curved fingernails.

Elaine's mother was a 60-year-old woman from a conservative Midwestern family who devoted her time to her husband, home, and daughters. She was in good health, but was preoccupied with fears of being fat and was always going on and off diets, although she was actually never more than 10 lbs. overweight. She was a chain-smoker. Elaine's father had been an American success story—a man from an immigrant Irish Catholic family who had built a small construction company into a very successful statewide business. He had been a hard-working man who doted on his daughters, but was away from the family much of the time because of his business. He had been in good health except for infrequent headaches, probably migraines. A chain-smoker, he had died of lung cancer during Elaine's 22nd year after a year's illness and a painful period of hospitalization. He had been a stoical man who never complained and did not like or go to doctors. His cancer had been diagnosed after it had metastasized. Elaine had bitterly mourned her father and wished that it had been her mother instead. After her father's funeral, she began dieting and in a period of three weeks lost one-third of her body weight. She then began an endless cycle of abstaining, vomiting, gorging, and excessive laxative use. For several months preceding the development of the anorexia, she had hardly talked to her mother; after developing anorexic symptoms, she had become close to her mother again.

Elaine had done well in grade school and high school, but had experienced extreme anxiety taking examinations. She was very sensitive to criticism and studied hard. In adolescence, she had shown musical ability and had attended a 2-year college, where she majored in music. Although she had developed into a promising young pianist, she had felt "unreal" about a musical career and had taken a series of jobs largely at a secretarial level with the goal of becoming a business executive.

Elaine had not masturbated in childhood and was inhibited about sexual matters. She had been frightened by a vertical scar on the abdomen of her aunt, which she had been told was caused by an operation after her "aunt's insides fell out" because of childbirth. At age 12, Elaine had had menarche, for which she was unprepared. In adolescence, she had had crushes on boys, been very popular, and had many dates. For several years, she had had intercourse with guilt and fear, using no contraceptives. She had been afraid to see a gynecologist, terrified of pregnancy, and constantly had watched her stomach for any swelling. She thought she would kill herself if she got pregnant. In late adolescence, after she had "gotten the pill" from a gynecologist, she had not worried so much about her periods or pregnancy. A close adolescent friend had been a sexy, precociously mature, rebellious classmate who had already had intercourse at age 12. The two girls had arranged double dates. Elaine frequently had disobeyed the family curfew rules and her father had criticized her for it. He also had disapproved of her first romance, which had led her to break it off. She had enjoyed visits from her father at college. When he would take her out, "it was like a date." As a young woman, she had had many boyfriends, several of whom wanted to marry her, but "something stopped her from marriage." Following her father's death, she had moved to another town, worked as a store manager, and begun an affair with her boss, a young married man. She had developed severe flu and been nursed back to health by her boss's wife, a close friend of hers. On recovery of her health, Elaine had moved back to her hometown.

THERAPY.* Underneath Elaine's compliant cooperative manner of relating to the analyst was the mistrust, suspicion, and hostility characteristic of patients who have undergone behavior modification therapy (Bruch 1974). In spite of the analyst's attempts to interpret her ego's defenses against admitting to negative feelings about him, Elaine denied any resentment, but soon forced her weight down to near half normal. She revealed that she had used hidden lead weights to fool the hospital staff into thinking that behavior modification had been successful.

After leaving the hospital, Elaine had become almost a recluse, living alone in her apartment, not looking for work, and seeing few people except for her mother, whom she talked to or saw daily. She spent most of her time fasting, gorging, vomiting, and taking laxatives. She said she would rather kill herself than go back into the hospital, as she felt her lengthy and expensive hospitalizations had been worthless and "a rip-off." Her medical treatment was with an internist, who prescribed dietary supplements. Gradually, the analyst ac-

---

* Each of the interpretations cited in the cases in this chapter exemplifies a series or a line of interpretations that was applied systematically as the defenses of the ego (denial, rationalization, belief in magic, acting out) unfolded. At times, because of space limitations, there has been a condensation of multiple interpretations.

quainted Elaine with her masochism and interpreted her defenses against admitting to her anger toward, and mistrust of, her previous therapist, the hospital doctors, and him. She began to come out of her isolation and consider work and socializing. Each of the following interpretations exemplifies a line of interpretation that was applied systematically as the defenses of the ego—denial, splitting, rationalization, belief in magic, acting in, and acting out—unfolded.

After the analyst's vacation break, Elaine said that she did not like his return, as she had done well at business school and had met a nice man who took her dancing. Away from sessions, she felt free; in her sessions, she felt strangled and hated treatment. The analyst interpreted her displacement; it was not the "treatment" she hated, but him. She left the office visibly angry and did not come to her next session. In the subsequent hour, she talked of how much she wanted praise; she had not come to the last hour because she was angry at the analyst for not praising her. In the next session, she accused the analyst of being cold and machinelike. She associated to hysterical symptoms that had been precipitated by smoking pot, by receiving anesthesia at the dentist, and by dating certain aggressive men. The analyst interpreted to her her fear of emotions and her excessive need to control. During the next week she revealed that she was dating more, stating, "I don't like European men who flatter and wine and dine me, but plain down-to-earth American men don't ask me out."

A second theme was her struggle with her studies: "Yesterday I came home so angry I was ready to jump out the window. Can I make an A grade? I hate myself. Nothing is ever good enough. I will never be satisfied. I do not know whom to hate more—you or the damn school." The analyst interpreted to her that she could face anger and did not have to get rid of it by not coming to sessions or by binging and vomiting. Elaine responded by saying that the longer she came to the analyst, the sicker she felt. She demanded that he change her hour because she "had to" go with her mother for their periodic visit to her senile maternal grandmother in a nursing home. The analyst asked Elaine why she had to go; perhaps her mother could go alone. Elaine became very upset and angry. The analyst also pointed out that, if it was so important to her, she could ask mother to visit at another time that would not conflict with her session. Elaine snapped, "The plans are already made," and did not come for her session.

On her return, she talked of how useless it was to visit her grandmother. She stated that her mother had once wet her panties (had been enuretic) in the car going to the nursing home. The analyst interpreted that Elaine had identified with her mother's extreme control. Elaine associated to mother's denial of all conflict; mother always had pretended that everything was all right, but it hadn't been. She was strict about manners and taught the children that yelling and getting angry were wrong. Control was the reigning word. Elaine had tried to be what her parents wanted, but it was not her.

In the next hour, Elaine bitterly criticized the analyst, saying that the analysis was psychological double-talk and that he did nothing for her. She had been anorexic for five years and so what? Near the end of the hour, she got up from the couch and went to the bathroom. She did not refer to her behavior in the next session, but subsequently said that she had felt nauseous and had thrown up in the toilet. The analyst told her that it was him and what he had said that she had gotten rid of by vomiting. She replied that she was sick and tired of living, that she affected no one's life and had no reason to be alive. The analyst interpreted to her that, in order not to know of her anger toward her mother and him, she was trying to kill herself with her use of laxatives—no one knew the lethal dose of Dulcolax and no drug company would do experiments with humans such as those she was carrying out on herself. Elaine left, slamming the door to the waiting room.

In the next session, she said she had been to her internist, her lab tests were better, but her potassium was still low. The analyst interpreted to her some of her denial of suicidal behavior. He said that she vitiated her internist's careful diet advice and the absorption of food and medication by her habits, that she denied making him and the analyst medically concerned about her, and that neither the internist nor the analyst would be surprised if she became sick and forced hospitalization.

In the following hour, Elaine was silent for 30 minutes; the analyst interpreted to her her strict perfectionistic conscience, stating that she controlled speech to avoid conflict if she talked, and that she vomited and took laxatives to avoid conflicts about being a woman and having a "figure." Elaine associated to having been a proficient ballet student—the best in her class. One day, she had had an anxiety attack and had given up dancing. At the end of the session, Elaine mentioned almost casually that her periods, which she had not had for years, had returned. The analyst's counterreaction was to feel that she was making more progress than she admitted to, but that she was denying emotions and conflicts about her periods. He also was resentful of her for withholding conscious information about such an important symptomatic improvement.

A series of sessions followed in which Elaine reported dreams and spontaneously associated to them. One dream was about her father. Her associations centered on the theme of her parents' reactions to her: father had appreciated her abilities, but mother had not. After reporting a nightmarish dream of being sent to prison, she associated to her favorite childhood story of Goldilocks intruding into the three bears' home and to her own feelings of sexual frustration. The analyst interpreted her guilt over sexual feelings and suggested that one purpose of keeping her weight so low was to punish herself by becoming unattractive sexually. Elaine's thoughts went to her father; he had had a bad back, but used to play tennis. She commented that she had been so strong, she had been an "athletic freak." Father had loved sports: he had gone to prize fights, watched football, and taken her to tennis tournaments. She used to love dancing with father at parties. He had been such a smooth dancer, incredible; he had been the life of the party. She turned to thoughts of diving, stating that she now went in the water feet first because it scared her to go in head first. She was afraid at the dentist's office because she couldn't see what he was doing. "I was told all my life a model falls face up; protect your face and hands."

At this point, the analyst informed her that the time was up. She had lost track of the time, which was uncharacteristic. She said as she left, "You should take advantage of it when I have things to say I may never say again." The analyst's counterreactions were that she was teasing him by giving him some apparently spontaneous associations, but that she really was after approval and control. He thought that she was telling him that if he gave her extra time, she would reveal herself to him. Such withholding and sadistic teasing with bits of information that the patient knows the analyst wants to hear is a characteristic anorexic resistance that can provoke intense countertransference reactions.

In the next session, Elaine reported a repetitive dream of a wall cracking; it was located in the family's old apartment. She had had the dream 15 years before, 8 years before, and once in the hospital. The old apartment had 16-foot ceilings. The room in the dream was the one in which Elaine and her sister had slept until the latter had gone away to boarding school. The room they shared had been big and nice, but Elaine had feared that someone would come in to get her. For many years as an adult, she had feared that someone would come onto her terrace and get her. In adolescence, she had had growing pains and mother had elevated her legs. The cracking reminded her of a mirror cracking. Her fear had been that someone would come through the glass window in her bedroom and get her. Her sister never had been in the dream. The interpretation was made that she felt she should be punished for having hostile thoughts about her sister. Elaine cried and said, "Cracked must mean crazy, murderous thoughts I had about my sister as a little girl."

In the next hour, Elaine resumed her cigarette smoking, which she had interrupted in sessions to try to uncover the impulses and fantasies it masked. The analyst interpreted to her that she must be afraid that if she did not smoke she would return to nail-biting; that, as a little girl, she had felt guilty and miserable at having anger toward her sister and had taken it out on herself in her habit. Elaine burst into tears and said that her sister could be so mean; she would tease Elaine, but Elaine never would fight back. In the next hour, she talked of visiting her mother: "Mother is bored to tears, says her teeth hurt, she is always going to give up cigarettes, she is always complaining about stupid little things; I wish she would die and get it over with. Mother's friend just had a breast removed for cancer." Elaine became silent and tense. The analyst interpreted to her that she tried to control thoughts and feelings magically by not talking and by cigarette smoking and her anorexic habits. Elaine said that it was all the same—the nail-biting, cigarettes, and anorexia were "a mish-mosh." The interpretation was made that she had to have conscious control—by putting her fingers and cigarettes in her mouth, her fingers down her throat to vomit, and laxatives in her mouth to control her bowels—but tried to make a mystery of her habits. Elaine's reply was: "Until 10 years of age, I had to sleep with light coming through the door of my room. I must have been afraid to be alone."

In the next session, she was silent for 20 minutes, and her need to control was again interpreted. She then burst out:

> The whole thing is mother. I am torturing her and can't stop, it is so stupid, I am getting back at her for all the things that were not her fault. I blame her for everything. I feel sorry for her, she is my victim. She doesn't know that I wind her around my little finger. I wonder if she does know. I tell her, don't give me things, but she does anyway. Everything ended when father died; he was the generator. Mother has done nothing since. You don't understand what I feel when I am cynical and bitter; everyone is divorced and bitter, few people are

happy. I gave up graduate school because I could not be the best. I think if my mother died all my symptoms would clear up.

The interpretation was made that, by hanging onto her habits, she wished to wrap the analyst, as well as the mother, around her little finger, and that she preferred the humiliation of her habits to the anxiety, guilt, anger, and fear of her neurosis, which she thought she hid from people. Furthermore, her symptoms and neurosis would not magically clear up if her mother died.

For the next sessions, which were prior to the analyst's vacation, Elaine dreamed of being late, and of her father being alive again and telling her to be on time. Her associations were to father's getting her up in the morning and to her not having feelings about the analyst's vacation. Indeed, she stated she was glad that he was going. Interpretations of her denial of anger at being left and not being able to control the analyst led to her thoughts that he was the father who would make her be on time in the dream. In a depressed voice, she said, "All of life and treatment mean nothing. The other day, after leaving, I thought of killing myself with sleeping pills." She laughed bitterly and added, "I'd probably botch that up like everything else." Interpretations were made of her need to control emotions. The analyst pointed out that depressed feelings could be faced—that they would not last forever, although it might feel as if they would. Elaine cried as she left the session. In this, the second year of her analysis, her weight was still below normal. However, she had improved; her periods had returned, and she was looking for work and was socializing.

When treatment resumed in the fall, Elaine said her vacation had been terrible; she had been angry with the analyst most of the time. "I can't face you and I can't face the laxative pills. I think of interrupting them to see what I think about and dream of, but I get angry and want to change all at once. My mother comes by and grabs at me. She is depressed. I've not seen her or called her so much." In the next session, Elaine was silent and visibly upset. She asked the analyst what had transpired in the previous session. His interpretation began with a reconstruction of the previous session: he stated that Elaine had said that she had not tried to interrupt her habits to analyze the conflicts they masked because she still wanted to change immediately and all at once. Elaine's associations were that she used to binge when she felt depressed and that her sister seemed like a stranger to her. Elaine stated that recently she had felt that she was more mature and wiser than her mother. In addition, she felt less guilty about her rivalry with her sister.

In the next session, Elaine was silent for many minutes. She ended the session by saying that measuring progress in anorexia by weight gain was "a crock of shit" and that camouflaging her thin figure with carefully chosen clothes for dates was "going through the motions." In the next session, she was again silent, and her need to control was interpreted. She then reported a dream in which she was anorexic and naked, and "a creep of a guy" and a doctor laughed at her. She said she now hated being anorexic and was eating to put on weight. She now noticed tons of anorexics on the street and they were disgusting fakes. Recently, she had met an old friend and they had laughed together, reminiscing. She hadn't laughed so enjoyably in 10 years. In the next session,

Elaine was silent for 40 minutes. The interpretation was made that she kept avoiding the analysis of her laxative habit by not talking of it and that it was a daily masochistic punishment to control emotions. Elaine said, "I feel hostile to the world. I feel if I stop my habits, I'll explode." The interpretation was made that she could have angry thoughts without carrying them out.

In one session, Elaine reported thoughts and memories of her father. Once she had had a fight with him after defying his curfew. She had said, "Why don't you hit me so that will show your interest?" The night before the session she had interrupted her laxative taking. She recalled her severe constipation in childhood. Her thoughts turned to a babysitter who used to beat her and her sister if they misbehaved. Mother caught the sitter punishing them and fired her. Elaine recalled that mother once had slapped her on the face for making a critical remark. Then Elaine said: "There are times when you move, Doctor, or you lean forward, that I think you are going to hit me; then I think, but you are my analyst. That sitter we had, I hated her so much. She had two faces, one real sweet and the other a son of a bitch. She told me such weird things."

In the analyst's counterreactions to Elaine's stubborn acting in and acting out, which included routinely coming to her sessions 15–20 minutes late, he felt like shouting at her and shaking her. He felt that he was reacting to her as one would to a stubborn, negativistic, provocative 3-year-old child. He also noted that she repeatedly provoked wishes in him to spank her or throw her out. The interpretation was made that, in analysis, she was recreating the battle for control that she had had with her nurse and parents. The analyst told her of the hostile feelings and fantasies she had stirred up in him. Elaine was silent and then said: "You know, my father was so controlled when he was angry, but he was shouting at me from underneath." In the following session, she reported a dream: "I was shouting at me." Her thoughts were of perfectionistic demands of herself and others. An interpretation was made of her identification with her father's excessive self-control. Her associations were to her father's illness, how thin and weak he had become; she left the session crying.

DISCUSSION. At the end of this phase of analysis, Elaine was putting on weight, her severe regression had lifted, and—most importantly—her body image had changed. She now hated both her own figure and the figures of other anorexic women. This change occurred before the oedipal aspects of her neurosis were analyzed. She could see that her nightmare of the cracked wall reflected conflicts about uncontrollable rage, but oedipal sexual fears about the female crack, the vagina, did not emerge until later. She had resumed her periods, but resisted exploring her pregnancy fears for another year, at which time she recalled sadomasochistic fantasies she had had about the scar on her aunt's abdomen. The changes in Elaine seemed to result from the analysis of her defenses against admitting to emotions and conflicts, particularly in the transference, with the liberation of anger and depression in sessions. Sperling (1955b) suggests that the occurrence of a "psychotic transference" in the analysis of such patients is not unusual and states that, although the relative strengths or weaknesses of the ego are important, the relationship with the analyst is the most potent force in the reconstruction or construction of the ego.

The turning point in Elaine's therapy was when she told the analyst of her fear that he would hit her. He then revealed to her his counterreactions and she dreamt of shouting at herself, which was an indication of her growing insight into her strict superego and her projective identifications. In Giovacchini's (1979) words, such patients recreate "a psychoanalytic ambience that is an approximate reproduction of the infantile environment . . . the analyst has to realize this state of affairs and be at times more intuitive, live with the patient's anger and complaints, and study his counterreactions and countertransference" (p. 475). Patience is essential in the analysis of addictive patients, whose habits, at their most primitive level, mask preverbal conflicts and traumas. Impulsive, psychotic, and psychosomatic patients, all of whom have preoedipal conflicts, have the means to communicate the impact and effects of their early preverbal traumas (Wilson 1968c, 1971, 1981; Chapter 2, this volume).

In analyzing habits, one has to be intuitive as to when to confront patients with their not bringing up the habit for analysis. One cannot ask them about it constantly or demand that they give up the habit. One should point out the reason for interrupting habits (i.e., to uncover fantasies and conflicts that are masked by the habit). Like obese patients, anorexic patients want and believe in magical control and want to stop the habit totally without analyzing it. The defensive purposes of habits, which mask suicidal and homicidal impulses and conflicts, have to be repeatedly interpreted. Some critics suggest that this induces masochistic transference in psychosomatic patients. However, if the analyst does not actively interpret and confront patients with the meanings of their psychosomatic symptoms and habits that serve defensive purposes, the symptoms and habits will become more intense, while patients' treatment behavior will continue to be too pleasant and nice. In the session where Elaine was silent for 40 minutes, the analyst made the interpretation about her laxative habit because she had not mentioned it for many sessions. Her associative responses confirmed the correct timing of his interpretation.

Gradually, basic changes were occurring in her body image and in her attitudes toward her symptoms. She noted with surprise that she had formerly thought herself to be beautiful when she weighed 52 lbs. Repeated interpretation of the unconscious reasons for inflicting such narcissistic mortification on herself was necessary (Eidelberg 1957, 1959). Elaine's acting out around time was intense: often, her response to an interpretation was to miss a session without even a phone call. The analyst realized that part of her anger was about her previous treatment, but when it reached the extent of not coming for two successive sessions and not calling, he pointed out her denial of reality and avoidance of emotions and emphasized that he would not go on seeing her if she was not responsible for her hours. If she felt she could not come, she should call him. Her response was to devalue the analyst by saying that he was paid anyway. He interpreted to her that she denied his interest in treating her. A second line of interpretation was that she treated him like food, which she unconsciously equated with the mother of the nursing phase. In the transference neurosis the analyst became an addiction (Flarsheim 1975), and she expected him to be available to her always, no matter what she did. Her response was to cry and say the analyst was throwing her out. He told her that she was blocking treatment and that he would refer her to another analyst, but that any experienced therapist would make the same request. Following this confrontation, Elaine stopped this aspect of her acting out.

In the initial sessions, with Elaine's permission, the analyst talked to her internist, who said that her weight was at a potentially dangerous level. He had prescribed dietary supplements to bring her blood chemistry to normal. With Elaine's weight at such a potentially life-threatening level, the analyst had a series of counterreactions: (1) Should he insist on hospitalization? (2) What was the lethal dose of Dulcolax? (3) Who else had treated patients at half their normal body weight? (4) What was the transference situation? The analyst consulted colleagues, who said that some of their anorexic patients had been at similar low weight levels. The analyst considered that Elaine had said she would kill herself rather than go into the hospital again. The negative transference was that described by Bruch (1974) in patients subjected to behavior modification. The analyst reflected that Elaine had agreed to analysis and was coming to sessions. He also knew that her negative feelings had not been interpreted in her hospital behavior modification therapy. The analyst learned of cases in which anorexic patients had taken up to 500 mg. of Dulcolax per day; there seemed to be no known lethal dosage of the medication. He considered what would happen with hospitalization. Hyperalimentation would increase her weight, but she would be released for treatment with more proof of her power to defeat the analyst by making him anxious. There did not seem to be any evidence of impairment of mental functioning secondary to starvation (Bruch 1982). Actually, in such regressed states, patients' denial and rationalization are so intense that the analyst can be deceived into thinking that this state of mental functioning is caused by the effects of starvation. The analyst made careful notes about his reasons for not hospitalizing Elaine, as he also was concerned about a possible malpractice suit if she died.

It is important for the analyst to differentiate between countertransference, which is unconscious and blind, and counterreactions, which are conscious reactions to a patient's situation. An important aspect of counterreactions is the normal concern for the patient as a physician and psychoanalyst. Analysts have to let themselves feel and react to these patients much as surgeons do with emergency cases. The key considerations for Elaine's analyst's decision were that she had agreed to treatment and was coming to sessions, and that he had the backing of her mother. It is important for the analyst to talk with colleagues who have treated such cases, to read the relevant literature, and to consult with other specialists. Once a decision has been made to proceed with analysis, it must be carried out boldly, but with awareness of the risks involved. The analyst will be stubbornly and perpetually tested by the patient. Some bulimics will abruptly stop analysis or go to another therapist, just when they have achieved basic healthy changes in ego functioning and body image. Unanalyzed residues of anger at behavior modification therapy are a frequent cause of this acting out.

CASE 2   Hospitalization for Anorexic Crisis

A 25-year-old woman was seen in consultation in the hospital. She was under combined psychiatric and medical treatment that included Thorazine and nutritional supplements. The history revealed that the anorexia of four months duration had developed after Frances terminated an affair, during which she had not used any contraceptives. She manifested symptoms of insomnia, fasting, amenorrhea, and difficulties in concentration while working. She had gone for office psychotherapy for three months prior to hospitalization. She had liked the psychiatrist, but symptomatically had gone downhill. She had developed suicidal fears of killing herself with a razor and had refused to eat anything but a little ice cream. When seen on the ward, she was being tube-fed per the nasal passage. The parents were seen together in consultation and, at the analyst's request, wrote up their observations on their daughter.

PATIENT'S HISTORY.   Frances was the second of two girls. Following a normal pregnancy, the mother had been unable to nurse Frances because of a fever of unknown origin. Frances was described as a "good baby," but she developed hair-pulling at age two, which continued until age three. A psychiatric consultation at that time yielded no specific therapeutic recommendations. At first, Frances had been a good eater, but then became difficult, forcing the mother to devise games to feed her. She was phobic about new situations such as getting haircuts, meeting strangers, entering stores, and taking train rides. Fire engines and ambulance sirens frightened her. She showed an early musical talent. A school phobia had appeared when she started kindergarten. The mother had stayed in school with her until she adjusted. At age five, Frances had reacted to the birth of a sister by hiding and crying. Analysis revealed that she had no preparation for the birth. From that time on, she had had a fear of hospitals. She had been an excellent student. The mother described her as "a complex, fearful, but basically cheerful child."

In the latency years, she had shown strong tomboy wishes, rejected frilly feminine clothes, and insisted on boys' clothes. She had played all contact sports, including touch football, and had been extremely competitive with boys. From three to nine, she had had a good friend, an effeminate boy three years her senior, who had played endlessly with her, inventing games, dressing up, and making believe. In later years, the boy had been used as a babysitter. Although on the surface, Frances was a conscientious older sister, she actually had been jealous and envious of her younger sibling until her college years. Throughout childhood, Frances had not been a big eater. During her college years, she had been 30 lbs. underweight.

At high school, Frances had had few friends and had not been close to any of her teachers; nor had she had any dates or crushes on boys. She had no memory of masturbation. She had been very conscientious about her studies, getting up at 4:30 A.M. to review her homework. She had excelled in sports and had enjoyed music and art. She had chosen a women's college to avoid problems of dating. Scholastically, she had done well at college and had gone on to graduate school, where she began to date.

Her first serious affair had eventuated in intercourse but had been marred by intense arguments because she refused to use any contraceptives. During the affair, she had begun to develop symptoms of anxiety, insomnia, hyperactivity, and anorexia nervosa. These symptoms had worsened until her roommate forced her to seek treatment. She had been in supportive therapy for three months before being hospitalized. In the hospital, she did not want to see members of her family and would not take any advice from them. The family had sought the consultation.

The father was a compulsive professional man who said that he "could not stand children." The mother was also compulsive. She had enjoyed many interests prior to marriage—e.g., biking, music, skiing—but had "given them up" for the sake of her husband. She was a strict disciplinarian at home. When deeply provoked, she would slap the children on the face.

PSYCHODYNAMIC HOSPITAL TREATMENT.   When first seen in the hospital, Frances was walking around the locked ward pushing an intravenous apparatus. With typical anorexic denial of conflict, she did not reply to questions. The analyst introduced himself, informing her that her parents had asked him to see her because he was an anorexia specialist. She made no reply and tried not to look at him. He told her that the problem in his work with her would be for them to find out why she felt forced to starve herself to death. She again made no reply. The next day, when the analyst came in to see her, she thrust her arm at him, saying in an angry voice, "Look what those interns did to me!" The intravenous needle had come out and her arm was black-and-blue and swollen from repeated attempts to reinsert the needle. The analyst had talked with the nurse and residents, who said that Frances had fought off their attempts to reinsert the needle. The analyst interpreted to the patient that her conscience was so strict that she could not admit to anger, that she fought with the residents but had to deny it. She burst out, "The nurses and interns are fascists!" The analyst made the interpretation that he knew the staff members were concerned with her health; that anyone who tried to control her made her angry, but her conscience did not permit anger. Her associations were to childhood; she had a "funny" memory that at eight years of age she had cut her sister with some scissors. The analyst asked her if she could remember her sister's reactions or what had caused the incident. Frances could not recall anything more. The analyst interpreted to her that her conscience was so strict that she could not remember mother's anger or her own, just as she disapproved of her own and the intern's aggression.

The analyst had a conference with the attending physician and informed him that Frances was developing a positive therapeutic relation. He asked the physician if he could delay on hyperalimentation, which was being considered because Frances's weight was near half normal. He said he could wait for a week. Then the analyst met with the hospital staff and explained that he wanted all attempts to encourage Frances to eat stopped because he wanted to make Frances responsible for her eating.

The next session, the analyst told Frances that as soon as she put on enough weight, she could leave the hospital and come to his office for analytic therapy, that behind her anorexic symptoms she had conflicts about men, marriage, pregnancy, and childbirth. She made no reply, but talked about her boyfriend who was coming to the hospital to see her; she did not want to see him as he upset her. The analyst interpreted to her that her way of dealing with conflict was to avoid it: food upset her, so she didn't eat; her boyfriend bothered her, so she avoided him; the analyst told her things that angered her, so she ignored him. Frances said she would see her boyfriend, but he had pushed her too hard to get married. The analyst pointed out that she had begun dieting when she was dating him because she was afraid of getting pregnant. Frances said that she had avoided reading about pregnancy in adolescence, that she used to think that pregnancy came from kissing.

Frances began to eat and gain weight. She called the analyst at his office to ask permission to leave the hospital to do special exercises. The analyst interpreted to her that she was denying how ill she had made herself. The next day, the nurses told him she was fasting and losing weight again. She reported a dream of being given the intravenous feeding again, but would not associate to it. Interpretations were made that she was angry with the analyst for not letting her do anything she wanted, that she hoped to defeat him by being fed intravenously again.

The next session, she said that she had had a fight with her boyfriend, that he was too demanding. The analyst interpreted to her that she wanted to control her boyfriend and him totally. She reported dreams of skiing and of having her periods again. She began to eat and put on more weight. The foregoing emergency phase of therapy lasted three weeks; in the subsequent three weeks of hospital therapy, she evidenced a developing positive transference. The content of her sessions largely involved her conflicts with her boyfriend and her work, and the analyst continued to interpret her wishes to deny conflict and anger with him because of his confronting her with her neurosis. She stopped fasting, intravenous feeding was not necessary, and she put on enough weight so that she could be discharged for office analytic treatment.

THERAPY AFTER LEAVING THE HOSPITAL.   After discharge from the hospital, Frances immediately began analysis. However, from the start, the therapeutic approach in the hospital had been basically analytic. Contacts with relatives were confined to the initial interview. For further problems, the relatives were referred to another analyst. The issue of discharge arose in analytic sessions. The analyst had been careful, when stating that he felt Frances was ready for discharge, to ask for her opinion about discharge. She had tried to evade the issue and make him totally responsible. He had told her that she could control her eating if she chose to do so. Later, in office analysis, she accused the analyst of being hard-hearted because he had released such a weak, helpless patient and he again interpreted to her that she had had conscious control and that, if she had told him that she did not feel ready to leave the hospital, he would not have discharged her.

Soon after starting office analysis, while riding home on the subway at 1 A.M., Frances became embroiled in an argument with two intoxicated men who wanted her to have a drink with them. They threatened to beat her up if she did not join them and she was terrified of being assaulted and followed when she left the subway car at her station stop. She revealed in analysis that her friends and relatives had often warned her against taking the subway alone at such hours, but that she denied realistic dangers in this and other situations. Her massive denial of internal and external conflict was persistently interpreted. A transference meaning of this incident was interpreted; that she wanted to frighten the analyst and force him to rehospitalize her for protection from her impulsive behavior. Frances and her relatives had been forewarned that symptomatic improvement might occur quickly, but that long-term analysis was necessary. Frances quickly regained her normal weight and her menstrual periods. Her acute symptoms cleared, she went back to work, and she resumed her social life. It was at this time, six weeks after discharge, that the basic analytic task began. It is only possible to discuss selected aspects of the analysis, which was terminated successfully at the end of the third year.

Brief episodes of anorexia and hair-pulling occurred during the first year and were analyzed in the context of the transference neurosis. These symptoms were provoked by separations from the analyst on weekends and holidays, and interpretations focused on the wish to make the analyst anxious and to control him as she had done with her parents.

Frances did not go over to a phase of bulimia, as is frequently the case with anorexics. Her extreme ambivalence appeared during the first year as a frequent strong wish to stop therapy and deny illness. Another symptom was a fear of being alone and a need to keep the light on all night; this fear was resolved by the end of the first year.

As with other anorexics, Frances's dreams reflected both oedipal and pre-oedipal conflicts, and the defense of denial had to be interpreted repeatedly for her ego to face the latent conflicts reflected in dreams. There was also a strong resistance to interpreting any of her own dreams, which reflected her need to control affects.

A repetitive anxiety dream was of being under water and not being able to get to the surface, which masked oedipal-phase fears of childbirth dating from the birth of her younger sister at age five. A regressive preoedipal fantasy of being the baby in utero was also expressed in the dream, as were conflicts about showing emotions (i.e., crying). In her childhood struggle with her implacable parents, Frances had cried repeatedly when her desires were frustrated. For a time, she had had the nickname of "crybaby."

In the course of analysis, the progressive development of a more benevolent superego, a stronger ego, and a stronger self-observing function of the ego was reflected in change in the manifest content of her dreams. Early dreams of being raped and attacked gave way to dreams of observing a rape or burglary. These were followed by dreams of being a hostage held by criminals who would probably release her. Then, frank dreams of mother, father, and the analyst dying reflected a shift from masochistic to sadistic fantasies. Finally, in the terminal phase, dreams of pregnancy, marriage, and intercourse appeared.

Dreams of rabid black dogs reflected oral- and anal-phase sadomasochistic conflicts. At the height of the working through of these conflicts in the transference neurosis, Frances dreamed of being assaulted and being robbed. In her associations, she said that she had seen a macabre off-Broadway play in which women had whole hands chopped off and tongues cut out. She had vomited at a scene in which a man was chopped up and served for dinner. This oral incorporative material was related to Frances's occasional aversion to red meat, and its analysis led to more relaxed behavior in the transference and in her object relations. Although such material is indicative of oedipal conflicts, in analysis it must be approached first from the point of view of preoedipal material.

The process of identification with the aggressor appeared in a dream in which

Frances "slugged" her roommate in the face. This reflected her identification with mother, who had often slapped her in the face for disobedience at the dinner table. She had a taboo against really "beating" anyone at tennis until she came to see that beating had a literal and sadistic meaning for her. Her parents, particularly the mother, were extremely controlling, as is universally the case with anorexic patients. As is typical of anorexics' parents, they never argued in front of the children. Decisions and rules were inflexible. Anorexics have less than normal opportunities to play one parent off against the other, or to turn to one parent for support and love when working through conflicts toward the other parent. Again, typically, the mother did all the cooking, even though she weakly suggested that the daughters learn to cook. The parents were very strict about sweets. While she was in the hospital, Frances asked for ice cream, which had been strictly rationed by the parents. When friends brought her this special food, she would not eat it. It was easy to see that the anorexia reversed an earlier battle that the parents had won: by starving herself, Frances brought about the offer of any food, in any quantity, at any time from everyone.

Frances's ambivalence was reflected in her having one foot off the couch for the first years of analysis and in recurrent wishes to stop treatment. Denial was a pervasive defense, with many ramifications in Frances's speech. A minimizing mannerism of speech was, "I just did not feel like doing it," which analysis revealed meant that she would not do it under any circumstances. "It was perfectly all right" meant that it was boring. Frances's tense readiness to run from the analytic room was a way of avoiding both her unconscious hostility toward the analyst (mother) and her fantasied projected retaliation from the analyst (mother and father).

Analysis revealed a strong latent homosexual conflict. Both consciously and unconsciously, Frances had wanted to be a boy. In latency, she had fantasied extensively about an adventurous boy with whom she identified. In adolescence, she had denied her femininity and held out against dating. She had chosen a women's college to avoid boys. Her anorexic symptoms had developed in adult life because of a delayed adolescent struggle in her three "affairs." A contributing cause of Frances's symptoms was preoedipal and oedipal seduction by the father, who bathed his daughter and toweled her off after her bath.

The symptom of hyperactivity, which is characteristic of anorexic patients, was manifested in Frances's increasing preoccupation with bicycling. She belonged to a bicycle club that arranged strenuous overnight trips. Prior to hospitalization, as her weight plummeted, she became more and more hyperactive. The all-or-nothing quality of this behavior is characteristic of anorexic patients. Later in analysis, after Frances had mastered her anorexia, her conflicts in sublimation still reflected this problem. For example, for a time she resisted spending some pleasurable hours swimming because she could no longer achieve her adolescent goal of being an Olympic swimmer.

The all-or-nothing problem involved other areas of psychic life. Frances either saw her family for long visits, at which times she felt compelled to do everything for them, or she did not see them at all. On weekends, she either did exactly what she wanted or she submitted totally to her boyfriend's desires. In the transference, the tendency to make interpretations into fiats had to be shown her. Her handling of money reflected this ambivalence. She saved money frugally for the first years of treatment, spending very little on herself; however, impulses to do the opposite emerged in the form of not being able to make purchases because she only wanted the best. While choosing a new apartment over a period of months, her fantasies and dreams of the perfect dwelling place emerged.

At termination, Frances showed marked structural change, with a stronger ego, a more benevolent superego, and a capacity for whole object relations and healthy sublimations.

DISCUSSION.   Since anorexic patients usually are negativistic and withholding, it is best, if possible, to obtain information from concerned relatives and any previous therapist in initial consultations. In addition, with hospitalized patients, further information should be obtained from the attending physician and hospital staff. Usually, anorexics deny their illness and will not ask their relatives for financial aid for therapy. As with borderlines and psychotics, the therapist often has to explain the need for therapy and the fees and arrangements involved with concerned third parties. In Frances's case, the analyst discussed treatment with the parents and obtained a developmental history from them.

The early interpretation of Frances's denial of suicidal behavior (masochism) parallels the technique of Sperling (1978) and Hogan (Chapter 9, this volume) with psychosomatic patients and correlates with the therapeutic technique used in the therapy of schizophrenic, borderline, and character disorders by Boyer (1975), Boyer and Giovacchini (1980), Kernberg (1975), and Volkan (1976).

First, one interprets anorexic patients' masochism—their archaic superego and the guilt they experience at admitting to any conflicts. Next, one interprets defenses against facing masochistic behavior; then, when the ego is healthier, defenses against aggressive impulses are interpreted. Such interpretations are inexact; frequently, patients' associations do not confirm the interpretation. These patients have an archaic, punitive superego and a relatively weak ego. The analyst provides auxiliary ego strength and a rational superego (Boyer 1975, 1980; Wilson 1971). Interpretations should be made in a firm, consistent manner (Boyer 1975, 1980). With such patients, the analyst needs to have authority. This is why Frances's analyst told her that he was a specialist in anorexia nervosa.

These patients' behavioral responses can be interpreted, as in the example of Frances's resuming fasting to punish the analyst for not allowing her to control him. Patients' dreams have to be utilized in the context of their psychodynamics. Early in treatment, patients do not usually offer useful associative verbal material, as is also the case in the analyses of children and patients with character disorders (Boyer and Giovacchini 1980). That Frances told the analyst her dreams was a sign of positive transference as, formerly, she had been silent and negativistic. The dreams of skiing and menstruating seemed to be indicators of a positive therapeutic alliance. At this stage of treatment, the analyst uses construction and reconstruction to respond to patients' silences. An example was the analyst telling Frances that behind her anorexia were fears of men, marriage, pregnancy, and childbirth. Like other psychosomatic patients, Frances developed an early strong positive transference and gave up some of her symptoms (i.e., began putting on weight) before she had any in-depth understanding of her conflicts. To facilitate this process, in the analysis of patients' masochism, the analyst must let patients know that they can express their emotions and conflicts in therapy.

Frances had received joint psychiatric and medical treatment, which had resulted in a splitting of the transference, anger on Frances's part at being controlled, and subsequent self-starvation and resistance to medical treatment. When the analyst was able to stop the forced medical treatment, the transference became concentrated on him. In this process, the analyst carefully studied his countertransference and counterreactions to Frances's negativistic behavior. He realized that if she resisted further, his treatment would be interrupted to save her life, as her weight had dropped to near half normal. Instead of worrying about Frances's dying, which was the affective state she wanted to induce in him, the analyst interpreted her masochism and suicidal impulses.

In discussing the problem of how far the analyst should go in interpreting intense denial, Anna Freud (1968b) refers to Bond's treatment of an anorexic girl where he countered her fantastic denial of self-destruction (extreme emaciation) by telling her that she would die. As with other anorexics, the effects of the self-starvation did not impair Frances's ego functioning. On the contrary, often when patients' masochistic impulses are most intense and the results of their behavior most pathological and self-destructive, the split-off, silent, rational part of the ego is ready for a confrontation and the potential for a positive transference is heightened. Alcoholics Anonymous (personal communication 1979) believes that some addicts have to experience "the gutter" before they will face what they are doing to themselves and battle their addiction. The psychological situation is similar to that seen in patients who have made a serious attempt at suicide. The analytic consultant brings out to patients, in the context of their life history and personal psychodynamics, that the problem is to find out in therapy why they want to kill themselves. Frequently, with such an approach, suicidal patients can be released from the hospital for analysis with no recurrence of serious suicidal behavior. In the case of Frances, she evidenced a positive transference throughout her analysis and did not resume any life-threatening fasting.

EGO STRUCTURE OF THE BULIMIC
AND THE ABSTAINER

Psychodynamics

The two cases presented provide a clear picture of the psychodynamic differences between the bulimic and the abstaining anorexic. The abstaining, hospitalized case evidenced a strict, archaic superego that restricted ego functioning at each developmental level. This patient overcontrolled her impulses; she didn't smoke, drink, or indulge in substance abuse. The expression of aggression was ego alien—she was a good, conforming girl. Analysis recovered memories of a phase of guilty masturbation at age 12, but she had no dates until after college. Her areas of successful adaptive functioning were schoolwork and athletics. In sports, however, her guilt at fantasies of "beating people" kept her from winning important matches. Her habits were hypernormal. She was always punctual because she planned her day so carefully. Her language was polite and ladylike; her affects, both aggressive and libidinal, were under strict control. The analysis in many respects was similar to that of a compulsive neurotic. Like other anorexics she had a split ego. She had to be confronted with manifestations of denial, split-off, aggressive and libidinal fantasies, impulses, and conflicts. Analysis of the many dreams she reported was fruitful and meaningful, but she resisted interpreting them herself. However, she was basically cooperative and trusting throughout her treatment. Acting out and acting in were limited and amenable to analysis. Her parents' behavior dovetailed with the psychological profile of other anorexic families (Chapter 2, this volume). Both parents were overconscientious, hard-working people who shared moral, ethical, and social standards. They overcontrolled their children. They did not argue in public but presented a front of united, hypernormal parental authority to their children. While this patient did not lie, she withheld thoughts and feelings. Silence was an analytic problem at times.

The bulimic patient evidenced a different type of ego structure and a less strict, though perfectionistic, superego. Her ego controls were deficient, and she shifted from abstinence to gorging, vomiting, laxatives, and habits and addictions such as smoking and drinking. She frequently acted out her transference anger by being late or not coming to sessions. To save face, she withheld information and lied about events. She would lose her temper, shout at the analyst, and, since the expression of aggression was ego alien, relieve her guilt by purging herself or by jumping up and leaving sessions. She always had split off and repressed aggressive and libidinal drives and fantasies by her intense nail-biting and cuticle-chewing. When in adolescence she stopped this habit, she replaced it with cigarette-smoking, which served the same psychodynamic purposes. Her language was replete with sarcasm, and she swore and cursed frequently even though these expressions of aggression were ego alien. She was bitter and cynical in contrast to the abstaining anorexic who was emotionally direct and idealistic. Like the abstainer, the bulimic felt guilty about "beating anyone." She, however, concealed such conflicts with a cynical devaluation of competitive activities. Analysis uncovered phases of florid sexual acting out in adolescence. She had had intercourse in her early teens without using any contraceptives and denied the possibility of pregnancy. She had had many dates and many boyfriends, some of whom had wanted to marry her, but as soon as a relationship became serious, she broke it off. She lied to her parents about these relationships. Unlike the abstainer, she discussed boys and sexual matters with her girlfriends and often avoided the transference by confiding in friends rather than in the analyst. Actually she had no consistent friendly relationships but shifted objects like a chameleon, depending on her mood and her needs of the moment. She was unorganized and impulsive compared to the abstainer. Her moods would shift from excited elation to bitter cynical depression. Behind this shifting ego functioning was a compulsive character structure that forced her, when she was "good," to be too hard working and perfectionistic.

Both patients had histories of childhood habits. For years, the bulimic bit her nails and chewed the flesh of the nailbeds. At age four, the abstainer was a hair-puller; however, she mastered this habit during the oedipal years. Her ego developed controls during this phase, and she channeled aggressive impulses into athletics. The bulimic didn't develop control of her nail-biting habit until adolescence, when she substituted smoking. Smoking was clearly a defense against nail-biting. She was a chain-smoker and for large parts of the day had a cigarette in her mouth. Although the athletic activities of both patients were pseudosublimations in that during their emaciated anorexic phases both gave up these activities, the abstainer resumed regular exercise as soon as she regained her health, but the bulimic had multiple conflicts which required months of analysis before she resumed exercise. Her all-or-nothing conflict was more intense than that of the abstainer. The bulimic periodically turned to alcohol and drank herself into a stupor, whereas the abstainer limited herself to two drinks at a party.

Many abstaining anorexics stubbornly persist in their anorexic behavior; others, like this patient, give up their self-starvation early in treatment. The bulimic case demonstrates that thorough, long-term analysis is necessary to enable gorgers and vomiters to master their pathological behavior patterns.

Countertransference

There has been no research differentiating countertransference in bulimics as opposed to abstainers. An overview of countertransference can be found in articles by Glover (1955), Orr (1954), Reich (1960), and Langs (1975a, b). A recent book on countertransference (Epstein and Feiner 1979) offers articles that are most pertinent to the problems encountered in the therapy of anorexics. Particularly relevant is Boyer's chapter on countertransference with severely regressed patients (1979), in which he details his inner experiences as analyst in selected difficult treatment situations (transference psychoses) and describes how he utilized an understanding of his reactions, fantasies, and emotions to resolve such impasses. Thomä (1967) notes the countertransference conflicts aroused in the analyst by a prolonged negative transference in an anorexic patient. He also describes a typical countertransference response to anorexics where the therapist becomes the overindulgent, infinitely loving mother.

Wilson's analytic experience with patients with severe characterological, psychotic, and borderline disorders (1967a,b, 1971, 1973, Chapters 1 and 2, this volume) correlates with and confirms Boyer's emphasis on the important role of projective identification on the part of the patient and counteridentification on the part of the analyst in the treatment of these difficult patients. Moreover, a remarkably consistent psychological profile of the anorexic family is evident.* The understanding of this profile is crucial for the analyst's comprehension of the anorexic's provocative acting out, which is actually reenactment behavior that symbolically informs the analyst of past activities, events, and relationships (Boyer 1979, Ekstein 1976, Robertiello 1976). Crucial for the analysis of these patients is the analyst's understanding of their nonverbal expressive behavior (Bruch 1973a; Mushatt 1980; Sperling 1960; Wilson 1971, 1973). The symp-

---

* This profile is the subject of Chapter 2.

toms of anorexia nervosa are a form of nonverbal behavior and the task of analysis is to make the patients aware on a verbal level of the conflicts that are masked by their eating disorder.

COUNTERTRANSFERENCE PROBLEMS

Sperling (1967) discusses and gives illustrations of countertransference problems in patients with psychosomatic disorders. She warns that the analyst has to withstand patients' perpetual testing, be aware of nuances and changes in transference feelings, and—most important—preserve the analytic role and avoid falling in with patients' wishes to turn the analyst into the image of the omnipotent mother. She notes further that these patients can pick up almost imperceptible nuances in the tone of voice, facial expression, movements, and even feelings of the analyst. Annoyance or irritation on the part of the analyst is taken to mean rejection and intensifies the need for control of the object (analyst) and situation (analysis) at any cost (exacerbation or return of illness). Worry or anxiety on the part of the analyst is taken as an expression of love—the kind of love patients have received from their mother, which means a reward (anxiety, worry) for being sick. Like the mother, the analyst is worried and expresses love toward the patients when they are sick. Sperling emphasizes that skillful handling of the transference, with correct, well-timed interpretations, is crucial. A last point is that the transference cannot be split with another medical specialist; rather, the analyst must be basically in charge of treatment.

The case reports presented in this chapter document Sperling's main points about countertransference and explore certain points that she does not touch on, such as the fantasies that these patients provoke in the analyst, and the problem of gaining a full therapeutic alliance with adult patients who start treatment under the domination of a medical specialist. One point of difference is with Sperling's statement that the patient tries to turn the analyst into the image of the omnipotent mother. This seems to be a global oversimplification of a series of projective identifications that range between two major extremes: the alternate attempts to turn the analyst into the complete source of pleasure (the breast-food-all-giving mother) and into the critical, punishing mother who demands perfection. Sperling's brief comments are on countertransference in the analysis of psychosomatic cases in general. However, the specific countertransference problems with anorexics are even more complex and difficult than those with other psychosomatic patients because part of their conflict is conscious, which means that, in addition to the development of a transference neurosis, there is a conscious battle with the analyst.

Bruch (1978b), a Sullivanian interpersonal relations therapist, emphasizes that the therapist must not be intimidated by the anorexic's manipulative behavior and thereby replay the role of the intimidated patient. Bruch gives examples of how she used the anger that anorexics stirred up in her for interpretive purposes. One technique was to interrupt the patient in a loud, angry voice in order to be listened to, and another was to withdraw to a defensive position and point out that the anorexic was a voluntary patient and could see someone else.

Selvini Palazzoli (1978) notes that few patients are better than anorexics at driving the analyst into a corner and provoking countertransference reactions. Mintz (Chapter 4, this volume) emphasizes the negative results of being over-anxious and phoning a patient, and of giving approval when the anorexic patient starts to eat more.

Hogan (Chapter 9, this volume) notes that drowsiness and educative or coercive tactics are common countertransference reactions to anorexics. Boyer (1979) and McLaughlin (1979) review countertransference reactions of drowsiness or sleep in the analyst. The core fantasy in anorexics' sleep-inducing associations and behavior involves fusion with the analyst as the mother in the transference. One chronically late analysand who was finally gaining some insight into her omnipotent resistance suddenly devalued analysis and the analyst and threatened to see an astrologist. The analyst had a countertrans-ference reaction of drowsiness, which the patient noted. His drowsiness was a sort of rebound phenomenon: if the patient was going to dismiss the analyst and his ideas, then he would dismiss her, too. The affect of drowsiness reflected the symbiotic fusion fantasies of the patient.

With respect to coercion, Hogan notes that the therapist of one patient threat-ened to discontinue treatment if she repeated her initial act of shoplifting. In response, the patient repeated and expanded her shoplifting adventures without ever informing the therapist again. She enjoyed typical anorexic "glee" at "getting away with it." Treatment was obviously useless, as she replicated her relation with her mother.

Flarsheim (1975) has written about the therapist's collusion with the patient's wish for suicide. One suicidal anorexic patient provoked hostility in him and he then wished that she would cease to exist (suicide). Flarsheim told the patient some aspects of his countertransference hostility and felt that this revelation improved the therapeutic relationship and contributed to the patient's improve-ment, although the patient had to be hospitalized. Flarsheim emphasizes that when anorexics give up their food addiction, they become addicted to the analyst in the transference. He also stresses that anorexic symptoms defend against sui-cidal impulses.

Another countertransference problem arises from patients' rationalization of their penis envy and conflicts with men, and accusation that the analyst is antifeminist. Many adolescent anorexics state that Freud was antifeminist, that penis envy is a discarded notion, etc. The analyst has to be very careful about countertransference in this potentially provocative situation and must keep in mind that this attitude is defensive and that underneath these patients are frightened. They have been repeatedly exposed to the oedipal and preoedipal primal scene and to extremely exhibitionistic parental sexual and toilet behavior, whose significance has been completely denied (Chapter 2, this volume). The major defense of the unconsciously terrified anorexic female is to control the objects and situations that provoke anxiety. All these patients lie about their sexual behavior, as well as about other matters. In the countertransference and counterreactions, analysts experience (1) resentment that their authority and professional training and knowledge are being challenged; (2) resentment that Freud's and their positions are distorted; and (3) above all, the feeling that patients are trying to pick a fight. One effective therapeutic technique is to analyze the patient's defensive rationalization. For example, analysts may point out that Freud never made up his mind about female psychology—that he changed his mind often, said different things at different times, and is widely misquoted; they may tell patients that they are in favor of women's rights and realize that women have been discriminated against; they may emphasize that little boys envy women; and so on, depending on each patient's character structure, history, and defenses.

Another important countertransference problem is the sudden devaluation of the male analyst and the expressed wish for a female analyst when patients' anorexic symptoms have cleared and they are analyzing their underlying neurosis. This wish expresses the desire to find in the analyst the early omnipotent breast-mother whom they can control. The resistance occurs when they have not effected a basic change in the quality of their object relations and have not worked through their symbiotic attachment to the parents. Analysts' counterreactions of resentment and anger can be intense. They may wish to get rid of patients in retaliation. With adolescent patients, the wish for a change to a woman analyst may be promoted by the parents, who unconsciously do not want their daughter to mature. This transference conflict requires careful and thorough interpretation. Women analysts encounter the same resistance when they refuse to be the symbiotic mother in the transference; patients will express the wish for a different, often a male, analyst.

A common characterologic defense of anorexic gorger-vomiters is an ego attitude of bitter cynicism and sarcasm. Interpretations are responded to with, "So what?" "I've heard that before." "You and your psychoanalytic crap." These defenses occur following a phase of positive transference and therapeutic progress. The analyst should pursue the interpretation of these patients' strict superego, which disapproves of the anger at the analyst and demands an iron control over it. Unhappiness, depression, hopelessness, loneliness, frustration, guilt, and suicidal ideas are masked by this defense of the ego. Cynicism and sarcasm reflect an extreme ego ideal of perfection that these patients demand of themselves and of other people. Understanding this aspect of the anorexic's character structure enables analysts to resolve their intense counterreactions and countertransference.

Finally, analysts should not be deceived by the appearance of healthy functioning in anorexics whose symptoms are gone but whose underlying conflicts are still unresolved. If such patients are allowed to go away to college before they are ready, dangerous suicidal behavior and the return of intense symptoms can be expected.

APPROACH TO
TRANSFERENCE INTERPRETATION

The approach to transference interpretation advocated here correlates with that of Boyer and Giovacchini (1980) and Kernberg (1975). The negative transference should be systematically elaborated only in the present, without initial efforts directed toward full genetic interpretations. Thus, Frances's return to anorexia was interpreted as an expression of anger at the analyst for not being able to get what she wanted from him (to leave the hospital prematurely), and Elaine's denial of anger at being left when the analyst went on vacation was interpreted.

The patient's typical defensive counterreactions are interpreted as they enter the transference. The anorexic's typical defense is massive denial, and both Frances's and Elaine's denial of the suicidal nature of their behavior was interpreted from the start. In Frances's case, to give the interpretation full impact, the analyst also interrupted medical treatment and the staff's efforts to encourage or force her to eat, thereby making Frances responsible for her behavior. With Elaine, the analyst interpreted the hidden suicidal impulses and fantasies that were masked by her massive doses of laxatives and other habits.

Some limit setting on acting out in the transference may be necessary to protect the neutrality of the analyst. When the analyst felt that Frances could be discharged for office treatment, he informed her of his opinion, but asked her what she felt about such a move, giving her autonomy, in that, if she had said she was not ready to leave, he would have continued her therapy in the hospital to resolve her fears. When Elaine acted out too much around time, the analyst set limits to her acting out to forestall a sabotage of the treatment process. A repeated line of interpretation was to point out how she devalued the analyst and treated him as she did food, which was something she could manipulate and control.

The less primitively determined, modulated aspects of the positive transference are not interpreted early, since their presence enhances the development of the therapeutic and working alliances (Dickes 1975, Kanzer 1975). However, the all-good/all-bad splitting of object relations is systematically interpreted as part of the effort to work through primitive defenses. Such interpretation was important in both Frances's and Elaine's treatment. Often, psychosomatic symptoms clear up long before their unconscious meanings have been analyzed because the analyst has become a new and different superego ideal for the patient, one who promotes instinctual control (Wilson 1971). Early interpretation of this early positive idealized transference is not advocated.

Interpretations should systematically clarify patients' distortions of the analyst's statements and of present reality. The highly distorted transference, which at times is psychotic in nature and reflects fantastic internal object relations pertaining to early ego disturbances, is worked through first in order to reach the transferences related to actual childhood experiences. An example of such an interpretation was the analyst telling Elaine of his hostile fantasies when she told him of her projected fear that he would hit her.

SUMMARY

This chapter focused on the analysis of a bulimic and an abstaining anorexic in order to highlight the similarities and differences in their ego structure and treatment. The countertransference was explored in depth.

The first case, a 28-year-old anorexic with bulimia and vomiting dating back five years, was presented to demonstrate the technique of interpretation, the transference, and the countertransference with a patient who for long periods of time was in office analysis with her weight at near half its normal level. Clinical material was presented to show the mistrust and suspicion in the transference of anorexic patients who have had previous behavior modification (coercive) treatment. Examples were given of the negative therapeutic response to successful interpretations and the complications of the analyst's countertransference with such masochistic patients. A particular focus was on the splitting and the projective identifications of the patient and the counterreactions of the analyst to these defenses.

The technique of interpretation and the handling of countertransference with these psychosomatic patients were shown to be similar to the methods used by Boyer and Giovacchini (1980) and Kernberg (1975) in the analysis of patients with borderline, narcissistic, and psychotic personality disorders.

In the second case, treatment of the 25-year-old patient began in the hospital, where the analyst's approach was to concentrate the transference on himself by interrupting—with the attending physician's cooperation—diets, medication, and force-feeding, by educating the psychiatric residents, nurses, and other staff members in the psychodynamics of anorexia, and by securing the cooperation of relatives. The hospital crisis therapy began with interpretations of the patient's masochism, which masked suicidal impulses. The focus was on the pregenital ego defenses of denial, projection, rationalization, belief in magic, control, externalization, and displacement. Details of the posthospital analysis were presented to show the gradual development of a positive therapeutic alliance. This patient's fear-of-being-fat body image was replaced by a normal, healthy, feminine body image so that, eventually, she was able to eat normally, work effectively, and achieve a healthy heterosexual relationship.

PART IV

Treatment

9
Technical Problems in Psychoanalytic Treatment

CHARLES C. HOGAN, M.D., D.MED.SC.

This chapter focuses on technical problems in the psychoanalytic therapy of anorexic patients because it is felt that this is the treatment of choice in the majority of cases. A comparison between psychoanalytic therapy and other contemporary treatment approaches is offered. Before turning to specific areas of technique, two broader aspects of therapeutic interaction will be considered: (1) the question of hospitalization, and (2) family involvement in treatment.

THE QUESTION OF HOSPITALIZATION

Many investigators have recommended hospitalization either to initiate weight gain (e.g., Bruch 1978a) or to treat the anorexia. Some, such as Dally (1969), recommend supplementing hospitalization with routine drug treatment. Others combine hospitalization with electroshock treatment, force-feeding, behavioral modification, etc. In some cases, hospitalization seems to be utilized not as an integral part of treatment or even as a necessary adjunct to it, but as a convenience in the workup or a means of collecting data (Minuchin et al. 1978, Thomä 1967).

Despite feeling that these patients are severely disturbed, Selvini Palazzoli (1978) is totally opposed to hospitalization and notes that "while hospitalization may benefit the patient physically, it can ruin an inter-human relationship that is likely to have a much more decisive and curative effect" (p. 119). Sperling (1978) observes that the group approach inherent in hospital treatment lends itself to a split transference, with all of the implicit complications of the anorexic playing one professional off against another. The uninterpretable regression to the patient's manipulation of the family is unavoidable.

The primary concern of treatment should be directed at the underlying psychopathology, rather than the symptoms of self-starvation, bulimia, vomiting, amenorrhea, etc. Overconcern with such masochistic, controlling maneuvers can help to perpetuate them and can interfere seriously with treatment. The repetition of mother's anxiety and not too subtle control only adds to the regression inherent in the neuroses. Nor should another physician be brought in before or during therapy to attempt to obtain and manage a weight gain. The anorexic symptoms serve to reconcile internal conflicts and to control the environment. It is important for patients to become aware of their own actions and impulses. They are overburdened by unconscious, inconsistent constraints on impulses. It is better not to sanction further external restraints unless the situation is critical. Provocative acting out with acute weight loss is part of the process.

There are occasions where self-destructive impulses push a patient to the brink of death or psychoses.* At such times, it may be necessary to hospitalize the patient temporarily, just long enough to deal with the immediate emergency. In situations where a patient has already been hospitalized by another physician and treatment has been initiated there, the patient should be transferred to outpatient therapy as soon as possible.

An initial general physical workup by a consulting physician is important, but this can be managed quite adequately on an outpatient basis. Anorexic patients should be followed regularly by an internist or a pediatrician, but therapeutic decisions must be made by the psychiatrist after consultation.

Authoritarian management, behavioral modification, force-feeding, parenteral feeding (with the exception of emergencies), and drug treatment, all of which are so commonly associated with hospital treatment, are absolutely contraindicated. It is the exceptional case where it is necessary to impose markedly restrictive parameters on treatment by psychoanalysis or psychoanalytic psychotherapy.

For the most part, these patients are neurotic with pregenital regressions and defenses. Although they are quite self-destructive, they usually can be treated with an interpretative outpatient approach. Selvini Palazzoli and others disagree with the view offered here and instead see all these patients as potentially psychotic. Masterson (1977) seems to include all these patients in the "borderline" category, while Sperling (1978) includes some patients in such a grouping. A minority of anorexic patients are inclined to occasional psychotic regressions. However, regardless of the diagnostic label, most anorexics are able to understand even the most primitive of their regressions and defenses when these are handled in an interpretative analytic fashion. The severe external constraint of hospitalization is seldom indicated.

FAMILY INVOLVEMENT IN TREATMENT

When members of the family are involved in concurrent individual treatment with separate therapists, it should not be considered a parameter imposed on the psychoanalysis of the anorexic patient. Indeed, with younger patients, this may be a valuable adjunct. As the mother becomes aware of her infantile attachment to the daughter, she modifies her manipulative behavior. The anorexic's treatment is facilitated by an alleviation of family pressures.

---

*See Chapter 8.

Sperling (1959, 1961, 1967, 1968a, 1978) has long advocated the treatment of mothers of children and adolescents suffering from psychosomatic illnesses in general, and anorexia nervosa in particular. In many cases, she has recommended treatment of the mother and child by the same therapist.

Bruch (1978a) often includes the family in her treatment schedule. She indicates the importance of the rigidly demanding and controlling mother in the family history of these patients. Bruch (1965, 1978a) is opposed to the psychoanalytic treatment of these patients because they have abdicated their independence to the mother.

Selvini Palazzoli (1978) places great stress on the family's participation in treatment. Her own approach seems to have evolved from individual therapy to family therapy. Like Bruch, she feels that psychoanalysis or psychoanalytic psychotherapy is not the treatment of choice.

Minuchin et al. (1978) feel that family therapy is the preferred method of treatment for anorexia. Over half of their cases were initially placed in the hospital and the decision to hospitalize was left to the pediatrician. Minuchin et al.'s experience that recovery from the major classical symptomatology is often quite rapid has been replicated by many others. However, in view of the relatively severe neurotic problems remaining, one can only suspect that such "psychosocial recovery" falls short of the resolution of emotional problems expected from a psychoanalytic approach.

PSYCHOANALYTIC CONSIDERATIONS

In the psychoanalytic treatment of anorexic patients, one must deal with pregenital regressions that have led various authors to categorize these patients as borderline, pseudoneurotic schizophrenic, narcissistic characters, and even schizophrenic or psychotic characters. These cases seem to be on a continuum, perhaps a multidimensional one, with the more serious psychopathological conditions. This continuum may even involve the psychoses. (Arlow and Brenner 1964, 1969, 1970). However, the majority of anorexic patients fall into a "neurotic" classification and quite clearly display pregenital defensive regressions from triadic oedipal problems.

Melitta Sperling has dealt more directly with the psychoanalytic treatment of psychosomatic disorders and anorexia nervosa than any other investigator. She (1978) does not believe that anorexia nervosa is a psychosomatic entity, but feels it is related to the phobias and hysteria and is an "impulse disorder." She does acknowledge its close relationship to psychosomatic disorders and indicates how frequently it is associated with psychosomatic conditions. She has repeatedly called attention to the needs of these patients to control their object representations and object perceptions (i.e., to use their objects as "fetishes"). She has also observed the demands of anorexic patients for immediate gratification and the omnipotent fantasies that accompany such demands. She (1959, 1967, 1968a, 1978) has noted the relationship of these defensive mechanisms to underlying incorporative and projective fantasies. She has shown that these character defenses are used in the service of denial, which helps to maintain the repression of depressive and sadomasochistic concerns. The latter, in turn, cover active libidinal oedipal interests and fears. Her contributions have helped immeasurably, and her observations correlate rather closely with my own.

Many other investigators have reported on the psychoanalytic treatment of individual cases of anorexia nervosa. Some of these findings have been summarized by Kaufman and Heiman (1964).

There is some difference between the analysis of preoedipal defenses and the interpretative analysis of the oedipal conflict. The approach advanced here goes back to Wilhelm Reich (1933) and has been reintroduced, expanded, and used by analysts in England, South America, and the United States (e.g., Arlow and Brenner 1964, 1969, 1970; Boyer 1961; Boyer and Giovacchini 1980; Fairbairn 1952, 1954; Kernberg 1975, 1976; Klein 1934, 1946, 1948, 1952; Kohut 1971; Riviere 1936a, b; Rosenfeld 1965; Searles 1965; Volkan 1965, 1976). In brief, the approach involves an analysis of more primitive defenses early in treatment with the anticipation of the presentation of the more repressed, but less primitive, oedipal and phallic concerns as treatment progresses. At one time, the preferred interpretation was one that condensed the patient's historical past, contemporary social and sexual life, and transference. In the milder transference neuroses, this still seems to be a valid premise.

However, as the complicated hierarchy of defensive postures in more regressed patients has been recognized, the necessity of interpreting the material in the context of the immediate motivation should be emphasized. This does not differ intrinsically from Freud's utilization of the concept "preconscious," but does involve more complex conscious and unconscious defensive maneuvers. These patients are totally unable to free-associate when they begin treatment, and consciously posture and maneuver through every session. It is only as they obtain an expanded view of themselves through an analysis of their defenses that they are able to trust the analyst and the analytic situation to the point of free association.

As free associations appear, interest can be directed more toward the content of the material. However, in the early period of treatment, the focus is more on the style and form of presentation. Constant attention must be paid to the posturing, manipulating, repetition for emphasis, attempts at dramatization, etc. It is important to call attention to such material and to interpret it if one can do so without humiliating the patient, or implying either an accusation or a reprimand for not following the "rules."

CASE EXAMPLE*   *Interpreting the Style and Form of Presentation*

One day fairly early in her analysis, Lila, a very verbal, intellectually sophisticated anorexic patient with a hysterical character structure, entered the room looking particularly frail in her demeanor, dress, and expression. She presented the following dream:

---

*The clinical material utilized in this chapter is derived primarily from work with seven patients: four have completed psychoanalysis, one has completed psychoanalytic psychotherapy, and two are currently in psychoanalysis. In addition, some references are to patients seen in consultation or observed through supervision. The first four patients, as

Something was coming out of my eye. I went to mother who informed me in a matter-of-fact way that my brains were coming out and that I should break them off. I was terrified and ran to father. He told me to lie down and the brains would go back into my head. I followed his directions and everything was all right.

The dream led to associations to castration, voyeurism, and exhibitionism with displacement of genital concerns to the head and eyes. Recently, Lila apparently had been frightened by an exhibitionistic incident. Her associations were not free, but clearly planned and thought out. She seemed to emphasize her helplessness. In addition, there had been many historical associations involving her love and admiration for her overidealized father, as well as her feelings of distance from her uncompromising, unsympathetic mother.

Certainly, one could justify the temptation to work with apparent oedipal or phallic concerns based on the content of Lila's associations. However, in work with patients who use regressive defenses, it is important to interpret their aggressive, sadistic, and masochistic defensiveness early in treatment. On a number of previous occasions, Lila had volunteered that she was most comfortable socially when she could present herself as a vulnerable, frail child. The analyst trusted his observations of her presentation of herself rather than the content of her associations.

The analyst interpreted that Lila felt she had to indicate that she would mutilate herself, "spill her brains," and compromise her intelligence to obtain his understanding and help. He added that she wanted him to see how ill she was, that the couch was not enough, and that she wanted his reassurance.

This interpretation was confirmed by associations to her apparently helpless, depressed mother of early childhood and her mother's frequent admonition, "Use your brains." The analyst then suggested that perhaps her mother had some of the same anxieties as Lila did about herself and her daughter. Lila also associated to her contemporary fears of lacking or losing her wit, ideas, and spontaneity (brain). She was afraid that analysis might render her a "run-of-the-mill nobody." She added that her associations during the early part of the hour had been in part consciously presented to please the analyst and indicated that she was "testing" him. For the moment, she conceded that maybe she could trust him as she could trust her father. In anorexic patients, such trust is obviously momentary.

The analysis of the phallic and oedipal concerns expressed in the manifest content of, and associations to, the dream was accomplished intermittently through dreams and associations during the ensuing years of Lila's treatment.

This vignette illustrates that frequently there are a number of levels of interpretation open in a given hour. It is generally important to interpret the defenses and attempts at control and manipulation early in the analysis. In particular, the early designation of masochistic self-destructive content and behavior is warranted. If one deals with these derivatives of primitive aggression early, the more repressed libidinal concerns will emerge later. Of course,

---

well as the two currently in treatment, were all analyzed on the couch: one at five sessions per week, five at four sessions per week, and one at three sessions per week. The patient in psychoanalytic psychotherapy was seen face-to-face twice a week. Three of these patients have had previous psychotherapy and/or hospitalization.

exceptions to the rule are not uncommon. When genital concerns do occur early in treatment, they must be handled appropriately. Conscious avoidance of such material should be noted wherever evident.

Style and Form of the Character and Defenses

Some of the outstanding personality traits of these patients, with the implied underlying defenses, are summarized below. Despite the apparent differences in patients' personalities, there are certain qualities that appear with remarkable consistency in case after case. The traits are closely related to each other and frequently overlap.

SUBJECTIVE FEELINGS OF, AND NEEDS FOR, THE ILLUSION OF COMPLETE CONSCIOUS CONTROL

Many of the anorexic's defenses, symptoms, and self-destructive character traits are quite conscious and seem to the patient to be consciously motivated. These patients see conscious manipulation of self- and object perceptions as a way of life. They can intellectually encompass the idea of unconscious motivation, but cannot accept it in themselves. They are often aware of mental mechanisms and dynamic constellations that are likely to be repressed in milder neurotics. Such conscious material is often self-interpreted and presented as the "unconscious." Such masochistic introspection, intellectual self-dissection, and conscious awareness frequently lead therapists to indulge in an unwarranted optimism as to patients' insight and as to the tasks and duration of treatment. This unwarranted enthusiasm eventually leads to unwarranted disappointment.

Underlying repressions are aided by extensive systems of denial which include a denial of the repressions. The patients invariably deny the seriousness, pathogenicity, and inappropriateness of their overall condition, as well as of individual stances, ideas, and behaviors. They will attribute all of these to conscious explanatory motives and refuse to consider other alternatives.

Conscious pride and a feeling of moral superiority are invested in this ability to control body, thought, and feeling. The pride and superiority are accompanied by mild elation and a sense of grandiosity that, in turn, aid in the denial. These patients aggrandize their suffering in the cause of morality.

There is a general attitude toward the analyst that "nothing is going on that I don't know about and understand better than you do." One patient was able to reject almost any interpretation, unless it was presented in the form of a question, for the first year of analysis. Another took unremitting pride in her control over sleep, academic efforts, and athletic activities. One patient maintained an omnipotent, virtuous pride that she had suffered more from her illness than her mother had from her political imprisonment. Most anorexic patients try to anticipate interpretations and repeatedly point out that they "knew" what the analyst was going to say beforehand. The usual response to an early interpretation of an unconscious motive is that of contradiction. What intellectual interest they do have in motivation will allow for a single exclusionary cause and will allow no room for overdetermination. As the analysis progresses, these patients are able to recognize the sense of power, elation, and omnipotent fantasies that accompany such contradictory certainty of thought and feeling. Beneath all of this is the overwhelming fear of losing control over any impulse, sexual or aggressive. As such impulses and their underlying fantasies appear in treatment, patients reluctantly become aware of their impulsivity and need for immediate gratification.

Until patients are well into the analysis, little or no attention is paid to even the concept of the unconscious. Attention is called to anger, masochistic needs, and destructive and sadistic behavior (when present). The aggression and sadism usually first appear in the need to control object perceptions.* Denial and isolating mechanisms are pointed out: "You have concentrated so hard on this minute question for the last 30 minutes that you forgot the original larger issue (the whole)"; "You want me to feel that you are not afraid"; or "You hate and desire to deny (this or that appetite)." Whenever the material warrants, suggestions are made as to how symptoms avoid feelings. Conscious affects are emphasized, particularly when they relate to symptoms (e.g., the shame and guilt associated with bulimia and vomiting). As treatment continues, increasing emphasis is placed on the displacement of feelings.

Such a need for a sense of conscious control at all times is dramatically represented in the constant attempts to control food intake and weight. Here other unconscious concerns are displaced onto the fear of being fat and are acted out in self-starvation, vomiting, etc. Some patients consciously resent their menarche and consciously nurse omnipotent fantasies of controlling their menstrual periods before losing them. Such material may be available and pridefully presented as early as the first weeks of analysis.

Anorexic patients soon become aware of their anger at the control exerted by the internal representation of the primary object. Phrases such as "She can make me do anything else, but she can't make me eat" are extremely common. The accompanying illusion of omnipotent pleasure in control is frequently accompanied by thoughts such as "I am making her (mother) feel more guilty than she ever made me feel" or "If she thinks I am weak enough to give in, she has another think coming." Elaborations such as "No one will trick me, I see through them" are extremely common.

Awareness of anger toward the mother is usually accompanied by a diametrically opposed ego state in which the maternal figure is seen as an absolutely necessary extension of the patient's own ego. This is frequently experienced as

---

*The terms "object perceptions," and "self-perceptions" or "subject perceptions," indicate a person's subjective total experience of the external object and self, respectively, at any given time. In many instances, they replace the more usual references to "self" or "object." "Reality" is a relative matter dependent on the past of the observer and/or participant. Even the contemporary object perception of the adult patient is colored by the projection and projective identifications of ghosts from the past. However, the analysis of pregenital regressions can and should allow for a broader, more distanced, clearer, and less scotomatized view of contemporary adult objects and representations of the primal object, including the transference representative. The same thoughts hold true for "self-perceptions."

a sense of intense identificatory love or understanding; all hostility is consciously denied. Clearly defined splits in the self-representation, the self-perception, and the object perception are demonstrable. Such ego splits should be interpreted whenever and wherever a line of cleavage is obvious and the two ego states are temporarily contiguous. At first, such interpretations are responded to with almost complete denial. Later, surprise and interest should replace the stubborn, defiant denial.

As the analysis evolves and the underlying impulses are interpreted ever so gently, outbursts of temper are frequent and sometimes include violent projections onto the analyst. Feelings of surprise, humiliation, and shame are acute in these patients. They will demand that the analyst be more understanding and protect them from such feelings. They will attack the analyst for making "unfair accusations." These transference disappointments are handled in traditional ways.

LACK OF FREE ASSOCIATIONS EARLY IN TREATMENT

Closely associated with the need to feel in conscious control at all times is the inability to free-associate. For the most part, trains of association are goal directed: they are used to seek gratification, shore up defensive fantasies, justify behavior and judgments, attack the analyst, etc.

Projections onto the analyst limit patients' participation in a free flow of associations. When such projections are patently and demonstrably false, they should be mentioned without challenge. When demonstrations would be equivocal, they should be ignored temporarily.

Spontaneity and free associations are briefly asked for at the beginning of treatment. They are not asked for again, but constraints on spontaneity are interpreted. The sense of humiliation associated with surprise or loss of control is repeatedly interpreted, but material relating to the anal and urethral sources is ignored until free association has been clearly established (i.e., occurs during most sessions).

Free association is not a consistent process with any patient. There are regressive episodes of conscious goal-directed verbalizations in the mildest of transference neurotics. In anorexics, intermittent free associations appear with greater frequency as the need for control over aggressive and sexual impulses is recognized. In general, this recognition follows an understanding of the need for control over object perceptions and object representations.

All of the attempts to maneuver and control, with their accompanying stubborn, contradictory, and defiant associative material, can take a toll on the unwary analyst. Countertransference reactions are common. Drowsiness, sleep, and attempts at educative or coercive measures are not uncommon reactions and may interfere with treatment.

Usually free association becomes generally available at about the time that the major somatic symptomatology is given up.

APPARENT LACK OF FANTASY LIFE

A shallow fantasy life is frequently ascribed to psychosomatic cases (Nemiah 1976, Nemiah and Sifneos 1970), but it is only a surface phenomenon. Early in treatment, associations continually involve behavior, motion, and judgments.

However, as regressive defenses are analyzed, underlying impulses and accompanying fantasies—sometimes of a very primitive nature—make their appearance. Then a rich, if sometimes seemingly bizarre, fantasy life emerges.

Only part of the anorexic population—those with obsessional character traits—displays this initial apparent lack of fantasy life. These patients usually present a dearth of dreams. They are frightened of acknowledging their own intolerance of frustration, their needs to act on impulse, and their hostility. They deny and repress wishes and fantasies. Wishes are often consciously dismissed with "What's the use. It wouldn't do any good anyway."

Two patients spent the first half-year of treatment reporting little more than their daily activities, self-starvation minutia, and fears of being fat. When underlying fantasies were interpreted, they would occasionally be acknowledged, but further elaborations were unavailable. Such patients cause many psychiatrists to turn to manipulative educational measures and lead others to write about the lack of a fantasy life in psychosomatic patients (Nemiah 1976, Nemiah and Sifneos 1970, Sifneos 1973).

Beneath such defensive ideational shallowness are layers of depression, impulsivity, and sadomasochistic fantasies that come to light as the constraints are lifted. At times, a fantasy underlying a piece of masochistic behavior may be recognized and implied or interpreted early in treatment. Caution must be used since these patients are wont to intellectualize and isolate such a piece of behavior at this point to maintain the illusion of conscious control. When this happens, patients may project, become "amateur analysts," and begin to attribute the identical motivation to acquaintances and the analyst—usually with pejorative connotations.

For example, one patient was given an interpretation about her need to control the analyst and the session. After she reported certain memories and associations, the analyst linked her contemporary obsessional control to childhood sadistic torturing activities toward her younger sister and gave a further interpretation as to what he deduced to be her fantasies, then and now, behind such controlling behavior. With an apparent lack of interest, she agreed to the possibility of "some such connection." During the following weeks, she began to notice "the rigidity" of the psychoanalytic procedure. She began to comment on what she felt were the analyst's needs to be omnipotent and have patients under his complete control. As time went on, she began to speculate on his childhood and on what a sadistic tyrant he must have been. Only after she reconstructed an event that she was sure must have happened to him and the analyst related it to an event that she had described in her own life did the whole projection collapse and allow her to admit that she had been talking about herself for the past several sessions.*

Even at this point, however, a diversionary projective identification occurred as she spoke with anger about the feelings of triumph the analyst was

---

*Kohut (1971) and his followers might well interpret such specific transference reactions as part of a more generalized transference. I have found the early analysis of any obvious anomalous transference reaction to be of value in obtaining anamnestic material leading to early fantasies and/or memories involving primitive conflicts that have contributed to current conflicts in the transference and other object relationships.

certainly enjoying at her expense—how he must get such pleasurable powerful feelings when he tore down patients' hard-won arguments and constructions. Even if he were right, his motives were untherapeutic and sadistic.

Once a patient has traced a defense to an underlying fantasy and impulse, the release of inhibitions can be spectacular and, at times, a bit chaotic. As an example, when the attempts to control the analyst have been traced to passive attempts to control mother and, further, to active sadistic fantasies of control of mother, with their attendant projections, the underlying impulses are frequently acted out. Depression is associated with frustrated attempts to control mother; the underlying hostility may intermittently appear either in the transference with rages, distrust, threats of termination, etc., or in life with masochistic acting out such as breaking up relationships, quitting jobs, and provoking verbal or physical retaliations.

In this group of obsessional patients, the treatment-induced acting out usually occurs only after some progress has been made. Early in the treatment, inhibition shadows every impulse and production. Anorexics who starve themselves but do not gorge and vomit are likely to fall into this obsessional group.

OVERIDEATIONAL FANTASY LIFE

Anorexics who do not present shallow ideational content are inclined to a more hysterical disposition and will at times flood the analysis with fantasies and dreams. In the early months (or years) of treatment, these patients have difficulty utilizing this material for analytic purposes. They are too intent on gratifications and symptomatic substitute gratifications. They are inclined to be bulimic vomiters who begin to act out early in analysis. Their impulses are closer to consciousness and are intermittently indulged rather than denied.

One such patient made "entrances" by coming late to every session. Immediately after her first psychoanalytic hour, she picked up a man outside the building where she had had her session. She would not tell the analyst about sexual activities with this man because of her certainty that her associations would excite the analyst. Throughout the early months of treatment, despite her vaginal anesthesia, she indulged in a succession of brief, meaningless affairs. The hours were filled with facts and fantasies about these repetitive experiments, but no overt genital expectations or disappointments were ever mentioned.

There does not appear to be any difference in the prognoses of the obsessional and hysterical groups. Treatment outcome seems to be more closely related to duration of illness, profundity of regression, and other factors than to the type of defenses controlling the character structure.

MORAL AND JUDGMENTAL SUPERIORITY

Anorexia nervosa is characterized by a severe, inconsistent, primitive superego that sometimes leads to violent judgmental attitudes toward others and the self (self- and object perceptions). This general state of affairs originates in incorporations of omnipotent maternal and paternal representations and is usually followed by a lifelong battle with mother for unimpeachable moral superiority. This struggle must be analyzed eventually.

In the meantime, however, these patients hide their hostility and fantasy life under a cloak of judgment and morality. They will not admit any aggression toward the analyst. The analyst simply is "incompetent" or "wrong." Judgments on, and sadistic verbal dissections of, the personalities of self and others may go on with no recognition of their fantasy quality or of the aggression involved. It is all done from a lofty position of omnipotent certainty of the "facts" of the case. Only with the greatest reluctance will patients occasionally admit the subjective nature of these productions.

Projections play an important role in this fantasy of moral superiority with its occasional judgmental rages. The relationships among judgment, projection, rage, and fantasies of fusion are obvious to any analyst and must be analyzed eventually. Interpretations should be as nonchallenging and nonjudgmental as possible.

After two years of analysis, one anorexic young woman had reached the point where she was free enough to verbalize her curiosity and her observations about the analyst and his office. These observations were not questions or perceptions, but rather, a series of conclusions about the analyst's personality, life style, and motives, accompanied by cautionary lectures, comments, or warnings. Many of these conclusions contradicted each other. They ranged from judgments about the analyst's indifference to accusations of sadistic sexual manipulations. This patient's denial of her underlying aggression, despite the rather pejorative nature of her conclusions, is characteristic of anorexic patients. Any possibility that the choice of observations was dictated by her, that the constructions that evolved were of her own authorship, or that both were related to her own fantasies was denied. To this patient, such judgments were factual descriptions of the analyst's fallibilities and she repeatedly implied how lucky the analyst was that she remained in treatment with him. Such implications were usually couched in the context of anorexic helplessness and innocence.

The characteristic certainty about her observations and the analyst's mental state indicated a certain lack of differentiation between analyst and patient. This patient was living out a dyadic transference that replicated a rather primitive, ambivalent relationship with mother. At this point, to allow herself analytic detachment or objectivity would be to admit defeat and humiliation at the hands of mother. All moral superiority would have to be relinquished. Analyst or mother would be in complete control. Fortunately, in most anorexic patients, the regressive defense is against the oedipal and phallic concerns of a neurotic triadic conflict.

Such aspects of this quality of personality can be particularly frustrating for the therapist if the nature of the process is not understood. Because of fragmentation (see p. 210), these judgments may be quite contradictory. The patient may berate friend or analyst one day for a quality that she feels is morally inferior and then accuse the same friend or analyst of the diametrically opposed quality, which she currently deems inferior, the next day. When the contradiction is pointed out, the patient may cover or totally repress her embarrassment with confabulatory explanations. When this happens, the fantasies of control and omnipotence are preserved, confidence is maintained, humiliation and helplessness are denied, the analyst has demonstrated his or her ignorance by questioning the judgments, and the analysis of the helpless hostility must await another day.

LYING AND STEALING

The judgmental predisposition, along with moral superiority and searches for ascetic perfection, carries with it an interesting contradiction evidenced by lying and stealing behavior.

Anorexic patients' continual propensity to lie in treatment has been noted by almost every investigator. While this lying may represent defenses and reenactments of aspects of oedipal conflicts, early in treatment it is a repetitious defensive maneuver and replicates the lying of the parental figures. More elaborate motivations are not evident at this time. As treatment progresses, the unconscious meaning of the content of some fabrications may make itself available for analysis. The use of lying to maintain denial is obvious.

The fantasied identification with mother is overdetermined in this particular defense. Patients want something to be true, and feel that if they can convince the analyst (mother, superego) of its truth, it will be true. This particular motive for the "fantasy" (lie) is usually readily interpretable early in analysis and is easily accepted by the patient.

Lying also is an attempt to control the analyst and the analyst's thoughts. This aspect is interpretable later in treatment, when patients are aware of their general need to control.

Patients attempt to appease the superego aspect of the internalized maternal representation by lying. They lie to deny responsibility and the accompanying shame. Lying may even take on an exhibitionistic character as patients attempt to paint a picture of moral superiority or social success and desirability.

The masochistic exhibitionism may be extreme: patients will fabricate something totally unbelievable and then defend it with fury. In social situations, this can lead to rejection and humiliation. Such deceit of self- and object perceptions plays a role in the fantasies (and/or isolated delusions) that these patients maintain about their own body images. Here the exhibitionism is in the implied content of the fabrication.

Lastly, the lies are a continued identification with the faulty superego of the mother or both parents. The mothers of anorexic patients are consistent liars who proclaim their own moral superiority. One patient called her mother a "sanctimonious liar" who "only lied in good causes." The mother has lied to control the child's activities and to justify her inconsistent behavior. As an adult, the daughter utilizes lies to control her object perceptions and representations. This particular determinant of lying may be inferred and later interpreted by the analyst without too much difficulty.

It is fortunate that anorexic lying does not have a sociopathic implication. It is so contradictory to these patients' general desire for moral perfection that it is readily given up by most patients relatively early in analysis.

Lying is often the result of a specific need to be discovered, humiliated, and punished. Certainly, when patients fabricate patent falsehoods in public they end up painfully ashamed. This provocation of punishment for the transgression may help in understanding another manifestation of their dishonesty—stealing.

Of four anorexic analysands who shoplifted in a manner reminiscent of kleptomania, only one evidenced overriding phallic connections. However, in all, associations to omniverous oral concerns were plentiful. These patients had conscious feelings of elation followed by guilt and shame over such "greedy" unlawful behavior. Punishment was often sought. One woman stole an article of clothing from a display counter while the clerk was standing there. She was detained by security personnel. Another ostentatiously placed an article of clothing on her body and walked out of a dressing room that she suspected was scrutinized by hidden observers. She was arrested and only escaped a jail sentence with the help of influential friends. After a period of humiliation, she was delighted to have "gotten away with it."

The thievery always involves clothing or food. Associations to clothing thefts repeatedly involve female siblings. Bruch (1978a) has noted a preponderance of female siblings among anorexic patients. In all four of the shoplifting anorexic analysands, there was an unusual amount of childhood and adolescent activity involving stealing and restealing of clothes between sisters; in fact, all of the female siblings were involved in such thievery. Some of these siblings were anorexic. The few male siblings of these patients did not seem to be involved in the relentless stealing, which was particularly aimless and often led to tears and recriminations. The parents were not involved and apparently were exceptionally ignorant of such continued, ostentatious dishonesty. In two cases, overt sadistic physical retaliations were part of the game. One patient physically attacked her sister with a pair of scissors at the age of eight. Another suffered a serious eye injury at the hands of an older sister at age six.

In these patients, the stealing represented an opportunity to act out aggressive, acquisitive impulses and sibling rivalry. The patients seemed to love "getting away with it." The repeated occurrence of such an extreme stylized activity reflected the family constellation. The mothers seemed compulsively involved in giving gifts of clothing to their daughters and enjoyed shopping for such gifts. The thefts and violence between sisters were, in part, a displacement of rage toward a generally depriving and controlling maternal figure whose reaction formations led to such gifts. The clothing represented mother, especially mother's love and food, and the stealing covered up the rage at deprivation.

These patients also acted out their desperate needs for food, and the guilt and shame associated with such impulses, more directly. At the beginning of treatment, two patients were unable to eat in anyone's presence. All four patients felt guilty and ashamed of eating in one or another context, and all associated eating with stealing. Two patients were obsessional "scrap stealers." When one young woman was in a hotel, she would invariably make the rounds of the corridors and steal scraps of food from trays left by guests outside their doors. Another would return to conference rooms after luncheons were served at her place of business and furtively steal from the unremoved leftovers. Such activities were accompanied by shame, as well as the fear and expectation of discovery.

Such compulsive dishonesty is an acting out of impulses and is common to all anorexics. Most anorexics have a history of childhood chubbiness or obesity. All have been covetous of food, particularly the food of others. Frequently, there is a history of food stealing from friends in early adolescence. All anorexic patients are involved in a constant battle between appetite and superego.

Scrap stealing may involve humiliation, but it is not potentially as dangerous or self-destructive as shoplifting. The latter also invites exposure, public humiliation, incarceration, and the consequent destruction of treatment. Unfortunately, vigorous attempts to educate the patient or to impose constraints on such a symptom almost invariably fail and compromise treatment. One patient whose previous therapist threatened to discontinue treatment if she repeated her initial act of shoplifting expanded her shoplifting adventures without ever again informing the therapist. She enjoyed a certain anorexic "glee" at "getting away with it." Treatment was obviously useless, as she replicated her relationship with her mother.

It is profitable to treat lying and stealing as one would treat any other symptom. Ask for associations, pose hypothetical questions as to the need for such self-destructive activity, and attempt to discover the meaning and source of the impulses. Such a detached approach does lead to patients' increased interest in their motives and increased understanding of their needs for immediate gratification. The frustration and anger are exposed, and patients are able to integrate their behavior with their generally "morally superior" view of themselves. Covert defiance and rebellion give way to analytic understanding. As with any acting-out patient, the stealing anorexic patient's welfare is in some jeopardy, but the jeopardy is less if the impulses are open to analysis than it is if they are perpetuated by constraints. Like other patients with pregenital problems, anorexics are usually quite surprised and gratified when they finally discover that they can control an impulse without "falling apart," without suffering intense frustration, and without the sense of envy and defeat characteristic of narcissistic injury.

FRAGMENTATION*

Fragmentation includes all isolations of parts of the ego and often occurs when patients are under internal or external stress. It varies in intensity and frequency and plays an important part in the ability to free-associate. It allows for contradictory judgments and facilitates the defensive use of lies. It ranges from major ego splits to repeated, isolated, often contradictory ideas that frequently take the form of fixation on some minute fragment of experience to the exclusion of the whole. The latter may create a fragmented feeling and confusion. It occasionally is accompanied by mild depersonalization. Such isolated areas of experience seem to be conscious manifestations of unconscious self- and object representations that are not integrated into the total personality and are used defensively. This mechanism may be pointed out early in treatment, but it is usually better to wait until patients are aware of how they use it as a defense. Early interpretation can lead to confusion or may compound the already existing confusion. Such internalizations, with their isolated "split-off" affects, always accumulate new content as they are projected onto contemporary figures. This produces contaminated object perceptions which contribute to the

---

*For in-depth discussions of fragmentation, see Chapters 5 and 6.

sense of confusion. One patient, after becoming clearly aware of such misperceptions, produced fantasies of internalized persecutory figures that would scold her, shout at her, and demand absolute compliance. She recognized her vomiting as an attempt to rid herself of the hated fantasied invaders and at times would plaintively ask how to get rid of them. With interpretation, she related each fantasied internalization to specific ego states. Later, when fragmentation was less of a problem, these internalized images were more clearly associated with fantasies of invasion by mother. As treatment progressed, such fears were seen to be amalgamated with fears of sexual penetration and finally to oedipal concerns with father and his transference representative.

When anorexic patients first become aware of their own hostility and wishes for sadistic control over the maternal figure, past and present, there is an almost universal ego split in their internalized object representations. Such major splits may also occur in other areas of patients' life experience. However, whatever other objects may be enveloped and consequently involved, the process seems to derive from the early ambivalence toward, and isolated part-object representations of, the primal object.

In less disorganized patients, the ego state of anger with its wishes for omnipotent sadistic control of the object representation and perception is seen consciously as a foreign body. Such a state contrasts dramatically with the anorexic's primitive wish for fusion with mother. The "positive" or part-object internalization of the "good" mother usually is represented by intense, loving, identificatory experiences with the idealized perception of mother, often replete with mild elation, e.g., "I am just like mother. I know everything she wants, thinks, and feels"; "Mother is just like me. She anticipates my every thought"; "We hide nothing from each other."

Obviously, a patient's search for pleasure in fantasied gratifying object perceptions allowed by the projection of gratifying idealized part-object representations is a denial of unpleasure associated with projections of frustrating object representations. Such a confusion of object perceptions of a single object or multiple objects can become cognitively accessible to, and understood by, the patient as he or she is able to acknowledge the contradictory split perceptions.

Fragmentation, whether it involves gross splitting or isolated unassailable preoccupations, should be demonstrated as soon as reasonably possible and should be handled as a defense. As patients become aware of its defensive nature, it should be analyzed and traced to its remembered or reconstructed analogues.

ACTING OUT

As in all patients with impulse disorders, acting out in anorexic patients is a common repeated defense against analytic understanding. These patients have an intense need for immediate gratification which is denied in many ways. In patients with hysterical personality traits, acting out may appear early in treatment. In the more obsessional cases, it generally appears as superego restraints are lifted.

Like other acting-out patients, anorexics pursue the mild elation and sense of omnipotence that accompany such instinctual indulgence. The self-destructive character of the instinctual indulgence is usually obvious and should be pointed out to patients as they indicate a willingness to understand. Such willingness is often slow to appear, since anorexics have such an ability to deny, rationalize, and even idealize their own self-destruction.

Very frequently, derivatives of a conflict seem to have to be acted out in outside life and in the transference before the conflict and its accompanying fantasies can be brought into treatment. For example, one woman had to find a lover of the approximate age of her father and analyst before she could acknowledge the loss of the idealized oedipal father. Another provoked an attack on herself immediately after reestablishing her menstrual cycle. Projections, rages, and complaints to friends and outside professionals are common behavior patterns. When handled without too much constraint by the analyst, these patients are able to verbalize and analyze the underlying conflict.

A word of caution is warranted in this regard. Too much authoritarian constraint can be very destructive emotionally and physically. One anorexic girl became psychotic after her parents took her out of treatment and placed her in a hospital where behavioral therapy was practiced. After she returned to her first therapist, he traced the psychotic regression to her separation from him and to the punitive hospital environment. Another patient attempted suicide a number of times in response to an inconsistent, inadequate, arbitrary therapeutic situation. Any relationship that infantilizes patients and forces them to submit to authority merely duplicates the mother-child relationship. All of the ambivalence is mobilized but remains unanalyzed. Acting out inevitably results. The high mortality rate in anorexia nervosa may be due, in part, to the anxious manipulations in medical or behavioral management.

There is no doubt that the provocation of the acting out can be most trying. One patient reveled in the thought that a loved one was suffering and feeling hopeless as she destroyed herself. She conceded she had similar feelings about the analyst. Another who cut herself with razor blades and burned herself with cigarettes initiated her analyst during the early months of treatment by carving "help" on her arm. One patient, when angry at the analyst, precipitated a confrontation with an attacker. The clear separation of the analyst from the patient's superego is of the utmost importance, and the repetitious interpretation of how patients utilize the analyst or others to represent their own primitive sadistic superego is a necessity.

These patients have little difficulty in becoming aware of their needs for immediate gratification when it comes to food, but their awareness of such needs, impulses, and anger in other areas is harder to establish. It is important that they see their acting out in such a context and become aware of the methods they use to deny their impulses.

Discussion

The recognition and analysis of the defensive maneuvers underlying these eight interrelated personality traits of anorexic patients is as important as the analysis of the content of the material. Any of these defensive postures may both represent and hide a particular impulse, wish, or fantasy whose content will become available only as the defense is interpreted, analyzed, and understood.

There frequently are points in the treatment when rather dramatic changes occur. After patients have become aware of their intense attachment to, and identification with, mother and of how they tried to control the maternal object representation that they now project onto the analyst, underlying dependent needs emerge. Anorexics are usually amazed at what arrogant, demanding, managing creatures they were hiding beneath their self-sacrificing, vulnerable, wraithlike asceticism. By this time, most analysands have recognized their vulnerability to shame and humiliation and are quite aware of their self-destructive wishes and behavior. With some variations in timing, the emergence of these underlying passive wishes is correlated with a relatively severe depression. Suicidal preoccupations seem to be a universal accompaniment.

It is important to thoroughly investigate and interpret the self-destructive wishes and suicidal impulses early in treatment. Manifestations of such wishes should be recognized by these patients in their general life style as well as in their anorexic symptoms. When the disappointment and depression reach consciousness, and intense suicidal wishes are felt, they can be understood more easily in the context of previous preparatory work. Acting out can be held to a minimum, but self-destructive neurotic acts still will be commonplace. For example, one patient chided a bachelor acquaintance about his latent homosexuality and provoked a retaliatory fist in her jaw. Another involved herself in an auto accident. A third provoked a sexual attack and attempted rape.

It is common for menstrual periods to reappear shortly before or after the beginning of this period of intense depression. There seems to be an attempt to renounce the regression, infancy, and mother.

Concurrent with these developments, material seems to become available for interpretations of the underlying sadism. Patients are already partially aware of their anger and how they direct it at themselves. Associations to the violence of the suicidal wishes and fantasies, along with the violent destructiveness of the neurotic actions, may lead to memories of sadomasochistic fantasies and acts in early childhood. In some cases, these fantasies had been acted out on younger siblings. Material usually includes violent, slashing, controlling, smashing, and cannibalistic fantasies directed toward self, sexuality, siblings, and mother. Patients begin to understand how they have tried to shut the beloved mother off from every gratification in life, just as earlier they had attempted to shut themselves off from such pleasures.

At this point, we are getting away from the form and style of presentation and becoming involved in content, which has been discussed thoroughly elsewhere in this volume.

Countertransference*

Obviously, the therapist and/or psychoanalyst is the recipient of all of the overt and covert anger of anorexic patients. The usual dangers to the analysis

---

*As this subject is covered extensively in a separate chapter (8), only brief mention of it is made here.

are involved. These patients provoke the analyst through their contradictory lack of cooperation, their judgmental superiority and contempt, and their acting out, as described earlier. Insofar as possible, the analyst should constantly be interested in the sources of the hostility and be in the position of interpreting the hostility rather than responding to it.

Frequently, the tendency toward arbitrary force (e.g., behavior therapy, forced hospitalization, imposition of drugs, electroshock therapy, leukotomy, lobotomy) in treatment is directly related to the effect of patients' covert stubborn lack of cooperation on the treating physician. The anorexic's self-destructive attempts to manipulate "authority" can be especially frustrating to the medical practitioner intent on "curing" the physical person.

For most analysts experiencing patient-induced anxiety, a greater danger than retaliatory force is hopeless, helpless resignation. It is more important to maintain reasonable analytic distances in anorexia nervosa than it is in the milder transference neuroses. Anorexics are acutely attuned to the anxiety and guilt they can mobilize in people around them. They will unconsciously attempt to do so with their transference objects, or at least in their fantasied transference object perceptions, in order to maintain the illusion of control.

Fortunately, as one accumulates experience with these patients and their pregenital manipulations, one also accumulates greater confidence in the ultimate strength of their egos and their integrative potentialities.

SUMMARY

This chapter focused on some specific technical problems of psychoanalysis or psychoanalytic psychotherapy with anorexic patients.

A critical study of the indications for hospitalization was offered. It was concluded that hospitalization is seldom necessary and should only be utilized in situations of particular emergency. It is definitely contraindicated in the vast majority of cases where no life-threatening crisis or psychotic breakdowns are at hand.

An attempt was made to determine what criteria, if any, should direct a psychiatrist to involve one or more members of the family in treatment. It is often helpful, particularly with younger patients, to have the mother and/or the father in psychoanalysis or psychotherapy, but it is by no means necessary. The important issue is the patient's understanding of the internalized parental object representations, subject representations, and self- and object perceptions —leading to the ultimate analysis of the triadic oedipal conflict.

Surgery, electroshock treatment, behavioral modification, and force-feeding are absolutely contraindicated, regardless of the circumstances. The primary concern of treatment is the underlying psychopathology. Symptoms of self-starvation, bulimia, vomiting, and amenorrhea are overdetermined, but do serve as masochistic, controlling maneuvers. Overconcern and anxiety about such activities help to perpetuate them.

Anorexic patients are characterized by pregenital regressions that delineate the clearly defined "final common pathway" of anorexic symptomatology. This clinical picture suggests to various authors such diagnostic classifications as "borderline character," "narcissistic character," "psychotic character," "pseudoneurotic schizophrenia," and even "schizophrenia." While the severity of regression varies widely with these patients, the prognostic implications so often associated with these diagnostic judgments do not apply to anorexic patients. The vast majority are clearly utilizing defensive regressions from a traditional oedipal conflict with an accompanying transference neurosis, and thus fall into the neurotic categories.

The style and form of anorexic defense mechanisms were considered and some very abbreviated observations were made on the general problems involved in the analysis of pregenital regressions. This material was followed by a listing of personality traits commonly observed in anorexia patients. Such personality traits are, among other things, representations of underlying defenses.

Included were (1) subjective feelings of, and needs for, the illusion of complete conscious control of mind, body, and impulse; (2) the closely related lack of ability to free-associate early in treatment; (3) in the early stages of treatment, an apparent lack of fantasy life in obsessionally defended patients as opposed to (4) a plethora of fantasies, dreams, and activity in those with overideational hysterical characteristics; (5) the fantasy and conviction of moral and judgmental superiority to others, particularly to the primary object and its transference representations; (6) lying and stealing, which have relatively little sociopathic significance in anorexics and readily lend themselves to analysis; (7) fragmentation, which includes defensive processes ranging from gross ego splitting to transitory, isolated affective or cognitive states; and (8) acting out, which often seems to be necessary before certain conflicts and accompanying fantasies can be consciously considered and treated. It was noted that too much authoritarian restraint can be damaging physically and emotionally and can contribute to further acting out.

Throughout this chapter, attention was directed at the defenses against pregenital sadistic impulses and fantasies, as well as their violently masochistic derivatives. The chapter concluded with a brief consideration of countertransference. An understanding of one's own reactions to these ingratiating, but demanding and provocative, patients is of cardinal significance in handling technical problems of treatment.

10
Psychoanalytic Therapy of Severe Anorexia: The Case of Jeanette

IRA L. MINTZ, M.D.

The treatment of anorexia nervosa has a long, dramatic, poignant, and tragic history. In 1689, Morton (reported in Thomä 1967) described the willful starvation of Mr. Duke's 18-year-old daughter who became a skeleton and died. Nearly 300 years later, anorexic patients still die. In 1873, Lasegue (reported in Thomä 1967) described the difficulties in treating such patients and keenly commented, "Woe to the physician who, misunderstanding the peril, treats as fancy without object or duration an obstinacy which he hopes to vanquish by medicines, friendly advice, or by the still more defective resource, intimidation" (p. 9). This warning still applies, but it is often ignored. Parents, friends, and often physicians continue to suggest, encourage, and coerce anorexic patients to eat, often without recognizing that the starvation represents the coalescence of a series of powerful forces arising from conflicts in childhood, swollen by the multitudinous cares of adolescence, and overdetermined by ambivalence surrounding aggression, sexuality, dependency, and regressed infantile yearnings.

In recent years descriptions of the treatment of this illness have been provided by many investigators, including Bliss and Branch (1960), Bruch (1965, 1970, 1973b, 1978a), Dally (1969), Minuchin et al. (1978), Selvini Palazzoli (1978), Sours (1969, 1974, 1979), Sperling (1961, 1978), and Thomä (1967). In my opinion, psychoanalytically oriented treatment is the most practical and effective approach, and provides not only symptom alleviation but personality changes crucial to the development of mature functioning.

REFERRAL

Jeanette was an 18-year-old woman with very severe anorexia nervosa. She was intensively treated as an office patient except for two brief periods of hospitalization in the very beginning of treatment before there had been an opportunity for a therapeutic alliance to develop. After the first 2–3 months, in

217

spite of many difficulties and severe crises, there was little question of re-hospitalization and Jeanette's treatment proceeded without interruption except for recognized vacation periods.

This case is presented to illustrate in detail the nature and therapeutic management of her illness, and to suggest that if such severe anorexia can be treated with minimal hospitalization, then perhaps the routine hospitalization of less severely ill patients deserves some reconsideration. Jeanette was treated in intensive psychoanalytic psychotherapy five times a week with no coercive procedures or behavioral modification techniques.

Jeanette was referred by another psychiatrist who had treated her for the previous five months and who had become increasingly concerned about her agitated behavior and increasing threats of suicide. At the beginning of her illness, she had seen a psychiatrist for about three months and a social worker for six weeks, and had attended a clinic for two months. Because of her age, the parents were not seen initially, but they were seen together after the fifth session when Jeanette had to be hospitalized.

FAMILY BACKGROUND

While most anorexic patients come from middle-class families, Jeanette came from a rather modest background. The father, an unsuccessful plumber, was described as a provocative, argumentative man whose work habits were erratic at best and markedly complicated by drinking, which had contributed to the loss of two previous plumbing businesses that had been financed by his brother. Jeanette felt that her father cared about her, but that he had such an inferiority complex and was so totally absorbed in his own difficulties that he couldn't pay enough attention to his children.

The mother was described as a controlling, manipulative woman who constantly fought with her husband and with Jeanette's two sisters and three older brothers. Although the father shouted at and insulted the mother, Jeanette thought that the mother was really in charge. The patient stated that her mother got her controlling ways from her own mother, who bossed her daughter around unmercifully. After the grandfather died, the grandmother spent six months of the year living with Jeanette's family and six months living with her son's family. The uncle was a wealthy man who would have preferred his mother to live in her own apartment with a companion. The grandmother would have no part of it, however, and insisted on living alternately with the two families.

The father's brother was a former policeman who ran a successful security company. When the analyst saw the patient in the mid-1960s, he was a wealthy man. This uncle paid for Jeanette's treatment. In a mixture of fondness for his relatives and a wish to demonstrate his financial success to them, he paid for all types of help for the family (e.g., camp for all six children, psychotherapy for Jeanette and two of her brothers, orthodontia for Jeanette). His largesse made the father feel demeaned, but he did not object because he could not afford to pay for such things himself.

THERAPY

Session 1

In the initial interview, Jeanette appeared very restless and agitated, was unable to sit for all of the session, and periodically got up and paced. While one could see that she must have been quite attractive before she became ill, in her current state she gave the appearance of a fluttering scarecrow. She was 5'5" and weighed 80 lbs. Her short hair was thin and dull, and hung limply about her neck. Her nose was beaklike, with its modest prominence accentuated by its thinness and by the flaring of her nostrils when she spoke. The zygomatic processes stuck out because of the lack of tissue beneath them, with darkened hollows replacing muscle mass.

She spoke in a loud, crude manner and appeared unkempt and disheveled. Her small-sized clothing hung on her sticklike frame. Her joints appeared large relative to the thin limbs emanating from them. She looked like a self-made concentration camp victim.

Her opening comments were as follows:

Look how messed up I am. . . . Let me show you how skinny I am. It's disgusting. [Pulling up her long sleeves] Look at my bones. I have to have something in my mouth all the time: gum, cigarettes, candy. I chew 20 sticks of gum a day. I don't eat regular food. . . . I stuff myself and then I vomit. I used to weigh 110, then I went down to 70. Now I'm up to 80. . . . I like to be with people constantly. You know, to have my feedings. . . . I'm happy when I'm told how skinny I am, that's how nuts I am.

Look at this. [Here she pushed down her jeans to reveal a mass of scar tissue on her abdomen.] I get this from burning myself with the hot-water bottle when my stomach hurts and I'm constipated. . . . I can't stand it when I'm constipated. I have to get it out. I take laxatives every night, sometimes 50 or 60. . . . Then I stay up most of the night exercising or smoking to keep up my metabolism so that I don't put on any weight. . . . I do everything to extremes. When I vomit, I jam my fingers down my throat so hard. . . . [Here she revealed a series of long-standing scars on the dorsum of her fingers where the upper teeth had gashed the skin from the violence of her thrust into her mouth.]

In her hyperactive, agitated state, she was almost oblivious to the analyst's presence and certainly was not attuned to his responses since thus far he had had almost no opportunity to make a comment. This was essentially the tenor of her early therapeutic contacts. She continued, "If someone doesn't call me, I get frustrated and act hysterical, . . . and then I go and eat the house up. . . . I have to always be in control. . . . When I get too frustrated, I get so depressed that I think of killing myself. . . . I can't be alone." She suddenly looked directly at the analyst, instead of talking to the air. "I feel that I'm not making contact with you. I really wanted to see someone else, you know, and because his office was in W_____, he thought that it was too far. I was furious. I really liked Dr. L. [her previous analyst] very much."

The analyst asked her why her previous therapy had failed if she had liked that analyst so much. She reflected for a moment, one of the first pauses in her outpouring, and then replied, "I don't know. I was very upset when he said that he couldn't help me. . . . He was very honest though." The analyst asked her if she had felt a sense of triumph at his defeat. "No . . . well . . . I don't know. Can you help me?" The analyst replied that she was so self-destructive that she might try to wreck this treatment, too. "No, I won't do that again. . . . You're pretty smart, maybe I did do that." So ended the first interview.

COMMENTS

At first glance, the analyst's early statements might appear intrusive, too challenging, and even precipitous. A brief explanation is in order. The analyst felt that Jeanette was so depressed and suicidal that it was important to make contact with her early, yet she treated him with indifference bordering on contempt. She made it clear that he was second rate and that she preferred the earlier analyst. She acknowledged that there was little contact between her and the current analyst. Her first response to him occurred when she was challenged as to why the last treatment had failed. Her reply, "I was very upset when he couldn't help me," suggested the hidden, defiant, negative transference so characteristic of these patients. The analyst felt that it was important to demonstrate to her that he was aware that she could also defeat him if she chose to and that he was not afraid of her manipulations through illness. That this attitude reached her momentarily was evident from her comment, "I won't do that again."

In addition, because she was so depressed and suicidal, it was necessary to attempt to establish a positive working alliance and relatively positive transference quickly in order to develop a libidinal tie to the analyst. This was not successful enough, however, and the patient subsequently had to be hospitalized, but the attempt was still necessary and, in the long run, was valid.

It is an error to wait with these patients for the transference and alliance slowly to develop, just as it is ill-advised to wait for the emergence of clear, obvious material prior to interpreting it. Anorexic patients may die before they talk because they are so self-destructive, so unused to revealing thoughts and feelings by speaking, and so prone to act out conflicts through symptoms. These patients usually have the experience in their lives of important people not listening to them or being sensitively attuned to their needs when they are well and speak normally. It was important, therefore, for Jeanette to feel that the analyst was listening very carefully and was attempting to understand her. These patients use their illness to get attention and to manipulate people. The more anxious others, including the analyst, become about a patient's threat of increasing illness, the greater the patient's tendency to exacerbate the illness in order to exercise control and achieve what are perceived to be necessary gratifications. The analyst wanted Jeanette to know that he understood this and understood her. Then she might feel that he could help her.

Sessions 2–4

The next three interviews continued in stormy fashion. Jeanette described feeling smothered by her mother, whom she felt ran her life. The mother constantly told her what to do and how to do it. It always had been that way. She felt that her mother was a good person who cared about her, but couldn't stop running every aspect of her life. She constantly told her to eat. Jeanette stated that she had to get away from her mother and that she wanted to be hospitalized. She had called all the major hospitals in the area to inquire about being admitted. If the analyst didn't grant her wish for hospitalization, she wouldn't return. This was stated repeatedly, both as an imperious demand and as an infantile whine. Her grandmother kept telling her that she was killing her father, who had bleeding ulcers, and she felt guilty after each attack of bleeding.

During momentary intervals in her agitated state, she described brief elements in her childhood. As a teenager, she had overeaten and been thought of as fat by friends, whom she felt had shunned her. When she was 13, she had weighed 114 lbs. In the next year, her weight had gone up to 150 lbs. She remembered disliking her sisters and most of her friends, who were thin. She became increasingly distressed following her comments about the anger toward her friends and sisters.

She again demanded hospitalization. In response to the analyst's attempts to discuss why she felt it was imperative, she again threatened to stop the treatment. When he pointed out her need to feel in control, and that she perceived any disagreement with her wish as a loss of control, she calmed down and said, "You understand about the control."

She spoke more about her turmoil and added that she "wanted to take the whole world in with my eating, . . . then I feel so guilty that I take 50 laxatives to get rid of it, . . . with the diarrhea and cramps." She again pointed to her scarred fingers and added that she masturbated every night in order to increase the pelvic muscle tone, which improved her control over defecation. She also exercised during the night and then took very cold showers to shock herself. In the fourth session, she reported taking only 30 laxatives instead of 50, and not inducing vomiting.

COMMENTS

Jeanette's comment that she "wanted to take the whole world in with my eating" reflected the close relationship between eating and people. Anorexics deal with food the way they would like to deal with people: i.e., they displace the control that they cannot achieve over people onto food. That this construct is accurate is evident in the frequent clinical episodes where frustration in a relationship, with the feeling of being helpless to control events, results either in sudden thoughts about consuming food or in an exacerbation of anorexic symptoms. These patients must gradually come to understand their difficulties and disappointments in relationships with people, especially family members.

The patient reverted to wanting to control the analyst by insisting on hospitalization. She wanted a different analyst, questioned this one's competency, and threatened to "fix" him by intensifying her starvation. She was momentarily receptive to the ideas that they could disagree but discuss their disagreement and that she could become annoyed without attempting to "fix" the analyst by starving or taking laxatives. This acceptance was followed by her associations to how guilty she felt over the hard time she was giving this analyst and had given to previous ones—she stated that they must be "nuts" to be willing to see people like her all day long.

When anorexic patients are permitted to manipulate and control the analyst and others in their life, the resultant guilt may be expiated by harsh primitive superego dictates for punishment via destructive acting out or increased symptom formation. On the other hand, if the manipulations are actively interfered with, the therapist may be seen as an extension of the controlling parents, and symptoms may become life threatening. Analysis of the behavior provides these patients with their opportunity to stop the behavior and the ability to deal with their feelings about it in a less regressive manner.

In Jeanette's case, the working alliance was evanescent, and her increasing agitation and suicidal threats required her hospitalization on the following day.

Hospitalization

In the hospital, Jeanette's regressed infantile behavior continued. She insisted on eating only low-calorie foods and also attempted to exercise excessively in order to insure losing weight. She brought her tennis racquet to the hospital and was enraged that there were no facilities for exercise. She found that on the most modest diet, she would gain a pound or two and this increased her distress. She walked about the ward in a pair of shorts and attempted to wear an open blouse that completely exposed her breasts. She was preoccupied with her anorexia and was unwilling to talk about anything that did not pertain to it. She insisted on discussing her diet, her severe abdominal cramps, her constipation and laxative use, and her exercise requirements. She was demanding, swore and cursed, was unable to tolerate any frustration, and, on three or four occasions, "fired" her analyst, told him that the treatment was over, and threatened to sign out of the hospital against medical advice.

Medical management, including decisions about food intake, was provided by the internist. This provided careful control over her metabolic requirements and deflected any resentment about intake requirements (in order to minimize negativistic behavior in the treatment). Jeanette was told that she would not be forced to eat because she was not eating for reasons that the analyst hoped they would uncover. At the same time, the internist would provide her with enough caloric intake to prevent life-threatening conditions. When she was rehospitalized, it was with the understanding that it was for psychiatric, not medical, reasons.

The internist never pressured or ordered Jeanette to eat; nor did he tell her what or how much to eat. Such authoritarian tactics are extremely inadvisable, as they cause the physician to be seen as a parental figure. Then patients' feelings of aggression, defiance, and negativism toward the parent are turned toward the physician, and they derive the same sadistic satisfaction in defying the doctor as they do in defying the parents. In addition, behaving in an authoritarian fashion prevents the analyst from analyzing patients' deep distrust and fear that any information they give the analyst will be used to dominate and control them. It is vital to obtain the complete cooperation and trust of patients to enable them to express fears and conflicts, and to tolerate and absorb the anxiety that emerges as they face their inner turmoil. If the physician or analyst does act authoritarian or controlling, it is very difficult later to disclaim any intention of dominating the patient. The analyst's role is to help patients understand themselves, not to tell them what to do.

In the hospital, the analyst attempted to get Jeanette to recognize that her preoccupation with the anorexia allowed her to avoid the thoughts and feelings that truly distressed her—that, in effect, the anorexia was a smoke screen for other upsetting problems. When she complained of weight gain, constipation, and cramps, the analyst pointed out that she could rid herself of these difficulties by talking about what really bothered her. Typically, she responded that nothing bothered her and that she had nothing to say. The analyst replied that she was not aware of what bothered her because she was constantly preoccupied with ideas about food, which interfered with the emergence of other thoughts into consciousness. If she thought more about her life, she would recognize some of her problems.

The other idea that the analyst attempted to discuss with her was the issue of control. He indicated that he thought it was a major problem of hers and that, for reasons yet unknown, she felt out of control over the important events of her life. Consequently, she shifted the area of control to eating, which she could and did control. She attempted to exert tremendous control over everyone in the hospital and became terribly agitated and distressed when she could not do so. She acknowledged that she tried to make the analyst do all kinds of things and would explode with anger if he didn't.

This discussion, which took place repeatedly, had a number of consequences. It permitted Jeanette to relinquish some of her infantile omnipotent attitudes in the transference so that she was not constantly exploding in rageful frustration and was therefore more amenable to rational discussion and reflection. It opened a window toward the recognition and subsequent discussion of one of her major problems. Finally, it provided a link between her current behavior and her symptoms, which were discussed as regressed attempts to control aspects of her bodily function when she felt that she had lost control over her relationships with external objects.

At times, these discussions were fruitful. Mostly, however, these interchanges were met with blanket hostility and derision, skepticism, denial, ignorance, or a "blank mind." Occasionally, she would respond for brief periods, sitting quietly and reflecting on what was said and or. some of her own thoughts. She would speak rationally for five minutes and then explode, deny everything that was said before, and indicate that it was all worthless, that there was no point in going on with this stupid, idiotic treatment, and that the analyst was "fired." She would then curl up in a ball, pull the blankets over her head, and terminate the interview. She repeatedly made requests to leave the hospital or to go to another hospital where behavior therapy would teach her how to eat. The following letter is a good illustration of her attitude.

Dear Doctor,
   I am leaving this morning whether you like it or not, so you better sign me the hell out of here. I think your psychiatry is pure and utter bullshit and even if some of the points you make may be true, absolutely nothing is getting solved. Every

patient here except me has been progressing but not with mere babble but with medication and electric shock—in other words, changing the brain. You can just about forget it with me; talking time is over. Don't waste my time, I won't waste yours. Sending me here was *your* mistake. I'll never forget you for it.

I am fucking starving now. I have been for many days. My weight has gone up. I am completely miserable. Now that you have destroyed me physically, as well as put me into deep depression, why don't you completely finish me off? My mind and feelings are still the same. I need control; I am dead without it. You killed me—you did your job and here I am in the city morgue at this hospital with all the nuts.

You can't understand my frustrations but you certainly can add to them; and you certainly have done so with great success. I hope you are as successful with all your patients—or should I say with all your victims.

When I get home I will go back to my same routine. At least I'll be able to eat and stay thin. Give up, and admit defeat for you have failed me miserably. I know I will probably not survive for long because of malnutrition, but gaining weight on liquids and candy in the city morgue is no fun either. At least at home I may be miserable within myself but there are people around that make me happy. Here I sit on my ass like a dead body. My brain is dead and so are my mouth, my eyes, my ears, my legs, my soul, and anything else a human being is made of is buried here, too.

I'm sick of seeing you in your tweed suits, happy-go-lucky as a lark running around with your "buddies" to your "confidential" big shit psychiatric meetings, consultations, dinners, ceremonials, or whatever you want to call them. OK so give up. Sign me out. We'll give up together. I can't stand seeing your face any longer. I don't trust you . . . I think you are incompetent as far as anorexia is concerned. I want to thank you for fucking up my life once more; for taking away all my controls. But starting from tomorrow my hell is over. Sign me out. Stay out of my room. Admit your mistake; I should've been put in Columbia-Presbyterian Hospital—and you damn well know it. Don't bother coming in because I can't look at your face again. Depression is a hard problem to cope with and I don't need any extras. Goodbye . . . maybe we will meet in another world under different circumstances, . . . I'll put you through the hell you are putting me through.

I'll expect 35 Ex-Lax at my door tomorrow. Don't give me any more lines. I don't care to hear them. I won't give up control so you had better quit now. I *hate* you. I honestly, honestly do.

Jeanette

P.S. I just stuffed my face and couldn't throw up. IF PARTS OF THIS ARE IRRATIONAL AND REPETITIOUS, . . . *THEN SO IS LIFE!*

If one looks beneath this angry letter, a certain involvement between patient and analyst seems evident. Jeanette clearly indicated that she felt the analyst couldn't stand her and wasn't interested in her. The analyst interpreted that Jeanette felt this way toward him sometimes and that her hostile provocative behavior made her feel guilty and made her fear that he would become disgusted with her, dislike her, and stop treating her. He pointed out that she usually "fired" him after a particularly violent outburst and that the "firing" was in anticipation of his annoyance and abandonment of her. Her statement "give up, and admit defeat" revealed the depth of her anxiety and her fear that the analyst would not understand either her testing of his resolve or the nature of her deep problems. The analyst's calling on her after one of these outbursts, and discussing her behavior while indicating that he could tolerate it and was not put off by it, was very reassuring to her.

There was a true threat in the letter, however. It centered on the issue of control. At one point, she stated, "I want to thank you . . . for taking away all my controls"; at another, "My mind and feelings are still the same. I need control; I am dead without it." It was obvious that she felt threatened by the relationship with the analyst. This threat had a dual source. First, she felt that a closer relationship with the analyst would result in her being controlled by him as he learned more about her. Second, he stood for her giving up control over food, which was a substitute for her inability to control people. She felt that she still needed it, and she experienced panic at its potential loss. This again raises the question as to the advisability of an analyst behaving in an authoritarian manner toward an anorexic patient. Being controlled is one of her major fears. For the analyst to attempt to regulate her eating is to verify her greatest fear and to unwittingly repeat in the treatment what the patient undoubtedly experienced as a child. Therefore, in an attempt to help the patient deal with conflict and early childhood trauma, the analyst retraumatizes the patient in the very way that she was originally damaged. This behavior neither encourages trust in the analyst nor provides the opportunity to analyze the patient's overwhelming fear of being controlled as expressed in the transference.

By the second week of hospitalization, Jeanette had put on 4–5 lbs. on her minimal diet. Although she was still agitated and frequently exploded with yelling and screaming, she more frequently acknowledged that there was something that bothered her but that she did not know what it was, and that her preoccupation with the anorexic symptoms covered it up. In response to the analyst's comment that if she were willing to think and to talk her abdominal cramps and constipation would subside, she acknowledged that she was afraid of her thoughts, that she forgot what they talked about, and that she was not interested in those thoughts. At a point of anxiety, she said, "I want the anorexia again; it's better than the thoughts."

In a subsequent session, she began to reveal what some of the thoughts and fears were. She reported that that morning, when she had put on her slacks and found that they were tight across her abdomen, she had become panicky at the implication of abdominal weight gain and had sworn and become agitated. In response to the analyst's query as to what type of people complain about clothing that is tight across the abdomen, she launched into a discussion about pregnancy. The summer prior to the severe exacerbation of her anorexia, she and her boyfriend had worried about her getting pregnant. She remembered telling him that if she got pregnant she would not want to put on weight and would starve the child. She would also starve herself and behave like a child— she couldn't be a mother when she wanted to be a child. She had carefully kept this fantasy from her previous and current analysts.

After this revelation, it was possible to discuss how her preoccupation with her anorexic symptoms in part reflected a concern about pregnancy and mothering. Her preoccupation with weight and an enlarged abdomen, her morning nausea and vomiting, her daily weighing, and her amenorrhea were related to the conflict over pregnancy. Jeanette suddenly felt very frightened. Tears came into her eyes and she began to sob convulsively and reiterate her fear. She then admitted that there must be something very wrong with her. She asked if the analyst would really try to help her—she wanted to depend on him. Would he continue to see her and come tomorrow? If he would see her, she would do what he asked and stay in the hospital. Earlier in the same session, she had demanded to leave the hospital and terminate treatment. That night, the nurses reported that Jeanette ate her first normal meal.

The following day, she continued to improve and to eat more normally. She continued discussing her preoccupation with pregnancy. When she awakened, she looked at herself in the mirror before she got dressed and thought that the woman in her was returning as she saw that her abdomen and thighs were beginning to fill out. She returned to her panic over constipation and her frantic need to take laxatives to get the stools out. She had the thought that she had to get the baby out and realized that the "stool baby" inside was what frightened her. It became increasingly clear that the idea of swallowing something that gave her a fat abdomen and then expelling it was directly related to her anorexic rituals. She added that it really did not have to do with food at all. She noted feeling a calmness and tranquility that were in complete contrast to her previous wild behavior. She also acknowledged feeling that she could tolerate frustration much better. The analyst pointed out that Jeanette had tried to kill the woman in her both physically, by changing her appearance to that of a preadolescent child, and psychologically, by behaving like an infant with temper tantrums, no frustration tolerance, unreasonable behavior, and an unwillingness to deal realistically with her problems.

Jeanette continued to improve and was discharged after 12 days of hospitalization to continue her five-times-a-week office therapy. Prior to discharge, she spoke about being afraid to go home, afraid of getting her symptoms back. "I'm afraid to lose my mother. She used to baby me and care for me. Now I'll have to be grown up." This idea emerged during a discussion of how her illness permitted mother to infantilize her and Jeanette to accept it under the guise of being ill.

Jeanette stated that she felt better after her discussions with the analyst because what they talked about made sense and she was able to think about it, and also because the analyst made the image of being a little girl less appealing. "Fellows used to say, 'You look like a little girl', and I'd say, 'I'm a woman', but I didn't really feel that way. Now I'll have to be."

In light of the seriousness of Jeanette's illness and her rehospitalization 10 days later for another week, a question may well arise as to whether her hospitalization was too short. However, it must be kept in mind that while the symptoms and behavior of anorexic and psychosomatic patients can seriously worsen very rapidly, they can improve just as rapidly. The total treatment is of long duration, but in the intermediate phase, temporary improvement in symptoms can occur quite rapidly. The problem is that it is not sustained because of continued conflicts, lack of solid ego strength and healthy defense, and persistent yearning for infantile gratifications. In general, short periods of hospitalization in conjunction with intensive analytic outpatient therapy may be helpful.

The interpretation of the conflict around pregnancy and mothering deserves some further elaboration. There are many clinicians who warn that active interpretative intervention in the acute phase of anorexia or psychosomatic illness is contraindicated and can result in accelerating the downhill course of the disease. My own feeling is that the intervention is not only warranted but crucial. The issue at question is not the intervention per se, but rather how the intervention is carried out. If it is carried out in the face of a persistent unanalyzed negative transference, then the patient undoubtedly will get worse. If, however, meaningful interpretations are made in consonance with a relatively positive transference, then the patient will improve. Nonanalytically trained psychiatrists and physicians are at a disadvantage in dealing with these aspects of the transference; as a consequence, their admonitions in the setting in which they find themselves do warrant prudent counsel. Jeanette's reaction to the discussion about the pregnancy conflict was one of anxiety, but it coexisted with a concomitant positive transference evidenced by her voiced dependency on the analyst, her desire that he continue to see her, and her willingness to adhere to his suggestions. In that setting, I felt that her temporary improvement was to be anticipated and that discharge from the hospital was warranted.

One additional point is worth noting. In dealing with the conflicts of anorexic patients, it is better to deal with those over aggression prior to those surrounding sexuality and to deal with the self-destructive aspects of the aggression before the destructive aspects. This sequence seems most amenable to these patients' strict, primitive, punitive superego, with its tendency for immediate self-punishment via symptom formation for imagined transgressions.

In Jeanette's case, the sexual conflict was dealt with first only because it emerged first and provided an opportunity to begin discussing some of her conflicts. The serious discussion of her fears of becoming pregnant interfered with her obsessional preoccupations with the anorexic symptoms and began to explain some of her behavior. The sudden undoing of anorexic symptomatology may be accompanied by a good deal of fear and anxiety, and a sudden dependence on the analyst. Bringing some of the unconscious determinants of the anorexia into conscious awareness permitted this patient greater understanding, a better sense of control, and a feeling of well being.

Rehospitalization

Ten days after discharge, Jeanette had to be rehospitalized for a week. In the interim period, she voiced considerable apprehension that she should have stayed in the hospital one week longer to solidify her desire to remain a grownup. On one occasion, she felt overwhelmed by upsetting thoughts and tried to rid herself of them by taking 14 Dulcolax and developing stomach cramps, but still could not get rid of the painful thoughts. It is important to recognize that these patients withhold a great deal of relevant information. Sometimes it is necessary to ask about material that one suspects may be withheld. She described feeling depressed about her life; she didn't feel that she could behave like an adult. She stopped eating and complained that her analyst did not understand her and did not care as much since she had been discharged from the hospital. He used to come to see her at the hospital and now she had to drive for over an hour to see him at the office. She became increasingly disorganized and was rehospitalized.

The rehospitalization resulted in a second meeting with Jeanette's uncle. During the first hospitalization, he had introduced himself with the comment, "I'm Jeanette's uncle, you know, the one who pays the bills." At the second meeting, he was less tractable and demanded to know why the analyst had failed. Considerable time was spent dealing with him and helping him to understand the problems of anorexia. It was to his credit that he did not interject himself again during the entire course of the treatment.

In the hospital, Jeanette again began to behave in an infantile manner, with temper tantrums, swearing, exaggerated responses to minor frustrations, and attempts at running the hospital procedures. On one occasion, she was enraged that she might not be able to go home for the weekend to attend to some college courses. The analyst pointed out that she was furious in advance without attempting to determine whether it would be feasible for her to get a pass. When the analyst agreed to give her a pass, she left. She returned in an elated state and stated that, from now on, she was going to work in treatment and that it was idiotic to have anorexia and to deprive herself of happiness. Instead of enjoying food, she was tearing her guts out. From now on, she was going to get better. The analyst asked her what had changed her attitude, and she stated that it was related to letting her go out on a pass: now that she trusted him more, she could believe what he said. He pointed out that it might also have been related to feeling that he listened to her and that she had some control over the events in her life. At the end of the session, she smiled at the analyst for the first time.

The analyst had to skip two days and discussed this with Jeanette beforehand. When he returned to the hospital on the third day, she appeared extremely negativistic. She had phoned the analyst's office and gone on at length about how she could not stand therapy any longer and hated the analyst. At the hospital, she stated that she was going back to stuffing herself and vomiting and to taking laxatives and that she never wanted to see the analyst again. In her ensuing temper tantrum, she appeared furious at the analyst and at herself for her infantile behavior. At the very end of the session, she provided the clue as to what had provoked the outburst: "You really don't care about me. I haven't seen you for two days."

When the analyst returned on the following morning, Jeanette was quiet and tractable. She voiced hopelessness, disinterest in the treatment, and a feeling that the analyst had betrayed her, but she was no longer in a rage. The analyst indicated that he thought that he understood what was upsetting her and why she had regressed. He pointed out that when he did not see her on those two days, she felt that he really did not care about her and thus lost hope, felt overwhelmed, and regressed. He added that it seemed very important for her to feel that he did care and that she so easily could feel that he didn't. He pointed out that this represented an infantile ego position, namely, that he should be at her beck and call. This stance revealed an unwillingness to recognize that he could have other commitments and involvements in his life. They had discussed in advance the strong possibility of a negative reaction and regressive behavior on her part, but she had readily accepted the 2-day absence and had made no objection.

The analyst pointed out that her intense abdominal cramps primarily represented tremendous feelings of hatred toward him that she felt unable and unwilling to accept fully and "swallow." In a sense, she had been attacking and destroying the analyst inside her (introjecting him) rather than attacking him directly with the full impact of her feelings of disappointment, frustration, and hatred. Jeanette calmed down, became more introspective, and was able to continue the session in a relatively attentive and positive manner. The marked change in her behavior was clearly the result of the analyst's transference interpretations, the hatred in the transference, pointing out the regressed infantile ego position, and indicating that she had introjected him and had attempted to destroy him in her somatizations. These transference interpretations are crucial in the early acute stage. While the usual analytic technique might require additional confirmatory evidence to fully validate the accuracy of the intervention, this luxury is not available in emergency situations and the analyst has to work on the basis of the apparent nature of the transference and experience with previous patients. This represents a difference in analytic technique and is applicable to the management of anorexic and psychosomatic conditions in general.

As the discussion continued, it was possible to indicate that her intense distress at feeling abandoned for two days must have reflected her childhood experience, which she was repeating, rather than remembering and understanding. The analyst added that the presence or absence of mother did mean life or death to the totally dependent infant or young child and that she seemed to be venting this early experience on him. In addition, a sister born 13 months after Jeanette might have required a great deal of the mother's attention, since Jeanette had just commented on her feelings of intense jealousy toward another sick girl on the ward who was getting a great deal of attention from the nurses. She acknowledged feeling conflicted, wanting and demanding a great deal of attention from the nurses because she was sick, but also recognizing that asking them to infantilize her was not healthy.

The following day, Jeanette was cooperative, optimistic, and eager to work things out further. She commented that she had remained "mature" all day, had been eating regularly, and had not let herself slide back. She noted with a great deal of apprehension that after she had eaten well the night before, she had become very fearful and anxious.

It was possible to point out that she became fearful when she ate because she realized that through the reestablishment of a normal eating pattern, she would be closing off the anorexia, which discharged all kinds of tension; without it, she would begin to experience distressing thoughts and feelings. She readily agreed and admitted that she had begun to worry about all kinds of things and had been unable to understand the source of her recent apprehension. The analyst recalled that when she had gone home after her first hospitalization and had attempted to eat normally, she had become depressed and had had suicidal impulses. Since anorexia is so self-destructive—in a sense, a suicide in stages—it would not be surprising to recognize that when she closed it off, it might be replaced by other self-destructive impulses, including depression. As the discussion proceeded, she described increasing feelings of anxiety and apprehension, along with fear that she would be unable to cope with her problems. The analyst pointed out that this would be surprising since all her life she had been trained to think clearly and to use her intellectual ability incisively to resolve academic problems. It would be ironic indeed if she could perform so well academically and not use the very same abilities to resolve her personal problems. After this discussion, she described feeling more relaxed and confident.

It seemed clear that, in the beginning of treatment, Jeanette required frequent contact with the analyst because of her severe separation anxiety, tendency toward sudden and severe regressions, inability to tolerate reasonable frustration, lack of understanding of her problems and urge to avoid dealing with them, and building up of tension as her anorexic symptoms were closed off. In retrospect, it seemed that, after discharge, daily telephone conversations with the analyst, in addition to treatment, might have prevented the decompensation and rehospitalization.

During the two periods of hospitalization, Jeanette frequently became enraged during sessions, swore and cursed at the analyst, and "terminated" the treatment. On those days, the analyst phoned Jeanette afterward, alluding to some difference of opinion during the past session and attempting to resolve it. Invariably she responded positively, talked things over, and thus prevented the feelings of guilt that she would otherwise have had when contemplating how shabbily she felt she had treated the analyst. For the analyst to call her in the face of such hostility certainly suggested to her that he cared and, moreover, that he could tolerate her hostile outbursts without retaliating and without becoming overwhelmed.

An obvious question is whether the analyst should have accepted the patient's statement that she felt the treatment was worthless, that she desired a different type of treatment, and that she wanted to end the therapeutic relationship. Some analysts, and perhaps some civil rights advocates, might have taken this patient's conscious requests at face value, ignoring the obvious unconscious pleas to the contrary. Without entering the field of legality and civil rights, but concentrating on the field of medicine, it becomes the obligation of analytically trained psychiatrists to follow their understanding of the patient's needs and to do whatever they deem best for the patient's welfare. This may include ignoring a patient's conscious statement when it is recognized that a deep unconscious attitude reflects the opposite position. The course of treatment seems to bear out this proposition.

Months 1–4: Dealing with Anorexic Symptoms and Behavior

In the first three weeks following her second discharge from the hospital, Jeanette was seen daily and, following stressful sessions, she would talk to the analyst in the evening on the telephone. The frequent contact served to minimize her separation anxieties, foster an increased dependence on the treatment, interfere with the tendency for sudden regressions, and promote an increasing sense of trust in the analyst.

Jeanette continued to create crises and attempted to maintain her anorexic rituals. She masturbated twice a day so as to increase her metabolism and lose weight, and exercised after each meal even if she only had soup. Her numerous complaints about physical symptoms (e.g., cramps and gas) were repeatedly interpreted as representing her unconscious wish for the return of the anorexia and her unconscious desire to avoid facing her problems. At times, however, these attitudes were quite close to consciousness and Jeanette either acknowledged the interpretation or volunteered similar information herself. With much swearing and agitation, the symptoms gradually subsided. Physical symptomatology alternated with recurring statements that she could not eat, would never find out what was bothering her, and would never get well because the treatment did not work.

In one episode, when she felt more confident and trusting, she confided, "I feel hungry now." Another time she noted: "When I eat three times a day now, the worries come out, but after I exercise, I can't think. I can't even read, or do homework." These statements represented clear clinical evidence of the defensive nature of her anorexic behavior: exercising, starving, or being mentally preoccupied with ideas about food served to prevent the emergence of psychic conflict. It also confirmed the necessity and validity of interpreting this behavior as defensive.

Jeanette became increasingly preoccupied with symptoms of constipation and again began to vomit repeatedly by putting her fingers down her throat. With considerable prodding, she finally recounted that her recent hospitalization had repeated a hospitalization exactly one year earlier for constipation. In very disturbed patients, the recognition and discussion of anniversary reaction behavior and symptomatology often provide enough understanding and insight to prevent an expanding decompensation (Mintz 1971). Jeanette went on to say that when she was very little she had been given enemas repeatedly and had hated them. She would be put in the tub and given an enema that would make her feel so full that she would defecate in the tub, all over herself. In the past two years, she had again begun to take enemas in the tub and to defecate all over herself. Her self-induced vomiting seemed to represent the same process from the other end. She related the constipation to conflict over the birth of her little sister and the desire to keep the "stool baby" inside. Concern over pregnancy in the relationship with her boyfriend had exacerbated the conflict.

In addition, the early traumatic experiences with the enemas seemed to play a considerable role in the development of anal fixations and character traits, later gastrointestinal symptomatology, and the quality of her object relationships. Certainly, issues of controlling and being controlled, and reversion to somatization, had some early roots in the relationship with mother and were connected to bowel functions.

Treatment sessions during the following month continued to be stormy. At one moment, Jeanette was quiet, tractable, and reflective, and was beginning to eat more normally. At the next, she was wild and depressed, voicing thoughts of suicide, quitting treatment, and hating the analyst. Dependence on the analyst increased. Fantasied rejections unearthed explosive diatribes. When she called the office at 6 P.M. and the analyst didn't call back until 9 P.M., she became furious, stopped eating, and accused him of complete indifference. "You know how important it is for me to hear from you."

For some time to come, Jeanette was extremely dependent on the analyst, and at the same time made inordinate demands on him. The full emergence of her insatiable dependency demands began to unfold. It was her unconscious awareness of this endless hunger and demandingness, and the anticipated rejection that they would invariably provoke, that had prompted her unwillingness to get involved in treatment in the first place. This kind of dependency had not been tolerated by parents or friends, and its various manifestations had been responded to by rejection. She had expected the same rejection from the analyst. Instead, her behavior had been interpreted and made more conscious, more understandable, and therefore more controllable.

One day Jeanette ate a sandwich for lunch and then had a normal dinner— her first in years. This was followed by feelings of panic and a bout of hysterical exercising. She then called the office seven times before the analyst got back to her. When he phoned she screamed that she quit, that she was fed up with the treatment, and that she would never get better. The analyst indicated that she was frightened partially because she felt that she was able to eat and that she could get better, but the sick part of her wanted to retain her infantile behavior, stay sick, ruin the treatment, continue to punish herself, vent hostility at the analyst for helping her get better, and avoid the worries that she would have to deal with once the anorexia no longer served as the repository of her conflicts. Many of these patients do regress in response to the inner awareness that they can get better, and it is very helpful to be able to point it out in order to interfere with the decompensation. Characteristically, Jeanette responded quickly, if temporarily, to these interpretations and quieted down. She acknowledged that she felt angry at the analyst for making her eat. The analyst hastened to point out that he could not make her eat and, furthermore, would not try to make her eat. If she ate it was because she thought about what was said and chose to eat. Her idea that the analyst was making her eat reflected both her suspicions that he was trying to control her the way that she felt others had, and her underlying wish of wanting to remain little, passive, and controlled. These comments were not made in shotgun fashion, but were presented in sequence during the ensuing discussion around her attitudes about the analyst.

Many of the negative and infantile elements in Jeanette's behavior have been discussed. The positive ones also deserve comment, as they reflect the split in her ego functioning. She had a keen intellect, and her excellent grades and academic accomplishment were not solely a result of endless drudgery. She was a leader academically and athletically. Her ability to analyze and to think incisively once she chose to do so contributed to her considerable progress in the treatment.

Jeanette began to wonder why she was eating and acting in so crazy a fashion. These reflections revealed the beginnings of an observing ego and transient moments of some insight, in contrast to earlier behavior characterized by little awareness of the pathological nature of her behavior. She acknowledged that often she felt crazy and became panicky. The analyst stated that he understood why she felt that her behavior was crazy and could recognize that anyone who behaved that way might well wonder if he or she were crazy, but that she could change her behavior whenever she chose to. It was clear that the patient was fearful that she was psychotic.

When a patient verges on panic and potential decompensation, it is important to communicate that the analyst does not share the patient's fears of her impulses and behavior, nor her fears for her sanity. If the analyst becomes anxious about the patient, then the patient feels that they both have lost control of the situation. This can result in a rapid decompensation, with a more flagrant psychosis. Discussing Jeanette's fears of craziness directly, and indicating that she could control it when she chose to, was immensely reassuring. An attitude of attentive concern is different from feeling as panicky as the patient. It can also be extremely helpful to discuss such crises with other experienced colleagues to retain one's perspective and to widen one's grasp of the situation.

The analyst asked Jeanette how she could develop any worthwhile image of herself or get involved with a man whom she thought was worthwhile if she thought she was crazy or feared that he would think she was. Such confrontations resulted in increasingly realistic behavior, further serious discussion, and further involvement in the therapeutic relationship. They did not prevent subsequent regressions, however, and progress was made by climbing up the mountain, slipping back, and climbing up again, each time a little further.

In a number of sessions, as the denial of illness was further eroded, Jeanette became increasingly fearful of dying from the anorexia. In one session, she became so panicky that she insisted on an immediate appointment with the internist. To the analyst's suggestion that, if she were afraid of dying, eating might be more beneficial than an instant appointment with the internist, she blew up, stated that the analyst did not care about her, and walked out of the office saying that she never wanted to see him again. In a further discussion in the waiting room, the analyst pointed out that she was furious because she felt that he was interfering with her desire to stay sick and because she felt that she could not control him by phoning the internist from his office.

In another session, after Jeanette described having eaten normally, she kept looking over at the analyst for signs of approval. He indicated that if he approved of her eating, then she might also feel that she could frustrate him by not eating and try to control him in that fashion. If she ate and got well, it was for her benefit. She admitted that she had manipulated her previous analyst by not eating. Approving or disapproving of patients' eating habits or other behavior encourages them to displace superego attitudes onto the analyst. A comparable situation is the teenager who lets the parents worry about him and blithely goes about dangerous activities without conscious reflection on the consequences. Conversely, when Jeanette's analyst left the responsibility with her, she was able to express her own worry about her health, as opposed to making the analyst worry: "It's me that I hurt when I don't eat. I'm scared to death that I might die."

At the same time, however, part of her did wish to eat to please the analyst, obtain his approval, and be close to him. In this sense, the wish to eat could be viewed as being controlled by the analyst. In addition, the desire to be close became frightening to the degree that it was associated with a loss of identity, a feeling of being fused with the analyst, and a feeling of death.

In the next few weeks, Jeanette continued to eat more regularly and to put on weight. She reported a reversal of a previously described pattern. For the longest time she had stated that when she did not eat, she felt well, and that eating resulted in gas, stomach pains, constipation, and general discomfort. Now she noted for the first time that when she did not eat, she felt ill and experienced stomach pains that were relieved by eating. At times now, eating made her feel better. She was surprised to recognize that when she did not eat, she had trouble thinking and speaking clearly, and that this tended to subside after eating. After not eating dinner one evening, ostensibly because she was working and did not have time, she had the nagging thought that she really should have eaten, that she actually felt hungry, and that the analyst would be disappointed in her for not keeping up her half of the treatment bargain.

The reemergence of her repressed hunger sensations, her awareness that the starving clouded her thinking, her guilt and discomfort about not eating, and her feeling that something was wrong with her emaciated condition were the reverse of her previous attitudes.

She needed to talk to the analyst every day—only what he said seemed to make sense to her. Even if her friends said the same things, they would be meaningless to her. She trusted the analyst. She was extremely attached to and dependent on the treatment, saw herself as helpless, and viewed the analyst as omnipotent. Within this framework, she was able to eat, to listen to the therapist, and to counter the strong regressive pull toward illness and infantile gratifications. Primitive superego guilt and punishment were in part ameliorated through the incorporation of what was perceived to be the analyst's superego, and reality testing was enhanced by identifying with his ego functioning. The potential for sudden severe regression remained, particularly in the face of perceived disappointment in the overvalued analyst, and in the continued presence of primitive aspects of ego functioning. Ultimately, it would be vital to analyze this infantile omnipotent view of the parent-analyst but at the moment the intense relationship could be utilized to counter the regression.

Jeanette reported an infantile relationship with a girlfriend who controlled her and bossed her about. Jeanette felt helpless to cope with her. She felt that the girlfriend took advantage of her, disappointed her, and made her feel weak and inadequate, but she could do nothing. The relationship with the girlfriend repeated the relationship with the mother, as is characteristic of anorexics' peer relationships in adolescence. When she got upset with this girlfriend, she wanted to starve, but found that she was unable to do so. She then tried to get rid of the distress by "exercising like a maniac and crying hysterically, but it didn't work and it was my best way." The anorexic syndrome, initiated when she could not control an external object, was no longer effective; the conscious awareness of her conflict interfered with the previously utilized repression. Jeanette further reported how weak and unassertive she felt when it came to realistically asserting her rights. All she could do was to yell helplessly and scream in a rage like an infant. Unable to repress the conflict, and feeling helpless about re-solving it, she released the full fury of her rage in the self-destructive impulse to kill herself, instead of the hated girlfriend-mother. This sequence is not atypical for anorexics or psychosomatic patients: inner awareness of the emerging depression when the aggression is no longer bound by the self-destructive psychosomatic symptoms occasionally prompts patients to develop an exacerbation of symptoms rather than to face the emerging depression.

COUNTERTRANSFERENCE

During the crucial weeks after Jeanette's second discharge from the hospital, when she was not eating properly and was constantly threatening to terminate treatment and attempting to coerce and manipulate the analyst, a subtle countertransference took place. The analyst became aware that he was calling Jeanette in the evening, instead of waiting for her to call his service. His initial rationalization that it was simpler and more expedient faded rapidly as he thought more about his concern for her welfare during the bouts of sudden irrational behavior without the protection of the hospital and his fear that she would die. This concern was unconsciously perceived by Jeanette, in whom it provoked both anxiety and an inner impulse to utilize this manipulative behavior increasingly to control the analyst.

With the more realistic change in the analyst's attitude toward Jeanette and her illness, she responded almost immediately and commented that he seemed to be behaving differently and did not seem to care as much about her.

Although analysts can be aware of their concern about a life-threatening illness, and their relative impotence in dealing with it by talking, this introspection has to be maintained constantly; otherwise, it will be eroded gradually by the patient's repeated, hostile, manipulative assaults as she relives in the transference the attempts to control the object through illness.

SYMPTOM IMPROVEMENT, EXACERBATION, AND SUBSTITUTION

In the next few weeks, Jeanette continued to improve. Her weight rose from 78 lbs. to 87 lbs. On occasion, after weighing herself, she would call up in a panic. She was frightened that she would continue to gain weight, especially after episodes of gorging when she feared that she could not stop. Bursts of exercise would follow. The impulses to starve were often dealt with by calling the analyst on the phone.

There were repeated episodes where she complained of gas, constipation, and/or nausea, usually citing the symptoms as a pretext for eating less and reverting to diet foods or starving. The symptoms were discussed as manifestations of her alleged need to remain ill, of her impulses to damage the treatment or frustrate the analyst, and of her fear of growing up. After these interpretations, her diet became more normal, exercising decreased, and symptoms lessened.

Her strong infantile attachment to her mother was dramatically illustrated in one session. The analyst stated that he would be unable to see her for the Saturday appointment because he had to be out of town. In the same session, the issue of driving to the office regularly with her mother was raised, and the analyst wondered about her not feeling comfortable driving by herself. She responded that perhaps it was time and that she would consider it. Minimal anxiety was acknowledged, and she continued discussing other subjects that bothered her.

That afternoon she called up hysterical. When the analyst returned her call that evening, she was enraged, stating that the treatment was worthless and that she was returning to her anorexia. She vowed not to eat and regressed to behaving in an infantile, hostile fashion with considerable crudeness and cursing. She appeared completely distraught and overwhelmed. She complained of stomach cramps, urges to vomit, an inability to deal with schoolwork, and depression. The analyst suggested that her turmoil might be related to his skipping the Saturday session. She calmed down and agreed to come in for the next session, where she explored further the possibility that her distress was related to the Saturday session, but was not sure. Later in the hour, the analyst suggested that she might still have some thoughts about considering driving to the session without her mother. She thought for a while and then added, "That's what it really is. When you asked me to consider coming up to the office by myself, I knew that I wasn't ready, but I was afraid to tell you." The analyst pointed out that it wasn't just that she was afraid to tell him, but rather, that if she spoke about it in the session, she would not worry about it as much and therefore would not have the excuse to hurt herself by wrecking things in the afternoon. He added that, even though she felt that she trusted him more, her attachment to her mother was still very strong. She must have felt that he was in a sense asking her to renounce the close relationship with her mother, which was available while she was ill, and at the same time advising her that he would not be able to see her on Saturday. She was reluctant to give up her mother and substitute a relationship with an inconstant analyst who would not always be there. This triggered the regression, the anger with the analyst, and the reinvolvement with the mother.

After three months in treatment, Jeanette seemed to be doing quite well. She had gained 15 lbs. and her weight was 93 lbs. One Sunday the mother phoned, stating that the patient was wild, swearing, and threatening to kill herself. On the phone Jeanette stated that she had had a fight with her boyfriend a few days before that she had not told the analyst about. In the next session she was hostile, suspicious, and accused him of laughing at her plight. After considerable discussion, which included dealing with her negative transference, she calmed down. She spoke about how upset she felt in the relationship with her boyfriend. He was pushing her sexually, at a time when she felt that he did not care that much about her. She felt taken advantage of, used, and worthless. Although at times, and in a superficial way, she could be hostile and insulting, she was really fearful of behaving in an appropriately assertive fashion. She was unable to deal with the boyfriend and felt devastated by what she perceived as his rejection of her. When he did not call back, she felt depressed and suicidal. She spoke of impulses to starve and was reminded of an earlier boyfriend. She described how a 2-year relationship with him had gradually deteriorated in her eyes. Both families were happy, however, and pushed the relationship. Her increasing unhappiness and insecurity were masked by a smiling face. She began to lose weight, recalling the thought that the boyfriend's family wouldn't want a sick girl. With a start, she realized that the previous Sunday was the

1-year anniversary of her engagement to him. This recognition produced a dramatic improvement. She reported feeling better, hungry, more in control. "This time I want to eat, and get better. I couldn't understand why I was getting sick. Usually when I get sick, I want to, but this time, I did not want to."

That afternoon an hysterical phone call again revealed her fear that she was going crazy and her desire to eat, vomit, and take laxatives. She screamed that she had to "shit Tom out . . . get rid of him." The analyst suggested that she could deal with and get rid of unpleasant memories by thinking about them without having to eliminate them through defecation.

In the next few sessions she elaborated on the relationship with Tom. She described how he constantly fought with her, insulted her, and argued with her friends, who hated him. He was indifferent to her anxieties during sexual relations and was not concerned if he hurt her. She remembered the first time, when it had hurt so badly that she fainted and awakened bleeding and with difficulty breathing.

It seemed evident that the anniversary of her engagement to Tom contributed to the argument with her current boyfriend in the need to relive that traumatic experience, including those aspects of the anorexic syndrome. The understanding of the anniversary nature of the behavior provided her with considerable relief.

Jeanette's eating continued to improve while her frenetic exercising tended to subside. By the end of the fourth month, she had become more interested in what was going on in the world about her. She weighed about 91 lbs. and continued to fear becoming too fat, which in her mind meant weighing 110 lbs. Her associations led to the idea that when she looked heavier, she would lose her waiflike appearance and, along with it, all the automatic attention and solicitude that she usually commanded merely by walking into a room. She would be like everyone else, would be judged equally and without special favor, and would be required to perform in mature fashion.

One night she developed a severe asthmatic attack and was rushed to the local hospital, where she was given oxygen and adrenalin. She recalled that she used to have asthmatic attacks as a child of five, but that this was the first attack since childhood. She then looked at the analyst and accused him of causing the attack. She stated that she was no longer able to starve or exercise excessively. She couldn't stop putting on weight.

It was clear that she felt that the asthmatic attack was a substitute for the aborted anorexia. Clinical experiences with other patients reveal similar circumstances in which one psychosomatic symptom is replaced by another or alternates with phobias, depression, or self-destructive acting out. While the overt illness shifts, the underlying conflicts, defenses, identifications, and type of object relationships remain relatively unchanged.

REGRESSIVE BEHAVIOR

As the weeks progressed, starving, laxatives, and vomiting became less of a problem. They were replaced by bouts of sudden regressive behavior in which Jeanette felt that she was acting crazy. She would look at her filling-out body in the mirror, especially at what she felt was her protuberant abdomen. She reported a fantasy that there was a "baby-fetus-devil inside with horns and a tail" and that she had to get it out by vomiting or through diarrhea, but couldn't. Instead, she behaved like a devil, yelling, screaming, and throwing objects about the house in an infantile, petulant manner; the fantasy was reflected in acting out instead of in anorexic symptomatology. The behavior clarified the underlying conflict and revealed the necessity for it to be analyzed after the anorexic symptomatology had subsided. She added that now she couldn't control anything. She couldn't get people to do what she wanted, and she no longer was able to control her own body with the starving, vomiting, laxatives, and exercises. She felt that she had to act crazy to control the analyst and to get others to pay attention to her, be concerned about her, and gratify her need to be babied.

The agitated behavior persisted over the next few days, with threats to injure herself or commit suicide. The analyst indicated that if she really felt that she could not control herself, she would have to be rehospitalized. She countered by berating him and accusing him of making her sick and no longer caring about her. At the same time, she indicated how desperately she wanted his attention. That night she phoned and realized that it was the anniversary of the onset of her anorexia.

After this anniversary, she calmed down somewhat, although there continued to be hysterical outbursts and temper tantrums. One such episode was followed by a bout of bulimia, which she compared to her previous wild, destructive behavior. She noted that both outbursts were similar: in one, she destroyed external objects with her hands and threw them about; in the other, she ripped foods apart and rapidly chewed them up and destroyed them internally. The bulimia was like a wave of destruction in which she ate five times as fast as normal and ate to destroy, not to enjoy.

Later Therapy: Dealing with Underlying Conflicts

By the fifth month, Jeanette had put on 20 lbs. and weighed 98 lbs. She complained that now that she appeared healthy, all kinds of demands were being made of her. When she had been sick, very little had been required of her. She knew that she had a report to finish and now the professor would tolerate no excuses. She also felt that her boyfriend was demanding more of her and no longer treated her as a helpless little waif. She could see that her worry about her weight really masked her anxiety about how she would be able to function in the world. In subsequent sessions, she stated that she would no longer go on eating binges now that she recognized that they represented outbursts of anger. She also added that she understood how much the anorexia stood for difficulties in her relations with people. She spoke again of how her previous waiflike appearance had elicited compassion from everyone without her having to say a word.

Now, however, things were different. She acknowledged how fearful she was of men. They looked at her differently now; they no longer babied her, but made sexual remarks to her instead. She realized that, as she filled out, she looked more womanly and more sexually desirable. She understood why she used to get so frightened whenever she began to put on weight and round out.

She also noted that now women saw her as more of a rival and were increasingly jealous of, and competitive with, her. She even described a different attitude about sexuality. When she had been emaciated, she would have sex quickly "and get it over with." When she looked more womanly, she behaved in a more sensual manner and did not rush about so frenetically.

In the middle of the fifth month, Jeanette further clarified the nature of her object relationships, as symbolized by her attitude toward food.

> I had such an urge to eat those cookies. They taste so good and I haven't had them in two years. If I eat one, I can't stop and I'll eat the whole box. Then I'll have to vomit, so I can't eat any. The urge is so great, just like the urge to swallow up gratifications in relating to people . . . but I can't control the people that way. I have better control over my relations with people now because they won't let me behave that way toward them. With food I can do what I want.

It was pointed out that that was what she used to try to do with the analyst to get intense infantile gratifications from him. She would call him and if he didn't reply instantly, she would explode, express hatred toward him, and feel that he hated her. Jeanette had set up an all-or-nothing relationship with food, which was rooted in her fear of losing control; furthermore, she had made the situation as frustrating and self-destructive as possible in order to discharge her aggression.

In the next few sessions, she revealed more about her self-image, her low self-esteem, and the nature of her object relationships. After revealing the fear that she would never get well, she spoke about fantasies of wanting to stay sick. In order to be successful, she felt that she would have to trust the analyst, which would mean "turning myself over to you. . . . that you will control me and make me better." One can see why these patients are fearful of a close, trusting relationship. Their needs to regress to obtain infantile gratifications and to repeat the earlier relationship with the parents require them to renounce their independent functioning and be passively controlled and dominated. This conflict is what they consciously fight and unconsciously accede to during the anorexia nervosa and its sequelae.

Jeanette's improvement continued. Her frustration tolerance increased. She developed and maintained a more realistic view of her life situation. She repeatedly spoke about the past anorexia as crazy and said that she would never do it again. She became more aware of bodily sensations of hunger when she did not eat. She also noted a sense of fatigue in the late evening, which in the past had been denied.

When she experienced abdominal pains, discussion with the analyst about how they stood for an interference with her newly acquired enjoyment in eating decreased the pains markedly. She spoke about her past use of a hot-water bottle, which had burned her abdomen, and indicated that the gas inside her abdomen reminded her of a baby who suffered when greedily swallowing air with milk; the voracious swallowing of the milk was similar to her insatiable binging attacks.

Subsequent to meeting a young law student through one of her friends, she was unsure about accepting a second date with him because of her insecure, unstable relationships with people. She toyed with impulses to regress and to get sick. She described how difficult it was to behave appropriately. "I run from being mature. I can't think and act mature for more than three hours; then I act 'waify and infantile'."

Nine months into treatment, she reported that, on the previous evening, both of her sisters had ganged up on her and been very critical of her. She felt devastated and overwhelmed by their remarks. She felt panicky and had the thought, "I'll tell them I'm sick and I'm going into the hospital, and then they will stop." She then experienced abdominal pains. Later that evening, she cried alone in her room and then noted that the abdominal pains had subsided. She went downstairs and, in a reasonably realistic fashion, attempted to rebut her sisters' criticisms.

SEPARATION FROM THE ANALYST

A crisis developed toward the end of the first year as the analyst's summer vacation approached. Jeanette was still quite dependent, but spent most of the sessions attempting to deal with her problems. Separation anxiety was a major problem and had been discussed many, many times as it related to her social relationships, her parents, and her therapeutic contacts. In one session, she arrived very upset and agitated. Her boyfriend had not called her and had deserted her, just as the analyst planned to do. She could not get better, the treatment was worthless, and she wanted to die. Self-destructive discharge of aggressive impulses alternated between feelings of depression and preoccupations with anorexic symptoms. Although she acknowledged understanding what was happening, she felt helpless to cope with it. She stated that she didn't know what she would do if the abdominal pains persisted all during the month that the analyst was away. He pointed out that her symptoms and attitude reflected anger at the analyst for leaving on vacation and attempts to coerce him to stay or to make him feel guilty about going. The behavior persisted for almost two weeks, with repeated interpretations of her repressed resentment toward the analyst as the reason for the symptoms and depression. Finally, she responded. One week before the vacation, she walked in enraged. She screamed, "Murderer! I'm going on vacation when you get back. You can put a flower on my grave," and then walked out.

In the next session, she was more quiet and tractable, and was able to converse without screaming. She acknowledged her feelings of hatred for the analyst, but stated that she felt less violent than in the previous session. It was helpful to her that the analyst had tolerated her aggressive assault without attacking her or collapsing. She could express aggression without terrible consequences and could identify with the analyst as the recipient of it without having to fall apart. She volunteered that she had been binging and taking diet pills for the past four days, but that she now planned to eat regularly. She phoned the analyst each of the four weeks of his vacation. Upon his return, she described episodes of anorexic symptoms, but no major regression.

THE "THINKING STAGE"

Jeanette reported that she was out of the "anorexic stage" and into the "thinking stage." She described two earlier pathological stages: the "waif stage" and the "cute stage." When she had been really sick and emaciated, she had been treated like a helpless waif. Everything had been done for her. "They just had to look at me, and I got sympathy." In the cute stage, she had been treated like a child. She had been encouraged, cajoled, helped along, not taken seriously, and dealt with as a little girl. "If I go over 90 lbs., they don't think I'm cute anymore, and I have to use my personality. I have to think, and speak, and behave like an adult, not just stand there and wait to be catered to."

She commented further on her mother's continuing infantilization, which she did not mind most of the time. The mother kept offering her special foods, as if to keep the preoccupation with eating alive and active in Jeanette's thinking and behavior. She insisted on washing her clothing, combing her hair, and straightening up her room. On occasion, Jeanette resented it and told her mother that she was an adult and that the mother should stop infantilizing her. While the mother did not openly object to Jeanette's giving up the anorexia and attempting to achieve independence, she continued to foster the dependency by always wanting to be with her, by being her confidante, and by attempting to erode her relationship with the analyst.

Early in the treatment, the parents had been advised to consult a female analyst in order to help them cope with their daughter's behavior and facilitate her recovery. The mother had been going on a relatively regular basis. At this point, she refused to continue, complaining that she really would like to see a male consultant instead. It seemed evident that the mother's increasing resistance was in great part due to feeling threatened by what she perceived as the impending loss of the symbiotic tie to her daughter.

Jeanette felt equally threatened. She reported that both sisters had suddenly begun to eat and vomit secretly. This distressed her greatly, because she felt that the sisters were bidding for the mother's attention and would get closer to the mother at Jeanette's expense. She felt that her position was being eroded at a time when she still could not tolerate separating from the mother herself, let alone being separated from her by the rival sisters.

Jeanette also felt that her social life was in turmoil. If she put on weight, she would no longer be seen as cute and appealing. Left to what she felt was her deficient, inept self, she saw little chance of winning friends and influencing people. Clearly, she would be ignored, neglected, and abandoned. The treatment was responsible. Discussing these issues in great detail brought her out of regressed states, and she could view herself more realistically for brief periods. Depression and thoughts of suicide alternated with insightful periods. She implied that there would no longer be external sources of gratification and attempted to evoke it from the analyst through her helplessness and vulnerability.

At a dance, she was complimented as a beautiful woman and thought to herself, "I'm fragile . . . can't be touched . . . a statue to be admired . . . not to get close to . . . and not to be treated like a woman." The sessions interfered with her impulses to become anorexic again. Although she agreed with the general tenor of the discussions with the analyst, she developed abdominal cramps. Again, they were interpreted as anger at the interpretations and as impulses to stay sick. It was pointed out that her fear of getting close was related to impulses to be cared for, along with fears that others would find out what an infantile, immature person she was. She couldn't be accepted as an adult and feel comfortable and secure in that role, but when she gave in to her yearning to act like a child, she feared discovery of her immature thoughts and behvior. These issues were continually worked through in the transference, as well as in social contacts.

These discussions seemed to effect changes in her ego structure. She went to a restaurant with her family and got food poisoning. "I was up all night with fever, cramps, and diarrhea. I was afraid that I might die. It was just the way I felt when I took the Ex-Lax. How could I ever have done it?" She vomited from antibiotics. "It felt terrible and I was so ashamed that I vomited." She began to deal more with separation and feelings of loneliness, and found that she was more willing to tolerate and think about her sadness. She often wanted to become anorexic, but wouldn't give in to the impulse, and instead thought about why she felt that way. She no longer regressed as often, as suddenly, or as deeply. She would speak with longing about the days when she was a skinny little waif. A new, transient phobia emerged in which she was afraid to go anywhere alone. She volunteered that now that she no longer acted like a little girl, she had thoughts of being one instead. "When I was thin, I could be attached to my mother. Thin is little. Now that I'm normal, I can't."

She reported a series of dreams about dying. In one, she thought of dying, but the analyst told her, "You can't die, you have to get better." She couldn't get sick and couldn't put her finger down her throat. This dream showed the impact of the therapeutic relationship—the internalization of the analyst's attitudes and the replacement of Jeanette's own primitive superego dictates.

Another series of repetitive dreams indicated Jeanette's desire to join the mother in heaven through death; she was unable to do so and fell back to earth crying. These dreams of reunion through death were reminiscent of the ambivalence expressed in her hospital letter, where she stated that she might meet the analyst in another world.

In the second year of her treatment, Jeanette got a job in an executive training program at a department store. She reported having conflicting thoughts and feelings about her relations with her coworkers and supervisors, and about being in the business world. Initially, she felt that the other salespeople were only interested in themselves and were either indifferent to, or critical of, her. Unable to control their attitudes toward her, she contemplated returning to starving or eating strange foods so that people would pay attention to her. Momentarily, she gave in to these impulses. With increasing frequency, she thought about it instead and concluded that to give in was infantile and crazy. She resisted and contemplated the thought that she was getting better. "I'm resigned to getting better. Treatment makes you grow up." Feelings of extreme loneliness and helplessness burst on her and were followed by bouts of crying and anguish. She had no one to be with and yet felt that she could not return to anorexia. She reflected on how infantile some of her demands were and resolved to deal with them. She felt better, but still was lonely.

She realized that occasionally her supervisors criticized her unfairly; at such times, she reacted with anorexic preoccupation, despondency, or anger.

I felt so terrible about the criticism, but I didn't binge. I was very anxious and tense and I kept pacing, but I kept thinking and I controlled myself. I had fantasies of wanting to beat them up, of wanting to kick the chair as if it were they, like the fantasy isn't enough. . . . When I was young, I used to be angry at everyone who teased me and called me fat. I had all these angry fantasies of revenge, and I used to yell at everyone. Then I lost so many friends that I stopped doing it, and instead I got anorexic and I began to hurt myself.

During periods of frustration, Jeanette reported binges of stealing that seemed to replace the binges of eating. When she became upset at work, she took sweaters and other items of clothing from the store instead of becoming preoccupied with anorexic fantasies or binging. These impulsive episodes were invariably followed by strong feelings of guilt that encompassed not only the stealing but also eating, enjoyable vacations she had taken, and generally everything that had previously given her pleasure.

Thus, it is possible to recognize a shift in the pathological impulsive behavior, but not in the underlying orality, dependency, and voracious, greedy impulses for immediate infantile gratification. The frustration of her insatiable needs that previously had been displaced onto food and anorexic preoccupations was now displaced onto impulsive stealing. This sequence was recognized and discussed by Jeanette. After a few weeks, the stealing stopped.

She continued to use her hot-water bottle on her abdomen, ostensibly to ease the abdominal pains. Its underlying meaning slowly emerged. That she viewed the hot-water bottle as a transitional object became increasingly clear when she attempted to cope with feelings of loneliness without resorting to further episodes of binging or starving. When she felt very lonely at night, she took the hot-water bottle to bed with her. The hot-water bottle clearly substituted for relations with people, especially when she felt anxious about a relationship and fearful that she couldn't control it: "I don't know whether I should go out with John or eat, vomit, and go to bed with my hot-water bottle." This dilemma occurred a number of times. When she felt comfortable with her boyfriend, she did not need the hot-water bottle. She volunteered that the hot-water bottle was like a security blanket. She remembered that, in the past, whenever she had a fight with her mother, she would run to use it.

Three months before the end of her treatment, she reported that she had given up the hot-water bottle. At that time, the relationship with her boyfriend had progressed very well. They had been going together for eight months and were planning to marry when he graduated from law school. Her weight was 110 lbs. and her anorexic symptoms were gone. She was still anxious in her relationships with people, but acknowledged that she preferred dealing with the problems directly rather than starving. Over the last year, she had confronted her parents more directly and with increasing success about their attempts to control her activities. Following her marriage, her husband accepted a position with a distant law firm and Jeanette was forced to terminate treatment. While the analyst felt that it would have been advisable for the treatment to continue longer, he also felt that she could work out her remaining problems on her own.

ADDENDUM

While the analyst did not hear from Jeanette following her termination, he did hear from her father and uncle every Christmas for the next five years. They reported that she was continuing to do well. With the birth of her first child, the analyst received a box of cigars from the uncle.

SUMMARY

The case of Jeanette, an 18-year-old woman with severe anorexia nervosa, was presented. The course of the intensive, psychoanalytically oriented treatment, with its difficulties, dynamic formulations, and technical problems, was described in detail. An attempt was made to illustrate the overdetermined and multidetermined aspects of the illness, as well as the necessity for analyzing these component parts to the greatest extent possible in order to ensure a successful outcome. The correlation between the anorexic symptoms and the underlying conflicts and character traits was stressed to demonstrate that the anorexic symptoms represent only part of the problem. Other treatment difficulties were discussed: the need to control people; the feeling of being passive and helpless; ambivalence about growing up and behaving in a mature fashion; conflicts about masturbation, pregnancy, motherhood, sexual identity, and reasonable self-assertion; the inability to tolerate aggressive feelings and channel them into realistic behavior; the inability to tolerate frustration; and the rigidity and harshness of the primitive superego, with its attendant low self-esteem.

The effective resolution of these issues makes the difference between a successfully functioning individual and one who remains immature, demanding, self-destructive, provocative, helpless, and compromised in the capacity to experience and maintain viable and mature relationships. Treatment modalities that are not psychoanalytically oriented may be able to modify or eliminate the starving and emaciation, but they do not attempt to correlate these symptoms with, and ultimately resolve, major disturbances in the patient's character.

11
Dream Interpretation

C. PHILIP WILSON, M.D.

There has been no in-depth psychoanalytic investigation of the dreams of anorexia nervosa patients. Hogan (Chapter 7, this volume) uses dream analysis to demonstrate (1) that anorexics do not free-associate in the first phase of their analysis and (2) that the analyst interprets anorexics' early clinical material in terms of the immediate motivation and transference relation to the analyst, leaving oedipal material until later. Thomä (1967) reports many dreams of anorexics and notes that they have "lying dreams" to please the analyst. He views the refusal of one patient to free-associate as resistance. Bruch (1973b) reports two dreams of anorexic patients that seem to reflect therapeutic progress. She does not report any extensive associations to the dreams, which are largely taken at face value, with no investigation of their latent meaning.

THE IMPORTANCE OF ANOREXICS' DREAMS

None of the contributors to this volume agree with Nemiah's concept (1976) of alexithymia—that there is a hereditary constitutional defect in psychosomatic patients that results in a failure of the ego's capacity to fantasy and dream. They feel that when anorexics and other psychosomatic patients don't report fantasies and dreams, it is a sign of intense resistance that can be analyzed.

Generally, anorexics who are hysterical neurotics readily report dreams and fantasies, whereas the compulsive anorexics resist revealing fantasies and dreams. M. Sperling (1974) reports the nightmare dreams of a 2-year-old anorexic girl who screamed in her sleep, "The fish are eating my fingers, the cats and dogs are biting me," noting that the interpretation of the projection of her oral sadistic impulses onto the fish and animals "brought to the fore her jealousy of her baby brother" (p. 176). This case report of Sperling's is important because it demonstrates the core psychopathology of anorexics. This little girl had animal phobias and anorexia. At such an early age, anorexia—not eating—is a phobiclike defense against oral incorporative conflicts.

Clinical Material

Dreams of anorexic patients are presented here to demonstrate a particular technique of interpretation which is determined by multiple factors such as the

245

transference and the quality of object relationships. A crucial consideration is the split in the anorexic's ego and the extent to which this split is comprehended by the self-observing functions of the patient's ego. The first phase of analysis involves making the healthier part of the patient's ego aware of the split-off, primitive-impulse-dominated part of the ego and its modes of functioning.

Typical anorexic defenses are: (1) denial and splitting; (2) belief in magic; (3) feelings of omnipotence; (4) demand that things and people be all perfect— the alternative is to be worthless; (5) need to control; (6) displacement and projection of conflict; (7) ambivalence; (8) masochistic perfectionism that defends against conflicts, particularly those around aggression; (9) pathological ego ideal of beautiful peace and love; (10) fantasied perfect, conflict-free mother-child symbiosis. Of course, these defenses overlap and commingle.

CASE 1   Undoing the Past

Joshua, a chronic anorexic 60-year-old rabbi, denied conflicts and was silent for a week. Each day, he would wait in the therapy room of the hospital, pull out the therapist's chair, give him a pad and pencil, and politely listen while the therapist constructed aspects of his life from the voluminous case record to show him his masochism. For example, his wife had left him, and his synagogue had ousted him, because he was too moral. On the seventh day, in response to this line of interpretation, he started scratching his forearm, to which the therapist called attention, making the interpretation that he made Joshua angry, but that Joshua took out this anger on himself by scratching. For the first time, his attitude of polite listening changed to one of excited interest, and he told the therapist a dream about a man who had burned himself to death. His associations were to a famous religious leader who had been burned to death as a martyr. Following this communication, for a time he flooded sessions with undoing dreams in which he succeeded in situations where he had failed in real life. Psychotherapy effected a resolution of Joshua's anorexic symptoms and improved functioning in his personal life and work. This type of case could be used by certain clinicians (e.g., see Nemiah 1976) to demonstrate alexithymia and, indeed, this man had been diagnosed as schizophrenic and had been given drug and electroshock treatment to no avail. His dreams demonstrated typical magical undoing, a pregenital defense of anorexic patients.

CASE 2   Belief in Magical Omnipotence

What could be called a prodromal dream of anorexia was reported by Colleen, a 19-year-old college student. Her dream was of pulling a breast into all kinds of shapes—long, fat, thin, etc. There was a genie in the dream; she and some other teenage girls climbed onto the breast, which had become flat and large, and rode away.

Colleen had had this dream at age 16 prior to the onset of her anorexic symptoms, but at a time when she was already dieting and struggling with an adolescent maturational conflict. At that time, she had had no boyfriends or dates. Away at college, she felt lonely and depressed. The dream expressed the preoedipal aspects of the anorexia. She had the breast and was omnipotent and magical. She could do anything she wanted with it. It was molded into a breast-phallus (i.e., fat and thin). It became the pregenital parent who could carry her.

These conflicts were repressed and externalized in the subsequent development of anorexia.

In reality, Colleen's mother had not breast-fed her daughter. In reaction formation against any hostility toward her daughter, she had given in to her every request and had "spoiled" her. The mother said that she could not stand the idea that adult children had to make homes of their own. Colleen's belief in magic was a major theme of her analysis and was particularly prominent in her wish that her analyst would be a genie in the transference, which was interpreted to her.

CASES 3 AND 4   Displacement and Projection

On Easter weekend, Teresa, a 30-year-old married anorexic patient, dreamt that she was gorging chocolates but could not vomit them up. Her associations were to a pregnant friend who might have a Caesarean section as the baby was in a breech position. She realized that vomiting meant giving birth through the mouth. She used to gorge until her stomach was swollen, which represented an oral pregnancy. She remembered that when she was eight years old, she had seen a pregnant woman's big belly and had not understood what caused the swelling. At this stage of her analysis, Teresa had given up her gorging and vomiting, which dated back 10 years. She had strong wishes to get her periods back and was gaining weight. Fantasies of oral pregnancy had appeared before, but now were being worked through.

This dream was an indication of structural change. Her bulimic habits were becoming truly ego-alien. Her ego was stronger, and her superego less strict. Internalization of conflict resulted in a transitory symptom of a stiff neck, which had a multitude of meanings. In self-punishment, she could not move her head to gorge; it was painful. Interpretations of her disapproval of masculine self-assertiveness led to a clearing up of her neck symptom, at which point she exploded with anger at her analyst, husband, and father. It required many weeks of analysis to work through these conflicts. This dream reflects the analytic principle that when patients dream of their symptoms, they are ready to give them up. The defense of displacement from below up is highlighted in this dream. This material illustrates the stage of analysis when the anorexic patient is able to free-associate and when the Oedipus complex is being analyzed.

The anorexic's fear of being fat frequently is verbalized as disgust with "flab," which is illustrated by 25-year-old Marla's dream. It clearly depicts typical anorexic displacement and projection of conflict onto fat. "I look at my arm in the bathroom mirror and to my horror see a vagina under my arm. I look at the other arm and see another vagina."

The day residue was Marla's having looked in the mirror the night before and noticed that she had some "flab" inside her upper arms. In her associations, Marla could not recall seeing her mother's genitals, but knew that she must have done so many times. That evening, she had been in a health club sauna and had anxiously looked at all the women's bodies.

She felt she avoided men because she was afraid of something. Then she recalled a dream in which she was sitting on the couch with her parents and was aware of rats and mice running under the couch. In her associations, she thought of other dreams of rats that reflected fears of being bitten and of being entered anally. She knew rats were penises to her. Interpretations were made that her fear of "flab" masked oral and anal sadomasochistic conflicts and, at the oedipal level, fears of mutilation by childbirth. The mice in the dream reminded her of children and of Mickey Mouse. The looking in the mirror brought to mind that in her childhood, when the family had gone on vacations, she had shared a motel room with the parents and had overheard and witnessed them having intercourse.

Marla had been exposed to overstimulating preoedipal and oedipal situations —nudity of the parents and the primal scene. She had had animal phobias, a sleep disturbance, and nightmares following the birth of her twin brothers when she was three years old. The dynamics were similar to those described by M. Sperling (Chapter 3, this volume) in the case of Linda, with Marla displacing and projecting her own oral sadistic impulses onto animals. The mirror aspect of the dream reflected a marked change and strengthening of the self-observing function of Marla's ego, with a concomitant healthy change in her body image.

CASE 5   The "Little Person" Phenomenon

Volkan (1976) described an anorexic patient with a split-off, archaic part of her ego—a "little person." He related this pathological ego structure to the "little man" phenomenon described by Kramer (1955) and Niederland (1956, 1965). In my experience, all psychosomatic patients, including anorexics, have a split-off, archaic, primitive ego. A conscious manifestation of this split-off ego is represented by the fear-of-being-fat complex.* In roughly one-third of the cases, this phenomenon is described by the patients. In the other cases, the split has to be uncovered in analysis. Bruch (1978a) notes that

> many anorexics feel their symptoms are caused by some mysterious force. Others feel they are split into two people. They are reluctant to talk of the split. This other person is described as a dictator, a ghost, or "the little man who objects when I eat." Usually this secret but powerful part of the self is experienced as the personification of everything they have tried to hide or deny as not approved of by themselves or others. . . . This different person is always male. (pp. 55–56)

In certain patients, the "little person" phenomenon is first revealed in dreams. This was the case with Susan, an impulsive anorexic high school student who denied all aggression in herself and other people to an extreme degree. She was always being taken advantage of by people. Her pathetic manner and threadbare way of dressing made other patients refer to her as "the waif" or "the orphan." She brought in a series of dreams containing images of an innocent, wide-eyed little girl that reminded her of current sentimental oil paintings that depicted an innocent, raggedly dressed child with tears in her enormous eyes. Susan was beginning to understand that these paintings showed how she tried to come across to people and to the analyst. After these dreams were analyzed, she had a dream of a little prince whom she wanted to control.

---

*See Figure 1, p. 22

Analysis showed this little prince to be her "little person"—the archaic split-off ego. The little prince was narcissistic, omnipotent, and magical. That he was male was a reflection of her secret wish to be a boy. For her, males were aggressive and magical while females were innocent, passive, and masochistic. The split-off part of her ego was filled with murderous rage and hatred.

CASES 6 AND 7   Masochistic Perfectionism and the Need to Control

Thirty-two-year-old Rebecca, another anorexic analysand, reported a nightmare in which a high school cheerleader saw blood trickling from under the bathroom door. She and other family members opened the door and shrieked in horror at the sight of the murdered father; his head had been severed at a weird angle and placed between his legs. The body was in a crucifix position. There was something vaguely obscene about it. Blood dripped from all the walls of the bathroom. The family wanted to hide the murder from the police but couldn't, as blood was seeping everywhere. Then Rebecca followed her mother through a trap door and came out into a beautiful, serene room with a view of the ocean.

Rebecca had resolved her anorexic symptoms except for her amenorrhea. Her associations were to the fact that she herself had been a high school cheerleader. At that time, her older sister had had a severe hemorrhage for which she had been hospitalized and received transfusions. She had been told that her sister had her menstrual period. Later in adolescence after Rebecca got her menses, she herself had prolonged menstrual bleeding and intense pain, but did not go to a doctor until she became anemic. The mother had not prepared her daughters for menstruation.

Returning to thoughts of the dream, Rebecca felt she was the one who did the murder; the head between the legs represented a wish that the man could give birth, the blood represented his menstruation and mutilation by childbirth, and the trap door was the birth canal.

Despite the oedipal themes of castration and childbirth, and the apparently healthy, womanly desires to menstruate and give birth, the preoedipal all-or-nothing theme was still prominent. Her feeling was that she did all the work and that women were masochistic slaves of men, a role her moralistic mother had portrayed. Prior to this dream, Rebecca had become angry at her husband for going to a men's glee club meeting and leaving her to do household chores. In addition, she had blamed her male analyst when she had not gotten back her periods. She said she wanted to get her periods, have a baby, and stop analysis. The wish in the dream was for both her husband and analyst to be Christlike, to menstruate, and to give birth. The all-or-nothing theme could be seen in the contrast between the bloody murder, on the one hand, and the serene room and masochistic crucifixion, on the other. Actually, Rebecca had not yet advanced to an oedipal level. Her object relations and transference behavior still were largely preoedipal in nature. The theme of blood pervaded the material—bloody castration, bloody childbirth, bloody menstruation, and bloody murder. One significant meaning of this dream was Rebecca's fear that if she menstruated she would bleed to death.

A taxing problem in the interpretation of anorexics' dreams is that while the manifest content and associations usually reflect both oedipal and preoedipal themes, until the anorexic symptoms and related pregenital behavior patterns are resolved and patients have accepted their neuroses, the analyst has to focus exclusively on the preoedipal data.

The following dream highlights the complexities of this problem.

Janet, a 28-year-old anorexic married woman, reported two dreams.* In the first, a great serpent was slithering up and down a flight of stairs. In the second, she was trying to get rid of a scabbed wound on the inside of her knee.

The night before, she had had intercourse with her husband on top. She usually preferred the superior position herself as it gave her control. Her associations were to gaining weight, to her breasts hurting, and to wanting her periods. Except for her amenorrhea, her anorexic symptoms had been resolved. Her body image was undergoing healthy changes. She no longer felt that to be thin was beautiful and at times had an almost visceral wish to be pregnant. The previous evening she had indeed felt that her husband was a snake because he had been so critical of her. She felt that, like her father, he got away with everything. For example, she bitterly resented his playing billiards with his new friends while she stayed at home. Although she had felt sexy before intercourse, during the act she had not communicated well and had not been orgastic.

Thinking of the dream, she recalled an early childhood memory of her mother killing a large snake she had found in a drain. She felt that her husband was clumsy making love, that she was more imaginative. She liked the top position because by writhing up and down and moving her nipples across his chest she could tease and excite him. She recalled her father saying that her mother "was positively toothsome." He loved mother's plump figure and never wanted her to lose weight. Before analysis, she had felt that this was horrible; now she thought it was nice. Her thought was that she must have believed that, like the snake, the penis could bite, and she must have been afraid of being bitten. To the dream image of a scabbed wound on the knee she associated a mutilated organ, the vagina.

Despite emerging oedipal wishes to be pregnant and to identify with her feminine mother, the crucial association was to her fear of a penis with teeth. A frequent pregenital fantasy of anorexics is that the vagina is a wound inflicted by a penis with teeth. This idea was evident in Janet's two dreams: the serpent represented the penis with teeth, and the scabbed wound represented a displacement to the knee of the fantasy of the wounded, bitten vagina.** Anorexic patients deny, suppress, and repress their oral incorporative impulses and fantasies, projecting them onto food.

Janet had a body-phallus-snake identification. It was she who was slithering up and down stairs in the dream. She was very proud of her lithe figure, did exercises daily, and went to a health club to work out. As a child, she had taken ballet classes and had loved dancing. She had begun to realize that she would

---

*The serpent dream is presented in condensed form in Chapter 1.
** For a discussion of penis dentata fantasies, see my stone symbolism research (Wilson 1967a).

feel narcissistically wounded if she lost her perfect figure through pregnancy and childbirth.

In the analysis of snake dreams, frequently one finds that the ontogenetic source of the snake image is a primitive gestalt of the shaft of the male organ devoid of testicles. This gestalt is established before the child's ego has advanced to a stage where it can cognitively integrate perceptual and kinesthetic data about the appearance and functions of the genitals.

In Janet's case, preoedipal identifications with the phallic breast-mother and the pregenital phallic father were fused with later oedipal fantasies and identifications. Although the scabbed-wound dream image is a typical oedipal castration dream element, this dream was interpreted in the context of the preoedipal fear of being bitten by a penis with teeth.

CASE 8   Displacement and Projection of Conflict

Claire, a 16-year-old anorexic high-school student in her third year of analysis, had put on weight and resumed menstruating, but still had not resolved her fear of boys and heterosexuality. She reported the following dream. "A man was a vampire in a house with me and another woman. He wanted to kill us or at least to suck our blood. My sister and father were there. Then we were driving somewhere on vacation."

In her associations, Claire said that she had a déjà vu feeling about the dream. It reminded her of a repetitive dream she had had since childhood. This dream was of a stone cottage with a beautiful lake to the right of it. Another repetitive dream was of trying to escape from a stone castle by a lake. There was a terrifying mushroom cloud: an atomic explosion. The patient associated to eating normally. She had trouble going to sleep and was upset that the analyst was leaving her for his summer vacation. She recalled as a 3-year-old child seeing her mother bathe her baby sister. She always used to be afraid of the dark and wanted all the lights on.

Utilizing stone symbolism research (Wilson 1967a, 1971, 1981), the analyst informed her that the stone element in the dream symbolized her teeth and oral desires. Claire thought of how she liked *red* meat and chewing bones and stated that she must be afraid of biting and being bitten. A further interpretation was made that she projected her devouring impulses onto men and the analyst in the transference when threatened by separation. She had previously dreamt that the analyst became a monster who was going to attack her. In Claire's fantasy, the dream lake and mushroom cloud represented a birth—her sister's birth, which had been a traumatic event as it brought about her first major separation from her mother.

DISCUSSION

The analysis of more than two thousand dreams of anorexics, including the examples given here, demonstrates that these patients have a rich fantasy life. In fact, a number of them were novelists.

Anorexics don't dream of food until they are in the process of giving up their symptoms and analyzing the conflicts masked by their bizarre eating. Teresa's dream of gorging chocolates is an illustration of such a therapeutic advance. Other anorexic patients have dreamt of "buffets." Such dreams reflected their growing awareness of their wishes to have food (the breast) available immediately and in infinite variety; to be able to have total control of food.

Claire's vampire and stone dreams highlight some of the technical problems of dream interpretation in these patients. Her dream symbolism of stone as the dreamer's teeth had to be interpreted by the analyst (Wilson 1967a). Although Claire had had typical stone dreams before, the analyst had not interpreted their symbolic meaning because her ego had been too weak to integrate such an interpretation. The following criteria indicated her readiness for interpretation: (1) Claire was eating normally, had regained her periods, and was facing her conflicts; (2) the multiple meanings of a transference resistance of coming late to sessions had been successfully analyzed; and (3) the self-observing functions of the ego were stronger, which was reflected in Claire's talking frankly about being upset by the analyst leaving her for vacation. Defenses against admitting to separation anxiety had been interpreted many times before, but this was the first time she had spontaneously mentioned such emotions.

SAND SYMBOLISM AND THE
ISAKOWER PHENOMENON
IN ANOREXICS' DREAMS

The analysis of sand symbols in the dreams of anorexics is of great importance. Spitz (1955) emphasized that infants feel thirst, but not hunger, in the hallucinatory state. In a recent paper (1981), I noted that sand can be used as a pregenital symbol in which repressed oral and anal conflicts are regressively represented. Sand symbolizes oral-phase thirst and/or the formless stool of the infant (diarrhea). Antithetically, it depicts a characteristic anorexic attitude, asceticism—the ability to do without mother's milk, to control impulse gratification. Sand representations in dreams can symbolize aspects of the conflicts and processes involved in smoking addictions. Smoking masks and expresses an Isakower-like phenomenon in that it induces a dry (thirsty) mouth.

Anorexic, and particularly bulimic, patients are beset with conflicts about thirst as well as hunger, as are all patients with addictive (oral) conflicts. For example, a 30-year-old bulimic anorexic woman reported the following material when she was mourning the recent death of her mother. She had just paid the bill for her mother's funeral and had expressed weary resignation at paying her analytic bill. In her analysis, she was trying to interrupt three habits—vomiting, laxative taking, and cigarette smoking. She stated:

> I have a dry mouth. Yesterday I was so thirsty I drank a quart of orange juice, but it did not help. For years while I've been anorexic, I've been thirsty. I would just take a sip of water. When I am depressed, I am more thirsty. I was crying yesterday. I miss my mother so much. Why couldn't I make everything up to her? Why did we have to fight so much?

An interpretation was made that she not only wanted her mother's love but wished that the analyst would love her, baby her, and give her gifts as her mother had done. This included not charging her for his services, but giving them as a "present." The patient cried and said, "Yes, mother gave me so much—she'd say, 'My money is yours.' I used to try to refuse her gifts, which I did not need, but she made me take them." A further interpretation was made that she denied wishes for tenderness and love from the analyst and from men she dated; instead she tried to be hyperindependent, "modern," and tough. The patient cried, became more depressed, and commented bitterly that there were no men worth meeting anymore. They were all divorced or neurotic.

At this stage of her analysis, this anorexic patient had resumed menstruating and was struggling to master her habits. In the first phase of treatment, when her weight was close to half of what it should have been and she was amenorrheic, she had many dreams of water, beaches, and sand. She acted out by going on frequent vacations to the Caribbean, where she spent most of her time lying on the beach as she felt "too weak" to play tennis or swim. These vacations were paid for by her doting mother. Glauber (1955; personal communication, 1965) and I (1967a, 1968b, 1971, 1981) have noted that sand and quicksand can symbolize the clinging mother who does not relinquish the symbiotic tie, but fuses with her child, who sinks, gets stuck, suffocates, and goes under. Sand and quicksand represent the weak, unstable state of the ego in these patients, whose infantile oral conflicts were never resolved and became overlaid with ambivalent all-or-nothing impulse control struggles at every subsequent libidinal and maturational phase. The anorexic ego state invariably involves conflicts with time.

A 25-year-old bulimic anorexic woman reported an explicit dream image of being in quicksand. She had resumed menstruating and had analyzed the conflicts underlying her gorging and vomiting habits. She had particular problems with time and impulses. For many years, she had come late to sessions and also had been late for other appointments and commitments. She had come to realize that in the transference she wanted the analyst to be the all-loving, tender mother of the first year of life and that she demanded of herself that she be a mother to everyone. Several dreams in which men she was interested in appeared as females had convinced her that she also wanted males to be maternal objects. This dream of quicksand reflected her growing knowledge of her unresolved symbiotic tie to and identification with her mother and the analyst in the transference.

Sand symbolism dreams are only amenable to analysis in the terminal phases of treatment of anorexic patients. The meanings of sand symbols—thirst and a dry mouth, diarrhea, conflicts with time, and its antithetical meaning of asceticism (impulse control)—should be interpreted in the context of the clinical material. The therapist usually has to ask these patients if they have a dry mouth and focus on this symptom, as they usually feel the dry mouth is normal unless it is intense and prolonged xerostomia.

While there may be intense characterologic resistance to facing dreams and fantasies, the fact that patients tell the therapist that they dream indicates therapeutic progress. Giovacchini (1979) describes a very negativistic, resistant hospitalized anorexic woman who had been diagnosed as schizophrenic. His patient began sleeping during sessions, but would not or could not communicate the content of her dreams. Giovacchini did not press her. In subsequent hours, she evidenced positive transference and talked of conflicts, whereas formerly she had been catatonic.

SUMMARY

Like other psychosomatic patients, anorexics suffer from pregenital fixations and conflicts, and the first phase of their analysis focuses on these problems. This is the therapeutic task whether the diagnosis is neurotic or borderline. These patients do not free-associate early in treatment. Dream interpretation is utilized during this phase to show patients their basic conflicts, part-object relations, all-or-nothing superego, and belief in magic, rationalization, and denial. The technique of interpretation is similar to that used in the analytic therapy of borderlines and psychotics and parallels the treatment methods utilized by Boyer and Giovacchini (1980), Kernberg (1975), and Volkan (1976). One can change from a technique of focal analysis of pregenital conflicts and dream material to a more classical oedipally-rooted psychoanalytic technique when there has been a shift from the anorexic symptom complex to a neurosis and when there has been a change in the quality of object relations. Case examples were given to demonstrate the pseudo-oedipal nature of these patients' dreams and associations, and the pregenital defenses of their egos, which receive particular attention and interpretation in the transference. The split in the anorexic's ego may be demonstrated by dream representations of the "little man" phenomenon. Sand symbolism dreams are important because they reveal the anorexic's conflicts over thirst, impulse control, and asceticism.

12
Psychoanalysis: The Case of Carol
GERALD V. FREIMAN, M.D.

Fenichel (1945b) stated:

> Anorexia can regularly be traced back to eating disturbances in childhood which under certain libido-economic circumstances are subsequently taken up again. Like the disturbances, later anorexia, too, may have a very different significance. It may be a simple hysterical symptom expressing the fear of an orally perceived pregnancy or of unconscious sadistic wishes. It may be part of an ascetic reaction formation in a compulsion neurosis. It may also be an affect equivalent in a depression in which the symptom of refusal of food makes its appearance before other signs of the depression are developed. It may be a sign of the refusal of contact with the objective model in an incipient schizophrenia. (pp. 176–177)

Since the treatment of anorexia involving the more malignant pathologies has been described in previous chapters, the following presentation focuses on the classical analysis of a predominantly hysterical anorexic woman. Emphasis will be placed on three particular factors whose importance in the treatment of psychosomatic syndromes was first recognized by Melitta Sperling (see Chapter 3, this volume). These factors are: (1) the mother-child relationship, (2) the importance of having the patient assume the responsibility and control of the psychosomatic symptomatology, and (3) the significance and importance of analyzing the preoedipal and pregenital material in order to effect a cure of the symptomatology.

REFERRAL

Carol, a 23-year-old single, white Jewish female of asthenic body type, markedly underweight but meticulously groomed and extremely attractive, was referred for analysis by her internist brother. She stated in her initial remarks that she was seeking treatment because of "a most annoying state of anorexia." When asked about this state, she described an inability to eat in public or at home for fear of vomiting. Carol explained that she did get hungry but most often got "a feeling of nausea" when she began to eat or even thought of eating. This had been going on for the past two years, causing her to lose about 35 lbs. (she was 5'6" and weighed 96 lbs.). The patient said she had had these episodes in high school and college, but they had subsided after a week or so (they had been diagnosed as virus infections and she had been advised not to eat—her mother would serve her tea and toast and in a few days she would be better). On questioning, she related that she had had eating problems all her life, in the sense that she had been on diets of various sorts—a vegetarian diet as a young child after she had learned how cows and chickens were slaughtered, a low-calorie diet, and a diet for her skin when she had had acne. (It later emerged that she also had a fear of her eating utensils being contaminated: she would insist that no one touch them after she personally washed them. She was particularly careful not to sit next to her younger brother, whom she felt never washed before he came to the dinner table.)

MENSTRUAL HISTORY

Carol experienced her menarche at age $16\frac{1}{2}$. She gave a history of always having had irregular cycles, sometimes going 3–4 months without a period. She joked that if she didn't know the facts of life, she would have thought herself pregnant. When she did experience her menses, they were invariably accompanied by cramps and marked irritability.

ONSET OF ANOREXIA

She associated the onset of her anorexia to an episode $2\frac{1}{2}$ years earlier when she had been on her way to work, and the subway had gotten stuck between stations for about 10–15 minutes because of an accident further up the track (she later learned that it had been a suicide). She had become extremely anxious and experienced a claustrophobiclike episode, with difficulty in breathing, palpitations, perspiration, and nausea that necessitated her going between trains to vomit. She had remained panicky until the train started. She remembered being consoled by some older woman. She went on to explain that since this episode, although she made it a point not to eat or drink prior to using the train, she would still feel some nausea (sometimes she would take Combid). Carol said she never really had felt comfortable using the subway, even as a child. Now she frequently used her own car, took a taxi, or drove in to work with a friend. She said if it weren't for the fact that she had an excellent job as an administrative assistant to a well-known TV producer and director in the city, she would take a job nearer to her home which wouldn't necessitate commuting (something her mother had suggested many times).

FAMILY HISTORY

Carol was the middle of three children, with a brother eight years her senior and a brother four years her junior (both of them extremely scholarly and the pride of the family).

Father

Her father was a professional man who was frequently away from home from early morning until late in the evening. More often than not, he worked on weekends as well. Her earliest memories of her father at home were of his being buried in his books and not available for questions or play. The only one who could reach him was mother and, later on, her brothers, who shared his scientific interests and whose careers were of the utmost concern to him. She felt that her father had been more readily available to her in her teens when he became concerned about her dating and her social life; he would constantly question her about her friends and warn her to be careful not to get too intimate with her boyfriends lest she become pregnant or acquire a venereal disease, and not to associate with girls who had a bad reputation. (Marijuana was another concern of his and her mother's.)

Carol expressed great love and admiration for her father and felt he loved her as well, but she also felt he never had been proud of her as he had been of her brothers. She recalled trying to engage him in conversations regarding her studies in English literature and the other humanities and feeling that he wasn't really interested and was merely being polite as he listened to her. She thought of her studies as "trivia" and fantasized that her father thought so too. (Incidentally, she had been an excellent student.) During Carol's analysis, it became evident that there had been a great deal of seductive behavior between daughter and father, much of which was quite annoying to her mother.

Mother

Carol's mother was described as a bright woman who was completely preoccupied with her home, children, and husband (in that order). Carol stated that her mother frequently would complain that she made a mistake when she interrupted her college education in order to get married, and that she should have gone on to some important profession such as law or medicine. She complained that instead she wound up a simple hausfrau—the servant of her husband and children. Carol felt that her mother lived vicariously through the achievements of her husband and children, especially her two sons—all the children had to be successful in school and strive for honors. The mother was described as a demanding individual who got her own way with little interference from her husband, even when she was unreasonable. She made most of the decisions in the house and was always confident that she was in the right.

During her consultation, Carol said that she "loved, hated, admired, and despised her mother all at the same time." She felt that her mother loved her, but only as her possession. She complained that her mother never allowed her to make important decisions on her own and was constantly interfering in her life. She said this was not true of her brothers, who seemed to be able to resist her interference and establish their own independence. Carol said that even in choosing a college, her mother's preference (a college near home) had prevailed over her own preference (an out-of-town school).

As if to undo these latter impressions, she added that she hoped that she didn't paint too bad a picture of her mother and that the analyst didn't "get the wrong idea." Underneath it all, she knew her mother meant to do the best for her and usually gave her good advice. Carol sometimes "marveled" at how bright her mother was and felt that her mother probably was the brightest one in the family "even if she isn't a college graduate or a professional." She declared that her mother was usually better at treating the anorexia than all the gastroenterologists and internists she had consulted, and jokingly remarked that the malted milks and cookies her mother made for her often worked better than all the antispasmodics, tranquilizers, vitamin shots, and concentrated protein food supplements she had been advised to take.

When asked how her mother felt about her consulting an analyst, Carol said that her mother was most concerned about the continuing loss of weight and was ready to try anything. Her mother would like to see Carol get married and have a family. She then went on to relate how "the anorexia" interfered with her social life and often caused her great embarrassment. The men she currently dated were good friends who knew about and tolerated her illness and never asked her to eat. But none of them wanted to get too seriously involved with a woman who had such a problem. In response to questioning, she said that since she had had the anorexia, she had had no intimacy with men. She had had two "brief affairs" in college and had petted heavily when in high school. When she related the latter information, she complained of feeling some nausea.

She always had looked up to her older internist brother; in many ways, he had acted as a father surrogate. As a child, she had not gotten along with her younger brother. She used to hit and tease him and was told that, when he was an infant, she had been very hostile toward him and at times had tried to hurt him. As she got older, she became friendlier and they now enjoyed a pleasant brother-sister relationship. She said that both of her brothers were very protective toward, and concerned about, her.

THERAPY

Early Sessions

After two sessions of evaluation, the analyst decided that Carol was analyzable. She began five-times-a-week analysis, which continued for three years and then was reduced to four times a week for the next two and a half years. It was a long analysis and, like all analyses, ran a complicated course with many side roads of exploration and interpretation. In what follows, the focus is narrowed to the analysis of the anorexia, with special emphasis on the three factors mentioned earlier.

During the first few weeks of treatment, Carol would lie down on the couch with a heavy sigh and frequent remarks such as, "Well if I have to" or "Here goes." She would lie there with her legs and arms crossed, almost immobile except for the movements of her mouth. She "recited" a medical history of "the anorexia" and her eating difficulties, which dated back to age four, the year her brother was born. Her recitations were almost affectless and were (as she told the analyst) well thought out before the sessions. The analyst's gentle suggestions that she seemed "frightened by the procedure" were met with "Don't be silly" and "I'm quite familiar with doctors and also with this type of treatment, which I read about before I came to see you." She would then continue with her recitation, filling in the entire hour with hardly a pause. She displayed her extensive knowledge of the medical diagnostic techniques and treatment for anorexia in a way calculated to impress the analyst.

After about two weeks, she ran out of this type of prepared material (which served her counterphobic needs), began to pause between her associations, and was much more visibly upset and fidgety while on the couch. She began to complain that "the anorexia" was worse than before she came for treatment—she couldn't eat at all and had unbearable nausea and vomiting. The analyst pointed out that the aggravation of her symptoms was a reaction to certain uncomfortable feelings and thoughts that were being stirred up in the analysis and that she was trying to suppress.

Following this, her symptoms apparently became even more aggravated—she was up all night retching and vomiting, could not sleep, and missed her session. She called her older brother, who insisted that she return to analysis as soon as possible. (He himself was in analysis and was most supportive of her treatment.) When Carol returned later that week (after missing two sessions) the analyst learned that her mother had stayed up with her and slept in her room for the previous two nights trying to comfort, console, and treat her.

At this point, lest, like all of Carol's previous physicians, the analyst be replaced by malted milk and cookies, he indicated more emphatically that she was using her symptoms of anorexia and vomiting in order to escape from certain feelings and thoughts being stirred up in the analysis. He also pointed out that she was enlisting her mother's support in her own wish to leave treatment. The analyst told her that she had to make a choice between remaining a semiinvalid with anorexia who was dependent on her mother's comforting feedings and remaining in analysis, no matter how uncomfortable, until she worked through her problems so that she could become a mature, independent adult. This type of confrontation had to be repeated on numerous occasions early in the analysis since there was mounting evidence in her productions that the mother was being seduced by Carol and, in turn, was seducing Carol to belittle the analytic treatment. The mother tried to sabotage the treatment in many subtle ways, especially by rewarding the patient in a most regressive fashion for being sick.

This type of narcissistically oriented, "psychosomatogenic" mother* exercises powerful, but covert, hostile aggression by interfering with her daughter's psychic separation, individuation, autonomy, and sexual maturation. The daughter develops a masochistic and/or sadistic identification with the mother and does not view her overindulgence as springing from the "wells of maternal love." In this masochistic identification, which is found in all psychosomatic patients, the patient assumes the roles of both subject and object in a regressive direction where the distinction between self and object is at times blurred.

Although the analyst's pointing out to Carol that she had a choice appealed to her realistic wish for psychic maturity, autonomy, and individuation on some level, the more immediate appeal (and an indication of the evolving transference

---

*See Chapters 1, 3, and 4.

neurosis) was revealed in her first dream. She was in a department store and a very handsome man—the manager—sold her some new type of false eyelashes. He assured her that all other women would "drool over" them and "burst with envy." This dream and the associations that followed made it clear that the more highly cathected appeal to her at this time was that the analyst would fulfill her wish for a phallus, which would be envied by her mother (and bring her closer to mother). The oral implications were quite manifest in the metaphors "to drool over" and "to burst with envy." The latter also were related to pregnancy fantasies and anal material, and are an example of the masochistic identification described earlier.

Still retaining her original symptoms, but not complaining or talking about them too often, Carol began to express more positive feelings toward the analyst and the analytic situation, which she at times likened to a "date" with her "understanding boyfriends." She filled in hour after hour with material she apparently thought the analyst would like to hear (in much the same way that she had tried to interest her father in her studies and, later, had tried to seduce him into questioning her about her social life). At the same time, she related material concerning her anger at her mother for having indulged her long-standing food idiosyncrasies and abnormal eating habits, as well as her transient phobias of school, the dark, and being alone. She repeatedly blamed her mother for "the anorexia" and "the vomiting."

Carol did not take any responsibility for these symptoms. They were mother's fault, and she constantly referred to "the" anorexia and "the" vomiting as if they had been visited on her by some evil spirit. In this respect, she regarded her psychosomatic symptoms much as a hysteric would regard her conversion symptoms—as "alien" to her conscious ego. Indeed, Carol's anorexia might be seen as more consistent with a conversion process than with a classical psychosomatic process. From the beginning of this analysis, the analyst repeatedly had to question her use of terms such as "the anorexia" and "the vomiting." He informed and then reminded Carol that these symptoms were hers and were her way of handling her emotional conflicts. It took time and constant interventions for her gradually to see that she was responsible and could control herself. She gained more conviction about this as the analysis progressed, and she was able progressively to understand the defensive function of these symptoms, particularly within the context of the transference neurosis.

Getting the patient to accept the responsibility for the symptom is the first step in retransforming the somatic expression into the conflicts that it masks. It is an attempt to change from primary-process to secondary-process expression, and from poor self-object differentiation to individuation. It is also an attempt to strengthen the observing portion of the ego and, in that sense, to strengthen the therapeutic alliance.

Later Sessions

After this initial period of relating positive feelings toward the analyst, which were accompanied by thinly disguised associations and dreams indicative of her positive oedipal longings for father (and older brother), Carol's negative feelings and thoughts began to emerge in the guise of masochistic, self-deprecatory material. For some time, in a state of mild depression, the predominant theme of her sessions was that of self-evaluations and self-reproaches. She referred to herself as a sick, helpless individual and expressed the feeling that no one thought much of her. She felt that her boss, father, mother, and analyst thought of her as an inferior being. During one session, she said she knew the analyst was bored by her. She felt that she wasn't as interesting a patient as the male patient who preceded her. She said she knew he was a physician because of the books he carried with him. He probably discussed things the analyst was interested in and the analyst liked him more. The analyst reminded her of telling him about her father discussing scientific subjects with her brothers and how she felt he was not interested in her schoolwork. The analyst confronted her with the fact that this must have made her quite angry at him, just as her thought about the analyst preferring the patient before her would understandably arouse feelings of anger toward the analyst. This type of confrontation was at first met with denial of her feelings, but after a while the whole masochistic defensive system of hiding her anger (rage) began to give way.

In one session a few days before Christmas, she came in and said that she felt depressed and discouraged and thought that after all this time in analysis she would be feeling much better. She complained that the analyst wasn't giving her the "fruitful" insights that could help her. She then related a dream in which her "boss or someone who looked like him" came into her office with a Christmas gift that was beautifully wrapped and had candy canes hanging from the ribbons. She became excited because she thought the gift was for her. He walked by, ignoring her, and gave the gift to Sonia (an actress whom Carol had spoken about many times and to whom she was very attracted—Sonia was working on a television production at the studio where Carol worked). The scene then shifted and Carol was in a hospital room that was furnished beautifully and she was taking care of her father, who had a hole in his jaw. She thought he had had some back teeth removed. Her associations dealt with her disappointment, her attraction to this actress, and then to some awareness of her anger and its relation to the second scene in this dream. As she spoke of her anger, she began to feel nauseous and became concerned that she might vomit on the couch.

During this session (and many others), the analyst had the opportunity to point out the connection between her disappointment and anger toward him, and her feelings of nausea and urges to vomit (these latter urges became more frequent during the sessions). About this time, she complained that her anorexia was worse and that she couldn't eat at home and was vomiting more than ever.

Carol gradually began to express her anger toward the analyst and other men in her life more openly. Sadistic fantasies of tearing, biting, and devouring the analyst, father, boss, and baby brother gradually gave way to specific fantasies and dreams of biting and incorporating the phallus. At this point in the analysis, there was some clinical improvement. She was delighted to report that she was able to eat out on a few occasions and began to date a new man. She also was able to express her oral incorporative fantasies and dreams without feeling nauseous. For instance, she related the following dream: "Someone, I think a man, gave me a box full of Baby Ruth candies. I ate some and was very happy. I then went into my mother's bedroom—she was in bed. I wanted to get close to her but she closed me out, saying she was too tired." Her associations led to these chocolate phallic-fecal-shaped candies—her coprophilic impulses and some material concerning early conceptions of anal birth. Ensuing sessions contained similar material—incorporating the filthy phallus and excreting it in the form of diarrhea were now verbalized without her feeling nauseous and without any aggravation of her anorexia outside the sessions.

The homosexual aspects that had been evident throughout the analysis became clearer and more manifest. Fantasies of being the analyst's only patient and of becoming friends with the female patient who followed her and replacing the analyst, along with some related material, gradually allowed the analyst to show her that her wish to incorporate the phallus and do away with her baby brother and father was for the purpose of getting closer to and possessing mother.

The preoedipal and pregenital factors involved in this case had to be analyzed before her symptomatic improvement became a real cure. A great deal of time was spent working through multiple fantasies, dreams, and associations dealing with her wish to eat her way into mother, tear her apart, devour her, and repossess the "real" phallus-baby-breast that was inside mother. Throughout this phase of the analysis, there were many tunnel, cave, and room dreams and fantasies, all of which expressed this deeply hidden, unconscious wish.

Only by working through his preoedipal material did she achieve her individuation and autonomy and come genuinely to work through (and resolve) the positive oedipal fantasies that she had expressed so easily at the beginning of her analysis.

SUMMARY

Most clinical material in the literature deals with anorexic patients who suffer from more malignant psychopathologies and who for the most part are not initially candidates for classical psychoanalytic treatment. This chapter is a clinical case vignette of a predominantly neurotic anorexic woman who was analyzable via classical technique. The emphasis of this presentation is on the analysis of the anorexic symptoms and on the importance of a thorough analysis of the preoedipal and pregenital material in the resolution of the core conflicts leading to the anorexic symptoms.

13
Anorexia Nervosa and Bulimia in Males

IRA L. MINTZ, M.D.

Bruch (1973b) quotes from the earliest report of an anorexic male, which was made by Morton in 1689:

> The Son of the Reverend Minister, Mr. Steele, my very good friend, about the Sixteenth Year of his age fell gradually into a total want of Appetite, occasioned by his studying too hard and the Passions of his Mind, and upon that into an Universal Atrophy, pining away more and more for the space of two years, without any cough, fever, or any other symptom of any distemper of his lungs. . . . And therefore I judg'd this consumption to be Nervous, and to have its seed in the whole Habit of the Body. (p. 285)

Morton's description of this patient was similar to that of an 18-year-old female patient of his (see Chapter 4, this volume). In both cases, he recognized the role of "the cares and passions of the mind," the perfectionistic studying, the lack of response to medication, and the chronic course. In 1868, Gull (reported in Hay and Leonard 1979) noted that the illness could occur in boys. Nevertheless, anorexia nervosa in males has been reported as rare (Screenivasan 1978), with a male:female ratio ranging from 1:10 to 1:20. Bruch (1973b) reported 10 male patients out of a series of 70 anorexics treated between 1942 and 1970.

A number of authors (Beaumont et al. 1972; Bruch 1971, 1973b; Crisp 1967; Crisp and Toms 1972; Deneux et al. 1977; Falstein et al. 1956; Hasan and Tibbetts 1977; Hay and Leonard 1979; Screenivasan 1978; Taipale et al. 1972) have reported on the most outstanding features of this illness in males. Premorbid features include childhood obesity, parental overprotection, excessive obedience, and a family setting with considerable strife and instability. Usually the anorexic managed to maintain a precarious psychic equilibrium until the stresses of preadolescence and adolescence proper destabilized it. Obesity and excessive preoccupation with food in family members were not unusual.

CHARACTERISTICS

The syndrome itself is characterized by the same features presented by women: a conscious refusal of foods, especially carbohydrates; a deliberate pursuit of thinness; difficulty in recognizing emaciation and other body-image difficulties; vomiting and purging; and a preoccupation with diets and cooking. A number of investigators (Bruch 1971, Hasan and Tibbetts 1977) have commented on the frequent restlessness and hyperactivity. Bruch has suggested that the hyperactivity is a pathognomonic sign of anorexia. Other clinicians (Crisp and Toms 1972, Dally 1969, Taipale et al. 1972) have suggested that anorexic males are sicker than anorexic females and more difficult to treat. Occasional bizarre symptoms have been reported, such as the 11-year-old boy who would not swallow his saliva because he believed that it contained calories (Screenivasan 1978).

In a 10-year follow-up of 11 cases of anorexia in males ranging in age from 14 to 46, Crisp and Toms (1972) emphasized the major symptoms: a fear of being fat, with pursuit of thinness to the point of emaciation; a preoccupation with food; a decreased metabolic rate; and day and night restlessness. Strikingly, three siblings of these anorexic males also had anorexia. As one boy recovered, his brother developed the disease. Similar findings have been noted with female anorexic patients (Chapter 4, this volume).

Bruch (1971) focused on the major body-image disturbance and the deliberate pursuit of thinness. She felt that other psychiatric conditions with weight loss could be differentiated from anorexia nervosa in part because, in the latter, "the relentless pursuit of thinness . . . represents a frantic effort to establish a sense of differentiated identity" (p. 32). Crisp and Toms (1972) also commented on the dynamic aspects of the weight loss, which aimed "to reshape appearance in pursuit of greater attractiveness, and self-confidence and a securer identity" (p. 337). Kay and Leigh (1954) believed that the illness was more frequent in girls because of the greater bodily changes and their resulting psychological impact and significance. Deneux et al. (1977) and Crisp (1967, Crisp and Toms 1972) commented on the presence of significant psychosexual conflict with unconscious homosexual conflict prior to the onset of the disorder. Bruch (1971, 1973b) commented on precipitating factors and mentioned seven success-oriented patients whose illness followed a threat to their continued success. She stated that four patients went to camp and three moved to different neighborhoods. She did not state that the illness was precipitated by conflicts over separation. She also noted that these male patients experienced alternate bouts of starving and gorging, the latter often followed by self-induced vomiting.

As is the case with female patients, these male patients had controlling mothers whose behavior toward them arose from the mothers' needs rather than in response to the needs of the children. Bruch felt that the syndrome was quite similar in males and females except that the onset in males tended to occur in prepuberty while the onset in females generally occurred later. Finally, she suggested that these boys did not develop sexually until they recovered from the anorexia. This suggestion contradicts the clinical observations reported in Cases 2, 3, and 5 of this chapter, as three of the males were in typical adolescence.

CONFLICTS

Sours (1974) described male anorexic patients, emphasizing their tie to, and identification with, the mother. He pointed out a developmental background of obesity, which was also present in three of the patients described later in this chapter. Psychodynamic considerations primarily revolved about intense conflict over sexual feelings toward the seductively perceived mother.

Sours (1980) commented further on the oedipal nature of one anorexic boy's conflicts, underlining his fear of his phallic-aggressive feelings and his erotic desire for the mother. Sours minimized the preoedipal cannibalistic destructiveness that is denied through starving, and the regressive omnipotent need to control eating that occurs in response to feeling overwhelmed and totally unable to control external objects. Prognostically, he felt that anorexic males were generally more difficult to treat than anorexic females. In my opinion, symptom removal and the achievement of some psychological insight are no more difficult to obtain with males than with females. However, a thorough resolution of the underlying conflicts is more difficult to achieve with males, as they withhold major aspects of their sexual conflicts and cling to their resentment over having been coerced into treatment.

Sperling (1978) noted anorexic behavior in males, but did not believe that true anorexia nervosa exists in the male. She cited two main reasons. First, the starving in the female is an attempt at independence from the mother while, in the male, the refusal of food makes him more dependent on the mother. (My own experience shows no such difference between male and female patients; both suffer from conflicts over separation and independence.) Second, males cannot experience amenorrhea and usually express their feminine wishes and identifications in pregenital conversion symptoms of the lower gastrointestinal tract (e.g., in colitis and hemorrhoids). However, the presence of coexisting syndromes is hardly unusual in psychosomatic conditions and does not eliminate the recognition of each specific disease. In addition, while amenorrhea is usually a cardinal symptom, it may be ill-advised to overemphasize any one symptom at the expense of the entire clinical picture. For example, there are female patients with classic anorexia nervosa who do not have body-image distortion. The preponderant clinical syndrome, unconscious psychodynamics, and developmental history in male patients are so similar to those of female patients that it is reasonable to conclude that anorexia nervosa can exist in the male.

Clinical Material

The following material presents the clinical course, symptoms, and underlying conflicts of five anorexic males, ranging from 10 years old to middle-aged. Two patients had chronic bulimia as well.

CASE 1   Acute, Moderate Anorexia in a Latency-Age Child

Eric was a 10-year-old boy referred for psychoanalytic therapy after a thorough workup by his pediatrician for unexplained weight loss as a result of a disinterest in eating. The parents stated that Eric had been quite well-adjusted and happy until about 10 weeks earlier.

ONSET OF SYMPTOMS.   His mother described the change:

He seemed unable to enjoy the vacation and became irritable and morose. In January, when he returned to school, he stopped eating. His aversion to food included all those foods that he had previously liked a great deal. . . . He used to love food, and often would take two and three helpings, so that he used to be stocky and a little overweight. At Christmas, he weighed 80 lbs. and now he weighs 55 lbs. He picks at his food and eats a little salad, half a bagel, and diet soda. He tells us that he just doesn't like food anymore, but at the same time he seems to have developed a curious interest in all kinds of food. He keeps asking what we're having to eat, but then he doesn't eat anything no matter what it is and tells us that he doesn't know what he wants to eat. He constantly opens the icebox to see what's inside and then rummages through the cabinets . . . but doesn't eat a thing. Sometimes he eats carrots and lettuce and jello.

He also watches every morsel that goes in our mouths, almost as if he'd like to eat, but something is holding him back. I've noticed that he tries to get me and his little sister to eat more. . . . He doesn't seem to care if his father or older brother eat or not. He especially asks his sister if she wouldn't like more, and he keeps pushing the dishes at her until I have to tell him to let her alone and not to force her to eat.

The mother spontaneously added that his personality seemed to change during this time. He became tense, fidgety, and somewhat irritable. He was in perpetual motion, pacing from the rec room to the library, to the kitchen, to his bedroom. He wouldn't even sit down to watch TV, but would stand in front of it. He used to love sports, but no longer engaged in them. The mother thought he might be too weak. At the beginning of his personality change, Eric would jog all the time and do 200 situps morning and night. At the time of the consultation, he was very weak and emaciated, but still rode mother's stationary bicycle for 45 minutes at a time.

The father added that he also noticed how withdrawn Eric had become. He used to talk freely and be eager to tell him the events of the day and what happened at school. Now he volunteered nothing and, when asked, had nothing to say or replied, "I don't know." He didn't seem as involved with his friends. They all used to play basketball on the driveway, and now he stood out there all alone. The mother commented that even though he was withdrawn and didn't talk, he hung about the house and followed her around. That was definitely different behavior. About a week before the consultation, after having lunch at McDonald's, Eric began demanding milk shakes. For the past week, he would only consume milk shakes. He would drink four or five at once, go to bed, and not eat again for almost 24 hours. Not a drop of food or water passed his lips.

PATIENT'S HISTORY.   The parents felt that, prior to this illness, Eric had gotten along well in school, been a good student, and been approved of by the teachers. He was a good athlete and had begun to enjoy playing tennis regularly with his father. He also had become interested in chess at an early age and was quite good at it, beating his father and four-year-older brother regularly. He always had had a good relationship with his older brother, but not with his sister, who was three years younger than Eric. She was very competitive and strong-willed, and seemed to threaten Eric's security. She often attempted to beat him in athletics, although she never succeeded. Frequently, she would either tease him and provoke a fight, or openly challenge him. Prior to becoming ill, he would take her on and at times hit her hard and send her off crying. Recently, however, he had avoided fighting and had submitted almost passively to her bullying. Eric's past history and developmental stages were reported as unremarkable. At age five, he had fallen while running and had broken a bone in his hand; he also had had a brief period of enuresis that year. The parents reported that there had been no feeding problems. Eric was described by both parents as a good eater.

A number of events, however, seemed to stand out in the mother's mind. About eight months prior to the onset of the starving, Eric had complained that he seemed to be too heavy and was troubled by it. His mother had replied that he was heavy like she was, while his sister and brother were thin like the father. The mother also had noted that he was beginning to develop a little pot belly. At the same time, the father's sister had become pregnant with her first child. Although the sister lived in a different state, her husband was a traveling salesman and would often drive her to Eric's home for a visit while he went out of town. Eric's starving seemed to begin just after his aunt gave birth to a little girl.

Eric was born on the West Coast, where he lived until age four. At that time, his father, a corporate lawyer, was transferred to the East Coast, where the family resided in a small suburban community. The mother preferred the new location because it reunited her with her family; she was very close to her three sisters.

The only family complications during the three-times-a-week two-year treatment were related to the father's frequent business trips to various parts of the world and Eric's brother's hospitalization for pneumonia. Eric suffered from separation anxieties when his father left home and was fearful that the plane might crash. When his brother developed a bad case of pneumonia during the second year of treatment, Eric became quite fearful that he might die. Other than that, there were no untoward complications. The parents were quite cooperative; there was little evidence of unconscious attempts to compromise the therapy, a situation that is not uncommon in these cases.

THERAPY. When seen in consultation, Eric was a taller-than-average 10-year-old with stylish black hair that hung over one eye and a somewhat noticeable scar on his chin from a bicycle accident. His outstanding characteristic, in addition to his emaciation, was a profound sense of sadness that contributed to his very forlorn appearance. He replied to questions or comments briefly in a monotonous, almost inaudible, voice. He agreed that he wasn't eating: he had lost all interest in eating and felt full whenever he ate. He added that when he ate he began to "feel weird inside" and the food would move around in his stomach. While he acknowledged that he had lost about 25 lbs., he did not feel or think of himself as thin. He spontaneously commented that he always felt cold no matter what he wore and that often he felt very tired. His major worry seemed to be school. Although he got mostly A's, he still worried that he would not do well, and he resented doing the required homework. In reply to questions about friends, he stated that he was much less involved with them now and didn't seem to care that he spent most of his time after school alone in the house. Prior to his illness, he had had many friends with whom he would play ball or chess. He noted that he had had no difficulty eating until just before Christmas. Prior to that time, he had had a "great appetite" and had enjoyed all kinds of food.

He began the second session with a request: "Can I stand?" He added that he had "to move back and forth, to walk in place," because he experienced tingling in the front and back of his upper thighs. He controlled the unpleasant feeling by constantly walking in place, 12 hours a day, even while sitting in school. "It's like walking while standing still." When he walked, he felt a little better. He had to watch TV standing. The tingling began shortly after the starving, and he couldn't stop or it would get worse. At that point, he began to cry. He said that sometimes at the end of the day, when he felt very tired after constantly "walking," he had to sit and tolerate the tingling. He was afraid to ask the therapist the first time because the therapist might be angry at him. Again, the therapist was struck by his sadness.

In the fourth session, Eric said he ate only milk shakes, but did not know why. When the therapist pointed out that not eating could result in his getting sick and that some children do die from this illness, he began to cry and said he felt that the therapist was pressuring him to eat. The therapist pointed out that he was not pressuring him and never would because that was not the way he worked. He added that if Eric was like other children with this illness, he had other problems that he was covering up by focusing on not eating. The therapist told him that whatever he spoke about would be confidential and would be told to no one, not even his parents.

Eric said that he did not think about food, although he ate nothing and drank nothing until his evening milk shakes. He did not believe that he was thin, but mentioned that the kids in school taunted him by calling him "little skeleton." He and the therapist spoke about the choice of milk as Eric's only food and, when Eric stated that he did not know why he had picked milk, the therapist pointed out that babies drink only milk. Eric added that his little cousin was born in December. He spoke more about babies, and the therapist suggested that Eric might be afraid of growing up and might wish to remain little.

The interpretations about identifying with a baby and wishing to be little were made on the basis of the patient's history, without waiting to obtain detailed confirmatory clinical evidence. The patient was already severely emaciated. Experience has indicated that a more active approach can stem the downhill course and prevent the need for hospitalization. Most prominent in the session were Eric's active pacing in place and his extreme fearfulness that the therapist would pressure him to eat, even after being reassured that he would not do so. The therapist responded to the latter concern by indicating that Eric was worried that he would try to control him by making him eat and that maybe Eric had difficulty controlling things in his life. At the end of the session, the therapist told the mother in Eric's presence that the pediatrician would continue to follow him and that it would be his medical decision as to whether Eric would have to be hospitalized if his weight continued to drop. This also permitted Eric to vent his anger at the hospitalizing physician rather than at the therapist who could continue to work with him in a hopefully positive fashion.

In the following session, Eric spoke a great deal about TV programs, especially one in which a guru remained all curled up in a small tank of water for an entire hour without breathing.

In the seventh session, Eric still remained standing for the entire session, rocking back and forth, plaintively complaining that he had told the therapist everything and didn't want to go over it again. He cried a good deal of the session, feeling that the therapist was pressuring him. He stated that the therapist was yelling at him, although he spoke quite softly to him, since he was standing about one foot from his chair. The therapist pointed out that Eric had difficulty finding something to say because he kept things in.

Eric then commented that it all began when he heard that his aunt was pregnant, and he began to think about being fat. (The actual starving began just after she gave birth.) The remainder of the session was spent discussing pregnancy and birth, with considerable tension and crying on Eric's part. He believed that the baby grew in the stomach, and that the stomach was cut open to let it out. The therapist wondered if this had something to do with his eating problem. Eric said, "Maybe." In the following session, he volunteered that before his aunt got pregnant, he had seen a TV special on how babies are made and knew that "you put this (pointing to his penis) into the woman."

In sessions 9–15, he spent a great deal of time discussing his little sister. He continued discussing the TV program about pregnancy. If only one egg appeared, how did his mother have him, his older brother, and his little sister? Clearly unhappy with his siblings, and especially his little sister, he implied that, with only one egg, there would be no siblings. He began to complain about his sister's intrusions into his life, especially the way she would tease and provoke him and destroy his possessions. He spoke about how she messed up his room, damaged his toys, and hid his chessmen. On one occasion, she broke the spokes in the front wheel of his new bicycle. No matter how much he yelled, she would not stop. When he punched her, she cried, but the next day she did it again. He added that it had been worse when she was little. During his agitated recounting of his sister's behavior, his endless pacing ceased momentarily.

In the next five sessions, he continued his complaints against, and his verbal abuse toward, his sister. When she was young, she used to climb out of her crib and jump on his bed and wake him up. She would throw her bottle at him and break many of his toys. Once, about a year ago, she had hit him in the head with a stone and, while he cried, his mother had spanked her. Usually the sister ran away and the mother chased her. In the 14th session, as he continued his tirade against his sister, he appeared more energetic and less sad. When the therapist remarked about his improved appearance, he agreed. He felt better. He didn't have to pace all over the house as much and was able to sit down for the first time in months. "I don't cry as much, and I hit my sister instead of crying. . . . I used to cry and ask my mother to punish her." In reply to the therapist's query as to why he did not punch her back, he commented, "If I hit her in the stomach where she might have a cut, I might hurt something inside." His previous comment about cutting the stomach open to get the baby out clearly suggested the repressed rage against the baby inside the pregnant aunt-mother. When he continued discussing his angry feelings toward his sister in the following session, the therapist pointed out that his fear of hitting his sister too hard had made him want to be weak so that he could not hurt her. He denied this and protested that he wanted to lift weights so that he could be strong. The therapist added that if he had no muscle tissue on his body, lifting weights could not make him strong—that maybe the front of his mind did wish to be strong, but since the back of his mind was afraid of hurting his sister, especially in her stomach, he needed to be weak.

He began the next session with the comment that he had so many ideas that he didn't know which one the therapist would like to hear about. He spoke at great length about his interest in lizards, especially those with teeth, about snakes that eat live mice, and about spiders. There was no pacing or rocking in this session.

In an interview, the parents reported a dramatic improvement. Eric's mood had improved, with a subsiding of his depressive, sad appearance. He had begun to talk with them again and to go out with friends after school. The school had also indicated a marked improvement in work, attitude, and sociability, except for his having beaten up the boy who used to call him "little skeleton." The parents noted a great deal of assertive and aggressive behavior, especially toward his little sister, with much less toward the older brother. The other day, when she had teased him, he had punched her in the head and sent her off crying. He had continued to ignore the new baby. He had stopped pacing at home and was able to sit and watch TV. His diet had not changed. The parents were still unable to remember any childhood feeding difficulties or any pressures that he might have experienced. They were encouraged to tolerate his emerging aggression and to consider any excesses part of a temporary phase. It was pointed out that such personality changes are often a prerequisite for changes in the eating pattern. Also, he had begun to gain weight, so there was little realistic medical concern.

The following week, in a discussion of Eric's resentment of his sister, the therapist pointed out that the birth of his little cousin probably made him remember how annoyed he must have been when his little sister was born. Talking about the new cousin, he commented, "You can't pick her up and throw—" and stopped. The therapist interjected, "and throw her. That's what you might have wanted to do with your baby sister." He spoke about how his sister once climbed into the clothes dryer and shut the door. In a subsequent session, he revealed that his worst thought about his sister was his fear of killing her and then being punished. A week later, he remembered that at age eight he had thought of getting a knife and stabbing her in the heart. During another session, he remembered wishing that she were dead.

In the third month, he described the movie "Pete and the Dragon," in which Pete was made a slave by his parents. He had an invisible dragon that protected him from his parents, his mean teacher, and the doctor who tried to steal the dragon. The therapist added that it might be nice if a boy had a dragon that protected him, and that maybe he wished he had a strong friend, instead of being strong himself. He then revealed that for a long time he had been trying to get an iguana as a pet, and that it was just like a Komodo lizard that was 15 feet long and ate deer and buffalo. He drew pictures of the lizard with its mouthful of alligatorlike teeth and the iguana as its miniature prototype.

By the 10th week, he had gained 11 lbs. just by eating milk shakes. Atypically, he was unconcerned about the weight gain. He described in some detail an eating ritual that was both compulsive and sadistic. He would begin eating at 8:00 P.M. every night and usually would take about two hours to consume the milk shakes because they were so cold. No one was permitted to interfere with any aspect of the ritual. The family would always have to be home on time, no matter what they were doing. Otherwise, he would not eat at all for the next 24 hours. The shake had to be eaten with a special silver spoon from childhood and with a certain kind of colored straw. Eric exercised the same tyrannical control over the family with his eating habits as do the typical anorexic adolescent females.

While he consistently denied ever being coerced to eat or being overcontrolled, his transference attitudes suggested a different picture. In the beginning of treatment, he was so fearful that he would be forced to eat that he became agitated over any discussion of his eating habits. Only after repeated reassurances that the therapist would not pressure him was he able to discuss his eating pattern without manifest signs of agitation. One can speculate about the nature of a therapeutic relationship where these patients are forced to eat prior to developing any understanding about why they need to starve. If they feel overwhelmed, they accede temporarily and then redouble their defiant starvation. Even though Eric's relationship with the therapist had progressed satisfactorily, and he spoke volubly, there was a marked distrust and fearfulness. He feared that the therapist would be angry if he did not talk about the right things and would resent his feeling that at times the treatment was boring. It later emerged that these fears were in great part projected transference aspects of parental coercive attitudes, particularly of oral rage and destructive cannibalistic impulses.

During the fifth month of treatment, as Eric described how he had avoided eating during his friend's birthday party, the therapist sympathized with him and suggested that he thought Eric would be so much better off if he weren't plagued by all these eating problems and could eat normally. He replied promptly and definitively, "I don't think so, because now no one tells me how much to eat, and I don't have to finish things. They used to say if I took an extra portion, 'you have to finish it. If you don't eat it all, you have to sit at the table, or you can't watch TV.' Now that can't happen." This discussion was elaborated on in the next few sessions. A picture emerged of a very fussy eater who had refused many staple foods for years, so that the refusal to eat anything during his anorexia represented the culmination and intensification of his long-standing conflict over food, his relationship with his parents, his oral sadism, and aspects of his masculine identification. He also described periods of sadistic teasing of the mother, who responded by spanking him. With his anorexic behavior, he was able to act sadistically under the banner of illness without fear of reprisal.

In one session, during an outburst of talk about babies, Eric spoke about a TV program in which a baby had died from a cord around its neck. He really knew that babies begin with a penis into the vagina and not by a seed. He also knew all about the umbilical cord and had seen the end of his little cousin's cord drying up. In another TV program, he heard about circumcision and how the end of the penis is cut off. He wondered recently if he was growing an extra knee, but his father said that it was just his muscle. He also read about a person who had three legs and saw a picture of a horse with three eyes. He heard there was a cow with five legs at a museum.

Eric seemed to be dealing with his castration anxiety and with compensatory attempts to cope with it. The misperception that he was growing an extra knee-penis and that all kinds of animals could have extra limb-penises represented a restitutive attempt to cope with castration anxieties. The sight of his little cousin's absent penis initiated castration threats which were then reinforced by the upward view of the remains of the umbilical cord: a displaced, withering penile stump. The muscle tissue in his body, unconsciously viewed by him as a symbolic penis, which was lost or dried up by starvation, reflected his ambivalent attitude about whether his identification was masculine or feminine. The starving and loss of tissue-penises might represent a flight from a masculine identity, while at the same time the loss of fat could be viewed as an attempt to rid himself of an inner picture of being pregnant and feminine. Thus, the tissue could represent aspects of both masculine and feminine identities, depending on how the ego viewed it at different points in time and in consonance with other aspects of life experience and the inner sense of self. He was already bewildered over threats to his masculine identification posed by identifying with the aunt-mother during her pregnancy, and he was filled with death-starvation wishes toward his little cousin-sister. These, in addition to the anticipated punishment for his hatred, coalesced into a self-destructive starvation syndrome in which he attempted unconsciously to clarify his identity and to starve and kill his little sister. The multiple symbolic penises were the current manifestation of this set of conflicts. Anorexic women have the same kinds of unconscious perceptions about their body tissue.

Increasing manifestations of Eric's oral destructiveness became evident in the fourth month of treatment, as he described his interest in biology and especially in rats and insects that "bite." He was particularly fascinated by a number of rat movies, including "Willard," in which a boy befriends rats, who then become his allies. He recounted with some sadistic glee how the rats would eat up and destroy anyone who mocked the boy in the movie or stood in his way. He spoke of having seen a number of rats come out of the storm sewers after a rain and having attempted to get closer to them before they ran away. These detailed descriptions spawned another association to the movie "Ben." Ben is the leader of the rats and is friendly with a boy. Ben and thousands of fellow rats attack, destroy, and devour people. In reply to the therapist's question as to whether he would like to be in that kind of a movie, Eric said he wouldn't mind letting the rats crawl on him because they were trained not to eat people. The theme of the rats was strikingly akin to his earlier story of "Pete and the Dragon" and his attempted identification with Pete through his interest in a pet iguana.

He spoke about visiting a farm and how the farmer caught rats in his house with traps. He remembered seeing them with their tongues hanging out, cut in the neck. The therapist pointed out that after he spoke about what a pest his sister was, he then spoke about how the rats got killed. He stated, "My sister is a rat." He no longer felt uncomfortable talking about thoughts of killing her. In another session, he remembered a Dracula movie where the vampire bites a woman three times in the neck and then is able to control her. He then bites two men in the neck and kills them. The therapist commented that if the vampire could control the girl by biting her in the neck, maybe he thought that it would also work with his sister. "No," he said, "You can't control her no m .tter what you do to her." The therapist added that if a person was worried about hurting someone with his teeth, he might not want to use his teeth and might just drink milk. Eric replied that he used his teeth when the shake was frozen.

In the fifth month of treatment, he spent two to three weeks discussing his preoccupation with sharks. He spoke about a TV program where a spear fisherman was bitten by a shark. He then went on to describe how sharks like to eat baby dolphins and how the adult dolphins attempt to protect them. He mentioned that he recently spent all Saturday afternoon in the library reading about sharks. He learned about their feeding frenzies when they eat everything in sight; he would never go spear fishing. He talked about visiting a friend who has a little cousin that bites. While at the friend's house, he was persuaded to put his finger near the cousin's mouth. His friend's sister then yelled to the cousin, "Bite it," which the cousin did. They called the cousin "Jaws 3." In one session, he spoke about a movie that takes place in the Amazon, where the piranha fish eat the muscles from a man's leg, and about a tribe that cuts the enemy's head off. He went fishing once with his friend and his friend's father, and they cut fish up for bait. He ripped out the insides of a fish and cut out the eyes. He denied feeling squeamish about it, except for one time when he felt sick to his stomach. He cut another fish open and found pink and white eggs inside. While he was unable to associate to the fish eggs, it was apparent that they represented babies and his murderous impulses to rip open his mother to kill his sister—impulses that were reawakened by the aunt's pregnancy. The erupting guilt resulted in his nausea at the time of the episode and contributed to the ultimate crystallization of the eating disturbance.

In another session, he recounted a scene from "Jaws" where the diver is exploring the hole in the bottom of the boat caused by a shark attack and a head with one eye comes tumbling out. This comment was related to his identification with the shark and cutting the eyes out of the fish. He then began to describe a whole series of frightening dreams over the next few weeks which he had never reported before.

I suddenly wake up and find a man standing over me with an ax. I stab him and run downstairs, and find my mother, . . . and later my father, dead.

I am being sawed up and I wake up scared. [Here, as the victim of the mechanical shark (the saw), he denied and projected his aggression.]

I am with a girlfriend, and the boat gets turned over, and we find ourselves on an island. We find cannibals who cut off people's heads and put them in a big pot and boil and eat them.

I'm on an island with a girl and we watch cannibals chasing someone and throw a spear at him, pinning him to a tree. Then they pull him apart and roast the parts of his body over the fire on a spit.

The last dream reminded him of a picture he saw about two months before his anorexia began of a sheep being roasted over a fire. He obliged by drawing a picture of the man's head, arm, and leg, skewered by the spit and being roasted over the fire. In another session, he confided that he had had these kinds of dreams since second grade and that he often had three or four a week.

At this time the patient was beginning the sixth month of treatment. Certain dynamics of his anorexia had already been discussed and explored: ideas about oral impregnation, his self-image in which he needed to be weak in order to minimize the impact of his aggressive impulses, his concern that if he were heavy it was too closely linked with his mother and a feminine identification, his aggressive and murderous impulses toward his sister, his wish to remain a baby drinking only milk, and his defiant self-starvation in response to being forced to clean his plate or be punished. These discussions had resulted in a great deal of improvement. He renounced his passivity and reaction formations toward his sister and schoolmates, he recovered from his depression, and he returned to an active play, school, and sports life. He put on 20 lbs. and was unconcerned about the increase in body tissue. His restless pacing behavior ceased.

At the beginning of the sixth month of treatment, despite dramatic improvement in behavior, affect, and physical appearance, as well as the uncovering and exploration of many of the underlying dynamics, Eric had not consumed a morsel of food or an ounce of water. He only drank milk shakes. The treatment seemed to be progressing satisfactorily, but the resolution of the cannibalistic impulses was essential before he would resume eating regular food with the use of his teeth. It was because of that crucial feature that the therapist was especially careful to make no premature interpretation about his oral sadistic impulses for fear that discussions about them would cease. Weeks passed as Eric progressed from descriptions of a desired alliance with a fantasied dragon, which was miniaturized into an iguana, to his interests in rats and snakes, with the beginnings of eating live animals and humans, to his preoccupations with sharks, and, finally, to the actual cannibalistic preoccupations in story and in dream. It should be noted that Eric's interest in biology was neurotically determined but resulted in his extensive knowledge about lizards, reptiles, and fish.

Once the sequences of associations had progressed to cannibalistic dreams, the therapist felt that it was appropriate to interpret Eric's cannibalistic destructiveness. In the beginning of a discussion of cannibals, the therapist pointed out that he thought he understood more of Eric's eating trouble. He stated that Eric had been talking about how people eat sheep and other animals, and at the same time talking about how cannibals eat people. He thought that, in the back of his mind, the idea of eating meat and regular food made him feel somewhat like a cannibal, and that was why he did not eat it. He reacted with perplexity and denial. "Why would I want to eat people?" The therapist told him that he felt angry with his sister and at times was so angry that he said he wished she were dead or thought about sticking a knife into her, and maybe in the back of his mind he also thought of destroying her by eating her. While the perplexity and the denial continued, his questioning and statements indicated that the ideas had made some connection.

I wouldn't do that because if I began to cook her, people would see the smoke from the fire [as on the cannibal island] and they would find out. Besides, my father is a lawyer and he knows judges who send you to prison. I wouldn't know where to bury the bones. They would dig them up, and then I'd go to jail.

The therapist acknowledged that the situation as he described it did indeed present him with a great dilemma and that not wanting to give in to his impulse to eat his sister resulted in his inability to eat all meat and other food.

He sat quietly, thinking. He then described an insulting poem which he used to recite to his sister.

I tried not to goof,
When I threw Lila off the roof.
She seems very ill,
Because she just stands still.

He provided associations to each line, the last one being: "She stands still whenever my mother asks her to do something. She never does it. . . . I do my work in the house. If I got caught and put in jail, later they would put me in the electric chair." The therapist wondered if that was why he would never sit in the chair—if he did, those "tingling" electric feelings would run through his thighs. During the first six months of Eric's three-times-a-week treatment, he always stood next to the therapist's chair throughout the entire session. He thought for a moment before the session ended.

The next morning, Eric's mother called to state that Eric had eaten his first meal in six months. Eric's eating of regular food continued as his diet expanded into an increasing range of foods, including all kinds of meat. He commented that his teeth felt "funny" when eating meat—a consciously perceived hypersensitivity to the use of his destructive teeth. Initial eating following the interpretation of the cannibalism, however, arose more from flight into health than from psychological insight, and considerable time was spent working through this conflict.

From a psychoanalytic perspective, the overt behavior of a return to eating was not necessarily synonymous with cure. Discharge of Eric at this time could have resulted in a return of the same symptoms and destructive character traits, which would have been even more difficult to deal with, or in the development of different, but equally pathological, symptoms and behavior. The return to eating represented change, but not understanding, and the treatment continued until Eric more completely understood all the motives behind his anorexic behavior and especially his concern over the destructive use of his teeth.

DISCUSSION. Conflict over aggression was clearly a major issue for Eric. Usually, the anorexics' aggression is directed primarily against the parents, especially the mother. Here, however, it was directed mainly against the little sister—his nemesis from the day she was born. This shift was not totally unexpected as fierce sibling rivalry and aggressive force-feeding of female siblings are common among anorexic girls (Chapter 4, this volume). Eric's hatred toward the sister was initially dealt with by ingratiating reaction formation, which was replaced by a healthier verbal and physical reaction following discussions in the treatment. The oral destructiveness was abundantly evident in his preoccupations with dragons, lizards, piranhas, rats, sharks, and, finally, cannibals. Initially, he used the animals as auxiliary destructive forces (friends); later he clearly identified with them as vampires who bit people in the neck and killed them. The denial of destructive use of his teeth was evident in the diet of milk shakes and in the later hypercathexis of the teeth while eating meat. The choice of *iced* milk symbolized the desire for warmth, closeness, and nurturing in what was perceived to be a cold, rejecting environment. The general choice of foods by anorexics reveals reaction formations against their underlying impulses. The diet sodas, lettuce, carrots, and empty, noncaloric foods, generally with the avoidance of meat, reflect the denial of cannibalistic urges (in addition to the fear of getting fat).

The interest in cold milk in some of these patients is not unusual. Schlossman (1979) described his experience with a 16-year-old anorexic girl who was ritualistically involved with milk. For a number of months, she ate no food other than iced milk. She would compulsively set up a series of little containers of milk in the icebox. Each container was given the name of someone she knew, who would then be symbolically devoured. The treatment of another 10-year-old boy was remarkably similar to Eric's. He also drank nothing but frozen milk shakes in the early months of his treatment to the degree that the pediatrician felt it necessary to determine their nutritional content. In addition, this child was preoccupied with the same kinds of cannibalistic conflicts channeled through the interest in lizards, rats, and other reptiles.

The symbolic use of the pig, while infrequent, does come up with what appears to be special significance in anorexic patients. The 10-year-old boy mentioned above reported that a relative of his told him about a feast that she had attended while on vacation in which a whole roasted pig with an apple in its mouth dominated the meal. This experience occurred two months before the beginning of the anorexic illness. The boy viewed the whole pig as an intermediate phase in his cannibalism, halfway between his eating bland, nonhuman food and his final concrete cannibalistic fantasies. Two anorexic male patients reported memories of seeing a whole roasted pig, with emphasis on the head, around the time they developed their illness. Patients frequently speak of a fear of being fat, as a fear of "blowing up," which seems to symbolically represent both the exploding of anger related to their aggressive conflicts, and a fear of becoming pregnant associated with sexual identity and mothering problems. Interestingly, the expression "fat as a pig" does not seem to be used frequently by anorexics.

Significance of the pig as a vehicle for the expression of symbolic conflict is worth considering. Pigs and humans are the only animals that are omnivorous and eat both animal and plant. Schlossman (1980) described the importance of swine in the lives of the early Egyptians and Hebrews. The Egyptians buried their dead in shallow sand graves from which pigs would uncover and devour the bodies. Egyptian mythology described the pig as a cannibalistic figure that epitomized their fear that the god, Set, would eat them. The Hebrews derived their fear of the pig from the Egyptians. The Hebrews' prohibition against eating pigs stemmed not only from the attitude that pigs are unclean and eat garbage, but also from the fact that their rooting habits permitted the unearthing of shallow desert graves and the consuming of dead relatives. Schlossman felt that this prohibition arose out of an unconscious, hostile, cannibalistic impulse against the father from unresolved oedipal conflict.

Eric's fear of his aggressiveness was reflected in his concern over damaging his sister in her stomach, where she might have a "cut." This "cut" could symbolize the vagina and his impulse to damage the baby through the vagina with his destructive penis, as well as his urge to "cut" her and kill the baby with a "stab in her chest"—an upward displacement of the urge to cut open her stomach-womb. The knife could symbolize one tooth, like the shark's tooth left in the hull of the boat in "Jaws"; similarly, in the dream, the saw that was cutting him up represented a series of knives, sharks' teeth, and punishment for his destructive wishes.

A second major problem was Eric's conflict over sexual identity. It intensified when he heard that his aunt was pregnant. He started to worry that he was too fat and was especially concerned with his pot belly. When he ate, the "food moved around" in his stomach like a viable fetus. The identification with the pregnant aunt was complete. When she gave birth and lost weight, he began to starve. Preoccupations with the pregnancy continued and were reflected in the description of the guru curled up in the tank of water, not breathing. Loss of weight as a symbolic castration has already been discussed. Restitutive features with masculine aspirations were also present in wanting to be thin and strong like his father and brother.

Finally, his wishes to be a baby, to be weak and helpless, to drink milk and then fall asleep, and to be cared for and replace his sister in his parents' concern were very much in evidence.

Typical anorexic fears of being controlled and assuming control over a part of the environment via not eating were clearly evident, but were not as prominent as in adolescent anorexics. These issues were present in a past history of picky eating, in the transference, and in some sessions where the resentment surfaced and then was minimized. Eric's great distrust was quite evident.

The treatment progressed satisfactorily into the second year. Eric, who was almost 13, grew taller, stronger, and heavier, and became increasingly assertive and aggressive. His sister no longer gave him trouble and was essentially ignored. He began to challenge his older brother physically and athletically. This resulted in some tension and fighting at home, to which the mother reacted with outbursts of rage or helplessness. Often she became depressed. Eric's emerging aggression in adolescence helped to clarify the mother's inability to absorb and deal with aggressive feelings in her sons. This undoubtedly contributed to some of Eric's earlier problems with self-assertion and the appropriate channeling of aggression. Shortly before Eric stopped treatment, the mother entered psychotherapy, which lasted about 18 months and helped her considerably. Soon after her treatment ended, the father was transferred back to the West Coast. The mother phoned after the family's move to inform the therapist that Eric was doing well.

CASE 2   Acute, Moderate Anorexia in an Adolescent

Thomas was a 16-year-old adolescent whose anorexia began seven months before he was referred for consultation by his internist.

ONSET OF SYMPTOMS. The parents were unaware of any problem until the beginning of the 10th grade, when Thomas moved up from junior high school to a much larger regional high school. Both parents gradually noticed that he wasn't eating and was losing weight. At the time of the referral, Thomas was 5'2" and weighed 78 lbs.

The father was a geologist who taught at various universities and worked as a consultant for different private corporations. He stated that Thomas was very concerned about being small, although he denied it and consistently avoided any discussion of it. The father was a tall, obese man whose weight averaged about 300 lbs. He had been told to lose weight for many years. After a heart attack four years earlier at the age of 47, his cardiologist had insisted that he go on a diet and, although the father had tried, he had been singularly unsuccessful. Recently, the cardiologist had put the father on another diet, which Thomas might have noted, as he began to eat similar diet foods.

The mother interjected that Thomas ate no breakfast or lunch—just dinner.

> He has stopped eating all the foods that he used to eat a great deal. He has stopped eating sweets, butter, milk, ice cream, pizza, and all the foods that boys usually enjoy. Now he eats the white of eggs, diet cottage cheese, melba toast, pears, and diet soda. Even when he has dinner, he leaves most of it. He constantly chews gum, however. The other day I found him chewing my antacid tablets at the medicine cabinet. I told him that it wasn't food, and then he denied taking it. He lies about what he eats and tells us that he eats much more than he does. When he goes to the doctor, he puts weights in his pockets to weigh more.

There was no reported gorging or vomiting.

The father, who had been a football player in college, stated that Thomas always had been interested in sports, but never had done well because he was so small. Since the starving had begun, Thomas had become preoccupied with exercising. He lifted weights twice a day. He constantly did situps and pushups, and swam 80 laps at a time, but was most obsessed with running. He ran miles every day, even in snow and rain. "We told him that he was crazy and that he'd get sick, but nothing stopped him. He looks so thin and weak, and seems to have no stamina, so that I can't understand how he runs six and seven miles a day." Both parents felt that he did not recognize how emaciated he was.

The mother commented spontaneously that Thomas had been an insecure, shy, and sensitive child who became tearful very easily. Even now, when the parents went out, he almost always asked where they were going and when they would return. The mother stated that he never resented their going out, but seemed to prefer that they stay home. The father added that Thomas seemed to be less interested in his friends these days and preferred to stay about the house and be with the parents. He was the only child left at home, since his two older sisters and brother had moved out.

In the second consultation, the mother volunteered that she felt that Thomas was anxious about going to the big high school and felt lost there. The other boys were so big and he was so little. He seemed to be fearful about growing up, because he was not eager to learn to drive. He also liked to go places with the parents more now than in the past.

PATIENT'S HISTORY. In describing Thomas's early life, the mother stated that everything had gone well with her planned, normal pregnancy. "His birth weight was 6 lbs., 11 oz. He was an absolute joy. We never had any babysitting problems because his two older sisters almost fought over who would take care of him." As the mother described all the developmental milestones as normal, and everything as "fine," the husband interjected firmly that his wife had pushed all the children about eating, just as her own mother had pushed her. The mother acknowledged that Thomas always had been thin and a picky eater, but she balefully ignored the criticism about the pressured feeding.

The mother then acknowledged Thomas's considerable separation anxiety. In the first three years of his life, she never had left him to go anywhere. The parents had taken him everywhere. He always had liked to be at home and never wanted to leave the backyard. All his friends would come over to visit him, as he would never go to their homes. He also used to climb out of the crib and come into the parents' bed for the longest time. In fact, he still liked to do it, but now the mother sat on the bed and told him that he belonged in his own bed. She remembered that he used to follow her all over the house, pulling on her dress. In kindergarten, she had to sit in the classroom with him for four weeks, but he still had to be taken out until the following year. He also had been "petrified" about going to camp at age 10 and almost had to be taken home. Thomas had been enuretic until age three, and again from age four to five.

In discussing their attitudes toward Thomas, the mother admitted thinking of him as "little" and, although the father denied similar behavior, he admitted calling him "my baby." With some embarrassment, the father acknowledged that his father used to call him his "baby." The grandfather, a talented but unsuccessful musician, had had great difficulty making a living and supporting the family. There were many arguments at home over money, and although the grandmother disparaged the grandfather, the father always remembered him as thoughtful, kind, and dominated by his wife. It seemed apparent that the father's fear of his own mother played a role in permitting his wife to dominate his life.

Thomas's 27-year-old sister had spastic colitis and had been treated at a local child guidance clinic for years. She was divorced and had three young children. The 24-year-old sister was a depressed, unmarried bookkeeper who lived in her own apartment near the family.

THERAPY. When first seen, Thomas appeared emaciated and his clothing hung loosely on his thin frame. He looked wan and pale, his nose was beaked, and he wore his dark hair in a ponytail down to his shoulders. He commented that he used to weigh 90 lbs., but now he liked to be skinny. He liked the way it looked. When he saw himself in mirrors he realized that he was skinny, that his body and legs were especially thin. He didn't want to be like fat people—like his father, who was so heavy that he had to catch his breath after he walked 100 feet. He denied eating diet foods, but did acknowledge that he had given up all the fattening foods he used to eat and, in addition, ate less food now.

He denied using laxatives or vomiting. He added that the past year at high school had been excellent. He felt that he had been treated in a more grown-up fashion and stated that he had enjoyed the increased freedom.

In the second session, in response to the therapist's general wondering about how he got along at home, he launched into a description of how his mother behaved toward him.

> She washed my hair in the shower or in the tub until I was 12, and now, after four years, she still wants to do it. I don't let her, but she doesn't give up. She wants to cut my toenails and occasionally I let her, when I get tired of her pestering me about it. . . . Everyone else can take his own food at dinnertime, but she puts my food on my plate, like I'm a baby. . . . When her friends come to the house, and sometimes in front of my friends, she introduces me as "my little baby" and kisses me.

As he spoke in more detail about his mother's infantilizing behavior, he got increasingly upset and annoyed. He stated that she still wanted him to come into bed with her and rub her arm, the way he used to when he was "little." Thomas's view of who asked whom into bed was clearly at variance with his mother's view.

In the third interview, Thomas's denial that he had any worries began to fragment. He spoke about his worries about his father—that he was afraid that his father could get another coronary and die. He worried about his father's smoking, which the doctor had told him to stop, his hypertension, his obesity, and his back trouble, which was caused by his obesity. He added, "It's not that I'm ashamed of him." Both sisters had phoned Thomas when they heard that he was ill. They had said that it was his mother's fault, that she bossed him around too much. He commented spontaneously, "I can't hate her all these years until I'm able to go away to college. Upset people don't eat." Up until this point, Thomas had been extremely reluctant to start treatment and had come only because of parental pressure. He added that he was willing to miss the math exam tomorrow in order to come in for the session.

In the fourth and fifth sessions, it was possible to point out to him that his "I don't know" responses were manifestations of an unwillingness to think and a need to avoid dealing with unpleasant issues. Further discussion led to his increasing awareness of pressure by the father, in addition to the mother. He felt that both parents watched him constantly while he ate and pushed him to eat. The father would take a bite of meat or potato and say, "Mm, this is good, why don't you try it"—"just like I was a little boy." As he elaborated more fully on his increasing recognition of the coercive, manipulative battle that went on between them and acknowledged that not eating seemed to represent defiance, he commented, "I'd go crazy if I had all these worries and not the anorexia." As he recounted his increasing resentment over feeling controlled and infantilized, it was pointed out to him that if he truly wanted to be as independent as he claimed, he should recognize that not eating provided his parents with the justification to worry about him, fuss over him, and baby him. He seemed to think about it carefully as the fifth session drew to a close. It was at that point that both he and his parents agreed to his coming for psychoanalytic therapy four times a week.

In the next half dozen sessions, he continued to discuss his problems with his parents, his feeling overwhelmed by his inability to deal with them, and his increasing recognition that he had fled from this conflict and displaced it onto the anorexic defiance. When he was seen initially in consultation, Thomas was planning to leave for camp in four weeks; at the same time, the internist was deciding whether he should be hospitalized. The therapist chose to see the decision about hospitalization as a medical one, although he remained in contact with his physician. In that way, he removed himself one step further from the role of the controlling, authoritarian parents.

Thomas began to try to assert himself with his father, but recoiled with anxiety as he "saw that mad look in his face, as if he were going to explode and bang his fist, so I stopped and got very quiet." He recounted episodes involving his father's violent temper. A few more aborted assertive attempts were followed by increased feelings of inadequacy and an increasing conviction that these types of problems were what truly bothered him. He acknowledged more awareness of his feelings of frustration and annoyance, concluding at one point that not eating must have been a good way of getting back at them. He added, however, that he just couldn't talk to them and needed a better way. The therapist pointed out that, in the past, his "better way" had been anorexia and that, while it undoubtedly had upset them, it also had been very damaging to him. He became preoccupied with his inability to be assertive and stated, "They can't shove the food into me." He spoke about the victory that they would feel if he began to eat. (At this point, he still hadn't.) The therapist never suggested that he eat, but rather, dealt with the emerging reasons why he didn't.

Finally, in the seventh session, Thomas volunteered, "I'll eat a little more." The therapist pointed out that this was a concession on his part to his own well-being, but that he clearly was not ready to renounce the starving in favor of dealing with the issues that distressed him. He then decided that he would again confront his parents, but this time chose to discuss it in advance. He planned to say that his therapist had said that "part of the reason I have my anorexia is because I need to get back at you." When the therapist wondered about that tactic, he readily admitted that such a maneuver would probably get them angry at the therapist instead of at him. Thomas and the therapist discussed his deflecting the attack, using the therapist as an ally and victim, and getting his parents angry at the therapist, which might enable him to avoid further painful confrontations with his parents if they decided to stop the treatment because of their annoyance. He indicated how insecure he felt about confronting them alone and wondered if he could talk things out with them in one of the sessions at the office. The therapist agreed and the parents came to the next session.

Thomas began the session with the comment, "The doctor wanted to see you and me together," and then modified it to, "We wanted to see you." He proceeded to tell them that his difficulties were not really with food, but with them—that he needed to grow up and that they were babying him and interfering with it. As he spoke, he looked at the therapist for reassurance. The parents seemed to accept his ideas, and he felt encouraged by their response. The therapist took the opportunity to suggest (for the second time) that the parents see another therapist for a number of consultations to help them understand the anorexia, which would facilitate Thomas's recovery. While they professed interest, they never followed through on the suggestion. By this time, the 11th session, Thomas felt a little better and was eating somewhat more. A beginning therapeutic alliance had been established, as evidenced by his changing behavior and willingness for treatment.

After some initial reluctance, most adolescents are quite willing to discuss coercive battles of control with their parents. To a considerable degree, the issues of growing up—behaving independently and pushing for increasing separation and autonomy—are a main thrust of adolescent development and the various manifestations are well recognized by most adolescents. The discussion of these difficulties is relevant and meaningful to the adolescent anorexic patient. The therapist's sympathetic support should never degenerate into attitudes that suggest to patients that they are viewed as weak, incompetent, or helpless. It should be pointed out that the difficulty arises from misunderstanding, misperceiving, not thinking incisively, and avoiding issues, rather than from weakness or defect. These patients are anything but weak, as can be seen in their tenacious adherence to their set course of action. At the same time, the therapist must be aware of the early impulses to defy the therapist (like the parents are defied), not to trust, and to attempt to sabotage treatment (e.g., as Thomas planned to, by encouraging the parents to dislike the therapist). Finally, the case material indicates the typical apprehension with which the patient views manifestations of realistic self-assertion.

Thomas's peaceful relationship with his parents was short-lived. When the parents returned from a brief business trip, Thomas reported that the mother again began to harass him about eating and tell him what to eat.

> I got so upset that I didn't sleep all night. . . . I kept thinking over and over that I won't eat. I'll get back at her. . . . revenge. To win means to escalate the battle. . . . to starve . . . the only way she'll listen. At the same time, I kept saying to myself, "You can't do it. . . . It's not good for you. . . . You can't hurt yourself."
>
> I was so upset thinking all night that I couldn't think or concentrate. I had a final in German, and I failed it. I usually get an A. I think that I also might have failed chemistry, too, and I'm good in it. I won't listen to her anymore and won't talk to her, and she'll hate me.

He concluded that "the only good thing that happened to me was that I didn't give in to it and I kept eating." The ensuing discussion permitted him to clarify how upset he was and how such distress dramatically interfered with his ability to think and to concentrate on his schoolwork. He reflected that when he had not been eating, all this upset had disappeared. He thought that he must have been depressed and that depressed people don't eat.

In the following month, Thomas alternated between further attempts at self-assertion and recoiling from the ensuing punishing attacks by the parents with regression to starving. He reported an episode where he had been asked to grill hamburgers for the family. The mother wanted him to have his soup before grilling the hamburgers, and he wanted to have the soup later. An argument resulted, and Thomas refused to eat his soup. When the meat was ready and Thomas asked for the soup, the mother stated that it had been thrown out. Thomas still saw it in the pot, however, and asked if he could have it; he was told, "No." The father sided with him, complaining that the mother was unreasonable, but Thomas was afraid to take the soup because the mother threatened that she couldn't stand it and that she wanted a divorce. In the following session, he pathetically described how terrible he felt about causing the blowup. His parents weren't talking and he felt guilty about ruining their marriage. Last week he could eat easily, but this week he couldn't eat. "I wanted to eat the lamb chops and the ice cream. It looked so good, but I said, 'You have to be thin . . . it's too fattening.' Then I thought, 'That's not the real reason, you're trying to get back at her. Eat.' But I just couldn't. I had a piece of cantaloupe." The therapist commented that he was speaking very softly and seemed to be keeping everything inside. He agreed, adding that when he spoke up, he got in such trouble, he just had to keep quiet, but he couldn't eat. "If I argue and talk up, will it be easier for me to eat? It's so hard."

A few days later, a group of Thomas's relatives were visiting and stayed for a chicken barbecue. Atypically, Thomas took two pieces of chicken and a large portion of potatoes. His mother requested that he share some of the chicken with his cousin, and he refused. The mother became furious and did not speak to him for the next two days. This occurred when Thomas weighed 80 lbs. At another point, the father responded to what appeared to be a reasonable question on Thomas's part with, "Don't raise your voice to me or I'll crack you across the mouth."

Months later, he acknowledged that not eating at the table when his parents watched him was like a chess game: a cat-and-mouse power struggle. After a big fight with his parents, he thought he was fat and shouldn't eat. At the same time, however, he realized that it was nonsense and that the burst of anger had set off the idea that he was fat and should starve. He was also afraid of talking with his father for fear of exploding with anger.

After six months of treatment, Thomas described repeated episodes where the mother interfered with his attempts to separate and act independent. He would attempt to assert himself, fail, protest weakly, and then regress to anorexic behavior. These events took place when Thomas wanted to change the appearance of his room, expressed the wish for more privacy, and asked to use the family car more frequently, but in a realistic fashion. He spoke of his running as "running to be free," not just to burn up calories. In the midst of an argument with the mother after Thomas had gained 16 lbs., she yelled, "You're no better! You look thinner than when you started! You're not going to that therapist anymore."

At the end of the first year, Thomas was able to recover early memories of force-feeding—sitting in the tub for hours, crying, angry, and refusing to get out because mother would force him to drink chocolate milk; not leaving the table because he would have to drink his orange juice first; and spilling his milk out, but putting a ring of milk around his mouth with his finger to deceive her. This vignette illuminates one probable origin of the almost universal deceitfulness in both male and female anorexics: the need to avoid an open confrontation with, and defiance of, the powerful mother of childhood out of fear of terrible retaliatory damage. Indeed, Thomas was still quite fearful of confronting his parents.

During the second year of treatment, he felt trusting enough to confide that it was his birthday. When he was 11, his parents had stopped giving him gifts or cards. He and his sisters continued to exchange gifts. One is able to recognize both the rejection by the parents and their marked inability to perceive the appropriate needs of the child.

At the end of two years of treatment, Thomas's weight had long been normal, but the fighting over separation and independence with both parents persisted. This in part contributed to Thomas's inflexible decision to go to college in Colorado. He never felt free of his parents' attempts to control him or of his inner impulses to accede passively to being controlled and then to regress. In addition, while some aspects of his sexuality had been discussed, these discussions were anxiety-producing, closely guarded secrets. He felt that continuing in treatment would result in his having to deal with these traumatic experiences.

The summer prior to his leaving for college, Thomas was 31 lbs. heavier than he had been in his anorexic state. Nevertheless, the mother, filled with her own conflicts over separation and loss of control over Thomas, phoned the therapist three times to complain that he was still emaciated and didn't even eat one meal a day. She told Thomas that he would "waste away to nothing" (not be there). The father's conflict also persisted, as was evident in his response to Thomas's statement, "I'm going to dinner at Susie's house, so I won't eat anything now." The father commented, "If he doesn't want to eat dinner tonight, just let him alone."

DISCUSSION.   Thomas's illness illustrates the intimate relationship between starving, defiance, and conflicts with the parents over aggression, the need to control his life, and separation. The oral sadism and cannibalism were more deeply repressed and less evident than in Eric's case. Thomas's suspiciousness, fears of trusting, and sexual anxieties were not reached and were avoided by his choice of a distant college.

The case material did reveal how the anorexic symptoms bind anxiety and facilitate the repression of thinking; conversely, eating results in the emergence of increasing tension, anxiety, concentration difficulties, and insomnia. Some patients who recognize that this turmoil is liberated by the eating and are unwilling to deal with the conflict do not report the changes to the therapist, but quietly regress back to the starving, giving the external appearance that progress has not occurred and that they have actually gotten worse. They play cat and mouse with the therapist the way that they do with the parents.

The behavior of both of Thomas's parents was striking. They were unwilling to see another therapist even for a brief time, because it was perceived as separating them further from Thomas. It was clear that the mother's own separation anxieties were mobilized whenever Thomas attempted to assert himself, become more independent, and separate himself from her. To a considerable degree, this problem was also present in the father. The parents' behavior resulted from intense, unresolved neurotic behavior rather than from malevolence. On occasion, this made it necessary for Thomas to starve, but remain under the control of the parents.

Thomas's early defiance in treatment (not talking) was part of his anorexic rebellion. On one occasion, he reflected on his not talking. He stated that he didn't talk with the therapist because his parents did not talk with him, except to order him about. He was doing to the therapist what he felt that they were doing to him. He perceived silence as a rejection and became quite poignant in his description of his feelings of sadness and loneliness.

These attitudes were voiced during the last four months of treatment and surfaced in part because he knew he was stopping shortly. On one occasion, he stated that he never had wanted to be in therapy and still didn't. He couldn't trust the therapist. He never told the therapist anything personal so that the therapist could never tell his parents. Even if the therapist told him personal things about himself, he still would never confide in him. He agreed that this attitude in part reflected how careful he felt he had to be. In another session, he revealed that he could not talk to any psychiatrist "because talking is doing what they want me to, just like eating would be." In the following hour, he spelled out with increasing clarity that the original defiant refusal to eat had been replaced by a refusal to talk: he had displaced the not partaking of the food onto the not partaking of the treatment.

He acknowledged that he worked very hard gathering information about the world, but that he was unwilling to gather information about himself. He was afraid to trust the therapist because the therapist could use the information against him in some way and get control over him. The therapist made many attempts to interpret this transference fear as having arisen from earlier life experiences where he felt overcontrolled, manipulated, and helpless to cope with the important events in his life. While he understood what was said, he acknowledged feeling powerless to effect any change in his attitudes. Some changes occurred, however, if only in his increased trust that enabled him to tell the therapist openly about his distrust.

> I could never tell you earlier how much I did not want to be here, that I really didn't want treatment, and that I still feel very coerced and controlled. . . . I have to be the best in everything . . . even if it's very silly, because then I feel that I'm in control. . . . I know that it's because I can't control things with my parents. . . . Sometimes I feel so terrible about being here that I feel I have to quit. I loathe it. I'd almost rather be sick than be here.

After a number of weeks of analyzing this negativism, Thomas responded somewhat with a lessening of the resentment. He agreed that it would be an intellectual challenge for him to be able to see that the treatment had been helpful to him. Another time, he said:

> I really want to tell you things but part of me just doesn't let me. . . . My father tells me to do things and then after I do them he expects more and more from me, telling me what he wants, but he never has time for me . . . to hear what I want . . . to help me. I asked him to help me with an engineering project and he fell asleep on me. And he wants me to do things for him. I hate him.

In this interchange, he became partially aware of the transference hatred and the fact that the therapist's listening to him patiently upset him because it reminded him of his father's inattentiveness. "I can really talk to you today. I tell you things that usually are not that important and I make a big deal of it, but certain things I tell no one, and I wouldn't tell you either, not in 200 years."

These outbursts over many weeks provided the opportunity to emphasize his transference attitudes, the extent of his deep, burning hostility, the degree to which he felt controlled and manipulated for so much of his life, and the pervading sense of sorrow and loneliness he experienced. Discussing these attitudes in detail resulted in a different attitude.

CASE 3   Acute Anorexia in an Adolescent

Ivan was 14½ when he was referred by his uncle, an orthopedist, for twice-a-week psychoanalytically oriented therapy. The initial consultation with the parents revealed that Ivan had seemed to be perfectly well until two years earlier. Before that time, he had been a solid, husky boy who weighed about 130 lbs.

ONSET OF SYMPTOMS. The father stated that some of the boys started to say he was fat, so he began dieting and in a few months lost 25 lbs. At the time of the consultation, he was 5'6" and weighed 96 lbs., his lowest weight. He added gratuitously that he probably could use a psychiatrist because he was so nervous. When he got a B in Social Studies he became so upset that he couldn't sleep that night. The parents commented that he had stopped eating all the foods that he used to like. While other children his age enjoyed candy, ice cream, pizza, meat, and potatoes, he ate only cottage cheese, carrots, celery, and skim milk. The mother continued:

> He doesn't eat any decent meals anymore. He just picks at his food. He is aware of the number of calories in every food and he rations himself with the most incredible self-control. Last night he didn't eat any food at all. He just moved it about on the plate. He has tremendous will power. He does whatever he decides to do. He wants to be thin and that is what he accomplished and we can't do a thing about it no matter what we say. . . . He exercises all the time. Three or four times a day he does pushups and situps, and lifts weights. The thing that bothers us most is that he seems addicted to running. He runs 10 miles a day even in the rain or snow. We tell him that he'll get sick, but he doesn't listen. . . . He doesn't seem to recognize that he's thin. Whenever he lifts his shirt and looks at his stomach, he complains that he's getting a pot belly and that he's getting fat. Then he redoubles his exercising. He occasionally complains that he feels dizzy and tired, but still won't stop exercising. He's like someone possessed.

The father interjected:

> He says that we're overprotective and I suppose that we are. My wife does everything for him, just like he's still little. She wants to pick out his clothes in the morning and tell him to wear his sweater or his coat, and he gets very angry about it. I think that she overdoes it, and I tell her, but she doesn't listen.

Rather than responding to the husband's allegations, the mother attacked her husband, pointing out how intrusive he was. She stated that he constantly told Ivan and his two younger sisters what to do. He was always in their bedroom picking things up and changing things around; he had to know every detail of their lives and would "quiz" them. The father seemed quite willing to acknowledge the truth of what his wife had said, but he attempted to minimize the impact of his behavior on the children's lives. He admitted that he was distressed about Ivan because he looked like a skeleton.

FAMILY BACKGROUND. Ivan's family was very comfortable financially, having inherited wealth from the paternal grandfather, who had made a great deal of money in real estate in Alaska. Ivan's father was in the real estate firm with the grandfather. This was a source of continuous parental strife because the grandfather exercised tyrannical control over the business and his four sons, all of whom worked for him. Ivan had two younger sisters. The oldest sister developed severe scoliosis requiring surgery during the second year of Ivan's treatment. Ivan had very little to do with his siblings and most of his conflicts centered about the relationship with his parents.

THERAPY. At the start of his initial interview, Ivan appeared quite tractable. In discussing his weight problem, he acknowledged that he was thin and should weigh more. He added that he was happy that he was light and did not wish to get fat again. He had been chubby for years, and the boys used to make fun of him. Now they no longer teased him, and he didn't want it to happen again. "When I realize how thin I am, I try to eat more, and then I say to myself, 'I'll get fat,' and then I can't eat any more. I always worry when I think that my stomach is getting fat." He stated that when he had started junior high school, he had thought that he should lose weight and had begun to diet. He claimed that he ate reasonably, consuming normal foods; he just ate small amounts.

He said that both parents had a weight problem and that, although they were not really fat, they watched what they ate. That was why they always had diet soda in the house. This led him into a further discussion about parental attitudes. He complained that his parents always wanted him to eat.

> They want me to eat when they want to eat. . . . They always want to stuff food into me. They used to put all the dishes in the center of the table, but now my mother puts all the food right on our plates and tries to get me to eat it all. . . . They say, "Eat what you want," but then when I don't eat it, they ask me why.

He became increasingly agitated as he described in more detail how he felt coerced into eating. In a loud, resentful voice, he blurted out, "If only my parents would let me alone! . . . They will only be happy if I gain weight, and I tell them to just give me time. . . . I try not to listen to them." He paused and then continued, "They keep trying to blackmail me. If I don't gain weight, then I can't go on a summer tour. I get so angry and I try to talk to them, but no matter what I say, it doesn't do any good. They are so stubborn."

At that point, the hour was up and the therapist suggested a second consultation. Ivan's anger spilled onto the therapist and, although he had been speaking quite volubly all through the interview, he refused all subsequent appointments. He arose, walked out to the waiting room, and peremptorily announced to his parents that they could not make him come back. The father indicated that Ivan would return for the next interview and they left.

In the second interview, Ivan appeared calmer. He discussed further his feeling pressured about eating and elaborated on how his parents coerced him into eating. While he was easily able to see that the issue of eating had evolved into a battle with his parents, it had not occurred to him that, while this was the main focus of difficulty, there were other aspects to the coercion and to his subsequent rebellion. He began to discuss being yelled at for the way he dressed, kept his room, and spent his money. At the end of the session, he acknowledged that he was willing to continue.

In the following five sessions, he further elaborated on his feelings of being manipulated by the parents and began to discuss his driven attitude toward school. He complained that his father invariably objected to how he spent his allowance. When he bought himself an art book at the museum, the father thought that it was too expensive. Long arguments ensued as the father attempted to get Ivan to return the treasured book, all the while labeling him a spendthrift. The father also objected to his spending money for concerts, theater, and museums. He complained that even though he was an excellent student, both his parents objected to the way he studied. They complained about his papers being scattered all over the room and, in attempting to "straighten out the mess," often mixed up everything and complicated his studying. They complained when he studied with the radio on and insisted that it be turned off. They rearranged parts of his room when they felt that the appearance could be improved. In a sudden moment of candor, he stated that he thought that he had chosen eating as the battleground because he could control it best.

In one session much later in treatment, he confided what he had meant when he had spoken about controlling eating. As a consequence of the treatment, his mother no longer piled the food on his plate and permitted him to help himself like the rest of the family. He would eye the baked potato in the serving plate and the parents would watch him looking at it. During some meals, he would just look at it from time to time but not take it, much to his parents' distress. On other occasions, he would place the potato on his plate and then neglect it for the rest of the meal. Frequently, he would slice open the potato—and stop—or open it, mash it, and then stop. He would sadistically toy with the potato the way he felt toyed with and manipulated. The detailed discussion about the potato became so graphic that Ivan became embarrassed, acknowledging that it seemed like crazy behavior and that he should stop it.

This is reminiscent of a hospitalized anorexic patient who lost consciousness on the ward. When she awoke and to her consternation saw an intravenous infusion going into her arm, she tried desperately to pull it out and moaned, "Now I don't have control over anything."

Ivan described a tremendous preoccupation with school, both in his need to achieve excellence in all his courses and in his involvement in all kinds of extracurricular activities. He complained that the school was not advanced enough academically, that the teachers were mediocre, and that the material was too simple. He got A's in everything. He was busy almost every day after school with all kinds of sports, clubs, and the school newspaper. In addition, he tried to get an afterschool job. Evenings were devoted to exacting, perfectionistic studying.

Another boy, two years older than Ivan, was equally perfectionistic in his studying. He stated that when he was not chosen as a National Merit Scholar, he felt so humiliated and so embarrassed that he couldn't face the other students in school. He spoke about his intense competitiveness: when he wanted something and couldn't get it, he felt overwhelmingly disappointed and might be upset for weeks. Further comments revealed that in addition to his perfectionism, competitiveness, low frustration tolerance, and fragile self-esteem regulation, he felt out of control.

> I need to know what's going on. . . . If I'm out of school because I'm sick, I have to make up the work, not because the teachers request it, but because I need to, for me. . . . I need to know everything that people talk about in school, even the work that was covered. I don't want them talking about what I don't understand, like it's behind my back. . . . I almost get paranoid about it.

It seemed clear that this student's push for academic excellence had many determinants. It arose in part from feeling helplessly victimized when his parents discussed events in his life without his knowing about it. To be an excellent, perfectionistic student meant to be in control of the material. To understand it and to know it is to control it. To not understand it is to lend oneself to being victimized by it. Dealing with the material in school was like dealing with the parents at home. Knowledge was power.

He equated control over his schoolwork with control over what he ate and could then understand why it was so vital to him. Academic mastery was the endpoint for appropriate adolescent thirst for knowledge, for increasing use of intellectual capacities, and for rewards for self-esteem regulation. It was also the endpoint for pathological, perfectionistic, displaced control over objects. This included defying the parents by studying too long and too hard, analogous to his way of eating.

Ivan's treatment progressed satisfactorily as he came to recognize the relationship between his anorexia and his conflicts about aggression, assertiveness, independence, separation, perfectionism, and control, as well as his difficulties in peer relationships and his inordinate feelings of guilt. Sexual conflicts were not reached during the two-and-a-half-year treatment. There was some ongoing resistance to the treatment in the form of conflicting activities during the therapy hour, resentment at being in treatment, having "nothing to talk about," and deliberately withholding information.

DISCUSSION.   Although Ivan did quite well in treatment—gained 30 lbs., felt less pressured, and became more assertive—there was little change in his attitude toward treatment, or in his willingness to be completely cooperative. Further discussion of what appeared to be indifference toward treatment resulted in this comment: "I could stop right now without a second thought . . . and I don't think that I got anything out of treatment." He added that he had grown up a great deal during the past year at school as a consequence of talking with his friends. It was only after further reflection that he realized he had displaced "valuable conversations" from the treatment onto his friends. He agreed that with all his provocativeness, uncooperativeness, and angry outbursts, he could count on the therapist to listen to him patiently, to point out what he thought he was doing, and to explain the reasons for his behavior.

The recognition of his unreasonable defiance and lack of appreciation of his improvement led to his realization of one of its main causes. "I was forced to come here against my will. I never wanted treatment, and even after two and a half years, I still resent it. . . . All my life I have been told what to do and coming to see you was just another part of it. If I came on my own, it might have been different." This outburst provided the opportunity to emphasize both the extent of his deep, burning hostility and the degree to which he had felt controlled and manipulated for so much of his life. Working through this aggression resulted in a different attitude at termination, but still left unanalyzed those conflicts that were not reached because of these resistances. Lasegue's dictum, "They never pardon," (reported in Thomä 1967, p. 9) is well illustrated by this case.

CASE 4   *Acute Anorexia and Bulimia in a Middle-Aged Man*

Carl, a 45-year-old married advertising executive with four children, was referred for treatment by his cousin, who was a physician, and agreed to it at the insistence of his wife, who stated that she would divorce him if he refused it.

THERAPY.   When seen in consultation, Carl was 5'10" and weighed 109 lbs. Seven years earlier he had weighed 140 lbs., and in college he had weighed 160 lbs. He stated that he had been losing weight gradually over the past four years, but that the weight loss had accelerated in the past year and he had "faded rapidly."

He added that, in recent years, food had become an obsession with him. He was constantly preoccupied with what foods to eat and when to eat them. He would think days in advance about what meals he would ask his wife to make and invariably would find fault with the food no matter how carefully it was prepared.

As an advertising executive, it was necessary to take clients out to lunch, and he found it increasingly inconvenient and embarrassing to avoid eating normal meals. He noted that he restricted himself to eating fruit salads and black coffee while his business colleagues ate regular meals. He noticed that over many months he had become less sociable, in part to avoid ordinary social relationships, in which he had lost interest, and in part to avoid having to eat dinners. He added that his wife always had enjoyed eating very much, and as a consequence she was about 5–10 lbs. overweight. Since his illness, she had lost much of her interest in food because he harried her so much about its preparation and then refused to eat. He had not had most of the foods that he used to enjoy (e.g., candy, soda, ice cream, pretzels, desserts, and pizza) for three or four years.

In the last five years, Carl had become increasingly involved with exercise, especially running, bicycling, playing tennis, and swimming. Frequently, he would skip a meal and jog while the family was eating. Initially, he had felt strong from the exercise, but recently he had felt so weak that he could hardly continue.

He was surprised to recognize that he enjoyed losing weight and couldn't understand what had prompted this reaction. He was particularly distressed when a colleague recognized that he had anorexia nervosa and told him that he thought that it only occurred in adolescent girls. He volunteered that during this period of weight loss, he had never thought of himself as thin, not even when he looked in the mirror. "At times I'd look in the mirror and see a big fat abdomen and I'd get upset, but in the morning you expel it." He was quite amazed to find that he weighed 109 lbs. as he had been sure that he weighed at least 127 lbs.

In a subsequent session, he added that his 15-year-old daughter looked much smaller and thinner than he did, but she weighed 124 lbs. One can see the typical anorexic disturbance in body image in this patient: he misperceived his appearance in the mirror, was unable to assess his body bulk accurately, and felt that he was heavier than his daughter.

In the middle of the first session, he mentioned spontaneously that his father had been operated on for carcinoma of the bowel two and a half years earlier. In the description, he slipped and said, "I was operated," but was not aware of this slip. Toward the end of the session, he added that his father had faded quickly, lost a great deal of weight, and died eight months ago. Two unwitting identifications with his sick father were evident. One was the unrecognized slip and the other was the similarity between his descriptions of his own illness and that of his father. He had "faded rapidly" in the past year and the father had "faded quickly."

In the second and third sessions, Carl spoke volubly. He began by commenting that it wasn't that he didn't want to eat, because he really was hungry. Instead of eating, he was obsessed with thoughts about eating. All day long he kept thinking about what he should have for the next meal, knowing that he probably would find fault with how it was prepared and not eat it. His wife had gotten in the habit of gearing the entire family's meals around his idiosyncrasies and went to great lengths to prepare his salads and other low-calorie foods the way he preferred them, only to have him find fault with them. Often he would arbitrarily refuse to eat the food she had prepared for no specific reason. While he exercised tyrannical control over the family's food and eating, he basked in the concern that people showed him because of his illness. He felt that his family and friends were preoccupied with his well-being; they constantly asked about his health. Just looking at him would evoke solicitous concern. "They all love me." The therapist pointed out that the preoccupation with eating could serve to prevent him from thinking about what really bothered him. With that comment, he launched into a bitter diatribe against his boss and members of his own family.

He said that he had been working for 14 years for the same boss at a small advertising company. When he started, the boss had just gone into business and had very few clients. In fact, the company had been in such dire straits that he hadn't been sure it wouldn't collapse. Carl had felt that this was his big opportunity and he had worked very hard. As a consequence of his endeavors, the firm had obtained an increasing number of clients and had begun to prosper. The boss had been very grateful and had treated him almost like a son, and Carl had been very happy. He had enjoyed working so much that he almost hadn't thought of it as a job. The boss would frequently invite him for dinner and had given a big party in his honor when he got married, along with a gift of a honeymoon cruise. Everything had gone fine until about four years ago, when the boss's son had come into the business. Prior to that time, as manager of the office, Carl essentially had directed the day-to-day activities of the business. With the arrival of the boss's son, Carl's work had been divided, and two vice-presidential positions had been created. Even though there was still a great deal of work to do, he felt as if he had been replaced and become number two again, just as he had been when he was little. Regarding the boss's son, he said, "I really felt jealous of him, and I haven't gotten along with him since."

He shifted into the childhood relationship with his younger brother. While he had gotten along reasonably with his older sister, he and his brother never had gotten along. The brother had been the parents' favorite. Everybody had liked him. He remembered hearing the brother's name echoing and reechoing throughout his life. The brother had been the brightest in the family—the valedictorian of his high-school class in the small midwestern town where they lived. He had been the school's best athlete. All the girls had liked him. Even the minister at the church had been particularly impressed with him. He had become a lawyer and moved from their small hometown to Chicago, where he currently had a successful practice.

Carl had always felt that there was no way to compete with his brother, so he had gone in the opposite direction. He had goofed off in high school and college, just managing to pass his courses. He had gone to a lot of parties and done a great deal of drinking and smoking, but still had managed to graduate from college.

He stated that his mother had died when he was 12 years old after a long and debilitating illness. At first, the doctors had thought that she had a brain tumor, but then it turned out to be multiple sclerosis. He didn't remember any particular feelings surrounding her death, but did remember that afterward he ate a lot and put on so much weight that the kids used to call him "Fatty." All through high school and college he used to love to eat and drink, especially steak, beer, and pizza.

His father had remarried a few years after the mother died and had become so totally preoccupied in satisfying the petty demands of his new wife that he showed very little interest in the children. The little concern that had been evident had been lavished on the brother. Carl remembered wistfully that he had been utterly unable to evoke any approbation from his father. After a while he had stopped trying.

He added that his sister also had been neglected and he felt that his father's behavior had something to do with her alcoholism. While the sister was bright and had done very well academically in college, she could never keep a job because of her drinking. She had married, had three children, and been divorced by her husband, a well-known surgeon, in part because he had found her public alcoholic behavior personally embarrassing and professionally damaging. Carl felt that his brother-in-law's prominent role in the community had enabled him to obtain custody of the children. Carl still felt responsible for his sister's welfare; he contributed to her support and helped her to find employment among the various corporations with which he did business.

He returned to the trouble with his job. He stated that he excelled at his work. He was very good at talking to prospective customers and getting new accounts. When the boss's son had come in, he had felt pushed aside and no longer needed. That was when he had begun to pay more attention to food, to eat less, and to exercise.

From time to time, his account was punctuated with momentary self-reflection.

I know that I'm losing my strength, . . . my ankles have swelled up almost every night for the past three weeks. My arms and legs look like sticks. Sometimes people who haven't seen me for a while don't even recognize me. . . . I used to do pushups but now I feel too weak. But I still try to jog every day. . . . I know it's crazy. I'm an intelligent and successful businessman, on the one hand, and yet I act like such a fool. My wife said that she can't stand it. I get her crazy with the food. Sometimes she even thinks of getting a divorce. I have four lovely children and I don't pay attention to any of them.

His eyes filled with tears. In another moment of candor and self-reflection, when discussing how demanding he was about his food, he wondered, "Is it really the food that I tell her I want, or is it my need to tell her what to do?" The anorexic's characteristic need to control through the use of "illness" and food was again evident.

After further complaints about his job, he acknowledged that he came home at night and argued with his wife about food, instead of arguing with his boss about the job. "When I begin to eat, I get more upset, . . . and when I eat less, I feel calmer." Many anorexic patients are aware of how their starving prevents them from experiencing upsetting thoughts and they hold on to it to avoid the experience of inner turmoil.

Carl's anorexia resulted from the coalescence of a series of conflicts that began in childhood with the death of his mother. The loss, abandonment, and resentment that he experienced was further compounded by his father's indifference and self-involvement. Seeds of the eating difficulty were evident in the obesity that developed following his mother's death.

Carl's later work situation recapitulated his early life experience. This time, by working hard, he was able to obtain a new set of benign parents who approved of him, instead of indifferent parents whom he felt neglected him. The anorexia seemed to develop just at the time that he felt replaced by the boss's son, an event that clearly reawakened the sibling rivalry with his own brother. Carl's frustration and aggression were displaced from the boss and his family to Carl's own family, and the attention that he no longer achieved as the favored "son" was now obtained as the "sick" patient. He also began to reject his wife the way he felt that the boss had rejected him. The rapidity with which the boss's son was able to achieve status and financial remuneration reawakened the rivalry with his hated, favored brother, resulting in enmity toward his new rival and withdrawal in the rival's favor, just as had occurred earlier in his life.

In the fourth and fifth sessions, Carl spoke a great deal about his deep resentment over work difficulties. The therapist pointed out that these were the realistic problems that were plaguing him, and that his starving was self-destructive in that he deprived himself of food and hid from himself the true nature of his turmoil. In the following session, he reported with considerable surprise that he had begun to eat more, including regular food, that he had enjoyed the food, and that he felt better. He also noted that the edema, which was being evaluated by his internist, had subsided considerably. He added that he couldn't remember exactly what he and the therapist had spoken about, but that it certainly had affected his appetite.

These early and often momentary bouts of improvement are not unusual and result from temporary periods of insight primarily related to the recognition that the dieting is a smokescreen for deeper and more pervasive problems. The improvement is usually evanescent, however, because the underlying conflicts are still unresolved, the pathological defenses and object relationships are unchanged, and the infantile omnipotent attitudes of helplessness, self-destructiveness, and sadism remain unchecked. In addition, many patients, including Carl, derive a great deal of secondary gain from the sickness in the form of attention. Finally, improvement by eating represents a threat, in that patients have to face long-avoided conflicts.

In the following session, Carl reported that he almost had called up to terminate. He felt discouraged, was again preoccupied with attitudes about food, and was behaving provocatively toward his wife. After he was unable to associate to the cause of the change, the therapist pointed out that, in the previous two sessions, he had reported feeling better and eating more normally. The therapist suggested that he had begun to realize what his real problems were and that the possibility of having to deal with them made the whole treatment a threat. He responded, "Maybe. . . . What would happen to me if I don't continue?" After the therapist pointed out the bleak possibilities, he continued,

What if I have to face my ideas about my brother? He used to treat me like dirt. He'd join the other kids at the YMCA when they'd taunt me and call me a fat slob. Or he never acknowledged that I existed, just like my father. What if I find out that I hate him? My father never wanted me. Just my mother. He only cared for my brother. [Pause.] All right, I won't act up. I'm going to listen very hard to what you say.

By the following week, his resolve had evaporated, as he returned to what became a perennial "I don't wish to continue, I don't need it, I'm eating better." Interpretations of spilling his self-destructiveness into the treatment served to mollify this behavior temporarily. As the self-destructive behavior was interpreted continuously, especially in the transference, Carl finally reported, "I feel so angry, I'm almost choking on it." He then reported a whole series of complaints about his wife that had been bothering him for years, but which he had never voiced. These outbursts of resentment were usually followed by temporary improvements in attitude, behavior, and eating habits. However, his pessimism about treatment always returned, usually within a few days. On occasion, he felt depressed, which substituted for his self-destructive starving. The depressive feelings frightened him and invariably threw him back into his preoccupation with eating. Eruptions of anger were substituted for by bursts of bulimia, a new symptom related to his perceived loss of control over his aggression. Such activity would be followed by feelings of guilt, self-recrimination, and further preoccupation with thoughts about food to avoid dealing with the aggression. This defensive posture was most obvious in his reply to one of the therapist's interpretations that the depressive moods and preoccupations with food were a smokescreen for problems: "I don't hear you. I've been thinking about what I'll have for lunch."

In the following two months, although Carl continued to improve in his mood, attitude, and eating, almost every session was initiated with the statement that he had thought of not coming or that this probably would be his last session. This behavior continued even after a number of enlightening and gratifying sessions. Many interpretations were made as to the reasons for this continued stance and, while they were of temporary help, he would invariably return to his pessimistic position.

On one occasion, he reported feeling distressed because his improved physical appearance resulted in his friends and acquaintances no longer asking about his health. In speaking about it, he remembered wistfully how concerned everyone had been when he had had to stop work for two weeks in the past. In one session, talking about his childhood and the impact of his mother's illness, he commented, "When I died, I mean, when she died, I felt so sad, like my whole world had ended. . . . Sometimes I feel like I've been waiting to die." These sessions were marked by considerable feelings of improvement. He commented that he felt much better mentally and physically, that he could see how much attention he demanded and how he was using being sick to achieve it. At the end of these sessions, however, he would still complain that he was not getting anywhere. Subsequent sessions revealed further identification with his sick, emaciated mother and further feelings of childhood rejection that he unconsciously attempted to deal with by evoking solicitous attention, rejecting his wife the way he had felt rejected, and evoking current rejection and hardship in his own life in an attempt to master earlier rejections. He reported feeling strangely upset when his friends commented on how well he looked.

In another session, he spoke about his mother's death, the extreme loneliness that he had experienced, and the tremendous eating binges that had followed. He realized that the same sense of rejection and loneliness had followed the feeling that his boss's son had replaced him, and that his early response to it had been to gorge. He understood that his need to starve defended against his urge to gorge, that he loved the food that he avoided, and that the gorging was in response to feelings of deprivation. He also recognized that the starving had been accompanied by a withdrawal from his friends, family, and interests.

DISCUSSION. It is reasonable to consider some of the unconscious motivations behind this man's anorexia. Early rejection by the parents and replacement by a hated brother fueled feelings of severe deprivation, which were responded to by gorging in an attempt to satisfy feelings of lack of love, emptiness, insecurity, and rage. Years later, when a similar picture redeveloped, Carl responded in similar fashion, with the initial gorging replaced by starving and a typical anorexic picture, with elements of loss of control, self-destructiveness, a sadistic identification with the aggressor, infantile regression, acting out, and strong secondary gain in the form of attention and pity.

By starving, Carl also identified with his dying mother of childhood and his dying father of later life. The anorexia appeared to be a substitute for depression and indeed alternated with depressive moods. The withdrawal during the anorexic illness paralleled a similar attitude in childhood during and following the mother's illness.

Carl remained in three-times-a-week therapy for about a year. He improved considerably, but terminated prematurely because of unresolved feelings of self-destructiveness and rejection in the transference.

CASE 5   Chronic, Moderate Anorexia with Bulimia
and Vomiting in a Late Adolescent

Henry entered analysis at age 18 during the summer after his graduation from high school.

ONSET OF SYMPTOMS.   The precipitating stimulus for seeking treatment was anxiety at the prospect of going to a college in Texas in the fall which developed after he suddenly realized that he was unable to stop his daily vomiting. He experienced near panic at the thought that he would be out of control and so far from home. He had been secretly gorging and vomiting for the entire four years of high school. A hearty eater in grammar school, he had been short and stocky at the time he entered a private high school. Not knowing any of the students in the new high school, he had felt distant, alien, and uncomfortable, and remembered feeling very vulnerable to a couple of passing remarks that he was "chunky." He had begun to vomit whenever he felt that he had overeaten.

At first, he had felt quite comfortable about it, since it enabled him to lose about 5 lbs. without having to curtail his rather enthusiastic eating. He enjoyed food and always had found it difficult to restrain himself, especially since both parents were somewhat overweight and kept the refrigerator stocked with the foods they all enjoyed. Almost without thinking about it, he had developed a habit of vomiting daily, usually at night, and especially after overindulging at dinner. He had felt distressed about the vomiting only when he thought he heard his parents outside the bathroom. He had recognized that his sudden silent behavior was an attempt to keep his practice a secret. His secret had been well-kept for the entire four years of high school, and the parents only had become fully aware of his eating difficulties at the time of graduation, when he had blurted out his anxieties and his associated fear of going away to college.

By that time, he had been gorging and vomiting regularly and had accepted his behavior as a matter of course. Toward the end of the first year of high school, in spite of his active eating habits and growth, his consistent vomiting had turned him into a tall, thin, gangling youth. During the following summer, he had taken a 3-week bicycle trip with a group of other boys. He had returned addicted to bicycling. This interest had persisted and intensified: during the evolving crisis in his senior year, he had felt it necessary to bicycle 40 miles a day. In his sophomore year, he had joined the track team and become a cross-country runner. This had interfered with his vomiting schedule because he felt that he could not run well after having vomited. He had adapted his vomiting to his coach's training schedule. It turned out that the summer panic had not been due solely to the inability to stop vomiting. After injuring his foot running, he suddenly had realized that he could not stop running or biking without feeling unhappy or tense. It was just like the vomiting. Henry's starving episodes alternated with secret bouts of gorging, although the latter never approached the intensity of most bulimic attacks. Rather, he would overeat, become anxious about putting on weight, and then vomit and/or starve.

Prominent anorexic behavior took the form of constant preoccupation with food, and ritualistic eating behavior. He would go to sleep thinking about what he would have to eat the next day. On awakening, he would lie in bed and think about the day's meals. Each meal would be anticipated with a voracious intensity. Whatever he chose to eat—and most of the foods were low-calorie, except during his overeating episodes—had to be prepared in the most exacting fashion and served at a certain time. Any deviation from his eating schedule would throw him into intense turmoil. He ate in precise compulsive fashion. The food would be arranged in specific patterns on the plate. Nothing could mix with anything else. Yet, when he ate, he would include two or three different foods in the same spoonful. This would necessitate all the food being cut the size of peas so that the diverse foods could all fit in the same spoonful. If the food was too hot or too cold, it was rejected. If a piece of fruit was not just to his taste, one bite would suffice and it would be thrown out. Another piece of fruit would be chosen, usually with the same result. His complete control over food was in marked contrast to his relations with people.

Henry had had two friends his age in grammar school, both of whom lived in his apartment building. They would walk together to the private grammar school three blocks away. After school, they would get together and play. The other two boys had gone to a different high school and Henry's relationship with them gradually had become more distant. Henry was a good athlete and played ball every day at school; he spent the evenings studying. He never invited his schoolmates home, nor was he invited home by them. Weekends were spent reading, watching TV, and being with the family.

FAMILY BACKGROUND.   Henry's family consisted of his parents, two older sisters, and a brother three years younger. The father was the president of a small high technology company. His work required moderate travel. He gave the impression of being intelligent, driving, and somewhat controlling, but also genuinely concerned about his family. The mother deferred to the father during most of the consultations, but did not appear cowed; on occasion, she differed with him in degree, but not in substance. The mother did part-time work at a social service agency in the city. Initially, they did not seem to fit the description of most anorexic parents. The typical overly close attachment and controlling behavior were not obvious. Salient features in Henry's past history did not include food problems, although the parents noted his compulsive attitudes about food over the past four years. Still, they had been unaware of the anorexic illness until Henry shocked them by revealing the vomiting. They also commented about his need to be compulsively clean, showering, brushing his teeth, and changing his clothing excessively. He had a past history of a fractured tooth from a fall, a broken wrist from a football game, and a fractured thumb from catching a baseball. He had been a shy, withdrawn child in school. The mother remembered some clinging and hanging about her at the time he entered high school.

The two sisters were out of the house at the time of consultation. They attended different colleges and seemed to be reasonably well-adjusted, though somewhat overindulged. Neither one was a perfectionistic, highly motivated student. The younger brother was described as a poor student who just got by; the mother perceived him as manipulating and somewhat exploitative.

THERAPY.   When seen in consultation, Henry was a tall, thin, wiry 18-year-old who appeared pale, anxious, and somewhat agitated. He was 5'10" and weighed 118 pounds. He appeared undernourished with sunken areas under the zygomatic processes. The skin about the eyes was darkened in response to his acknowledged sleeplessness. He was most unhappy in describing his alleged inability to stop his vomiting, running, and biking. He felt out of control—that something must be wrong with him since he could not control his own body. He stated that he could not control the eating, either, and consequently often would only eat at 9 P.M. Then he could curtail excessive eating by going to sleep. (Eating at night and then falling asleep were also a prominent pattern in the case of Eric.)

At the end of the second interview, the analyst acknowledged that he could understand his concern about his behavior and that it might be feasible to enter a local college and continue his treatment. He agreed, and the treatment began during the summer and continued in the fall while he attended a local university.

In the first session following the decision to enter analysis, he reported that "since deciding to come here, for the first time I awoke in the middle of the night nauseated, and I vomited twice." He appeared surprised, and associated to doing it without guilt since now he was sick. In the past, he had to use his finger to vomit. He never had been nauseated or vomited spontaneously before. The analyst pointed out that Henry realized that it was related to accepting treatment, and that being sick was now his excuse to vomit. He added that it also suggested that he viewed the treatment as a threat that might remove his symptoms, and that the nausea and vomiting signaled his unconscious assertiveness and defiance against the analyst and the treatment. Henry responded with the comment that he made his food exactly the way he wanted it, and he described his cooking procedures in some detail. The analyst added that while he could control his food, he might be concerned that he could not control his life; he might worry that the analyst would try to control him, but that would not happen.

While such interpretations of fears of being controlled and emerging defiance in the transference might be viewed as precipitous in the introductory phase of the usual analytic procedure, they encouraged the development of a positive therapeutic alliance with Henry. They also indicated to Henry that his defiance was acceptable and understandable, and could be discussed without fear of danger to, or retaliation from, the analyst.

In the second session, some manifestation of a positive transference was evident in his comment that he was surprised he was able to talk so freely to the analyst. In the next few sessions, he juxtaposed the extreme control of certain aspects of his life with the chaos and uncertainty of other aspects. He described in great detail how he attempted to plan all the activities in his life whenever possible. Before falling asleep each night, he would schedule the following day's activities, including the most minute elements, his meals (what and when he would eat), and his running and biking (how long, how fast, what routes, which side of the street). This was followed by considerations of what time he would get up, where he would sit in summer school classes what TV programs he would watch, etc.

By contrast, however, major issues in his life were in flux, out of control, and, in his mind, beyond resolution. Friends of the family would ask what he wanted to study and the fact that he did not know was overwhelming to him. He had no friends and felt that he would be completely isolated, anxious, and lonely so far away in college. The analyst attempted to encourage a discussion about what he perceived to be the reasons for his lack of friends. He became silent and appeared more distant than a few moments earlier. The analyst commented that Henry's silence prevented him from understanding how Henry was thinking about the questions. After a pause, he looked up and replied that he was thinking of the bread and cake that he was planning to buy at the bakery. The analyst pointed out how his response illustrated what he thought was one of his problems: his discomfort about contemplating his difficult relationships with friends resulted in his avoiding dealing with the issue and focusing instead on thoughts of eating. He liked to think about eating because he could control every detail of it—it was a refuge from thinking about problems over which he felt he had no control. This was why his thoughts about food were so all-consuming and protected him from facing major issues in his life. He acknowledged that he truly did not want to think about them.

In the fall, still feeling discomfort because he could not control his vomiting, he decided that he would stop the vomiting with self-control, and he proceeded to do so. The following few days were a source of great satisfaction and increasing self-confidence. A week later, he reported that, ever since he had stopped the vomiting, he had had stomachaches and headaches, particularly during or after sessions. The analyst suggested that the previous discharge of tensions and problems through vomiting was now being dealt with by stomachaches and headaches and that when he was able to more fully absorb the tensions associated with facing and dealing with the conflicts, the stomachaches and headaches would probably subside. He continued to report stomachaches and headaches for a few more weeks.

Henry had been driving for about a year. With the mother's part-time work schedule, it was suggested that he drive his younger brother back from school when the bus did not run, and to and from his tutor when the mother was not available. Henry acquiesced without the slightest objection, although the chauffeuring assignments were obviously tedious. In one session, he described a whole afternoon of driving his brother about while the brother behaved in an insolent and provocative fashion. He reported the episode with no conscious sign of resentment. As the analyst wondered aloud about how he might have felt at various times during the afternoon, he suddenly reported experiencing a splitting headache that began while the analyst was speaking. The subsequent discussion led to the analyst pointing out that the headache seemed to be a substitute for painful and resentful thoughts about his brother.

The analyst also felt, but did not state, that the headache reflected a transference attitude, namely, that his unconscious unwillingness to hear what the analyst had to say had set off the impulse to attack the analyst's head, the source of the unpleasant information. Anxious about those hostile impulses, he attacked his own head instead. Subsequently, this interpretation was made to him and led to discussion of his problem of repressed aggression, especially toward his brother. In many patients with somatic symptoms, especially headaches, when this interpretation is made, the symptom recedes. In the sessions following the transference interpretation, a whole series of similar occurrences were described, so that it became increasingly clear that the younger brother was a source of intense envy and hatred. He began to speak more openly about how he felt that his brother—and, to a lesser degree, his sisters—got more than he did. They were indolent and never worked, so his parents gave them things. By comparison, he had worked at a newspaper route all through high school and now was an assistant manager in charge of 12 newspaper boys. He paid for his own hi-fi set, but his parents bought sets for his siblings. He paid for his bike, while his father bought his brother's. He began to speak about how he had resented his brother ever since he was born. They all thought he was so cute when he ingeniously demonstrated how adept he was at avoiding work.

He had kept his vow to stop vomiting, but noted that not vomiting meant that he had to run and exercise more. He also was aware of more difficulty in controlling his voracious appetite. In one session, after discussing with some agitation his fear of gorging and getting fat, he reported the following dream:

> I was at a big party. The banquet tables were full. I didn't know what to eat first. I began to eat and eat. Suddenly a rat that was hidden in the salad tried to jump into my mouth. I was disgusted and, as I threw him away, I began to vomit up rats one after the other. My mouth felt dirty. There must have been at least seven or eight and I got frightened.

He associated the party to the recent 25th anniversary party for his parents, where there had been a lavish display of food. All the parents' friends, including the priest who had married them, had been there. Both sisters had drunk too much and he had been disgusted at their boisterous behavior. As usual, his brother had acted like a spoiled brat. The rats reminded him of the pet hamsters that he had as a child. He thought that they were rodents and used their teeth a great deal. One got out once and chewed a hole in the cellar door. They had babies all the time, and he worried that the babies would die. "If I think of rats in my mouth, maybe that's why I brush my teeth so often." The analyst suggested that a foul mouth had additional meaning. Henry remembered that when one of the hamsters died, he got upset and gradually lost interest in caring for them and finally gave them away.

The dream seemed to represent Henry's concern over his cannibalistic destructive feelings toward his brother. Additional confirmatory evidence emerged in the subsequent two sessions. The voracious appetite that he had difficulty controlling was fueled, not by his gourmet interest in food, but by destructive impulses toward his brother. The impulse to gorge stood for the unconscious impulse to destroy. He identified with the omnivorous rodents. Where overt cannibalistic fantasies emerge, the presence of snakes, lizards, and rats is not uncommon. The case of Eric is a vivid example.

In subsequent sessions, it was possible to link his eating preoccupations and intense anger at any disappointment about food with his displaced preoccupations with people. His repressed feelings of resentment, displaced onto the food, would result in eruptions of anger when the food wasn't ready on time. His fear of blowing up and becoming fat represented the fear of losing control over his temper and exploding with stored-up aggression. The vomiting symbolically discharged rage and, when he curtailed it, the tension had to be discharged by exercising. Passive wishes were also present in disguised form, with the eating of the rat babies reflecting a pregnancy fantasy, a vain attempt to hold on to the baby in him, to stay little and not grow up, and to continue to be cared for by his parents rather than to leave home for a distant school. He also identified with the hamster babies in his wish to be cared for when he was replaced by his hated brother. Vomiting also symbolically revealed his conflict over renouncing infantile identifications, with attempts to eject these childish identities. The anxiety over what he wanted to be hid the immature wish not to grow up at all and to be little.

In the fourth month of treatment, Henry spent a great deal of time discussing his difficulties in making friends at the local college. He would stay at the periphery of any group, an onlooker with little or nothing to say. Occasionally, he would come out with a single, carefully censored phrase. The analyst pointed out that he was afraid of what might pour out of him, that everything had to be carefully digested before he would let it out. He then remembered a time years ago when he had wanted to yell and scream at his brother and to hit him. When he was eight, he had hit his brother at every opportunity, which had infuriated his parents. At age 10, he had kicked his sister and bruised her shinbone. She had had trouble walking for a few days. He acknowledged with some apprehension that at times now he had the urge to go outside and scream. He also had thoughts of smashing one of the beakers of acid in chemistry class. In an attempt to control by denying the emerging aggressive feelings, he added, "I'm just not convinced of all this."

By the fourth month of treatment, Henry felt considerably better. He was less tense, was sleeping better, and was able to concentrate on his studies. He still had difficulty eating regular foods.

Henry had joined the college cross-country team and was chagrined to find out that he was the slowest runner. He would practice and exercise regularly, but without noticeable improvement. The analyst suggested that his difficulty was in part attributable to not having strong leg muscles and that all he had was tendons and bones. He added that all athletes recognize that they need meat to build muscle, and that he wasn't eating any. He revealed that he was constantly preoccupied with the appearance of his body. He exercised to build up his muscles and did endless pushups and situps, along with general calisthenics.

He was also concerned about what he perceived to be his pot belly. Every morning, he would look in the mirror at his abdomen and then attempt to starve or exercise the little pot belly away. With this preoccupation, the male anorexic reveals the same conflicts as the female. He stated that he did not wish to be thin, but that he was just afraid of becoming fat. He feared that the food that he ate would not develop into muscle, but rather, would enlarge his abdomen.

After considerable discussion about eating to build muscle, he mentioned that he had been testing out his strength and realized that when he was heavier, he was indeed stronger. He then decided to eat meat to increase his muscle. That night, he had his first steak in over a year. From that night on, he ate regular food consistently.

DISCUSSION. The discussion about building muscle illustrated a number of theoretical and technical points. Henry's preoccupation with the physical appearance of his body symbolized his ambivalence over active and passive impulses, destructive and receptive feelings, and his masculine identity. Unconsciously, to be masculine meant to be destructive and to be able to kill his brother. To be physically strong meant that he would have the power to carry out aggressive impulses. To be weak meant that he could hurt no one and need not fear the eruption of aggressive impulses. This is a common developmental problem in adolescents, as their biological growth provides them with increasing strength that often frightens them. To be physically weak also meant to identify with the pot belly, to be pregnant, and to be feminine. It would follow then that, with these types of underlying conflicts symbolized by the physical appearance of the body, it would be therapeutically appropriate to provide Henry with a degree of insight into his aggressive feelings and concomitant awareness that his aggression could be controlled before insisting on his gaining weight, which unconsciously might mean that he could destroy his sibling. At the same time, however, clarifying for him that eating meat would increase his muscles (masculine), rather than his pot belly (feminine), encouraged his masculine identification. It was these shifts in internal identifications that contributed to his willingness to eat. Treatment continued for a total of three years with a successful conclusion.

SUMMARY

A detailed description of the clinical syndrome, psychodynamic conflicts, and psychoanalytic treatment of five anorexic male patients was presented.

The clinical picture was similar in the 10-year-old boy, the adolescent males, and the older man, and clearly paralleled the illness in females. The same conflicts over independence, dependency, aggression, and psychosexual identity existed in all the male patients, but the overt manifestations of these conflicts varied depending on patients' stage of development, degree of intrapsychic instability, ego strength, defenses, and environmental experience.

The major conflict in the 10-year-old boy arose out of the need to deny very primitive aggressive drives of a cannibalistic nature related primarily to his sister instead of his parents. In addition, conflicts in psychosexual identity and the need to rid himself of an overidentification with the heavy, pregnant aunt by starving were paramount.

In the teenage boys, aggressive conflicts were also a major issue and were manifested in adolescent rebellion against the parents. Fear of and anger toward the father, who threatened their emerging masculine identity, were also of considerable importance. Two of the boys responded to having been coerced into treatment with great resentment. Their hostility and suspiciousness were never fully resolved, in spite of the positive results of the treatment. The crucial issue of being controlled—being made to go for treatment—never subsided, although every attempt was made to analyze it, and no attempt was ever made to make these patients eat or tell them what to do. Their long-standing resentment parallels a shorter phase in many anorexics who transform the decision of not eating into the decision of not talking, often with some consequent improvement in eating. These reactions underscore the complications arising out of therapy programs centered around coercing patients to eat.

The third adolescent's problems were similar to those of the other two. His severe obsessive-compulsive character structure attempted to deal with this aggression prior to the anorexia. The denial of sibling rivalry was marked and interfered with the development of friendships. There was clear demonstration of the use of exercise to discharge aggression. Dependency problems were a major difficulty; they accounted for his entry into treatment and were present in the transference.

Finally, issues of dependency in the older man far outweighed other conflicts. These dependency conflicts reemerged from the reawakened memory of the loss of the mother and within the context of a new sibling rivalry toward the employee-brother. The sadistic, coercive rage was displaced onto the food and starving, and indirectly expressed hatred toward the wife-boss-father.

14
Psychoanalytic Therapy: The Case of Martin

HOWARD K. WELSH, M.D.

Martin began twice-a-week psychoanalytic treatment at the request of his family members, who were extremely concerned about his weight loss. At the beginning of his two-and-a-half-year treatment, Martin was 35 years old, 6' tall, and 113 lbs. He dressed oddly in old, unfashionable clothes. He often wore Woody Allenish, brightly colored sneakers or workboots. Generally, he conveyed a clownish appearance. He had been dieting strictly for at least two years, eliminating all sweet and rich foods in a careful effort to keep his weight down. Although he looked ghastly and emaciated, Martin did not feel that he was too thin. He felt attractive and was angry at his family, particularly his mother, for being so concerned and for nagging him constantly to eat and gain weight. He expected that treatment would consist of further entreaties and orders to eat.

THERAPY

By the end of the first interview, it was clear that Martin's marked weight loss, approximately 60 lbs. over the past two years, was due to his severe and peculiar dieting, rather than to any physical illness. He had a horror of gaining weight and becoming fat. After gaining a few pounds, he would starve himself, drinking only water for the next day or two, until he more than made up for the gain. At times, he would completely give up his strict diet and abandon himself to eating binges. He would eat several boxes of cookies at one sitting. Then, with his stomach bloated, he would walk to the pastry shop and eat cakes until he was in pain or felt sick. After gorging, he sometimes would induce vomiting and take laxatives. He was very frightened by these periods of total loss of control and was afraid that if he began to gain weight, he would not be able to stop. He had the fantasy that one day, in the midst of a binge, he would find the pastry shop closed. Totally out of control, he would break into the shop and be caught by the police. Although he would try to explain that he only had entered to get some pastries, the disbelieving police would usher him away.

At the end of the first interview, the therapist told Martin that, although he was curious about the reasons for his unusual eating habits, he had no personal interest in whether he was fat or thin. However, he thought that if Martin lost another 10 or 15 lbs., his health might be in serious danger. Martin thanked the therapist and said he would contact him if he wanted treatment. The therapist did not expect to see him again since his motivation for treatment appeared nonexistent. He had come merely at the urgent pleading of his family. To the therapist's surprise, Martin called a couple of weeks later. Apparently, he had become concerned enough about himself to agree to twice weekly psychotherapy.

Martin was an extremely isolated man. He had no friends and had not dated a woman in several years. His social contact was primarily with his family. He visited his parents, who lived in another state, saw his younger sister, who lived nearby, and had dinner with his aunt and uncle occasionally.

Martin spent most of his time thinking obsessively about food. He planned and replanned his meals for the coming week. He structured conversations with others around the topic of food. In spite of his peculiarities, he usually was liked by people. He was voluble and friendly and had a good sense of humor. As isolated as he was, he did not seem withdrawn or affectless. He led a meticulously routinized life and became extremely upset when it was disrupted. For example, when the subway train was a few minutes late and his usual schedule was thereby altered, he became distressed. He went to sleep early and arose early. He usually walked to work, a trek of several miles, in order to keep active and thin.

Martin's profession involved exacting work and he was capable of being quite competent. However, he had been laid off or fired from three previous jobs because he stubbornly had refused to advance beyond a certain level of skill and would take no initiative on the job. He tried to do as little work as possible and invariably became the office clown. He felt that he was just a child, and he wished his bosses would expect no more of him than he did of himself. Furthermore, he believed himself to be brain-damaged and felt that he could function only at a minimal level. He maintained this belief in spite of his previous training and college education, his achievement on advanced exams, and his proven competence and exceptional ability in certain areas. In reality, Martin was of superior intelligence.

In addition, Martin had moments of paranoid thinking where his reality testing was severely impaired. For example, while walking down the street, he believed that a woman who looked his way was thinking how attractive he was. Immediately this changed to another thought—the woman was really thinking that he was a fool and an idiot. He felt ridiculed and humiliated. At times, with his odd and clownish dress, he indeed looked foolish. It seemed, however, that these feelings had no relation to the reality of his dress and that he felt he was ridiculed only by women. This was clearly the projection of his own feelings about himself at the time.

Another area of impaired reality testing involved his fear of sweet foods. He was convinced that eating sweets would cause him to develop diabetes. The therapist learned that his dieting had started 10 years earlier, after his mother had developed diabetes. At that time, he had been quite heavy, weighing in excess of 200 lbs. After learning of his mother's diabetes, he had suffered a bout of spastic colitis for the first time. The physician he consulted had recommended a special diet and also had suggested that he lose weight. Martin's mother had told him that diabetes was caused by eating too many sweets and that if he were not careful he, too, would develop diabetes. In spite of being informed that people do not develop diabetes from eating too much sugar, but rather, have an intolerance to sugar after developing diabetes, his mother's pronouncement was not doubted and she was held to be the highest authority.

His mother's diabetes aroused intense separation anxiety. He identified with her and her illness and dieted as if he, too, had diabetes. Two years before he entered therapy, his mother had begun to have a series of other difficulties: circulatory problems, phlebitis, and arthritis. His anxiety had increased and his identification with her had become more pronounced. He had adhered to his "diabetic" diet even more strictly and had begun to lose a great deal of weight. He had assumed all of his mother's illnesses. Once, when his mother was having an attack of arthritis, he literally hobbled in and out of sessions.

There was no evidence of early traumatic separation experiences. His mother had been doting, overconcerned, and overinvolved. She either would give strict instructions on how to behave and what to do, or she would take care of everything, so that Martin felt no need to take any responsibility at all. He had rebelled against his mother's domination in passive-aggressive ways, for example, by dirtying his clothes after she had warned him against doing so. Martin's father was an extremely anxious and excitable person. Unusual events or responsibilities were too much for him to handle. Most of the time, Martin's father withdrew from the family and spent time with his friends. Father and son had absolutely no relationship. Fights between father and mother were daily occurrences, although the father never intruded in Martin's involvement with his mother. Nothing had intruded until his sister's birth, when he was 11 years old. At that time, he had developed asthmatic symptoms, which had lasted for several years. Except for this and eczema in infancy and early childhood, Martin had not been troubled by any other illnesses.

As his attachment to the therapist grew, his separation conflicts emerged more clearly in the treatment. He again began to have eating binges, usually on the weekends. He mixed concoctions of various foods in a blender until they had a smooth, milklike consistency. He found these mixtures particularly soothing and comforting. The connection between his feelings of loneliness and emptiness on the weekends and his urge to binge and eat his soothing, pasty blends was discussed. He never thought of satisfying his need for human relationships with a girlfriend; he always turned to food. He told the therapist a joke during this period which illustrated how his orality served as a regressive defense against incestuous wishes.

Morris was not feeling well and went to see his physician. His doctor told him that he knew the very thing that would cure his problem. The patient needed mother's milk. He sent Morris to a wet nurse, who supplied his need. As Morris was partaking of his medicine, the wet nurse began to become aroused. After several more minutes of Morris happily indulging himself at her breast, she asked if there were anything else she could do for him. She would be glad to oblige. Morris looked up and quickly responded that a few cookies would go along just fine.

The therapist continued to focus on Martin's fear of loss and separation from his mother and from the therapist in the transference, leaving oedipal interpretations in abeyance. As his defensive identifications with his mother's diabetes and her fear of eating sweets were clarified, his eating symptoms became much less extreme. He binged less frequently, and he allowed himself more sweets in a fuller diet. Over a period of three to four months, he gained approximately 45 lbs. and stabilized his weight between 150 lbs. and 160 lbs.

Martin began to elaborate on his special horror of becoming fat. He felt that fat men had rounded body contours like women and that their penises were smaller than those of thinner men. He wanted to have a skinny, phallic body. He felt the same horror and anxiety when viewing a woman's body. He always had the feeling that women were awkwardly constructed and deformed. Their way of walking struck him as peculiar. He fantasized what it would be like if he had been born on another planet and did not have to contend with the differences between the sexes. The creatures of his fantasied extraterrestrial race were unisex or hermaphrodites, free of castration anxiety.

Martin also had a fixed, delusional belief that his own penis was abnormally small, deformed, and mutilated. In spite of the reality testing provided by comparisons to other men and by medical examinations, he maintained this belief, usually on an unconscious level. Often, he displaced this idea onto his brain, viewing it as damaged and inadequate. This explained his conviction that he was stupid, incompetent, and could only function in a minimal or severely compromised way at his job.

A crucial part of his treatment was the discovery of the origin of Martin's belief about his penis. This occurred through the analysis of a reaction in the transference. After months of treatment, Martin noted that the therapist did not have any diplomas or certificates on his walls. He wondered whether he was really a certified psychiatrist or even a physician. He feared that the therapist was incompetent or a charlatan and that he was putting himself in his hands to be damaged rather than helped. This reaction came at a particular point in the treatment and led to a significant childhood memory. His castration anxiety, with the therapist as the feared castrator, had been a theme in his treatment for several weeks. In dreams and fantasies, the therapist was "Dr. Miracle," a villain out of a beloved opera who continually thwarted the hero and robbed him of his loved one. It seemed that the therapist was the feared father who, uninvolved though he was with Martin and the mother, still prevented Martin from maintaining his early attachment to his mother forever.

The therapist encouraged Martin to think about why, at this time, he was so concerned about the therapist's qualifications and was feeling such mistrust. He then remembered that his mother had told him that, in order to save money, his father had hired an unqualified and second-rate mohel to perform his circumcision in the traditional Jewish ceremony. His mother said that the mohel "cut off too much" and "did a botch job." He mutilated the patient's penis. At first, it wasn't clear whether his mother had told him this or whether it was a screen memory that reflected his castration anxiety. After a number of sessions, as he remembered more details, it became clear that his mother had actually told him this on a number of occasions. In fact, it was a major preoccupation of hers throughout his growing up. His earliest memories of this began at age six or seven, but he was certain that this concern of his mother's had begun at an earlier age. He remembered his mother talking frequently about his deformity, discussing it with neighbors, and announcing that he would have to go to a doctor. When he did see a physician, he was assured that his penis was perfectly normal. This preoccupation seemed to have the intensity of a delusion for the mother, resulting either from the projection of her own feelings of genital damage and castration onto her son or from her own castrating wishes. She made it clear that she had wished to have a daughter instead and often told her son that he was as pretty as a girl. However, in the story she told her son, the father was portrayed as the castrator. He had hired the unqualified mohel and was responsible for the maiming.

Martin's view of himself reflected his mother's view of him. He maintained two contradictory views of reality that existed separately and split off from one another. On the one hand, he knew that his penis looked like any other man's and was quite normal. On the other hand, he consciously believed what his mother had said—that the mohel had "cut off too much." As a corollary, his mother had told him that he never would amount to very much, that he was second rate. This had colored his entire self-representation. His paranoid projection onto the women he passed in public places—that they thought he was pretty and then thought that he was a fool—exactly reproduced what his mother thought of him. He was as pretty as a girl and was castrated, too.

Intense homosexual conflicts accompanied his feminine identification. He was afraid that becoming fat meant having body contours like a woman and a smaller penis. His unconscious wish to acquire a whole and more potent phallus combined with a feminine longing to be penetrated. Invariably, on any job, he would begin to feel that his boss was "trying to screw him." This would make him angry and he would retaliate by doing less work. This would make the boss angry, and Martin would feel with greater conviction that the boss was singling him out "to give him the shaft." The cycle would continue and escalate. This cycle, coupled with his desire to behave like a child with little responsibility, resulted in Martin's inability to keep a job.

As the memory of his mother's belief in his mutilated state emerged, along with their folie à deux, Martin's conflicts over aggression unfolded and became paramount. The distortion of his reality testing to match his mother's view that his penis was mutilated defended against his murderous rage toward her. To see himself as not castrated meant that he would have to face a more frightening reality—that his mother was a castrator and was horribly destructive to him. Unconsciously, he had to contend with this rage in any case. He constantly was afraid that she might die, particularly when he was with her. He was afraid he would kill her. His assumption of her illnesses was an identification that also served his unconscious guilt and need for punishment. Throughout his life, his frightful anger toward his mother had contributed to his separation anxiety.

She would be destroyed because of his rage and he would be alone. Yet, his hatred of women and sadistic impulses toward them were so great that he was impotent and kept himself isolated. He was afraid that he would become another "Son of Sam," a murderer of women. It became clear that his eating binges, where he experienced complete loss of control, gave vent to his unconscious murderous rage toward his mother and at the same time gratified his fantasy of incorporating her. He described his eating binges as devouring, destructive rampages. They were the regressive oral expression of his unleashed and uncontrolled aggression. His fear of these binges and his stringent efforts to control them resulted in his extreme dieting and anorexic symptoms. His true fear involved his need to control the rage felt toward his mother, which was now defended against and disguised by regression to orality and displacement onto food.

During this period in the treatment, he had a dream in which he was about to enter a subway tunnel when a large, terrible black dog emerged, snarling and showing its teeth. He awoke from this dream in a state of great anxiety. In his session, he recognized the subway tunnel as his unconscious and the black dog as the projection of his own frightening aggression. His wish to remain a child was also a wish to be harmless in his aggression. His mother's statement 10 years earlier that he would get diabetes if he ate sugar paralleled and resonated with her earlier proclamations about his penis. Again, his mother was presenting him with a frightening and false reality, but this time the threat was of death rather than castration. The reality of his own separateness and individuality again was denied, and he felt that his mother's death would mean his own.

His treatment came to a difficult stage as his conflicts shifted from the arena of his anorexic symptoms to their sources. He no longer stringently dieted, nor was he unusually thin. He still sometimes binged on the weekends when he felt particularly lonely. His understanding of himself had increased greatly, but he was still an unhappy and isolated person. He was still afraid that he would become another "Son of Sam" if he got too close to a woman. In addition, the nearly lifelong view of himself as damaged and crippled continued to permeate his whole self-representation. His work in the psychotherapy was compromised by the same problem. He felt incapable of utilizing his insight for change. Only the therapist could change him by his potency and magic. His maternal transference resulted in an extremely strong attachment to the therapist. He imagined that he and the therapist would continue to see each other until they were both old.

Along with this attachment, the therapist became the focus of his rage. He would defeat the therapist by defeating the treatment. He would thwart him and show him to be incompetent, even at the expense of continuing his masochism and illness. After one and a half years of treatment, in response to this therapeutic stalemate and the therapist's frustration with his negative therapeutic reaction, the therapist agreed to decrease his sessions to once weekly. In retrospect, this appears to have been a major mistake and a tacit agreement on the part of both Martin and the therapist to relinquish ambitions for further progress. At the time, the therapist rationalized his own counter-reaction by feeling that it was wrong to see him twice weekly when he did not want to go further in therapy. Once-a-week treatment would suffice for more supportive goals. The therapist failed to appreciate that Martin would gladly confess to a lack of motivation in order to avoid rocking the boat any further and unleashing his enormous rage. The therapist played into Martin's resistance. Realizing this mistake, the therapist tried to reinstate twice weekly treatment, but Martin refused. After a year of once weekly therapy, Martin stopped his treatment completely, feeling satisfied with the results.

DISCUSSION

Martin's history confirms the findings of psychoanalysis and psychoanalytic therapy with other anorexic patients (Sours 1974, Thomä 1967). Conflicts involving oral drives and impairment of separation-individuation appear to be of primary import in many patients. Except for those aspects of Martin's reality testing that were directly involved with his delusional view of his mutilated penis and his intense separation anxiety (he felt he could not survive if his mother died), his reality testing was not impaired in any pervasive way. He was not overtly or globally psychotic. The impairments in his reality testing, object relations, and impulse control, as well as the degree of his masochism, were within the borderline range of ego pathology. He did not have a thought disorder or any signs or symptoms characteristic of schizophrenia, nor did he have a major affective disorder. His preoedipal fixation and regression, which resulted in a more-than-neurotic degree of ego pathology, appeared to be typical of a large group of patients with classical anorexia nervosa.

The case of Martin may be compared to the two cases of boyhood anorexia nervosa described by Falstein et al. (1956). In all three cases, the onset of bulimic episodes during the treatment marked the beginning of therapeutic improvement. Furthermore, all three patients began dieting by identifying with a dieting mother who encouraged her son to imitate her. All three patients were obese prior to the dieting. Falstein et al. hypothesized that the mother's encouragement of her son's dieting implicitly encouraged his growth and masculinity, provoking a reactive panic and regression to a more infantile and dependent relationship with her. With Martin, however, the covert communication was just the opposite. Essentially, Martin's mother said, "You and I are one and the same. If I have something wrong that needs to be corrected by dieting, you must do the same. I never told you to diet before, although you have been fat. In fact, I encouraged you to eat. But now that I have to diet, you should, too."

Unlike the cases reported by Falstein et al., Martin's treatment did not reveal a pregnancy fantasy as a significant underlying dynamic. However, this might have been due to a therapeutic oversight or blindness and would not have been at all implausible, considering Martin's wish to be a member of a unisex, hermaphroditic race, presumably capable of self-impregnation.

As is often the case with male anorexics, while Martin was dieting and enforcing strict control over his impulses, he did not masturbate (Beaumont et al. 1972). He began masturbating again after his bulimic episodes reappeared during his treatment. His conscious masturbation fantasy was always the same: he fantasized performing cunnilingus on a large, unknown black woman while she stood over him. He never was able to associate to or elaborate on this fantasy, but it seemed that, unconsciously, the black woman represented the phallic mother and he was attached to her orally, as her feces-baby-penis. The fantasy symbolically captured the lifelong unconscious symbiotic relationship between Martin and his mother.

It appears that the core conflict for patients with anorexia nervosa is the enormous fear of losing control over their impulses and forbidden wishes from all levels of development. The anxiety over controlling these impulses is displaced onto eating and the fear of being fat, with focal distortions of body image and impaired reality testing. An attempt is made to relieve the anxiety by the reassurance that eating and body weight can be mastered and controlled.

Every form of psychological and somatic therapy has been tried with anorexia nervosa patients (Crisp and Roberts 1962, Hay and Leonard 1979, Roussounis 1971). Behavioral therapy and family therapy have enjoyed particular popularity recently. The treatment of Martin demonstrates the complicated interplay of conflict, defense, fantasy, and disordered object relations in the pathogenesis of anorexia nervosa. It is difficult to imagine any treatment other than an intensive, analytically oriented individual psychotherapy or psychoanalysis that would be able to uncover and address the material that was revealed in this case. Interpretation and insight helped Martin to understand a good deal about the psychological causes of his unusual eating behavior. He achieved significant symptomatic improvement. He gained 45 lbs. and stabilized at a normal weight. He modified his severe dieting and the whole cluster of typical anorexic behaviors related to the fear of becoming fat: vomiting, taking laxatives, and hyperactivity. He stopped being susceptible to bulimic episodes, and he resumed his usual masturbation practices.

Most therapists interested in symptomatic or behavioral change would have considered Martin "cured." However, his therapist had hoped for a deeper resolution of his conflicts and for more ego growth. Nonetheless, there was some ego development that came from the insight and working through in the treatment. He understood enough about his feelings and conflicts so that he no longer feared an absolute loss of control. His impulses were not so frightening and potentially overwhelming. Martin was left with a greater sense of mastery that came from self-knowledge, rather than a false and pathological mastery of his eating and weight. With insight into his homosexual conflicts, rage, self-punitiveness, and need for omnipotent control, his masochism became less severe and he was able to keep his job without provoking his boss into firing him. However, he was too afraid to venture further in treatment, which would have upset his schizoid, but stable, existence.

The problem of motivation can be expected in the treatment of most anorexics (Crisp and Toms 1972). Characteristically, anorexic patients do not see themselves as troubled or as needing help, nor do they see themselves as too thin even when they are emaciated. They consider their relentless pursuit of thinness to be in the service of physical attractiveness, virtue, self-control, and independence. They usually do not seek out consultation or treatment themselves, but are led by concerned family members to a nonpsychiatric physician who may hospitalize the already seriously wasted patient. The typical symptoms of the anorexic are ego-syntonic and therefore do not afford motivation for treatment, especially for self-exploratory therapy.

What really motivated Martin to begin treatment seemed to be his great fear of loss of control. This fear, shared by most anorexic patients, needs to be addressed by the therapist in the initial consultation sessions. Such an approach helps the patient to feel understood. The therapist can say something such as, "Although everyone else is worried about how little you eat and weigh, I think you feel your thinness protects you from losing all controls, protects you from binging and becoming endlessly fat. Perhaps that is the problem for which you would really like help." This interpretation taps the source of the patient's own anxiety, thereby enhancing the potential desire for treatment.

The problem of motivation also caused Martin's therapy to founder at the end. When he had understood and worked through enough of his conflicts to feel more mastery over his impulses, he no longer wanted to use his psychotherapy to make further changes within himself or in his life. It was the therapist's ambition that Martin should attempt to alter his schizoid life style. It was the therapist's confronting him a bit too persistently about this issue that caused him to stop therapy. He made the same mistake that Martin's family had at the beginning: he was pushing him to give up yet another, more characterological, defense against his fear of loss of control. Martin's schizoid avoidance of human relationships protected him from stirring up desires and impulses that he feared would destroy the other person and/or himself. The therapist should have been tolerant of his ego-syntonic schizoid defenses and his disinterest in doing anything about them, as he had been tolerant and merely curious about his eating habits. He should again have related Martin's fear of loss of control to his choice of self-isolation, gradually stirring up the anxiety and motivation necessary for further therapeutic progress.

The most consistent and characteristic feature of Martin's transference was his continued wish for, and fear of, the therapist's omnipotent control. His analytic attitude of neutral curiosity was reassuring to him at the beginning of treatment, but later became depriving. He wanted the therapist to be the fearsome and powerful "Dr. Miracle" who could control his life. He wanted to take on the therapist's desires, attitudes, and view of reality as he had done with his mother. At the same time, he desperately wanted to be in control of his own self and destiny. His transference reactions repeatedly vacillated between these two conflicting trends. It sometimes was difficult to switch gears and understand that his experience in the transference was just the opposite of what had been manifested one session before. The emergence of his passive wishes often triggered hostile, resistant, and rebellious reactions in subsequent sessions. He wished to continue in therapy always. At the same time, this wish frightened him. That he could make the therapist so essential to his life and give up control to him made him want to stop therapy. If he saw the therapist as able to manipulate, control, or abandon him, the therapist became dangerous. He experienced the confrontation of his schizoid defenses as a threat that the therapist would abandon him if he did not change, so he left first.

SUMMARY

A sketch was given of the psychoanalytic therapy of a man with anorexia nervosa. Historical data, features of the transference and countertransference, and the importance of specific unconscious fantasies were emphasized. The patient's anorexia nervosa originated from a displacement onto eating and body weight of the need to control his frightening impulses. These impulses derived from oedipal and strong preoedipal fixations. A description of the central organizing function of a delusion shared by mother and son was offered. Specifically, its role in representing an overwhelming castration threat and a barrier to a cohesive sense of separateness and masculine identity was discussed. Certain difficulties in the treatment were highlighted, especially the ego-syntonicity of anorexic pathology, and some suggestions were made to enhance and maintain the anorexic's motivation for treatment.

15
An Analytic Approach to Hospital and Nursing Care

IRA L. MINTZ, M.D.

The increasing clinical incidence of anorexia nervosa has been noted by many investigators and has been manifested in the emergence of self-help anorexia nervosa societies and the development of anorexia nervosa treatment centers and hospital care units. Inpatient hospital care can be a crucial treatment requirement, either on an emergency basis or for more prolonged care.

WHOM TO HOSPITALIZE

Further scrutiny of differing approaches is therefore warranted. Some therapists and hospital treatment centers feel that a 3-month hospitalization in the beginning phase of treatment is necessary for all anorexic patients. The view of the contributors to this volume is that hospitalization should be reserved for acute, severe regressive behavior where either medical or psychological reasons indicate that the patient is in danger of dying or becoming severely ill from marked emaciation, convulsions from electrolyte imbalance, cardiac arrhythmias, or severe depression with suicidal impulses or psychosis. Selvini Palazzoli (1978) emphasized the importance of attempting to treat the patient out of the hospital whenever possible and in spite of marked weight loss. She pointed out that therapists might contemplate hospitalizing patients for their own peace of mind—to avoid the stress of outpatient treatment. Mild to moderate anorexia nervosa can be successfully treated in outpatient clinical services or in office practice.

THE PURPOSE OF HOSPITALIZATION

The period of hospitalization should be as short as possible. The goal is to provide massive hospital support systems to carry the patient through the severe regression and to restore a reasonable modicum of health so that the patient is able to function with safety outside the hospital. This would include correcting any electrolyte imbalance or other blood chemistries, resolving severe depression, suicidal danger, and psychosis, and improving body weight to a level that is no longer dangerous and that can be worked with in treatment (Chapter 4, this volume). This general approach also applies to the treatment of psychosomatic diseases such as asthma and ulcerative colitis. This attitude is beneficial to the patient and cuts down on hospital costs. It also tends to emphasize to the patient that the primary goal of the treatment is not weight gain, but the resolution of the conflicts that have resulted in the development of the anorexic symptoms.

PATIENTS' ATTITUDE TOWARD THE HOSPITAL AND STAFF

An essential feature of the psychoanalytic treatment and hospital management of anorexic patients is the recognition of these patients' unconscious conflicts. This permits therapist and hospital staff to understand patients' feelings and problems thoroughly, and to act rationally and incisively help patients to resolve them. The more clearly therapist and staff understand patients, the more help they can give them.

In reviewing the medical regimes at different hospitals, Bruch (1973b) emphasized the difficulty in making effective comparisons among the different facilities, but did emphasize that good results in the hospital seemed to be correlated with the skillful abilities of the staff personnel. She also pointed out that hospital staff members often feel overwhelmed with anger, frustration, and anxiety in response to these patients' difficult behaviors. Bettelheim (1975) described in detail the important effect of the staff's conscious and unconscious reactions to patients on the progress of treatment.

Cohler (1975) described a residential treatment for anorexia nervosa and emphasized the complex feelings of the treating therapist. He stated that because anorexic patients are so difficult to treat, "the therapist's feelings of anger and hopelessness . . . [are] a genuine and intrinsic part of the treatment process and not, as is often believed, an element of countertransference" (p. 387). He felt that the therapist's ability to tolerate these feelings helped patients to change. It is true that not every reaction of the therapist is a countertransference. Some reactions may stem from not understanding the patient's problem. It is rarely therapeutic for a therapist to feel helpless, hopeless, frustrated, and angry in dealing with patients, and anorexic patients are no exception. If anything, such feelings are counterproductive and provide patients with a sense of increased sadistic gratification from their hostile antagonistic behavior, increased doubt about the therapist's capacity to understand and treat them, and intensified feelings of being overwhelmed by and guilty about impulses. It is crucial to be able to absorb and try to understand any feelings that patients express without a sense of frustration, anger, rejection, or abandonment. The importance of this attitude will be discussed later in the chapter.

Cohler (1975) later reported how one anorexic patient succeeded in repeating her undifferentiated, fused relationship with her mother with her female therapist. She was verbally abusive to the therapist and attempted "to bind her therapist to her by not differentiating between their personalities" (p. 403). The therapist felt "confused and completely smothered and overwhelmed" by the patient. She lost her appetite, became anorexic and amenorrheic, and fantasied that she was pregnant with the patient, "who would live forever inside her body" (p. 404). The therapist became increasingly afraid of merging with the patient, and the patient became increasingly disturbed.

Silverman (1974) reported on the hospital treatment regime in a pediatric ward and emphasized a firm approach in correcting severe medical abnormalities with concomitant four-times-a-week intensive psychotherapy. He felt that hospitalization was required for a period of three months. He also emphasized the importance of a careful evaluation of the patient's metabolic status.

Sours (1980) reported on the hospital care of anorexic patients in an acute stage; he emphasized the importance of focusing on the needs of the individual patient and using experienced staff. He commented on the important role of the nursing staff and the danger of nurses identifying with, or coercing, anorexic patients.

In discussing countertransference, Wilson (Chapter 8, this volume) agreed with Sperling (1978) that anorexic patients constantly test the therapist and try to induce intimidation, anxiety, and rejection. He emphasized that anorexics expect the therapist to worry about them when they are sick just as the mother did. Agreeing with Bruch, he underlined the need not to be intimidated by the patient.

Anorexic patients who are hospitalized for severe, life-threatening symptoms are considerably regressed psychologically. As with most regressed states, ideas, attitudes, behavior, expectations, goals, frustration tolerance, and object relationships are all affected. Previously thoughtful, realistic, and considerate behavior fades away and is replaced by infantile, hostile, provocative, demanding, and petulant attitudes. Independent, goal-oriented behavior is replaced by coercive, manipulative, and unrealistic demands. In a general way, patients behave toward therapist and staff as they behave toward their authoritarian parents.

Anorexic patients, who have a major and overwhelming fear of being controlled, unconsciously resort to controlling food because they cannot control their own lives or other people. They learn they can control people by frightening and coercing them with the threat of becoming sicker. This unconscious attitude may not be clearly perceived by hospital staff, who can be subtly manipulated and coerced by these patients.

PATIENTS' BEHAVIOR
Regressed Goals

Anorexic patients attempt to achieve regressed, infantile, dependent, and sadistic goals. The need is to be helpless and dependent on the one hand, and manipulative and sadistic on the other, with the guilt from the latter behavior assuaged by immediate punishment in the form of starving and depression. There is the wish to be treated as someone special, to get extra attention and concern, to be catered to, worried over, and indulged. These attitudes and conflicts have been present for years and are intensified during the anorexic syndrome. This behavior is not premeditated, but rather, arises out of deeply felt needs and requirements associated with feelings of marked weakness and, often, feelings of total inability to cope with the world. These feelings are completely out of keeping with patients' true abilities and capacities. The regression accentuates the state of helplessness and, to a considerable degree, this intense helplessness subsides as the regression recedes and patients improve. Anorexic patients often have difficulty making the simplest decisions, organizing daily activities, and exercising even a modicum of independence or assertiveness.

Displacements of Major Issues

These patients attempt to engage therapist and nursing staff in endless discussions about food, eating, dieting, and thinness. Patients may admit that they think about nothing else during their waking hours. To the degree that patients are able to engage staff in food preoccupations, patients' displacements from major issues onto food are reinforced and progress is impeded. The more these topics are discussed, the less the possibility of getting to the real sources of concern.

Struggles with Control

The problem of who controls whom is a major source of concern.* These patients feel that they have been told what to do all their lives, that they have been overcontrolled and have behaved like obedient little robots or, as one patient put it, like little puppets with someone else pulling the strings. They are both terrified and desirous of being controlled. Being controlled is equated with being cared for, but on an infantile level. This ambivalence takes the form of alternating, opposing behavior and attitudes (i.e., withdrawn, defiant, and sadistic behavior at one moment, followed by activity that serves to encourage sympathy, help, and concern at the next).

A teenage boy acknowledged that he had to obtain perfect grades because knowledge is power and he could control events with it. It was therefore not surprising to hear him state that he would never reveal certain personal information because he felt that the more the therapist knew about him and his vulnerabilities, the more control the therapist would have over him (Chapter 13, this volume). A 17-year-old girl offered all kinds of rationalizations as to why she did not wish to continue treatment. A more thorough discussion of her fears revealed that she was growing fond of the therapist, and this frightened her into wishing to stop. She reasoned that the more that she liked him, the more she would wish to please him, and by wanting to please him, she would then fall under his control. She added that she recognized that the therapist might not try to control her at all but that she would still be victim of being controlled.

Although patients may be primarily obedient and "controllable," the seeds of inner unrest are evident in early obsessive-compulsive character traits that

---

*See Chapter 4 for a detailed discussion.

serve the purpose of control. The exacting, perfectionistic quality of their work illustrates the need to control their academic performance. Frequent compulsive rituals also reveal this controlling propensity. Here, too, lie the seeds of the defensive displacement from large issues to small ones that is so characteristic of compulsive behavior. Long before their anorexia, patients have often learned to shift what they could not accomplish in one area of life to controlling how their books are arranged on the shelf. The anorexic syndrome follows the same pattern, displaced now onto food. When patients cannot deal with an important event in life, they control how the food is arranged on the plate, or what they eat. Patients' behavior in the realm of control is of far-reaching psychic relevance and importance, and should not be trifled with casually.

Punitive Conscience

Anorexic patients have a very strict punitive conscience that contributes to a rigid critical attitude toward their own and others' behavior. Therefore, they are very sensitive to criticism, feel guilty very easily, and expect to be criticized frequently—perhaps as harshly as they criticize themselves. Just as they are the recipients of severe feelings of guilt, they are experts at evoking guilt in others by their appearance, behavior, and comments. People tend to feel badly about how patients look, what they do, and what they say, and usually tend to compensate for these feelings by babying them and catering to their whims and needs.

Feelings of Aggression

Finally, these patients have a tremendous problem with their feelings of aggression. During most of their lives, they have been obedient and compliant. They have been unable to be firm or assertive, to stand up for their rights, or to be unruly, difficult, uncooperative, irritable, or angry at times. They have feared that any expression of aggression would be uncontrollable and would be met with punishment and disapproval. Therefore, there is very little outward evidence of aggression until the treatment begins to shift the aggression from self-destructive anorexic behavior or depression to an externalized form, such as irritable, sullen, or uncooperative behavior.

ATTITUDE OF STAFF TOWARD PATIENTS

Medical care by the internist or pediatrician should be directed toward correcting the emergency situation that prompted patients' hospitalization. Toward that end, accurate weekly weighings, some awareness on the part of the nursing staff about how patients eat, and intravenous supplementary feedings and fluids may be indicated. These procedures can be accomplished, however, without attempts to coerce patients to eat or to put on weight. Any sense of desperate concern and worry over patients' condition is ill-advised and very counterproductive. Patients unconsciously view such concern as the consequence of their ability to control the staff through illness. Thus, their urge to stay sick or to get worse will increase, since control over the staff is unconsciously more important than getting better. A hard-hearted, indifferent, cold, or rejecting attitude toward patients is *not* advocated: all patients have the right to medical care by a thoughtful, considerate, and sensitive hospital staff. However, patients must recognize that the doctors and nurses are quite capable of dealing calmly with the situation, without conveying any sense of undue apprehension or panic. As most of the hospital care is performed by members of the nursing staff, their attitudes, behavior, and actual nursing care are of great importance in facilitating patients' recovery.

Dealing with Patients' Dependency

The nursing staff should deal with patients' dependent, helpless, waiflike appeal for attention, affection, love, and special consideration. Understanding patients' dependency problem helps one decide how to deal with it. Patients who are sick physically and regressed psychologically require the help of a very thoughtful, sensitive, and caring person, but someone who can help without overindulging, who can be sensitive without being seductive, and who can be considerate without being fearful. These patients require thoughtfulness with encouragement, responsiveness with realism, and calmness with strength.

It is helpful to recognize the disparity between the helpless, waiflike attitude that patients present and their true underlying capacity. These patients have intellectual ability and many areas of ego strength that they neither recognize nor utilize. The tenacity that is evident in the stubborn need to starve can be channeled into the dogged pursuit of getting well. The intellectual capacity that is manifested in consistently obtaining excellent grades can be used toward the thoughtful resolution of life's problems. These patients are not without resources. They just do not use them in a healthy fashion. It is helpful and important for the staff to recognize these abilities and not be seduced into undue sympathy by patients' woeful appearance. Rather, staff members should encourage patients' assertiveness and ability to make decisions, to tolerate frustration, to work hard to get well, to face and discuss difficult problems, and to see their own strengths. Despondency and helplessness can be countered by indicating to patients that they can get well if they work at it. Furthermore, patients are more encouraged by the display of a quiet, consistent, and firm recognition that they have the necessary ability to get well than through any vociferous pep talks.

Most anorexic patients are aware of many problems that they consciously refrain from discussing. They become pessimistic and complain about not improving without acknowledging that improvement in great part is a result of problem solving and working in treatment. Unrealistically and in infantile fashion, patients expect to get better just by being in the hospital. Their complaints of lack of progress arise out of regressed thinking and behavior, and can serve to evoke sympathy and indulgence from the staff, along with guilt that they aren't doing more to "make" patients better. This guilty response can be displaced onto the therapist, with feelings of resentment toward the therapist for not "curing" patients. This curious staff attitude can take place even when the nurses recognize that a patient is not being cooperative, talking effectively, or working in treatment. The patient has subtly evoked enough guilt so that they cannot clearly perceive that there is little reason for improvement. Guilt can obscure staff's objectivity as much as undue sympathy.

It should be helpful and reassuring to the hospital staff to recognize that, under almost all circumstances, they should be able to help patients medically and prevent death. This is especially true if they are objective about medical findings and are not manipulated by patients into permitting them to enter a dangerous medical phase that then remains untreated. The internist and pediatrician can remain watchful and relatively unintrusive as long as patients do not present a critical medical problem. They can be quite thin without being perilously ill or close to death. By being unobtrusive yet firm, staff members offer patients reassurance that they are not attempting to control them. When their condition deteriorates dangerously, however, the physician and nursing staff must be firm and consistent in doing whatever is medically essential to save patients' lives.

If the staff enters into discussions about food with patients, and patients will attempt to promote this, then the staff unwittingly helps patients avoid the confrontations necessary for them to get better. In addition, patients and staff have divergent goals: patients talk about food so as to avoid eating it, while nurses talk about food in the hope of encouraging patients to eat. Patients will never comply; in fact, they unconsciously use the discussions about food to sadistically toy with, provoke, and antagonize the staff. Ultimately, as the discussions about food proceed endlessly, the staff becomes aware that nothing positive will be achieved, and the frustration and impotence of the staff members to be helpful to patients lead them to feel pessimistic, discouraged, and resentful. One cannot forbid patients to talk about food and diets since they have the right to talk about whatever they choose. But one does not have to become the unwitting victim of a ploy that is antitherapeutic and frustrating. It is possible to listen politely, and with interest, yet with the recognition that to encourage this type of discussion will lead nowhere.

Dealing with Patients' Self-Starvation

Forcibly coercing patients to eat serves a short-term goal of weight gain and produces a long-term liability of weight loss and increased defiance. Patients angrily comply with the authoritarian requirement that they eat in the hospital and then revert to starving as soon as they leave. To force patients to eat as a therapeutic modality flies in the face of their entire life experience. They already feel that they can't control their lives—that they never have been in control. As one patient succinctly put it, "Not eating is all I've got." Sperling (1978) has warned that force-feeding without consideration for personality change can result in decompensation and psychosis.

The hospital staff should take a very specific position on this issue. Patients should be permitted to eat whatever they choose; no attempt should be made to influence them. They should be told that they will in no way be forced to eat. However, they must also recognize that starving is the somatic equivalent of suicide and that it is the duty of staff members to attempt to prevent them from dying. If their weight reaches a point of acute danger, then the staff members will provide them with supplementary nutrition. Patients may wish to know what weight loss is necessary for such nutritional supplements so that they may feel free self-destructively to lose further weight, or sadistically to attempt to get just above or below the specified weight to see what the internist will do. Spelling out these details is unwarranted and only falls into the trap of focusing on weight loss instead of on problem solving. The reply should be left vague; e.g., the weight will be determined by a series of medical and hematological circumstances.

Dealing with Patients' Conflict over Control

It is imperative that patients realize that the staff is available to help them, rather than to control them. A great deal of these patients' life experiences has left them feeling quite the opposite: that people are out to control them. In the hospital among a group of strangers, they feel even more helpless and vulnerable to the demands of others. The staff should recognize and be aware of patients' fear of being controlled and not do or say anything to increase it. Patients will fear and complain about being controlled even when no attempt has been made to control them. It can be pointed out that the hospital staff is available to be helpful and not to order them about or make all their decisions. In individual conversations with patients and in group meetings, the staff members should encourage patients to express their own ideas and to consider various alternative solutions; they should not fall into the attitude of "helpfully" providing solutions for patients. Patients often approach a staff member and ask what they should do. The staff member should be adroit enough to encourage patients to figure it out without making them feel rejected or antagonized. Infantile needs to be helpless, to be told what to do, and to be controlled take over and tend to preclude independent reasoning. The hospital staff should not unwittingly reinforce these regressed behavior patterns.

Dealing with Patients' Punitive Conscience

It is certainly important not to be critical of these patients' attitudes or behavior, no matter how frustrating they seem to be. The most inoffensive comment about patients' attitudes or behavior can be silently perceived and responded to as a critical remark. If such an interchange comes to the attention of the nurse, it is helpful to indicate that the remark was not meant to be critical and that perhaps the reaction reflects a sensitivity on the patients' part.

If one recognizes that a strict punishing conscience sets in force a series of self-punishing reactions, then one should be prepared to look for and recognize the various manifestations of self-destructive behavior. In anorexic patients, the primary self-destructive behavior is the starving. These patients truly enjoy food and wish to eat, but deprive themselves of the enjoyment and satisfaction of eating.* Most anorexics are able to tolerate the starving because the feelings of hunger are repressed and not experienced. When the repression fails, the

---

*See Chapter 13.

hungry feelings return and patients binge. The gorging is then followed by feelings of extreme guilt, which often set off vomiting.

Self-destruction takes many forms, however, including psychosomatic diseases such as asthma, which can be associated with subclinical anorexia. Other forms of self-destructive behavior can take place within the hospital setting and should be recognized as such. For example, patients may get moody or depressed. This indicates a shift in the self-destructive trajectory from self-punitive behavior (suffering through starvation) to self-destructive behavior (suffering through self-recrimination). The different clinical forms of the self-destructive drive and the underlying ego structure and defenses have been described in more detail elsewhere (Mintz 1980). This depression should not be viewed with alarm, particularly if it is associated with a tendency to eat more. It suggests that the conflict is shifting from food preoccupations to psychological manifestations and therefore should be welcomed as a sign of progress. It is easier to treat a patient suffering from unhappy feelings and ideas than one who has no complaints other than a fear of being fat.

In a few patients, the self-destructive attitudes are so strong that anorexic starving, depression, and suicidal feelings are all present at the same time. Here the presence of the depression signals a self-destructiveness so intense that it is not absorbed by the self-destructive starving alone; the punitive conscience requires additional penance in the form of severe depression. These patients are usually more ill and more difficult to treat.

Another manifestation of this self-destructiveness takes the form of uncooperative, provocative, and antagonistic behavior. To provoke and frustrate the very people whose job it is to help when one is sick, hospitalized, and separated from friends and family, and realistically subject to the rules of the hospital staff, is truly a self-destructive act. If staff members are not well trained and alert to the possibility of this type of behavior, they may respond consciously or unconsciously with retaliatory actions. Or, equally inadvisable, they may feel unduly frustrated and give up trying to help patients at a crucial time. The provocative, antagonistic behavior may reflect the beginning of an intrapsychic shift from the anorexia to difficult behavior patterns; if so, it should be recognized and accepted as such, and considered in a potentially positive light, rather than with despair. This concept can be considered further in discussing the problems of aggression.

Dealing with Patients' Aggressive, Hostile Behavior

There is overwhelming clinical evidence that self-destructive behavior is an alternative to externalized aggressive behavior and represents the other side of the same coin. While staff should never attempt to provoke hostile reactions in patients, increasing manifestations of anger can indicate an intrapsychic change and herald an evolving improvement. More specifically, expressing anger toward the staff is more beneficial than acting self-destructively provocative with the staff.

Characteristically, these patients have always had difficulty in being reasonably and firmly assertive, in standing up for their rights, and in tolerating other people's anger and criticism. The aggressive drive can take the form of unruly, uncooperative, surly, and procrastinating behavior. This behavior is in marked contrast to previous behavior, which characteristically was cooperative, obedient, and submissive. In addition to recognizing that this type of change can be positive and that these "difficult" patients are beginning to deal with their conflicts over aggression, the staff needs to be able to tolerate and absorb patients' aggression without feeling threatened or defensive, without attempting to minimize the seriousness of their feelings, and without retaliating. It is of tremendous help to patients to realize that they can express feelings of anger without being punished, ignored, or abandoned. It increases their self-esteem, improves the quality of their relations with people, accentuates the value of verbal communication, improves mastery, and aids sublimations.

However, it is not enough for patients to externalize various aspects of their aggressive drives. To be able to act unruly, obnoxious, and provocative may be a necessary intermediate phase in treatment, but it should not be viewed as the end point. Otherwise, one can end up with permanently obnoxious individuals. It is hoped that the accompanying treatment will provide patients with sufficient insight into their problems over aggression to enable them to channel the aggression into more socially acceptable behavior.

SUMMARY

Given the importance of the hospital setting, an attempt was made to illustrate how some of the major conflicts of anorexic patients are expressed toward hospital staff. It was emphasized that the better staff members understand patients, the better they can cope with them in an effective, therapeutic fashion.

PART V

Special Issues

16
Derivatives of Latency

CHARLES A. SARNOFF, M.D.

There is a point during the emergence from latency when one expects to observe a maturational process involving a burgeoning of secondary sex characteristics and a shift in primary love attachement from parents to peers.

ANOREXIA NERVOSA: AN ALTERNATIVE TO ADOLESCENCE

In young people with anorexia nervosa, this expectation is interdicted by a cessation and regression of normal development. In effect, these young people turn the clock back. Physical maturation slows, weight is lost, menses cease, and the figure recedes. Emotional involvement with the family intensifies and that with friends becomes secondary. Usually a strong ambivalent quality pervades peer ties. Peers are viewed as externalized rejecting and condemning superego figures. Therefore, the anger-laden relationship to the mother is intensified for lack of peers to relate to and to trust.

The cessation and regression of the normal developmental process is the result of a configuration of defenses that takes the place of adolescence. Anorexia nervosa is not so much a disease or a syndrome as an alternative organization of the ego that is chosen over the often chaotic, always challenging, and sometimes frightening confrontation with adolescent sexuality. Of the other adjustment patterns usually seen in adolescence, the ones most closely allied to anorexia nervosa are the withdrawn and ascetic patterns. In both, the child shies away from intense sexualized socialization, and the parents remain more important than peers in the area of close personal relationships. All three adjustments (asceticism, withdrawal, and anorexia nervosa) may be transient sexual adaptations that later give way to a more mature experiencing of life. For many, however, the pattern persists to become the basis of their future adjustment and character.

All three adjustments allow disengagement from sexual encounters. The withdrawn person has no contact with potential sexual partners and so develops no skills to deal with sexuality. The ascetic person confronts social situations and partners and learns to cope with sexual feelings through repression and denial. The anorexic person changes his or her bodily configuration to that of a younger child and thus is not seen by others as a sexual object. Female

327

anorexic patients universally have a fantasy involving their psychic body image: the nonscaphoid abdomen is a sign of pregnancy. Manipulation of the true body image through starvation supports denial of sexuality from within at the same time that it fends off sexual approach by others.

TRANSIENT VERSUS INTRANSIGENT ANOREXIA

There is a wide spectrum of anorexia nervosa, ranging from transient cases that clear up after a few sessions of psychotherapy to intransigent cases that persist through many years and many therapists. In all cases, behavior and defenses are organized around specific fantasies involving body image which lead to self-starvation.

The easily reachable transient anorexic adjustment is associated with a discrete, thinly repressed, and well-organized body-image fantasy in the context of a competent ego organization. The intransigent anorexic adjustment involves a bizarre, poorly organized body-image fantasy filled with contradictions that do not bother the patient in the context of an ego organization that shows impaired reality testing, narcissistic deformations, and the impress of the mother in both ego-ideal content and object relations. All of these elements carry the characteristics of latency ego states into the organization of the personality mobilized to confront the challenges of adolescence. The reason for the imprint of latency on regressed adolescent adjustment is obvious. When the intensified sexuality of puberty appears, the tried-and-true defenses of latency are at hand to help counter and stifle drive discharge through fantasy, regressed, sadistic, and cruel interactions with parents (who retain center stage), and narcissistic deformation of object relations.

When confronted with insights into these patterns, intransigent anorexics readily agree, but see no reason to change their ways. The regression is conscious, is felt to be justified, and, as a result of support from the mother, is apt to provide secondary gains. Their refusal to eat is a form of impulse disorder with an emphasis on overcontrol. Transient anorexics, on the other hand, find insight a help. Much of their fantasy activity is repressed, leaving them bewildered at their state and unaware of the reasons for the starving. Their pathology is related to repression. In essence, they are food phobic and have anxiety associated with eating, with little understanding of its cause.

Clinical Material

The following case material illustrates the two extremes of the anorexic spectrum.

CASE EXAMPLE   *Transient Anorexia*

Millie was 13 years old when seen in consultation at the hospital where she had been sent by her pediatrician for evaluation of her refusal to eat. She sat by her bed reading. She wore street clothes. She appeared to be of normal weight and her development was that of early puberty. Millie was not overly thin. She informed the consulting psychiatrist that she had lost 15 lbs. in the last few weeks; she had been much heavier before that. At 5'3", she weighed 110 lbs. Millie's pediatrician felt that the rate of weight loss was a source of alarm. He had admitted her for a general workup for the causes (organic or functional) of the sudden weight loss. Uncovering no positive organic findings, he had attributed her starvation diet and weight loss to anorexia nervosa. He then had called for a psychiatric consultation.

Millie's mother had first called attention to the weight loss and the starvation diet. The mother was cooperative with the hospital, but not over involved in the treatment. Many "get well" cards from friends were observed in Millie's room. The child was somewhat impatient with the psychiatrist's presence because she expected some of her friends to visit momentarily.

During the course of the consultation, the psychiatrist asked Millie whether she worried about her stomach. Did it bother her if it protruded? Anorexic females are preoccupied with keeping the stomach flat. No matter how thin they are, they will intensify their self-starvation if the abdomen protrudes in any way. Behind this preoccupation is the fantasy that the protuberant abdomen is a sign of pregnancy. Starvation keeps the abdomen flat and hides from the world the sexual fantasies and preoccupations that cause a protuberant abdomen to be seen as a pregnant one. Millie associated to the psychiatrist's questions with a recollection of her concern at a party that someone would think she was pregnant because of her tight dress. The psychiatrist posited a relationship between her fear about eating and her concern lest her figure take on the configuration of a pregnant woman. "I think that's it," she said. "I probably could eat now." She did, and soon went home. There were only a few sessions, and these were related to her concern about how to behave with boys. The psychiatrist never saw her again. Her pediatrician reported nothing unusual for the rest of her adolescence.

This child is remarkable in that she came to someone's attention. Transient anorexic adjustments to the sexual challenges of adolescence are frequently undetected by physicians and often are masked as ordinary dieting. In these cases, the body-image-oriented fantasy is the decisive factor in determining anorexia as the avoidance technique to use in coping with the pubertal intensification of sexual drive energies. For all intents and purposes, there was no involvement or even awareness on the part of Millie's mother of the true nature of the child's condition. Loss of appetite and weight loss were considered by the mother reasons to take the child to the doctor for a workup. Millie's cognition was normal for her age. She could apply abstract thinking to free-standing ideas. She could understand and apply abstractions to new situations in such a way that she could see them in a new light. As a result, she could differentiate the words of fantasy from the false reality that the words created when this situation was pointed out to her. These skills made it possible to set aside the latency style of functioning through fantasy that had reassumed dominance at the time of her anorexia.

The capacity to differentiate reality from fantasy when confronted with the difference necessitated the use of repression. Without repression to mask the fantasy from rational challenge, Millie could not have acted on the basis of an untenable hypothesis. In brief, she had a characterological *neurotic* cognitive style of ego organization. Thus, her condition, which consisted of a food phobia, was amenable to uncovering therapy. When the irrational fantasy was stumbled on and exposed by the psychiatrist, her rational faculties were brought to bear on it. Then, like Freud's ancient cities exposed to the light and air, it crumbled.

CASE EXAMPLE   *Intransigent Anorexia*

Sonia was 16 years old and had been quite a beauty before her anorexia nervosa. In latency, she had been the ideal child to her mother. Her latency-age fantasy life had been rich. However, when she had reached puberty, the cognitive changes of maturation had wreaked havoc with the effectiveness of fantasy as a discharge pathway. The symbolic population of her persecutory fantasies had been replaced with real teenagers, who had become her persecutory protagonists. Sonia had placed herself in the role of the persecuted one. She could not make friends or go to parties. She feared she would be considered dull or boring, or that she would be ignored. In actuality, she could not differentiate herself from the internalized bad mother imago of her childhood and had projected this confusion onto the thinking of her peers. This was intensified by her ambivalent relationship to her mother.

Sonia's father had disengaged himself from the family and had devoted himself exclusively to his business at the first sign of crisis. As the result of the loss of accessibility of others, Sonia's relationship with her mother became her only object tie. Though her mother often spoke of the burden of her constant contact with the girl, she did little to minimize it. She gave a sigh of relief whenever her daughter was hospitalized, but never actively initiated separation. The closeness of the two intensified Sonia's ambivalence toward her mother. This, in turn, reinforced the negative aspects of the internalized maternal imago.

As a result, Sonia's misinterpretations of her peers' behavior were magnified. The more time she spent with her mother, the more apt she was to rail at her own passivity and her mother's constant attendance and advice. Then these negative feelings were projected onto peers. Thus, fighting with the mother resulted in an intensification of the bond with her.

Of course, much of this situation with her mother had been present before the age of 12. In latency, the relationships with the mother and peers had been preserved by the ability to project the conflict onto a fantasy, which had been manifested clinically in the form of night fears. That is the way a latency-age child manages to be "perfect." The depressive affect that accompanies such a situation is also dealt with within the personality. One sees anger or anxiety, rather than depression, when the mechanism of projection is actively involved in fantasy formation that incorporates fantastic symbols. When real people are used to populate the fantasies, depression surfaces. Actualization through the fancied detection of feared situations in the reactions of peers justifies depressive affects. At age 12½, Sonia had experienced a marked manifest depression, coupled with a feeling that she could not make friends and was disliked by her peers.

Sonia's parents had decided to get psychotherapeutic help for her. Although the family had had sufficient funds, her father, who put little stock in psychotherapy, had asked her pediatrician to make as low a fee as possible a prerequisite. They had been referred to a Mr. M., whose distant office had consisted of a desk and chairs in the garage of his home. No attempt had been made to alter its appearance from that of a garage and it was never cleaned. The mother described cleaning her clothes after each visit. His abilities as a therapist were reported by the child to be as dilapidated as the setting. Mr. M. had spent the 18 months of twice-a-week therapy telling Sonia about himself and had offered her rewards if she would go to parties. She had tried, but had continued to interpret the reactions of peers as rejections.

In the meantime, Sonia's figure had matured and she had begun to attract the attention of young men. One day, she had decided that she was disliked because she was fat. She had decided on a diet. Her mother had been delighted by her "fashion model" appearance. Sonia had had mixed feelings about the whole situation. She had liked her slimness, but not the hunger, the empty-space feeling inside her stomach, and the constipation and interference with bowel habits that had accompanied the starvation. She especially had disliked giving up her favorite food, chocolate cookies, so she hit on a compromise. She would eat all she wanted of cookies and candies and then either spit it out without swallowing or vomit it up.

In this way, the impulse to eat could be responded to at will, while the feeling of emptiness within could be considered a product of her own design. Sonia had a true disorganization and disorder in impulse control. She overcontrolled and undercontrolled her eating with little pattern or reason other than the urge to eat and the need to stay thin. Her mother had considered the vomitus and the packages of spit-out food disgusting. Sonia had considered these practices justified since, in her own mind, the chocolate tinge that pervaded it all made it look "just like shit," with the implication that the food had been digested. She had begun to lose weight rapidly. Her therapist had declared the situation beyond him when her weight dropped to 68 lbs. At 5'4", she was gaunt and skeletal. Her skin had a yellowish cast. People who met her casually became fearful and withdrew, reinforcing her own fears.

There followed a series of hospitalizations during which Sonia was threatened with intravenous feeding. In response to these threats, she had agreed to eat and had gained sufficient weight to go home. Her mother had been quite fearful during this period. She had claimed not to know what to do. Her response to this situation had been to placate her daughter while begging for her cooperation—certainly a mixed message. The girl had followed her impulse of the moment.

The anorexia nervosa was undoubtedly affected by the genetic influence on behavior of late-latency object relations. In late latency, children begin to look beyond their parents for superego contents. Peers and social influences, such as magazines, TV, and films, provide children with idea resources that can be called on to challenge parental guidance and to fuel rebellion against passivity. As often as not, the parents themselves, seeing the child's maturation, encourage development in sexual areas and others that they formerly forbade. In essence, the late-latency child comes in conflict with old parental imagos, sometimes even with the current parent as an ally.

These are internal conflicts whose resolution results in some of the more disquieting, though transient, psychopathological symptoms of late latency. Obsessional symptoms, paranoid reactions, hives, and gastrointestinal symptoms are common (see Sarnoff 1976). The point is that, specifically at this age, internal conflicts between oneself and parental imagos stir up guilt that may be dealt with through the use of body functions as primitive symbolic forms. Thus, the child withdraws from the conflict on a verbal level and becomes preoccupied with cathexes turned toward the self. In the process, the world is devalued and the form and functions of the body become more important than relations with others. The situation is analogous to that of a general who devotes his attention to the shape of his supply ships in the heat of battle.

Even Sonia's thoughts about her body changed as her attention was turned inward. She ceased to worry about weight as a deterrent to others' esteem and began instead to seek the perfection of a personal ideal filtered through an immature and distorting cognition. All of this was conscious. She accepted contradictions between the reality of her thinness and her interpretation of what she saw in the mirror without a qualm. Conscious contradiction formed a part of a new "rationalism" that she had developed for her own use (e.g., "No matter what you see in the mirror, I see the same thing and to me it is fat"). Sonia became anxious and fearful when forced to eat. She enrolled in a program of voluntary hospitalization that placed little faith in insight. Instead, there were rules about eating that emphasized discipline: weight loss was recorded and responded to with loss of privilege. She became quite anxious under this regime and asked her mother to give her another chance with psychotherapy. She entered dynamic psychotherapy at age 16.

She explained to her new therapist that she had rejected the program because she felt fat if her abdomen protruded at all. She was so thin that any food ingested could be perceived as a relatively massive distortion of her scaphoid abdomen. In her intuitive response, this little part that was seen as fat stood for a whole body that was fat and pregnant. Her cognition in the area of perception of her body was so distorted that all input was shaped to support her delusion. Since it was conscious and rationalized, interpretation could not avail her of new insight and confrontation could not diminish her invariable response to all she heard or saw. She unquestionably loved the power she had over those who loved her or wanted to help her. Her power was the result of her personal, irrational, and unassailable "logical" system.

There was more than a touch of sadism in Sonia's refusal to give up her "rationalism." She was the center of attraction in an adult world. The alternative, in her mind's eye, was to become a wallflower in a world of young teenagers. Narcissistic overcathexis of her own ideas, fantasies, and distorting cognition helped her to preserve her self-created world. In this way, she was able to select a moment in her life and stop time there. It was a moment when she had been praised for her asexuality, a time predating her body roundings and menstrual period, which would lead toward adult sexuality. It was a moment when she could live in fantasy rather than reality. Finally, it was a moment when learning was by rote and she didn't have to understand the intrinsic essence of a process.

Sonia had stopped time in latency. Wilson (personal communication, 1979) points out that, in his extensive experience, he has found that parents encourage this.

The parents, because of their character structure, admire their children most in the latency phase, and do not accept the aggressive and sexual changes of adolescence. The parents unconsciously like the latency figure and are repelled by the roundings of the female figure.

In addition, the parents engage in fighting with the children. The children respond in kind. This interferes with separation from parents and the establishment of relationships with peers. There is a mutual interplay aimed at keeping the child forever young.

Sonia's cognition interfered with interpretation. She could not learn from psychotherapeutic work in those areas involved in her complex. She had withdrawn from reality object ties. She learned by memorizing words and phrases by rote. The only exercise of logic known to her consisted of twisting words to fit her needs. Her long, thin arms and legs gave one the impression of a spider. Indeed, spiderlike, she had woven about her a web of words through which she would not see. Soon the word-web alone became her world. No matter how her therapist tried to free her, she would not leave the safety of her web. It tangled close about her. Reality receded. Predator became prey to its main device. Her web of words served as both hiding place and prison trap. Her loneliness was devastating; yet she reveled in her ability to outsmart others and to twist reality to suit her needs in a contest of wills whose sole judge was herself.

Within four months, Sonia worked through her use of projection to fend off peers and reestablished contact with old friends. She began to feel anxious in the treatment. She told her mother that she thought therapy put too much of a burden on her and she demanded to drop out of therapy. She wished to return to the program that offered external controls. When her mother called to tell the therapist what was afoot, she explained that she could not argue with her daughter. She feared Sonia's rage if she defied her wishes. The therapist met them four years later. They were shopping. Sonia appeared to be essentially unchanged, except that her affect was flatter.

SUMMARY

Anorexic symptoms most often make their first appearance during the emergence from latency. The hypercathexis of fantasy in latency and the undemanding nature of the latency-age bodily configuration make regression to the latency state a sanctuary from the sexual demands of puberty and from adolescent turmoil. Withdrawal and asceticism are other common examples of such a response to adolescence.

Those with neurotic character defenses use the anorexia as a transient adjustment to sexuality—a means of causing the body and the menstrual cycle temporarily to regress to the form and function of the latency child. Their unconscious fantasy that fat means pregnancy can be dispelled through interpretation. At the other end of the spectrum are the intransigent anorexics, whose heightened narcissistic cathexes of fantasy at the expense of reality, and primitive cognition and understanding of causality, allow them to establish a cognitive style that permits an indefinite continuation of the regression. Since the illogic and contradictions are consciously accepted by these patients without challenge, the process of interpretation offers no new insight and only slow progress in psychotherapy.

Case examples of the extremes of the anorexic spectrum were presented. The external characteristics and symptoms of anorexia nervosa do not define the disease entity, but rather, are the products of a reaction pattern. The psychiatric diagnosis and prognosis depend on the status and nature of ego functions. The more pathological the cognitive impairments are, the more likely it is that an intransigent form of anorexia nervosa will develop.

The severer forms of anorexia involve intense aggressive interaction with parents. This encourages physical regression and interferes with separation. The emotionality and high noise level of the verbal interactions give the parents no time to convey and encourage the development of more mature levels of abstraction and other logical processes. Failure to achieve some mastery of sexuality leaves the anorexic without the interpersonal skills acquired through gradual exposure. Thus, the longer the anorexia lasts as a defensive configuration during the emergence from latency, the more entrenched and necessary the reaction becomes. For this reason, early psychotherapeutic intervention is indicated.

17

The Relationship between Self-Starvation and Amenorrhea

IRA L. MINTZ, M.D.

Amenorrhea has been recognized as an essential feature of the syndrome of anorexia nervosa for 300 years (Thomä 1967), but its far-reaching and manifold psychodynamic meanings have been only partially considered. Society's reaction to menstruation has always been that of taboo and horror, with avoidance and seclusion of menstruating women. These attitudes date back to the earliest written history. Deutsch (1944, p. 153) referred to Chadwick's quotation from Pliny's "Natural History": "The menstruating women blighted crops, blasted gardens, killed seedlings, brought down fruit from trees, killed bees, caused mares to miscarry. If they touched wine, it turned to vinegar; milk became sour."

Frazer (1959) cited the behavior of innumerable primitive tribes throughout the world who view women as dangerous and filled with frightening destructive powers while menstruating. When Zulu women begin to menstruate, they must run to the river and hide among the reeds, where they remain secluded in a hut for two weeks. During this time they cannot drink milk lest the cattle die. During menstruation, Australian women are forbidden to touch anything used by men under pain of death. In Uganda, pots that the menstruating woman touches have to be destroyed. In Costa Rica, it is believed that drinking out of a cup used by a menstruating woman will cause the drinker's death. In almost all of these tribes, the menstruating woman is kept in seclusion, occasionally for months, with very strict taboos observed in an attempt to protect the rest of the tribe from her mysterious and harmful effect on them.

MENARCHE

Deutsch (1944) described the psychological effects of menstruation on women in considerable detail. "The most important event of puberty is menstruation. . . . The first genital bleeding mobilizes psychic reactions so numerous and varied that we are justified in speaking of the 'psychology of

335

menstruation' as a specific problem" (p. 149). She described the importance of menstruation in the lives, fantasies, and behavior of premenstrual children, and felt that premenstrual girls are preoccupied with secrets about menstruation. Furthermore, "All observations suggest that, whether or not the girl is given intellectual knowledge, even when she has the best possible information about the biological aspects of the process, and despite its wish-fulfilling character, the first menstruation is usually experienced as a trauma" (p. 157).

Over the years, however, sex education courses in the schools and the women's rights movement have helped to dispel some of the previous misconceptions about menstruation. Kestenberg (1965) pointed out what she felt was the overemphasis of the traumatic aspect of the first and subsequent menstruations, and focused on "the positive aspect of the menarche as a turning point in the acceptance of femininity" (p. 19). When earlier pregenital and oedipal conflicts are not overwhelming, this is undoubtedly true, but when there is a great deal of earlier conflict, the menstruation serves to intensify anxieties and reopen old wounds associated with feelings of helplessness, loss of control, bodily damage, and problems in feminine identification.

Ritvo (1977) commented that "the menarche is an important landmark in early adolescence because it has all the characteristics of a normal developmental crisis" (p. 128) and added that the crisis may be a stimulus for further progress or an impediment that sets off regressive anal and castration conflicts. Both Ritvo and Deutsch cited cases where menarche had been overwhelming, including one suicide attempt. Ritvo described girls who reacted to menarche at age eight or nine with rage, temper tantrums, shame, and bizarre attempts to conceal it. He felt that the short latency period did not permit the establishment of strong ego structures to cope with the regressive pull to pregenital experience, especially that of anal soiling. In his opinion, concealment is "a widespread, if not universal, reaction to the menarche" (p. 129). All tribal taboos against menstruation include concealment of the girl during menarche.

Deutsch (1944), Kestenberg (1965), Ritvo (1977), and others described the unconscious perception of the menstrual process in oral, anal, and genital terms. Deutsch described girls' varying attitudes toward menstruation. Early, it is seen as an additional excretory function that is unclean and dirty, with this dirty feeling spreading to other parts of the body. The cloacal excretory concept is particularly frequent in girls who were enuretic earlier in life. Other girls use menarche to regress into childlike helplessness and be cared for by their mothers. Kestenberg (1977) stated that "menstruation becomes associated with fecal masses of bloody urine, with castration, and with the loss of the generative inside. . . . A wish to expel or injure what is inside combines with masochistic fantasies of bleeding as a result of rape, becoming impregnated, and delivering a phallic product of an oedipal union" (p. 226).

Women with ulcerative colitis tend to get exacerbations of the bleeding at the time of their menstrual periods. The colitis attacks in part reflect conflicts over feminine identification. The bleeding from the colon is an unconscious attempt to deny the menstrual process and to displace it onto the colon, where it loses its sexual feminine connotations. Conversely, one colitis patient intent on stopping the bowel bleeding unwittingly became amenorrheic for five weeks. In her discussion about it, her associations led to cloacal fantasies, which were then reflected on and clarified. The patient's period began 10 minutes after leaving the office.

MENSTRUATION AND LOSS OF CONTROL

Ritvo (1977) commented on and emphasized the important issue of control. "The memories of puberty in the analysis of some women show that the experience of the menstrual flow, which, in contrast to the experience with urine and feces, cannot be controlled by voluntary sphincters, contributes to the character traits of helplessness, and passivity" (p. 128).

This loss of control and its attendant helplessness can reawaken memories of earlier conflict over the initial inability to control sphincters and people. Anxiety over loss of control can be compensated for by character traits that emphasize obedience and respect prior to decompensation, and excessive control and manipulativeness during the illness. Thus, some anorexic adolescents who have acceded to dominating and controlling parents all their lives rebel in areas related to the anorexia. Under the guise of illness, they become very stubborn and manipulative. Chronic anorexic patients can exercise an almost demonic control over their food and their parents' lives in the realm of eating.

The perception of menstruation as a loss of control over soiling reactivates unresolved oral and anal conflicts, especially the sadistic control over fecal objects. Anorexic patients frequently have a preanorexic history of easy-going, compliant behavior in which the impulses for anal defiance and overcontrol were well concealed. Under the influence of passive illness and helplessness, this controlling, manipulative behavior emerges. Anorexic patients demonstrate many anal characteristics in their exacting, compulsive attitudes about food. This control is in part sphincteric in the sense that patients are almost totally preoccupied with their food, what enters their mouth and what does not, and what they do with it once it is inside. One anorexic patient would eat foods in a certain order—green salads, red meat, and milk—and then attempt to vomit the food back in reverse order, without mixing the different foods, and stop prior to regurgitating gastric juices.

Control over the feces through excessive laxative use can be as exacting and tyrannical as control over food. By comparison, menstrual control is silently but effectively dealt with by amenorrhea. Although we cannot speak of an anatomic sphincter, nothing leaves the uterus, just as nothing enters the mouth. The control is exercised at different levels: voluntary with the eating, and neuroendocrine with the menstruating. The need to control is present in both cases and can be relinquished in both cases by insight. During the course of a successful analytic type of treatment, the patient begins to eat and to menstruate.

If permitted, patients will attempt to achieve the same type of control over people that they exercise over eating, defecating, and menstruating, particularly in the area of food.

Sperling (1978) has pointed out that control in anorexic patients is so important that if it is removed precipitously before compensatory changes can take place in ego functioning, dangerous acting out or decompensation may result.

Menstrual bleeding reawakens turmoil from all levels of development: loss of control over body contents, body damage, a missing organ. Prior to menarche, bleeding is associated with body damage and injury; the site of the bleeding is usually visible and attempts can be made to control it. This does not happen with menstrual bleeding: no injury precedes it, its location is deep within a vulnerable part of the body that cannot be seen, and it cannot be stopped. The loss of control is total. One usually cannot start it, stop it, or see where it's coming from. It is therefore not surprising that menstruation should play so decisive a role in psychic functioning. It encompasses and reawakens aspects of early ego control over the body, the libidinal drives, object relations, and, most crucial, psychosexual identification—all areas of extreme conflict for anorexics.

PENIS ENVY

Deutsch (1944) commented,

> Unless the genital trauma has been greatly intensified by individual experiences, it is mastered by the feminine tendencies mobilized by the first menstruation. Emotional contents of a decidedly feminine character take the place of the penis wish and penis envy. Fears of defloration and rape, mobilized and strengthened by the onset of menstruation, accompany the young girl's sexual fantasies at this time. Menstruation becomes a decisive experience in this process of feminization. (p. 171)

In the anorexic female, the conflict over penis envy has not been fully resolved and is acted out repeatedly in the symbolic loss of penile equivalents (muscle tissue). The patient is unable to accept the adult femininity that menstruation represents. The persistence of penis envy and its denial takes the form of the continual loss of penises through loss of body tissue which resonates with the inability to accept a feminine identification so intimately wound up in the menstrual process.

Mushatt (1980) commented on the multidetermined aspects of constipation and defecation in anorexic patients. He stated that defecation can express riddance and destruction of the object, as well as separation. Constipation can express holding on to introjected objects and retention of attachments.

Menstruation and amenorrhea also have multiple symbolic representations. In addition to arousing conflicts over pregnancy, castration fears, penis envy, and destructive fantasies, menstrual bleeding can represent loss and separation, loss of a part of oneself, loss of "the child" in oneself, and separation from one's childhood attachment to the mother. Amenorrhea can serve to retain the childlike self-image and childhood attachments—to deny maturation. Menstruation can symbolize deprivation or depression over not being pregnant. During pregnancy, some women identify with the fetus in order to vicariously achieve symbiotic reunion with their own mother; menstruation can disrupt such a fantasy and confront these women with the reality of their separation from mother.

Ritvo (1977) stated that the pubertal girl's feelings and behavior around menarche are strongly influenced by her ego's response to the original pregenital and phallic instinctual strivings, and by her object relationships with the parents. Her initial reaction may be shame, fright, and disgust, followed by reaction formations. Girls with unresolved penis envy and feelings of castration are predisposed to develop severe body-image problems in puberty. How an adolescent resolves body-image problems determines later sexual pleasure. The sexually mature adolescent body serves as a focus for the acceptance of femininity and sexuality, with its attendant conflicts over pregnancy and childbirth. Anorexics deal with these conflict-laden issues by starving themselves into a regressive preadolescent body image, renouncing femininity with amenorrhea, creating infantile dependency through illness, denying threatening aggression via helplessness, and losing the symbolic sought-after penis with tissue loss.

ADOLESCENT CONCEALMENT, SECRETIVENESS, AND POPULARITY

The concealment and secretiveness that Ritvo (1977) stated has its roots in pregenital anality, with strong repression of the absence of a penis, is also associated with a more pronounced concealment of masturbatory activities and fantasies in girls than in boys.

This secretiveness, beginning with the earlier needs to conceal the loss of the penis and the body damage associated with it, is reactivated in early adolescence. Clannish, secretive behavior is commonplace. Young adolescent girls congregate to discuss secrets arising out of sublimated forms of the concealment of the menarche and menstruation, which hark back to the earlier penis envy. The early adolescent reaction formations to the menstrual soiling, and its associated genital damage and penis envy, take the form of a preoccupation with physical appearance and popularity. To be popular, sought after, and worthwhile is to undo the feelings of shame, worthlessness, and damage so closely linked to the menstrual process. Thus, the concern with beauty, cliques, and popularity contests is much more frequent among adolescent females than it is among their male peers. At the same time, the highly critical, catty, and derogatory remarks that characterize the behavior of some adolescent girls represent an attempt to deny and project damage onto others. Adolescents who do not deny and project defects onto others are often severely self-condemnatory. The defects are related to conflicts over menstruation, body image, and identity.

Clinical Material

CASE EXAMPLE   Anorexia Developed in the Course of Analysis

Diane, age 12, came from an intelligent, talented, but highly neurotic family. Both parents were musicians, and while the father was more recognized and gave concerts throughout the country and abroad, the mother was just as actively concerned about her career and was often jealous of her husband's success. As a result, the patient was neglected as a child, her care being delegated to maids. When the mother was available to the patient, her narcissism prevented her from intuitively and sensitively responding to her daughter's needs. As might be expected when the family was together, there was a great deal of bickering about music and careers. The mother suffered a depression following the birth of the first son and required psychiatric treatment. There was no difficulty with the second son, but the mother again became depressed following the patient's birth. This depression lasted for a number of years and interfered with the relationship to the patient and with the mother's career. When depressed, the mother became withdrawn and uninterested in the children. At the time of the patient's analysis, the older brother had a history of antisocial behavior and drug usage and had been in treatment for two years.

Diane was a reflective girl who attempted to deal with her feelings of marked inferiority, obsequiousness, thoughts that her personality was defective, and feelings of physical ugliness. In previous sessions she had described in detail why she felt that companions thought little of her. Her personality wasn't good. She wasn't comfortable around friends. She couldn't speak well with them. She felt that her hair was too thin, her ears too big, her face too square, her lips too big, her cheeks too fat, her skin damaged by little pimples. Her eyes were the wrong color, her neck too short, and her thighs too fat.

In actuality she was a very attractive young girl whose described blemishes were almost nonexistent. She was poised, verbal, and had a great deal of charm.

A number of weeks later, bringing up her physical defects and her concern over her unattractiveness, she stated that she needed to get rid of her "flab," slapping the outside of her thighs. "They're too fat." As she spoke about her discomfort with herself, she suddenly slapped her puffed-out cheeks, deflating them. The motion was the same as the slapping of the thighs. She then attempted to change the size of her abdomen by controlling her muscles. She returned to her preoccupation with her thighs with the comment, "I'd like to get a knife and cut off the flab just like that, and sew it up, but it would look ugly."

On the next day she returned to the same theme. She was feeling contented because the boys were paying attention to her by chasing her and her friends. She punched her thighs, stating that they were too "blobby," too fat, and then hit the inside of her thighs. "If I exercise I can lose weight, but I can't get the blobs off my thighs." She again pursed her mouth, filled it with air, and slapped her cheeks to expel the air. "My face and thighs are too fat. The rest is OK, but my face has those little pimples and I can't get rid of them." She paused momentarily and, with her hand resting between her legs, put her finger at the center of her genitals. A moment later she again commented that she needed an operation to remove the fat. It should be noted that this behavior and ideation were reflective of fantasy and not indicative of any reality-based decision. Then she said:

> When I read *Seventeen Magazine* I'd like to be a model and be thin but I can't be pretty. . . . My arms are all right. The chart in the magazine said that they are supposed to be twice the size of my wrists, so that's OK. My waist is the right size, and my thighs are supposed to be five inches smaller than my waist, and they are, but they are still too fat.

The clinical material reveals a correlation between feelings of inferiority and physical ugliness, and conflict over sexual identification. It seems plausible to conclude that feeling ugly is related to feeling fat. Diane was primarily concerned with the lumps on the external upper thighs that were displaced from the inner thighs, and this preoccupation was revealed in her behavior. Additional displacements were primarily to the head, especially to the cheeks. She acted out in fantasy a castration of the fat cheeks, which were alluded to in comments about the thighs. The overconcern about minute blemishes on the cheeks represented a miniaturization of the conflict previously represented by the fat thighs. Here, too, she was concerned with something that was ugly and protruding and had to be eliminated. Lesser conflict was represented by concern over the size of wrists, arms, etc. In total, however, it represented ambivalent feelings about being female.

It is of interest that Diane felt that her thighs were too fat, even though by her own measurements they corresponded to normality. It suggests that a disturbance in body image reflects an attempt to deal with unconscious conflict and is related to ambivalent feelings about accepting a feminine identity and its suggested castrated state. Diane's unconscious feelings about wanting a penis— represented symbolically by the muscle tissue of the thighs, arms, body, and face—were countered by conscious desires to rid herself of this tissue. The intensity of the conflict and its attempted unconscious solution overrode her conscious perceptions of her body. In this context her attitudes were quite similar to those of anorexic patients who also reveal distortions in body image, see themselves as too fat during emaciated states, and deal with their unconscious perception of fat not only as a pregnancy but as a phallus.

This conflict was even more graphically illustrated by a very emaciated 19-year-old anorexic patient who would get very panicky any time that she felt that she was putting on the slightest amount of weight. She would squeeze the muscle mass on her legs and arms and want to get rid of it. She was especially distressed by the tissue on the inner side of her thighs and would squeeze it, complaining that she "couldn't stand it hanging there" between her legs and "had to get rid of it." This same conflict was symbolized by, and displaced onto, other parts of the body. While, on one level, the weight loss represented the loss of feminine curves and the conflict over a feminine identity, on a deeper level, it also seemed to symbolize the loss of multiple displaced penises (various parts of the body), which stemmed from unresolved penis envy.

Six months later, Diane began her session by describing how she lost her ring, but then found it lying in the grass. She went on to comment that, during the previous year, she had lost five rings and three bracelets and that her mother was very annoyed with her because some of them had been expensive. She just didn't know why she kept losing them.

She associated further to attempts to lose weight; she was back on a diet. During the spring, she had felt too fat and had asked the pediatrician if it would be all right to lose some weight. He had assented, but had cautioned her that since she was 5'2" and weighed 102 lbs., she shouldn't lose more than 5 lbs. Instead of losing 5 lbs., she had eaten a lot of food while visiting her cousin in Arizona and thought that she had gained 5 lbs. Her girlfriend was 5'2" and had weighed 95 lbs. when her mother asked her to go on a diet; now she weighed 91 lbs. The mother wanted her to stop, but the daughter wanted to keep going.

The analyst then commented about the diet that Diane had described and wondered why she was on a diet of figs and lettuce for breakfast, and salad and skim milk for lunch, without even knowing what she weighed. She replied that she weighed 107 lbs. and needed to be thinner for gymnastics. "We won gymnast ribbons yesterday. We got blue, I mean pink, ribbons." As Diane was unable to associate any meaning to the slip, the analyst suggested that it might stand for male and female, and that her slip might indicate her preference for being a male. She denied this possibility, although on previous occasions she had volunteered some jealousy of men, and the idea that they had it better than women—they were more appreciated, less gossipy, less preoccupied with popularity worries, and more confident.

The analyst attempted to connect the preoccupation with weight loss to questions of her psychosexual identification, suggesting that maybe losing weight and the curves of a female might have something to do with wanting to be thin and more like a male. She associated to the attitudes and behavior of her two brothers, stating that her older brother was always nasty and critical of her. She felt that both brothers acted as if they were better than she was.

About eight weeks later, she returned to the same theme, which now included the conflict over menstruation. She spoke about all the birthday presents she had received from her parents and two brothers, and said she didn't deserve them. She added that she had her period and couldn't stand it. She hated it and didn't wish to discuss it. She described feeling very guilty about necking with her new boyfriend. She'd like to join the Hari Krishnas, but "it's a stupid religion." She thought about the Moonies, but they are a "dumb, sick bunch," too. She stated that, "As a Catholic, I want to be a part of Jesus." The analyst suggested that maybe she felt that she was having trouble controlling herself and that these organizations that exercised strict controls over a person's behavior might help her to control herself. She acknowledged the comment with half-hearted agreement, adding over and over, "I want to be different, I want to be different." The analyst commented that she might also think that she would be different by being male. "Possibly, I know that I told you before, but guys have difficulties, too. They get pressured to drink and smoke." When the analyst replied, "But they don't get periods," she responded angrily, very upset and crying, that she didn't want to talk about it.

The following day, she reported receiving an elephant pin, her favorite symbol, which she happily fastened to her shirt. She described how contented she had felt all day in school and alluded to the pin as the source of the satisfaction. She again spoke about the vulnerabilities, sensitivities, and insecurities of her girlfriends, of how easily they were slighted and how little it took to upset them—e.g., the lack of a greeting, not being recognized immediately as they joined the groups.

"I'm still too fat," she stated as she hit her stomach repeatedly with the palm of her hand. "Yesterday, you probably felt grouchy because of your period," the analyst commented. "Yes, I hate it, I hate it, I can't stand the cramps, and we're not going to talk about it," she said loudly, beginning to cry. The analyst added that they didn't have to talk about it, but if she could get rid of the cramps by talking about it, she would feel much better.

> Yes, I know, but I don't want to get rid of my fat and my periods by becoming an anorexic. A girl in school did that, but I don't want to stop eating. I told you I don't want to discuss it. All my girlfriends hate it, and I hate it most of all, washing the blood out, the stains. I don't like to wear the pads. My pants don't fit. Why do I have to have all these fucking things?

The analyst attempted to interject, "But if you're so unhappy with it," but was interrupted with a violent outburst of crying and anger. "I don't care, I can't stand it, I'm not going to talk about it, I hate you, you bastard!" In reply to a casual comment of the analyst noting her annoyance, she laughed, "I sure insult you, and I curl up in the chair. Why do you think that I go through all this if I don't want to get better?" [still crying]

In the following session, she offhandedly commented that she had gotten rid of the cramps just after yesterday's session. She continued talking about the discomfort of her period and all the mess that it produced. The analyst suggested that it was not only the physical complication that troubled her, but also the inner mental worry that accompanied the menstruation. He added that, all during her life, whenever she had bled, it always had meant that she had an injury or an accident, but that now, when she menstruated, the bleeding was normal and healthy. She immediately interjected, "It isn't bleeding, it's not bleeding, it's a *period*. If you bleed, it means that there is something wrong inside. Besides, none of my friends talk about it as bleeding. It's just a period." In discussing this further, she refused to acknowledge that menstruation was accompanied by bleeding and was unwilling to continue the interchange, remaining quiet, troubled, and baleful for the last few minutes of the session. Her response validated the assumption that menstruation is a manifestation of inner body damage, castration, and injury. She and her friends were unwilling to acknowledge the possibility of normal, healthy bleeding and accepted the process without acknowledging its components.

The following spring, she broke up with her boyfriend after an argument about how far they should go sexually. That summer, she went on an 8-week teen tour of Canada. Returning to analysis in the fall, she described how hard she had tried to lose weight during the summer, but to no avail. She then added that she had missed her periods for June, July, and August. The patient remained amenorrheic for seven months although there was no actual weight loss. She became increasingly preoccupied with food and her weight, thought that she was fat, attempted to diet unsuccessfully, and jogged four miles daily. The anorexic symptoms subsided during the course of the analysis, and her periods resumed with additional insight about her conflicts over femininity.

Discussion

Diane's unconscious attitudes about losing weight and about menstruation are not atypical for adolescent females and tend to suggest that those with anorexia nervosa fall on one end of a continuum that includes many other adolescents and women with similar, but less intense, conflicts.

While this chapter has focused primarily on the intrapsychic conflict surrounding the menstrual process, it should be recognized that parental attitudes about femininity and menstruation can affect the child's attitude during early development, as well as during adolescence. C. Karol (personal communication) described one case in which a parent suddenly rejected the daughter's femininity. In response to her first period, the daughter became very excited and put on her mother's lipstick and rouge, and borrowed her high heels. The father became enraged at the sight of what he perceived as wanton behavior, and angrily ordered the daughter to remove "that paint" and take off those shoes. The daughter's periods ceased.

In light of the underlying dynamics of the menstrual process, it seems evident that any therapy should have as one of its goals the clarification of these multiple conflicts if the patient is to achieve normal functioning in sexual behavior, the menstrual process, feminine identity, pregnancy, and motherhood.

SUMMARY

An attempt was made to correlate starvation and amenorrhea in anorexia nervosa. It was noted that the intertwining of menstruation with anal excretory functioning contributes to anal sadistic character traits in anorexia. The anorexic's conflict over menstruation reactivates penis envy, and the ambivalence is expressed in tissue loss: a series of symbolic penises. Menstruation is disturbed or absent in anorexia and stands for an unwillingness to accept femininity.

Treatment goals should be directed toward correcting major intrapsychic conflict rather than just resolving its symptomatic consequences (e.g., not eating, not menstruating). Otherwise, the patient is left with major disabilities associated with her ability to enjoy her sexuality and feminine identity. In addition, her capacity to deal with pregnancy and motherhood will be impaired.

18
Psychodynamic and/or Psychopharmacologic Treatment of Bulimic Anorexia Nervosa

C. PHILIP WILSON, M.D.

The contributors to this volume feel that psychoanalysis or analytic psychotherapy represent the most comprehensive approach to the treatment of restrictor and bulimic anorexics because their central focus is on the resolution of the underlying personality disorder. It may be appropriate in some cases to use medication, particularly antidepressants, to treat restrictive and bulimic anorexics. Such appropriate situations might include life-threatening electrolyte imbalances, severe states of starvation, treatment stalemates, or cases where cost and therapist availability are problems. However, the use of drugs may be a trade-off with potentially disadvantageous consequences that are explored in this chapter.

In their eclectic volume on the psychotherapy of anorexia nervosa and bulimia, Garner and Garfinkel (1985) conclude that medication remains a controversial issue. Studies of chlorpromazine, cryptoheptadine, lithium, bromocrytine, naloxone, and cannabis showed that no single drug has a generalized application in the treatment of anorexia nervosa. Garner and Garfinkel note that the role of anticonvulsants in the treatment of bulimia is unclear. They emphasize that, of all drug treatments, the role of antidepressants remains the most hotly debated.

There have been an increasing number of reports of the use of antidepressants, particularly in the treatment of bulimic anorexics (Brotman et al. 1984, Jonas 1983, McGrath et al. 1981, Mendels 1983, Pope et al. 1982, Pope 1983, Pope and Hudson 1984, Sabine et al. 1983, Walsh et al. 1982, 1983, 1984). In view of this development, I shall (1) explore the psychodynamics and etiology of the bulimic anorexic's depression, (2) outline our psychoanalytic technique with bulimics and document the psychoanalytic resolution of depressed affects in the course of treatment, and (3) describe in detail the dangers, risks, and consequences of the use of medication.

The rationale for the use of antidepressant medications is that in some cases they achieve dramatic resolution of symptoms which seem related to the finding of affective disorder in the family (Pope and Hudson 1984, pp. 54–56, 89–107). On the other hand, Altshuler and Weiner (1985) seriously quesion the research methodology that links restrictor and bulimic anorexia nervosa to a family history of major depression. Whatever genetic, constitutional factors there are in bulimic anorexics (Pope and Hudson 1984) they do not preclude psychoanalytic treatment. Some of our cases would have been diagnosed as "endogenous depression"; however, they were analyzable. The parallel may be with asthmatics, some of whom have a constitutional genetic allergic predispositon. Such asthmatic patients can be successfully analyzed. After analysis they may still test positively for allergies, but they no longer experience asthmatic attacks in conflictual situations (Sperling 1978, pp. 184–185).

Anorexia nervosa is a generic term that includes both the restrictor and bulimic syndromes. The restrictor, part of whose ego structure resembles that of the compulsive neurotic, overcontrols both the impulse to gorge and other impulses because of punitive superego demands and intact ego controls. The bulimic, whose ego structure is an admixture of hysterical and compulsive traits, has the same fear of being fat. Because the bulimic's defective ego is unable to carry out the punitive strictures of an archaic superego, the bulimic is unable to contain the impulse to gorge as well as other impulse gratifications. In this chapter, I focus on the bulimic anorexics.

It is a central hypothesis of my research (1980, 1982, pp. 9–27) that restrictor and bulimic anorexia symptoms are the result of an overwhelming fear of being fat, which has been determined primarily by an identification with a parent or parents who have a similar fear, and that anorexia (fat phobia) is secondarily reinforced by the general fear of being fat which afflicts most women and many men in our culture.

My central purpose here is to emphasize that bulimic anorexics suffer from an impulse disorder (pp. 10, 18, 115). Their fat phobia masks an addictive personality disorder (pp. 26–28). The goal of psychoanalytic treatment of the disorder is to strengthen the patients' ego so that they can tolerate both realistic and neurotic depression. Precipitous relief of depression by means of medication can lead to a loss of motivation for treatment. As noted by others (Sperling, Hogan, Mintz, Wilson; pp. 2–3, 55–56, 60–61, 77–80), if the etiological unconscious conflicts have not been resolved, bulimic symptomatology may be replaced by other psychosomatic symptoms such as asthma (Mintz, p. 237), or by other neurotic symptom formation, acting out, and/or suicidal impulses. A psychological addiction to medication can develop in such addiction-prone patients. Bulimic patients in "hyper states" may use any available substance, including medication, for suicidal purposes. This has been particularly noted in their overdosing themselves with laxatives (Wilson, Chapter 8). Other complications are discussed in the case material.

THE COMPONENTS OF DEPRESSION IN BULIMIC ANOREXIA NERVOSA

Sours (1980) believed that the depression of the restrictor anorexic was related to a discrepancy between the ego and ego ideal which resulted in shame, humiliation, inadequacy, weakness, and inferiority. In contrast, he thought that the bulimic was more apt to experience depression stemming from the oedipal phase, with guilt and moral masochism generated by strict superego demands. In my experience, and in that of my colleagues (Wilson, p. 36; M. Sperling, p. 81, *1959* ref.), the depression of bulimic anorexics is induced by unremitting pressure on the ego of repressed and unsublimated, aggressive and libidinal drive derivatives, conflicts, and fantasies that have both preoedipal and oedipal sources.

The psychodynamics of the personality disorder that underlies the depressive symptomatology of bulimia are complex. With the emergence of any of the conflicts described below, a patient may manifest symptoms of depression.

PSYCHODYNAMICS OF BULIMIA

An unresolved preoedipal fixation on the mother contributes to difficulty in psychosexual development and to the intensity of the oedipal conflict. Bulimic anorexia nervosa, fat phobia, can be considered a specific pathological outcome of unresolved oedipal conflicts in a child whose preoedipal relationship to the mother has predisposed him or her to this particular reaction, under precipitating circumstances.

The genetic influences on this complex are parental conflicts about weight and food specifically, and about aggressive and libidinal expression generally. Such neurotic and/or addictive parents are, in addition, perfectionistic. Significantly, they deny the impact on the developing child of their exhibitionistic toilet, bedroom, and related behaviors. Other psychogenetic influences on this complex are cultural, social, and medical, as are secondary identifications with women and/or men who share the fear-of-being-fat complex.

The terror of loss of control (i.e., of becoming fat) lies in a conscious fear of overeating and in an unconscious fear of incorporating body parts; smearing or eating feces; bleeding to death, mutilating or being mutilated; masturbating and/or becoming nymphomaniacal, both possibly leading to orgastic pleasure. All these feared drive eruptions are displaced onto the fear of being fat, with a struggle to contain impulses to gorge, a giving in to voraciousness, and then an attempt at self-punishment and undoing by vomiting and/or the use of laxatives. In the bulimic, there is an attempt by the ego to suppress and repress libidinal and aggressive fantasies, drives, and impulses. There is a parallel attempt by the ego to surrender to these impulses and to masochistic behavior which also expresses self-punishment and undoing.

From a structural point of view, considerations of the part played by the ego are central. In the preoedipal years, the ego of the bulimic anorexia-prone (fat-phobic) child splits. One part develops in a pseudonormal fashion; cognitive functions, the self-observing part of the ego, adaptive capacities, and other ego functions appear to operate normally. While the restrictor anorexics in childhood are most often described as "perfect" and have excellent records in school, the bulimic anorexics have more evidence of disobedience and rebellion at home and school. In adolescence they show more antisocial behavior, sexual promiscuity and addiction. Repression, denial, displacement, externalization, and projection occur in the fear-of-being-fat complex. In many cases, conflicts are also displaced onto habits such as thumb-sucking, enuresis, encopresis, nail-biting, head-banging, and hair-pulling. In other cases, there is a concomitant displacement and projection of conflict onto actual phobic objects. In some patients, bulimia anorexia alternates with other psychosomatic disease syndromes, such as ulcerative colitis (Sperling, pp. 60–61), migraine (Hogan, p. 146), and asthma (Mintz, p. 237). The split in the ego manifests itself in the intense, psychotic-like denial of the displaced wishes, conflicts, and fantasies. In other words, the split-off neurotic part of the personality is denied in both the fear-of-being-fat complex and in the bulimic symptoms.

The conflicts and defenses associated with bulimics appear at each maturational and libidinal phase. Conflicts in separation-individuation (Mushatt 1975, 1980, 1982) are paramount but are denied by both the parents and the developing child. Normal adaptive conflict is avoided and denied. Many parents of bulimics raise their children in an unreal, overprotected world. Perfectionistic parents impair the decision-making functions of the ego with infantilizing intrusions into every aspect of the child's life. In each case a focus of therapy is on the pregenital object relations.

Unlike M. Sperling (pp. 71–72), my colleagues and I (p. 4, pp. 263–314) include males in the diagnostic category of restrictor and bulimic anorexia nervosa. Mintz and Walsh (1983) have shown that male bulimic anorexics have oedipal and preoedipal fixations and unresolved problems in separation-individuation, severe latent homosexual conflicts and a feminine identification, and the same fear-of-being-fat complex seen in the females in identification with a mother's and/or a father's fear-of-being-fat.

PSYCHOANALYTIC TECHNIQUE IN THE TREATMENT OF BULIMIC ANOREXIA NERVOSA

Whether the patient is seen twice a week in analytic psychotherapy or five times a week in analysis, the same psychodynamics and technique of interpretation are used, with modifications that are determined by the frequency of sessions.

Therapeutic technique has to be adapted to the varying defenses of the ego. The bulimic patients resort to acting out, rationalization, denial, withholding, and lying more intensely and more persistently than do the restrictors. There are of course many varieties of ego structure in bulimic anorexic patients. Accordingly, technique varies with the degree of regression encountered, and with the individual style and experience of the therapist. Most of my colleagues and I tend to see the patient vis-a-vis in the first diadic phase of treatment. However, some bulimic anorexics can be analyzed along more classical lines with the couch being used from the beginning.

The technique of interpretation is determined by multiple factors such as the transference and the quality of the patient's object relations. A crucial consideration is the split in the ego of the bulimic anorexic and the extent to which the split is comprehended by the self-observing functions of the ego. The first phase of therapy involves making the healthier part of the ego aware of the split-off, primitive-impulse-dominated part of the ego and its modes of functioning.

Typical defenses and character qualities of the bulimic anorexic are: (1) denial and splitting, (2) belief in magic, (3) feelings of omnipotence, (4) demand that things and people be all perfect—the alternative is to be worthless, (5) need to control, (6) displacement and projection, (7) intense ambivalence, (8) masochistic perfectionism, particularly relating to conflicts around aggression, (9) a pathological ego ideal of beautiful peace and love, and (10) a fantasy of a perfect, conflict-free mother-child symbiosis.

The bulimic anorexic also makes extensive use of the defense of projective identification (Bion 1956, Boyer and Giovacchini 1980, Carpinacci et al. 1963, Carter and Rinsley 1977, Cesia 1963, 1973, Giovacchini 1975, Grinberg 1972, 1976, 1979, M. Klein, 1955, Ogden 1978, Perestrello 1963, D. Rosenfeld and Mordo 1973, H. A. Rosenfeld 1952, Searles 1965). Unacceptable aspects of the bulimic's own personality—impulses, self-images, superego introjects—are projected onto other people, particularly the therapist, with a resulting identification based on these projected self-elements. The extreme psychotic-like denial of conflict of the bulimic anorexic is produced by primitive projective identification onto others of archaic, destructive superego introjects.

Sperling (1978) noted that part of the conflicts of restrictor and bulimic anorexic are conscious. Conscious withholding, conscious rationalization, distortion, and lying are all characteristic behaviors of the bulimic anorexic. The lying and stealing are instituted, basically, by rebellion against primitive archaic superego demands for absolute perfection. It is repeatedly necessary to interpret the projection of the archaic superego introject onto the therapist and other objects. This pseudopsychopathic behavior is analyzable (Hogan, pp. 208–210; Wilson, pp. 186–189).

A key to therapeutic technique with bulimics is translating the anxiety aroused by the patients' self-destructive behavior into interpretations of their masochism. Thus, the persistent interpretation of defenses such as denial and rationalization can bring them to accept responsibility for the sometimes irreversible tooth and gum damage they have caused and/or the life-threatening secondary effects of their bulimic habits, such as low potassium blood levels.

TECHNIQUE IN THE DIADIC PHASE

The following problems and techniques of interpretation are used in the first diadic phase of treatment. (1) These patients usually do not free associate, as also happens in the analyses of children and of patients with character disorders (Boyer and Giovacchini 1980). (2) The therapist therefore takes an active stance, frequently using construction and reconstruction. (3) Behavioral responses can be interpreted. (4) Dreams have to used in the context of the patient's psychodynamics. (5) First, one interprets the masochism of these patients—their archiac superego and the guilt they experience in admitting any conflict. (6) Next, one interprets defenses against facing masochistic behavior; then, when the ego is healthier, one interprets defenses against aggressive impulses. (7) Such interpretations are inexact and frequently are not confirmed by the patients' associations. (8) For these patients who have an archaic, punitive superego and a relatively weak ego, the analyst provides auxiliary ego strength and a rational superego (Boyer 1980, Wilson 1982, 1971, p. 185). (9) Interpretations should be made in a firm, consistent manner (Boyer 1980). (10) With such patients, the analyst needs to have authority.

Because bulimic anorexic patients, in their projective identifications, can pick up almost imperceptible nuances in the tone of voice, facial expression, movements and even feelings of the analyst, they provoke intense counter-transference reactions (Sperling 1967, Wilson, pp. 189-191).

Another special technique in the analysis of bulimic anorexics is to demonstrate to the patient his or her need for immediate gratification (the impulse disorder, i.e., the primary narcissism) early in treatment (Sperling 1967, 1978, Wilson, p. 18 Hogan, p. 158-159). Thus the patient is shown that the symptoms are manifestations of a split-off, impulsive part of the ego (i.e., the fear-of-being-fat complex).

A useful acronym for the technique of interpretation in the initial phase of therapy is MAD. M = masochism, A = aggression, D = diadic transference.

The analyst can begin to interpret triadic oedipal material only when the patient's archaic superego has been modified, when the ego has matured so that there is a capacity to tolerate libidinal and aggressive conflicts, and when there has been a shift from part object relations toward whole object relations.

It is important that the psychiatrist be in charge of the treatment process (Sperling 1978, Wilson, Hogan, Mintz, p. 186, pp. 197-198, pp. 315-324). A split transference with the medical specialist can vitiate treatment. Hospitalization should be reserved for true emergencies.

As with other psychosomatic symptoms, when bulimic anorexic symptoms subside, acting out increases. Patience is essential in the analysis of bulimic patients, whose habits, at their most primitive level, mask preverbal conflicts and traumas. Impulsive, psychotic, and psychosomatic patients, all of whom have preoedipal conflicts, have the means to communicate the impact and effects of their early preverbal traumas (Wilson 1968, 1968c, 1971, 1981).

One must be intuitive about when to confront patients regarding their withholding of relevant information about binging. One should not ask about it constantly or demand that the habit be given up. Instead, the therapist should point out the reason for interrupting a habit (i.e., to uncover fantasies and conflicts that it masks). Bulimic patients, like those who are obese, want and believe in magical control and want to stop the habit without analyzing it. The defensive purposes of habits, which in these patients mask suicidal and homicidal impulses and conflicts, have to be repeatedly interpreted. If the therapist does not actively confront patients with the meanings of their symptoms and habits that serve defensive purposes, the symptoms and habits will become more intense, and the patients' negative transference will be split off and expressed in exacerbations of symptoms and habits, while the patient will manifest pseudo-respect and compliant behavior in their verbal communications.

THE RELATIONSHIP OF BULIMIA
TO THE ADDICTIONS
AND THE CHILDHOOD HABITS

To treat bulimic anorexics effectively, it is necessary to understand the impulse disorders, the addictive personality structure (Wurmser 1980, Wilson 1981; p. 26), and the habits of childhood which are frequently the developmental forerunners of bulimia. I have emphasized that bulimia is a food phobia, an addiction (p. 26). In bulimics I have noted (p. 18) the frequent occurrence of childhood thumb-sucking, nail–biting, cuticle–chewing and eating, head–banging, hair–pulling and eating, and other impulse disorders such as encopresis and enuresis. Some patients report no habits and a childhood history of excessive good behavior. Therapy, however, uncovers isolated episodes or phases of rebelliousness. The ego makes use of the same defenses in its struggle with a childhood habit or a childhood impulse disorder as it does later on in efforts to cope with bulimic anorexia nervosa or other eating disorders. Thus the defenses of denial, splitting, displacement and externalization, and conscious withholding and lying are deeply ingrained in the ego structure of the bulimic anorexic. In some cases we see a chaotic ego structure, as when a childhood habit coexists with bulimia and an addiction.

In my research on the fear-of-being-fat complex (Wilson 1980, 1982; Chapter 1), it has usually been found that this fear becomes intense in adolescence, the time when bulimia most often occurs. The fear of giving in to a habit, or not being able to control it, is the forerunner of the fear of being fat. When a habit or an addiction is interrupted patients are afraid of becoming fat, of overeating, and also of losing control in other ways, such as losing their temper and/or acting out.

BODY IMAGE

In the fear of being fat (anorexia), the basic conflict is rooted in a massive preoedipal repression of sadomasochistic oral-phase conflicts. These conflicts have been elaborated by the ego with new defensive structures at each subsequent libidinal and maturational phase of development. It is the surface of the mother's breast, and by extension her figure, that has been projected in the bulimic anorexic's body image. The fear of being fat reflects the terror of oral-sadistic incorporation of the breast of mother and later of other objects (Wilson, Chapter 1).

A few restrictors and a number of bulimics do not evidence a clearcut body image disturbance (Mintz, p. 90), although they are all fat phobic. In these cases the ego is healthier and the psychopathology primarily oedipal.

PATHOLOGICAL WEEPING AND
BULIMIC DEPRESSION

The vicissitudes of the analysis of depressed affects in bulimia can be viewed in terms of what Greenacre (1945) described as pathological weeping. In the analysis of certain bulimics and addictive patients (Wilson 1981), I was able to confirm Greenacre's findings that pathological "stream" weeping can be a substitute for an expression of fantasies of male urination displaced upward to the eye and the lachrymal system. I was also able to confirm her finding of an extreme body-phallus identification. As analysis makes these conflicts conscious and they are worked through in the transference neurosis, pathological weeping, of which silent tearing is one example, is replaced by normal crying and sobbing with appropriate affects. Of course, with many bulimics crying has an exhibitionistic aspect and they have learned to act out emotions, a behavior that has to be analyzed.

CLINICAL MATERIAL

The following clinical material highlights the emergence and the analysis of depressed affects in the treatment of a bulimic anorexic.

The patient was a 26-year-old single woman living with her family and working as an editorial assistant in a publishing firm. In the fifteenth session of her analysis she was late to her session for the first time. Her associations were that she missed the bus because she had been enjoying talking to her friend. She thought about not being efficient and not allowing time to get to appointments. She also does not take care of things; she lost her bag when she went skiing. She procrastinates on sending in her medical health insurance forms that will get her payment for sessions. She realizes that she does not do the things she should do. Her car needs to be taken in for an oil change, but she does not do it. She knows she waits until her parents and others get impatient with her. The interpretation was made that chores and details of living are not exciting; that one part of her wants immediate pleasure and resents tasks; that it was more fun to talk to her friend than to come for her session.

Her associations were to childhood: her father was a perfectionist who would make up chores for her to do. He would save up his anger when she did not do the things he wanted her to do, then he would explode. "Even now when I'm an adult," she said, "he yells at me." The interpretation was made that she keeps most of her anger to herself, but that she has a safety valve for it: her binging. The patient said, "It is funny I don't think about what I am doing when I binge." The interpretation was made that her strict conscience does not let her know about things that she is angry about and that she feels she has to get rid of conflicts by binging. At this point, for the first time, she became upset and cried. She said that she had never realized before how unhappy she was.

In subsequent sessions her associations and dreams unfolded aspects of her neurosis, her dependence on her parents, her agoraphobia, and various age appropriate realities that she avoided (such as having a bank account and check book of her own). A number of dreams revealed her wish to be back in high school, to remain a teenager with no adult responsibilities. She talked about age and time; she hated the idea of anyone growing old; she refused to accept the possibility of her parents ever dying. As she faced more and more of her conflicts she also began to exert will power to interrupt her binging. The frequency of her binging decreased to every other day from once or twice a day.

The underlying depression that is masked by bulimic symptoms began to emerge. She cried in sessions and expressed hopeless feelings. She wondered if anything could be done for her; and asked if analysis would be forever. She had suicidal ideas, and was aware of wishes to not come to sessions. She wanted medication to relieve her depressed feelings. Interpretation was made focusing on her intolerance of anxiety and depression. She remembered that as a girl she used to be called "princess" by her father, that she was his favorite and knew she could get anything she wanted from him. Feelings of hopelessness emerged as she thought about the fact that she did not have many friends, and those few she had, she felt, used her. She talked of not wanting to grow up. She ignored the idea of people dying; her parents were ageless to her. Recently she had refused to go to the funeral of her cousin's grandmother. Her family was angry with her but told others that she was sick with the flu. Although she was 26, she said she thought of herself as a college girl and dreaded the idea of her next birthday. With further maturation of ego capacities to face and tolerate conflicts and affects, particularly depression, binging frequency decreased to once or twice a month.

DETERMINANTS OF DEPRESSION IN THIS CASE

What were the determinants of the bulimic depression in this case? They were:

1. Unhappiness because of failure to achieve mature object relations. The patient said that she had few friends and those she had took advantage of her.

2. Unhappiness and anger because of a failure to actualize magical narcissistic fantasies. The patient talked more and more of the princess in her and how much she wanted to dominate and control people.

3. Unhappiness at adaptive failure. Increasingly, she associated to ego deficits, forgetting and losing things, not being adult and responsible.

4. Unhappiness because of her failure to achieve normal separation-individuation from parents or parent surrogates. From the first sessions she spoke of her dependence on her parents, one manifestation of which was her inability to think of their death and her avoidance of funerals.

5. Unhappiness because of her failure to achieve the perfectionistic goals required by the archaic superego. She showed growing awareness of this problem in her references to her father's perfectionism and her inability to achieve control of herself.

6. Unhappiness because of neurotic guilt inflicted by the archaic superego, which legislates against the expression of libidinal or aggressive impulses and fantasies. She was becoming aware of this conflict in her reference to keeping most of her anger to herself when her father yelled at her.

THE ANALYSIS OF DEPRESSIVE AFFECTS IN BULIMIA

Emerging depression is described by Mintz (p. 95), who notes that some patients become depressed *after* they begin to eat. "The self-destructive conscience that dictated suffering by starvation shifts to an alternative form of criticism, suffering by feeling worthless and depressed." In the bulimic anorexic the ego cannot maintain the attempt at self-starvation. The patient submits to the impulse to gorge and then tries to expiate by vomiting. When this habit is interrupted, intense depression surfaces.

Mintz (p. 240), describing the analysis of a severely regressed bulimic anorexic, notes conflict about separation from the analyst as his summer vacation approached. The conflict caused by this separation promoted self-destructive discharge of aggressive impulses alternating with feelings of depression and anorexic symptoms (binging and vomiting). From the analysis of a 45-year-old man suffering from anorexia nervosa and bulimia, Mintz (p. 294) reports, "On occasion, he felt depressed which substituted for his self-destructive starving. The depressed feelings frightened him and threw him back into his preoccupation with eating. Eruptions of anger were substituted for by bursts of bulimia. A new symptom related to his perceived loss of control over his aggression." In this case (p. 295) the anorexia (and bulimia) appeared to be a substitute for depression and indeed alternated with depressive moods.

Freiman (p. 261) describes the emergence of depression in a bulimic anorexic in the initial phase of analysis. "For some time in a state of mild depression, the predominant theme of her sessions was that of self-evaluations and self-reproaches. She referred to herself as a sick, helpless individual. She felt her boss, father, mother and analyst thought of her as an inferior being." At first the patient responded to genetic and transference interpretations with denial, but then the masochistic defensive system that masked her anger (rage) gave way. Depression was replaced by aggressive thoughts, fantasies, and affects.

Mintz (pp. 112–113) also describes graphically the vicissitudes of depressed emotions in an adolescent girl. Thelma typically felt that she was both fat and ugly. When she ate, she felt fat in her stomach and thighs. (Most anorexics are particularly concerned with the belly and thighs.) She also stated that her face, arms, wrists, fingers, back, and toes were fat. All these body parts have symbolic meanings.

As she provided details of her gorging, she acknowledged that it seemed to happen when she was upset and that the upset feeling disappeared during the bulimic attack. It was pointed out that if she could think about what upset her, she might not have to gorge. One month later, Thelma reported that she had gone for three weeks without gorging, until the previous night, when she had binged and vomited. When she had defended her older brother's choice of a college, her mother had yelled at her, and hit her across the face. The mother had become enraged, had called her daughter stupid, and had told her to get out of the house. Thelma had run upstairs sobbing, overwhelmed by the feeling that no one cared for her. Later that night, she had eaten all the food in the icebox, felt stuffed, vomited, and then had eaten again and felt sick. The dorsum of her hand had bled from the violent thrust into her throat. She admitted that the gorging episode had eliminated the previous depression and sense of panic. Now, she hated herself for her eating and vomiting. She had hated her mother and then felt guilty, but after the vomiting she had felt "purged" and relieved. The vomiting seemed to serve both as a somatic eruption of anger and a punishment. The patient remained in treatment and eventually was able to resolve her conflicts.

Similarly, Hogan (p. 145) comments, "In each of the five patients presented here (a mixture of restrictor and bulimic anorexics) as the above defenses and impulses were reluctantly acknowledged and understood there were temporary rather severe depressions. These depressions frequently followed the relinquishment of the major anorexic (bulimic) symptomatology." I give an example (pp. 252–253) of emerging depression in a bulimic anorexic at a point in analysis when she was controlling her binging and facing her unresolved symbiotic need for her mother and the analyst in the transference.

My (pp. 30–31) emphasis is on the repression of emotions in the restrictor and bulimic anorexic family. The parents are intolerant of libidinal and aggressive manifestations and of depression in their children. They do not promote normal separation-individuation, i.e., the developing ego's capacity to tolerate depression.

With reference to sand symbolism in the dreams of anorexics (pp. 252–254). I observed that bulimic anorexics, in particular, are beset by conflicts about thirst as well as hunger. The xerostomia (dry mouth) they suffer from masks oral phase depression and the wish for the breast and mother's milk (love). Sand symbolizes oral phase thirst, and the repressed affects related to it, which emerge in the analysis of bulimic anorexics, range from anger, sadness, and despair (depression) to compassion, gratitude, and ecstasy (elation). This mixture of opposing affects reflects the ambivalence of the oral phase (Wilson 1981). Hogan (p. 145) notes the self-destructive behavior, aggression, and sadism that characterize the emergence of the underlying depression of bulimic anorexics.

THE USE OF MEDICATION
IN BULIMIC ANOREXICS

The incidence of bulimia seems to be increasing in the United States. A recent study (Halmi et al. 1981) reported that five percent of women seen at a university health service received a diagnosis of "bulimia." Another paper (Stangler et al. 1980) reported that 19 percent of college women had symptoms of bulimia.

It is the purpose of this volume to describe in detail specific new methods of psychodynamic therapy for bulimia that have been found to be successful. This book emphasizes that the crucial therapeutic problem is the treatment of the underlying masochistic personality disorder. The number of publications in the *Index Medicus* referring to *Bulimia* increased from 9 in 1979 to 51 in 1983. A recent double blind study by Walsh et al. (1984) concluded that while there were serious side-effects in patients, including orthostatic hypotension, diarrhea, sleep disturbances, and hypomania, a significant number of patients had a clearing or a reduction in bulimic symptoms and depression. The patients were, however, carefully selected; those who were addicted to drugs or who were suicidal were not included in the sample. A recent paper by Brotman, et al. (1984) noted, in contrast, that only 27 percent of the total group showed an antibinging and antidepressant response to drug trials. Although the data showed a relation between bulimia and depression, successful treatment of depression often did not eliminate binging activity and a reduction in binging was not always accompanied by a remission in depression. Although the study by Brotman et al. was retrospective and uncontrolled, the results confirm the complexity and chronicity of bulimia and its resistance to treatment. These authors point out that an exploration of the personality characteristics of bulimic patients would be helpful, because personality disorders appear to contribute to the chronicity of the syndrome.

A paradox emerges from a study such as that by Walsh et al. (1984). Where the clinician is forced to use medication it should only be used in relatively healthy bulimics who can adhere to a diet. Yet it is just these patients, with more mature egos and strong motivation, who should have the most favorable prognosis for psychotherapy or analysis.

The following clinical vignettes highlight negative aspects of medication:

MOTIVATION FOR INSIGHT VITIATED BY ANTIDEPRESSANT MEDICATION

A psychiatrist consulted me about a 30-year-old bulimic female. Her bulimia dated from adolescence when she put on weight to avoid sexual feelings with men that aroused anxiety. Unable to control her appetite, she gorged and vomited daily and was obsessed with fears of being fat and attempts to diet. Her personality was split into a pseudo-normal functioning ego and a compulsive fear-of-being-fat ego. The pseudo-normal functioning was manifested in excellent performance as a social worker. She was beloved at the agency where she worked long hours with problem children. In her other bulimic self, she was a kleptomaniac, stealing food, money, and articles of clothing.

The childhood history revealed an overworked mother and an alcoholic father who left the family when the patient was five years of age. During the initial phase of her analytic psychotherapy, as she came to recognize many of the conflicts that she avoided by her binging and vomiting, she decreased her binging, put on weight and became sexually attractive to men who started to ask her out. On these dates she experienced intense anxiety, and so resumed her bulimic habits. The therapist became discouraged by the regression and prescribed Nardil. The patient's chronic depressed feelings were relieved, however, her bulimic behavior was basically unchanged. The content of sessions was markedly changed, that is, she felt well and had little to talk about. The therapist asked her to go for consultation, but she refused. Therapeutic change was vitiated and a stalemate ensued.

MEDICATION PERCEIVED AS PUNISHMENT BY THE ARCHAIC SUPEREGO

The depression of bulimic anorexics masks suppressed and repressed libidinal and aggressive conflicts and affects, but the masked anger is central. Medication that relieves the depression also conveys the unconscious idea of a punitive stricture of the archaic superego, which prohibits rage and anger. For example, in another context (p. 247) I described a bulimic anorexic woman who, in the course of analysis, gave up her gorging and vomiting. She had come to realize that one of the meanings of her gorging was the achievement of an oral pregnancy and that to vomit meant giving birth through the mouth.

Her bulimic habits had become ego alien, but as occurs frequently in such patients, another psychosomatic symptom appeared; she developed a stiff neck. Her associations to the stiff neck were that it developed when her husband came home late from a poker game with his buddies. In the sessions she exploded with anger at me, at her husband, and at her father. The theme of her anger was her resentment of male authority. Her father had dominated the household; her mother had been the perfect wife submitting to father, and doing all the household chores including cooking and cleaning. The analytic fee and the frequency of sessions reminded her of her father's power. Her husband, she felt, got away with everything; he went out gambling while she washed dishes. At this point the patient laughed and said, "I guess part of me is a stiffnecked New England woman who does not approve of pleasure for anyone else or myself. Actually, I make myself my husband's slave. He has asked me to hire a cleaning woman and I really should arrange some singing lessons and get together with my friends instead of glueing myself to the house as my mother did."

The patient's stiff neck cleared up in the session, but it took many months of analysis for her to work through her anger and resentment towards men. She had the typical bulimic anorexic's devalued internal representation of the mother and a masochistic view of femininity. Considering that her repressed anger was a major component of her depressed moods, to relieve them with medication would not resolve the patient's underlying neurotic conflicts. On the other hand, she, like most bulimic anorexics, was intermittently impatient with analysis and guilty about her emerging anger. She would readily have taken medication to dispel her symptoms, and would have perceived this as a carrying out of the prohibitive strictures of her archaic superego.

MEDICATION AS IT LEADS TO ACTING OUT

When bulimic anorexics have partially resolved their bulimic symptoms but have not yet analyzed their preoedipal part-object relations, they often abruptly devalue the analyst, stop therapy, and seek treatment by medication. The case of a 35-year-old bulimic woman executive is illustrative. She came to treatment on the urgings of her internist, who repeatedly told her she was masochistic. Her father, a banker, born and brought up in California, was known as the Christ of the bank. As a workaholic and perfectionist, he did everything for everyone, consequently having little time for his daughter. Contrastingly, the mother, a religious Catholic, devoted herself to her daughter, showering the girl with moral instruction and intrusive attention. Mother and daughter spoke to each other daily on the phone. The patient developed bulimic anorexic symptoms at 20 years of age, at the time she began her first love affair with a brilliant young lawyer. After she married him she discovered that he was alcoholic. After five years of a sadomasochistic marriage, during which she lent him money, took him to hospitals for treatment, and was verbally and physically abused by him, she secured a divorce.

Following the divorce, her bulimia worsened; she stopped any dating of men and became a recluse. Her life was split between hard work as a department store executive and binging and vomiting alone in her apartment. In the analysis, the masochistic nature of her behavior and character structure were the focus of interpretation. She began to decrease the frequency of her calls to her mother. The frequency of her binging decreased from five times a day to once a week. She then approached her employers for a raise in pay, as she realized she was grossly underpaid for her work, and she began dating an advertising executive. Intense depressed emotions developed, however, and she abruptly terminated treatment and went to a psychopharmacologist for medication to relieve her depression. The prognosis for this patient to resolve her problems in analysis had been favorable. Her acting out by taking medication interrupted treatment. Whether or not the medication eased her depression, she was left with an underlying masochistic personality disorder.

MEDICATION AS EFFECTING CHANGE
IN BODY IMAGE

A major criterion for a cure in dealing with anorexia nervosa is for the patient to experience a change in the psychotic-like fear-of-being-fat body image, and in the obsession with being thin. Bruch (1973b), although using a technique of treatment different from mine, does correctly emphasize that a realistic body image concept is a precondition for recovery in anorexia nervosa. I have described in detail (p. 177) the change in body image of a woman in analysis for chronic bulimic anorexia nervosa. This patient, who was seriously underweight and using laxatives in potentially suicidal amounts when she began analysis, had begun to put on weight; her regression had lifted and she reported that she now hated her thin figure and the figures of other anorexic women. This change occurred prior to the analysis of the triadic oedipal aspects of her neurosis. The changes occurred consequent to the analysis of her defenses against admitting to emotions and conflicts, particularly in the transference, with the liberation and expression of anger and *depression* in sessions.

At one point the patient's acting out around time was so intense that I told her that I would not go on seeing her if she did not show me that she was responsible for her sessions. Her response was to devalue me by saying that I was paid whether she came or not. I interpreted to her that she was treating me as she did food, which she equated with the mother of the nursing period; that she wanted me to be available to her no matter what she did. The patient's response was to cry and say that I was throwing her out. Again I confronted her with her need to act out, and she stopped it.

What were the components of her depression? One was anger because her narcissistic demands were thwarted; I refused to be the mother in the transference. A second component was depression because she had to face and work through conflicts in separation-individuation with me in the transference and with real objects in daily life.

It should be noted that in publications about therapeutic results from the use of medication there are no systematic reports by psychoanalytically trained investigators of body image changes.

MEDICATION AND COGNITIVE IMPAIRMENT

A case example illustrates the interference with therapy and the psychic shifts that occurred as a result of medication. A 23-year-old bulimic in psychotherapy showed little change in her bulimic behavior but developed considerable insight into her masochism in the first year of therapy. Pressure was brought by her family to discontinue therapy and go on medication. The therapist, instead of discussing the disadvantages of medication, prescribed Nardil. The patient's depression improved; her bulimic behavior, however, continued, and she developed serious cognitive difficulties. She could not concentrate at work, became amnesic and made many parapraxes. The therapist took her off medication, she became depressed again but her cognitive functioning returned to normal.

In my consultations with this patient another frequent reaction to being medicated was verbalized: she said she was secretly very discouraged, as she felt the therapist had lost confidence in her ability to resolve her problems when he put her on medication. The therapist's countertransference conflict had led him to medicate the patient, as he acknowledged in supervision.

THE USE OF MEDICATION:
FURTHER COMPLICATIONS

Other patients seen in consultation have attempted suicide with aspirin, Nardil, Tylenol, Ipecac, and Tofranil. One experienced a resolution of her depression and bulimic symptoms following the administration of Nardil, but developed a manic toxic psychosis, became noncommunicative, and acted out sexually. Another possibility, as indicated before, is the development of a split transference between the psychopharmacologist who may give the medication and the therapist. In several instances bulimic anorexics were observed to experience a dramatic clearing of symptoms with Nardil but acted out transference anger at the therapist by disobeying the MAO dietary restrictions, inducing hypertensive crises that required hospitalization.

COUNTERTRANSFERENCE

The therapist has to be able to withstand what can seem like perpetual testing by the bulimic anorexic (see pp. 189–191). Sadistic behavior on the part of the patient can set off increasingly strong countersadistic feelings in the analyst. If the therapist is unable to contain the aggression, this inability to deal with it can result in a need to medicate the bulimic in order to tranquilize the patient into decreasing their sadistic attacks on the therapist. Such patients want, above all, to turn the analyst or psychiatrist into the image of the omnipotent mother. In addition, with bulimics as with other addictive patients, there is a conscious battle going on with the therapist. To give the patient medication means to the patient that the battle has been won and the patient has succeeded in turning the therapist into the omnipotent mother who can take away the patient's symptoms with pills. The result is that the patient is left with an unchanged personality disorder.

MEDICATION AS IT MAY LEAD TO SUICIDE

Suicidal use of medication is exemplified in the case of a hospitalized bulimic anorexic. The patient was a 30-year-old woman who had come to New York to escape from her dependence on her mother, who was her only friend and confidant, and with whom the patient had an unresolved sadomasochistic tie. Relationships with men ended in rejection, unhappiness, and despair. The patient had attempted suicide several times by cutting her wrists. The psychiatrist treating her offered her supportive psychotherapy twice a week and Elavil. When he went on vacation for two weeks, which to such a patient meant that she was being totally deserted and unloved, she tried to kill herself by overdosing with a massive dose of Elavil. Supervision resulted in the transfer of the patient to analytic therapy without the use of medication. Follow-up shows that she has developed a positive therapeutic relationship with marked analytic progress.

DISCUSSION

A crucial goal of the psychodynamic treatment of bulimia is that through the analysis of the transference neurosis the patients' ego can mature so that they develop the capacity to face and tolerate both realistic and neurotic depression. Like the restrictor, the bulimics are obsessed with fantasies of remaining young forever and being free of any conflict, realistic or neurotic. They deny the conflicts they manifest, like their dependence on their parents, who usually have similar conflicts. They believe in magical solutions to problems, are intolerant of delay, and ambivalent about such lengthy learning experiences as analysis or analytic psychotherapy. The foregoing case illustrations document the complications of giving antidepressant medication to patients in therapy. As the discussion of bulimic depression and the case histories demonstrate, it is the analysis of depression and its resolution that are crucial for lasting results with bulimics.

In chronic bulimics, as I noted (Chapter 8), gorging, vomiting, and use of laxatives, humiliating as they are, serve as defenses against conflicts, impulses, and affects that the patient fears more than the eating disorder. In the case of Carol (Chapter 8) the bulimic symptoms replaced the patient's nail biting, cuticle and flesh chewing. No matter how severe her bulimic behavior, she never returned to her nail biting and was extremely proud of her long nails. With such a patient one can expect that bulimic behavior will not be given up early in the course of therapy. In contrast, with some adolescents bulimic symptoms of recent origin clear in a relatively short time, and analysis of the underlying conflicts does not take so long as it does with chronic bulimia.

However, with an epidemic number of bulimic patients we have to ask if, given the cost of analytic treatment and the limited number of trained analytic therapists, some patients, those with healthier personalities, can be treated by antidepressants successfully and safely. Can some inaccessible patients become motivated for therapy as they see the dramatic effect of a psychiatric intervention with the medication? The answer would seem to be that medication can only be used with any degree of safety with patients who demonstrate relatively healthy ego functioning. Walsh et al. (1984) in their research only select bulimics who can adhere to a diet and who are not addictive or suicidal. Yet it is just such patients who would benefit most from analytic psychotherapy or psychoanalysis. Moreover, if medication is used to resolve bulimic symptoms in supposedly selectively healthy patients, this can prevent them from mastering the symptoms by will power and understanding without medication, which is actually the experience of many bulimics. In addition, those patients whom we have seen in analytic investigation, who have a seemingly healthy ego, evidence an underlying masochistic character structure, (Mintz, pp. 104–107) and, because of their unresolved oral conflicts and belief in magic, no group of patients is more prone to believe in a symptomatic cure and to minimize, withhold, or lie about neurotic symptoms and conflicts.

In those situations where the use of medication, particularly antidepressants is necessary, i.e. medical crises, or when patients cannot be motivated for psychotherapy, in treatment stalemates, or where cost and therapist availability are problems, the use of drugs is a trade off with potentially disadvantageous consequences. Therapeutic stalemates can occur in cases of chronic bulimia where there has been a long term resistance to insight and change in analytic therapy.

While medication in some intractable cases may facilitate therapy, we have found that even in severe regressed states knowledgeable interpretations have resolved the impasses. The effectiveness of our technique in these crisis situations has been documented in Mintz's (p. 217–244) detailing of the analysis of such a severely regressed hospitalized bulimic, and my (p. 169–193) analysis of an emaciated bulimic's repeated provocative, brinksmanshiplike, suicidal use of laxatives. Before resorting to medication, consultation and/or supervision are advisable. In cases seen in consultation and supervision and in cases presented to the psychosomatic study groups of the Psychoanalytic Association of New York and The American Psychoanalytic Association, such therapeutic impasses have been resolved by a (1) deeper psychodynamic understanding, (2) a review of the countertransference conflicts of the therapist, and (3) an exploration of the often subtle treatment sabotage on the part of the patient's parents, who frequently are unable to accept self assertive behavior by the enmeshed bulimic anorexic. It must be kept in mind that, at best, medication may make the patient more amenable to dynamic therapy but it cannot change the underlying impulsive, masochistic personality disorder.

The "golden years" of psychoanalysis are not in the past, but in the present and future application of our new therapeutic techniques to the treatment of bulimic anorexics and other patients with severe preoedipal psychopathology. Hopefully, the shortage of analytically trained therapists will be alleviated by the estimated 5000 candidates (Limentani 1985) who are in training in the institutes of the International Psychoanalytical Association.

SUMMARY AND CONCLUSION

Faced with the recent epidemic increase in bulimic cases and the increased use of antidepressants in their treatment, this chapter discussed in detail the psychodynamic causes of bulimia, the symptoms of which can be considered as depressive equivalents. The psychodynamics are complex, multidetermined, and have both oedipal and preoedipal roots. The multiple unconscious determinants of bulimic depression have been enumerated and traced to family psychopathology. Our psychoanalytic technique with bulimics has been reviewed. Case material has been cited to document the rise and fall of depressive symptomatology in the course of analysis, and particularly in the transference neurosis, to underscore the point that it is the analysis of depressive affects and their resolution in the transference neurosis that is crucial for therapeutic success. The focus of an analytic treatment is on the resolution of the underlying masochistic personality disorder.

Further clinical examples have been presented to substantiate the opinion of the contributors to this volume that conjoint use of drugs and psychodynamic therapy are contraindicated. Among the negative consequences of medication are acting out, alternate symptom formation including toxic psychosis, vitiation of motivation for therapy, the use of drugs for suicidal attempts, split transference to the psychopharmacologist, and psychological addiction to the drug. Drugs can be resorted to because of countertransference conflicts of the therapist. It is emphasized that while there may be situations where the use of medication, particularly antidepressants, is appropriate, (i.e., medical crises, treatment stalemates, or when patients cannot be motivated for psychotherapy, or where cost and therapist availability are problems) the use of drugs may be a trade-off, with potentially dangerous consequences. Psychoanalysis or psychoanalytic psychotherapy without the use of medication are the treatments of choice for bulimic anorexia nervosa.

REFERENCES

Altshuler, K.Z., and Weiner, M.F. (1985). Anorexia nervosa and depression: a dissenting view. *American Journal of Psychiatry* 3: 328–332.

Anthony, E.J., and Benedek, T., eds. (1970). *Parenthood: Its Psychology and Psychopathology*. Boston: Little, Brown.

Arlow, J. (1957). On smugness. *International Journal of Psycho-Analysis* 38: 1–8.

Arlow, J., and Brenner, C. (1964). *Psychoanalytic Concepts and Structural Theory*. New York: International Universities Press.

——— (1969). The psychopathology of the psychoses: a proposed revision. *International Journal of Psycho-Analysis* 50: 5–14.

——— (1970). Discussion of "The psychopathology of the psychoses: a proposed revision." *International Journal of Psycho-Analysis* 51: 159–166.

Asbeck, F., Hirschmann, W.D., Deck, K., and Castrup, H.J. (1972). Lethal course of anorexia nervosa: alcohol and laxative abuse in a female patient. *Internist* (Berlin) 13: 63–65.

Beaumont, P.J.V., Beardwood, C.J., and Russell, G.F.M. (1972). The occurrence of the syndrome of anorexia nervosa in male subjects. *Psychological Medicine* 2: 216–231.

Benedek, T. (1938). Adaptation to reality in early infancy. *Psychoanalytic Quarterly* 7: 200–214.

Berlin, I.N., Boatman, M.J., Shiemo, S.L., and Szurek, S.A. (1951). Adolescent alternation of anorexia and obesity. *American Journal of Orthopsychiatry* 21: 387–419.

Bettelheim, B. (1975). The love that is enough: countertransference and the ego processes of staff members in a therapeutic milieu. In *Tactics and Techniques in Psychoanalytic Therapy*, vol. 2, ed. P.L. Giovacchini, A. Flarsheim, and L.B. Boyer, pp. 251–278. New York: Aronson.

Bibring, E. (1953). The mechanism of depression. In *Affective Disorders: Psychoanalytic Contributions to Their Study*, ed. P. Greenacre, pp. 13–48. New York: International Universities Press.

Bion, W.R. (1956). Development of schizophrenic thought. *International Journal of Psycho-Analysis* 37: 344–346.

Bird, B. (1972). Notes on transference: universal phenomenon and hardest part of analysis. *Journal of the American Psychoanalytic Association* 20: 267–301.

Bliss, E.L., and Branch, C.H.H. (1960). *Anorexia Nervosa: Its History, Psychology, and Biology*. New York: Hoeber.

Blitzer, J.R., Rollins, N., and Blackwell, A. (1961). Children who starve themselves: anorexia nervosa. *Psychosomatic Medicine* 23: 369–383.

Blum, H.P. (1976). Masochism, the ego ideal, and the psychology of women. *Journal of the American Psychoanalytic Association* 24(Supplement): 157–191.

―――― (1977). The prototype of pre-oedipal reconstruction. *Journal of the American Psychoanalytic Association* 25: 757–785.

Boskind-Lodahl, M. (1976). Cinderella's stepsisters: a feminist perspective on anorexia nervosa and bulimia. *Signs: Journal of Women in Culture and Society* 2: 342–356.

Boskind-White, M., and White, W.C. (1983). *Bulimarexia: The Binge Purge Cycle*. New York: Norton.

Boyer, L.B. (1961). Provisional evaluation of psycho-analysis with few parameters in the treatment of schizophrenia. *International Journal of Psycho-Analysis* 42: 389–403.

―――― (1966). Office treatment of schizophrenic patients by psychoanalysis: *Psychoanalytic Forum* 1: 337–356.

―――― (1975). Treatment of characterological and schizophrenic disorders. In *Tactics and Techniques in Psychoanalytic Therapy*, vol. 2, ed. P.L. Giovacchini, A. Flarsheim, and L.B. Boyer, pp. 341–373. New York: Aronson.

―――― (1978). Countertransference experiences with severely regressed patients. *Contemporary Psychoanalysis* 14: 48–72.

―――― (1979). Countertransference with severely regressed patients. In *Countertransference: The Therapist's Contribution to the Therapeutic Situation*, ed. L. Epstein and A.H. Feiner, pp. 347–374. New York: Aronson.

―――― (1980). Working with a borderline patient. In *Psychoanalytic Treatment of Schizophrenic, Borderline and Characterological Disorders*, ed. L.B. Boyer and P.L. Giovacchini, pp. 171–208. New York: Aronson.

Boyer, L.B., and Giovacchini, P.L. (1967). *Psychoanalytic Treatment of Schizophrenic, Borderline and Characterological Disorders*. New York: Aronson.

―――― (1980). *Psychoanalytic Treatment of Schizophrenic, Borderline and Characterological Disorders*, 2nd rev. ed. New York: Aronson.

Brenner, C. (1976). *Psychoanalytic Technique and Psychic Conflict*. New York: International Universities Press.

―――― (1979a). The components of psychic conflict and its consequences in mental life. *Psychoanalytic Quarterly* 48: 547–567.

―――― (1979b). Working alliance, therapeutic alliance and transference. *Journal of the American Psychoanalytic Association* 27(Supplement): 137–157.

Brillat-Savarin, J.-A. (1825). *The Philosopher in the Kitchen*. New York: Penguin, 1981.

Brody, S. (1956). *Patterns of Mothering: Maternal Influence during Infancy*. New York: International Universities Press.

Brotman, A.W., Herzog, D.C., and Woods, S.W. (1984). Antidepressant treatment of bulimia: the relationship between binging and depressive symptomatology. *Journal of Clinical Psychiatry* 45: 7–9. Abstract, *Intelligence Reports in Psychiatric Disorders*, 3: 3, pp. 4–5.

Bruch, H. (1961). Transformation of oral impulses in eating disorders: a conceptual approach. *Psychiatric Quarterly* 35: 458–481.

―――― (1962). Perceptual and conceptual disturbances in anorexia nervosa. *Psychosomatic Medicine* 24: 187–194.

―――― (1965). Anorexia nervosa and its differential diagnosis. *Journal of Nervous and Mental Disease* 141: 555–566.

―――― (1970). Psychotherapy in primary anorexia nervosa. *Journal of Nervous and Mental Disease* 150: 51–67.

——— (1971). Anorexia nervosa in the male. *Psychosomatic Medicine* 33: 31–47.

——— (1973a). Anorexia nervosa. In *American Handbook of Psychiatry*, Vol. 4, 2nd ed., ed. M.F. Reiser, p. 791. New York: Basic Books, 1975.

——— (1973b). *Eating Disorders: Obesity, Anorexia Nervosa, and the Person Within.* New York: Basic Books.

——— (1974). Perils of behavior modification in the treatment of anorexia nervosa. *Journal of the American Medical Association* 230: 1409–1422.

——— (1978a). *The Golden Cage: The Enigma of Anorexia Nervosa.* Cambridge, Mass.: Harvard University Press.

——— (1978b). The tyranny of fear. In *The Human Dimension in Psychoanalytic Practice*, ed. K. Frank, pp. 83–98. New York:: Grune and Stratton.

——— (1982). Anorexia nervosa: therapy and theory. *American Journal of Psychiatry* 139: 1535.

Carpinacci, J.A., Liberman, D., and Schlossberg, N. (1963). Perturbaciones de la comunicación y neurosis de contratransferencia. *Revista de Psicoanálisis* 20: 63–69.

Carter, L., and Rinsley, D.B. (1977). Vicissitudes of "empathy" in a borderline patient. *International Review of Psycho-Analysis* 4: 317–326.

Cesio, F.R. (1963). La comunicación extraverbal en psicoanálisis: transferencia, contratransferencia e interpretación. *Revista de Psicoanálisis* 20: 124–127.

——— (1973). Los fundamentos de la contratransferencia: el yo ideal y las identificaciones directas. *Revista de Psicoanálisis* 30: 5–16.

Cohler, B.J. (1975). The residential treatment of anorexia nervosa. In *Tactics and Techniques in Psychoanalytic Therapy*, Vol. 2, ed. P.L. Giovacchini, A. Flarsheim, and L.B. Boyer, pp. 385–412. New York: Aronson.

Crisp, A.H. (1965). Clinical and therapeutic aspects of anorexia nervosa: a study of 30 cases. *Journal of Psychosomatic Research* 9: 67.

——— (1967). Anorexia nervosa. *Hospital Medicine* 1: 713–718.

——— (1968). Primary anorexia nervosa. *Gut* 9: 370–372.

——— (1969). Psychological aspects of breast-feeding with particular reference to anorexia nervosa. *British Journal of Medical Psychology* 42: 119–132.

——— (1979). Early recognition and prevention of anorexia nervosa. *Developmental Medicine and Child Neurology* 21: 393–395.

Crisp, A.H., and Roberts, F.J. (1962). A case of anorexia nervosa in a male. *Postgraduate Medical Journal* 38: 350.

Crisp, A.H., and Toms, D.A. (1972). Primary anorexia nervosa or weight phobia in the male: report on 13 cases. *British Medical Journal* 1: 334–338.

Dally, P.J. (1969). *Anorexia Nervosa.* New York: Grune and Stratton.

Deneux, A., Sans, P., Le Clech, H.G., and Messak, E. (1977). Three cases of mental anorexia in men. *Revue de Neuropsychiatrie de l'Ouest* (Rennes) 14: 83–95.

Deutsch, H. (1944). *The Psychology of Women: A Psychoanalytic Interpretation*, Vol. 1. New York: Grune and Stratton.

Deutsch, L. (1980). Psychosomatic medicine from a psychoanalytic viewpoint. *Journal of the American Psychoanalytic Association* 28: 653–702.

Dickes, R. (1975). Technical considerations of the therapeutic and working alliances. *International Journal of Psychoanalytic Psychotherapy* 4: 1–24.

Eidelberg, L. (1957). An introduction to the study of the narcissistic mortification. *Psychiatric Quarterly* 31: 657–668.

—— (1959). A second contribution to the study of the narcissistic mortification. *Psychiatric Quarterly* 33: 636–646.

Eissler, K.R. (1943). Some psychiatric aspects of anorexia nervosa, demonstrated by a case report. *Psychoanalytic Review* 30: 121–145.

Ekstein, R. (1976). General treatment philosophy of acting out. In *Acting Out*, 2nd ed., ed. L.E. Abt and S.L. Weissman, pp. 162–171. New York: Aronson.

Engel, G.L. (1962). *Psychological Development in Health and Disease*. Philadelphia: Saunders.

Epstein, L., and Feiner, A.H., eds. (1979). *Countertransference: The Therapist's Contribution to the Therapeutic Situation*. New York: Aronson.

Escalona, S.K. (1954). Emotional development during the first year of life. In *Problems of Infancy and Childhood*, ed. M.J.E. Senn. New York: Josiah Macy, Jr., Foundation.

Fairbairn, W.R.D. (1941). A revised psychopathology of the psychoses and psychoneuroses. *International Journal of Psycho-Analysis* 22: 250–279.

—— (1952). *Psychoanalytic Studies of the Personality*. London: Tavistock.

—— (1954). *An Object Relations Theory of Personality*. New York: Basic Books.

Falstein, E.I., Feinstein, S.C., and Judas, I. (1956). Anorexia nervosa in the male child. *American Journal of Orthopsychiatry* 26: 751–772.

Fenichel, O. (1945a). Anorexia. In *The Collected Papers of Otto Fenichel* 2: 288–295. New York: Norton, 1954.

—— (1945b). *The Psychoanalytic Theory of Neurosis*. New York: Norton.

—— (1954). Neurotic acting-out. In *The Collected Papers of Otto Fenichel* 2: 296–304. New York: Norton, 1954.

Ferrara, A., and Fontana, V.J. (1966). Celiac disease and anorexia nervosa. *New York State Journal of Medicine* 66: 1000–1009.

Flarsheim, A. (1975). The therapist's collusion with the patient's wish for suicide. In *Tactics and Techniques in Psychoanalytic Therapy*, Vol. 2, ed. P.L. Giovacchinii, A. Flarsheim, and L.B. Boyer, pp. 155–195. New York: Aronson.

Frahm, H. (1965). Results of somatic treatment of anorexia nervosa. In *Anorexia Nervosa*, ed. J.E. Meyer and H. Feldmann, pp. 64–66. Stuttgart: Georg Thieme.

Frazer, J. (1959). *The New Golden Bough*. New York: Criterion Books.

Freud, A. (1958). Adolescence. *Psychoanalytic Study of the Child* 13: 225–278.

—— (1968a). Acting out. *International Journal of Psycho-Analysis* 49: 165–170.

—— (1968b). *Indications for Child Analysis and Other Papers, 1945–1956*. Vol. 4 of *The Writings of Anna Freud*. New York: International Universities Press.

Freud, S. (1887–1902). *The Origins of Psychoanalysis. Letters to Wilhelm Fliess, Drafts and Notes: 1887–1902*. New York: Basic Books, 1954.

—— (1893–1895). Studies on hysteria. *Standard Edition* 7: 3–122. London: Hogarth, 1953.

—— (1905). Fragment of an analysis of a case of hysteria. *Standard Edition* 7: 3–122. London: Hogarth, 1953.

—— (1909). Notes on a case of obsessional neurosis. *Standard Edition* 10: 155–257. London: Hogarth, 1955.

—— (1914). Observations on transference-love. *Standard Edition* 12: 157–171. London: Hogarth, 1958.

—— (1918). From the history of an infantile neurosis. *Standard Edition* 17: 7–122. London: Hogarth, 1955.

—— (1923). The ego and the id. *Standard Edition* 19: 13–66. London: Hogarth, 1961.

—— (1925a). An autobiographical study. *Standard Edition* 20: 7–74. London: Hogarth, 1959.

—— (1925b). Negation. *Standard Edition* 19: 235–239. London: Hogarth, 1961.

—— (1932). New introductory lectures in psycho-analysis. *Standard Edition* 22: 1–193. London: Hogarth, 1964.

Friedman, S. (1978). A discussion of Wilson's paper on "The Fear of Being Fat and Anorexia Nervosa" at the meeting of the New Jersey Psychoanalytic Society, October 13.

Galenson, E., and Roiphe, H. (1976). Some suggested revisions concerning early female development. *Journal of the American Psychoanalytic Association* 24(Supplement): 29–57.

Garner, D.M., and Garfinkel, P.E. (1985). *Handbook of Psychotherapy for Anorexia Nervosa and Bulimia.* New York: The Guilford Press.

Gedo, J. (1977). Notes on the psychoanalytic management of archaic transferences. *Journal of the American Psychoanalytic Association* 25: 787–803.

Gero, G. (1953). An equivalent of depression: anorexia. In *Affective Disorders: Psychoanalytic Contributions to Their Study*, ed. P. Greenacre, pp. 117–189. New York: International Universities Press.

Gill, M., and Muslin, H. (1976). Early interpretation of transference: *Journal of the American Psychoanalytic Association* 24: 779–794.

Giovacchini, P.L. (1963). Somatic symptoms and the transference neurosis. *International Journal of Psycho-Analysis* 44: 143–150.

—— (1975a). Self-projections in the narcissistic transference. *International Journal of Psychoanalytic Psychotherapy* 4: 142–166.

—— (1975b). Various aspects of the analytic process. In *Tactics and Techniques in Psychoanalytic Therapy*, vol. 2, ed. P.L. Giovacchini, A. Flarsheim, and L.B. Boyer, pp. 5–94. New York: Aronson.

—— (1977). The psychoanalytic treatment of the alienated patient. In *New Perspectives on the Psychotherapy of the Borderline Adult*, ed. J. Masterson, pp. 1–39. New York: Brunner/Mazel.

—— (1979). *Treatment of Primitive Mental States.* New York: Aronson.

Glauber, I.P. (1955). On the meaning of agoraphilia. *Journal of the American Psychoanalytic Association* 3: 701–709.

Glover, E. (1955). *The Technique of Psycho-Analysis.* New York: International Universities Press.

Goitein, P.L. (1942). The potential prostitute: the role of anorexia in the defense against prostitution desires. *Journal of Criminal Psychopathology* 3: 359–367.

Goodsitt, A. (1969). Anorexia nervosa. *British Journal of Medical Psychology* 42: 109–118.

Gordon, M. (1978). *Final Payments.* New York: Random House.

Greenacre, P. (1945). Pathological weeping. *Psychoanalytic Quarterly* 14: 62–75, No. 1.

Greenacre, P. (1954). The role of transference: practical considerations in relation to psychoanalytic therapy. *Journal of the American Psychoanalytic Association* 2: 671–684.

—— (1958). Early physical determinants in the development of the sense of identity. *Journal of the American Psychoanalytic Association* 6: 612–627.

—— (1968). The psychoanalytic process, transference, and acting out. *International Journal of Psycho-Analysis* 49: 211–218.

Greenson, R.R. (1965). The working alliance and the transference neurosis. *Psychoanalytic Quarterly* 34: 155–181.

—— (1971). The "real" relationship between the patient and the psychoanalyst. In *The Unconscious Today*, ed. M. Kanzer, pp. 213–232. New York: International Universities Press.

Greenson, R.R., and Wexler, M. (1969). The non-transference relationship in the psychoanalytic situation. *International Journal of Psycho-Analysis* 50: 27–39.

Grinberg, L. (1976). *Teoría de la Identificación.* Buenos Aires: Editorial Paidós.

—— (1979). Countertransference and projective counteridentifications. *Contemporary Psychoanalysis* 15: 226–247.

——, ed. (1972). *Prácticas Psicoanalíticas Comparadas en las Psicosis.* Buenos Aires: Editorial Paidós.

Groen, J.J., and Feldman-Toledano, Z. (1966). Educative treatment of patients and parents in anorexia nervosa. *British Journal of Psychiatry* 112: 671–681.

Grossman, W.I., and Stewart, W.A. (1976). Penis envy: from childhood wish to developmental metaphor. *Journal of the American Psychoanalytic Association* 24(Supplement): 193–212.

Grotstein, J.S. (1981). *Splitting and Projective Identification.* New York: Aronson.

Gull, W.W. (1868). The address on medicine. In *Evolution of Psychosomatic Concepts. Anorexia Nervosa: A Paradigm*, ed. M.R. Kaufman and M. Heiman, pp. 104–127. New York: International Universities Press, 1964.

—— (1873a). Anorexia nervosa (apepsia hysterica, anorexia hysterica). In *Evolution of Psychosomatic Concepts. Anorexia Nervosa: A Paradigm*, ed, M.R. Kaufman and M. Heiman, pp. 132–138. New York: International Universities Press, 1964.

—— (1873b). Meeting of the Clinical Society. *Medical Times and Gazette* 2: 534.

—— (1888). Anorexia nervosa. In *Evolution of Psychosomatic Concepts*, ed. M.R. Kaufman and M. Heiman, pp. 139–140. New York: International Universities Press, 1964.

Guntrip, H. (1961). *Personality Structure and Human Interaction: The Developing Synthesis of Psychodynamic Theory.* New York: International Universities Press.

Halmi, K.A., Falk, J.R., and Schwartz, E. (1981). Binge-eating and vomiting: a survey of a college population. *Psychological Medicine* 11: 697–706.

Hasan, M., and Tibbetts, R. (1977). Primary anorexia nervosa (weight phobia) in males. *Postgraduate Medical Journal* 53: 146–151.

Hay, G., and Leonard, J. (1979). Anorexia nervosa in males. *Lancet* 2: 574–575.

Heimann, P. (1942). A contribution to the problem of sublimation and its relation to processes of internalization. *International Journal of Psycho-Analysis* 23: 8–17.

Hoffer, W. (1950). Development of the body ego. *Psychoanalytic Study of the Child* 5: 18–23.

Jacobson, E. (1964). *The Self and the Object World.* New York: International Universities Press.

Jawetz, I.K. (1976). Discussion of S. Ritvo's presentation. Panel on "The psychology of women: late adolescence and early adulthood," reported by E. Galenson. *Journal of the American Psychoanalytic Association* 24: 640–641.

Jessner, L., and Abse, D.W. (1960). Regressive forces in anorexia nervosa. *British Journal of Medical Psychology* 33: 301–311.

Jonas, J.M., Pope, Jr., H.G., and Hudson, J.I. (1983). Treatment of bulimia with MAO inhibitors. *Journal of Clinical Psychoparmacology* 3: 59–60.

Kanzer, M. (1975). The therapeutic and working alliances. *International Journal of Psychoanalytic Psychotherapy* 4: 48–73.

Kaplan, E.B. (1976). Panel on "The psychology of women: latency and early adolescence," reported by E. Galenson. *Journal of the American Psychoanalytic Association* 24: 155.

Karol, C. (1980). The role of primal scene and masochism in asthma. *International Journal of Psychoanalytic Psychotherapy* 8: 577–592.

Kaufman, M.R., and Heiman, M., eds. (1964). *Evolution of Psychosomatic Concepts. Anorexia Nervosa: A Paradigm*. New York: International Universities Press.

Kay, D.W.K., and Leigh, D. (1954). The natural history, treatment and prognosis of anorexia nervosa, based on a study of 38 patients. *Journal of Mental Science* 100: 411–419.

Kay, D.W.K., and Shapiro, K. (1965). Prognosis in anorexia nervosa. In *Anorexia Nervosa*, ed. J.E. Meyer and H. Feldmann, pp. 113–117. Stuttgart: Georg Thieme.

Kernberg, O.F. (1966). Structural derivatives of object relationships. *International Journal of Psycho-Analysis* 47: 236–253.

—— (1972). Early ego integration and object relations. *Annals of the New York Academy of Science* 193: 233–247.

—— (1975). *Borderline Conditions and Pathological Narcissism*. New York: Aronson.

—— (1976). *Object-Relations Theory and Clinical Psychoanalysis*. New York: Aronson.

—— (1980). *International World and External Reality: Object Relations Theory Applied*. New York: Aronson.

Kestenberg, J. (1965). Menarche. In *Adolescents: Psychoanalytic Approach to Problems and Therapy*, ed. S. Lorand and H. Schneer, pp. 19–50. New York: Delta.

—— (1977). Regression and reintegration in pregnancy. In *Female Psychology*, ed. H. Blum, pp. 213–250. New York: International Universities Press.

King, D.A. (1971). Anorexic behavior—a nursing problem. *Journal of Psychiatric Nursing* 9: 11–17.

Klein, M. (1934). A contribution to the psychogenesis of manic-depressive states. In *Contributions to Psychoanalysis, 1921–1945*. London: Hogarth, 1948.

—— (1946). Notes on some schizoid mechanisms. *International Journal of Psycho-Analysis* 27: 99–110.

—— (1948). *Contributions to Psychoanalysis, 1921–1945*. London: Hogarth.

—— (1952). *Developments in Psychoanalysis*. London: Hogarth.

—— (1955). On identification. In *New Directions in Psychoanalysis*, ed. M. Klein, P. Heimann, and R. Money-Kyrle, pp. 309–345. London: Tavistock.

Kohut, H. (1971). *The Analysis of the Self*. New York: International Universities Press.

—— (1977). *The Restoration of the Self*. New York: International Universities Press.

Kramer, P. (1955). On discovering one's identity: a case report. *Psychoanalytic Study of the Child* 10: 47–74.

Kramer, S. (1974). A discussion of Sours's paper on "The anorexia nervosa syndrome." *International Journal of Psycho-Analysis* 55: 577–579.

Langs, R. (1975a). The patient's unconscious perception of the therapist's errors. In *Tactics and Techniques in Psychoanalytic Therapy*, vol. 2, ed. P.L. Giovacchini, A. Flarsheim, and L.B. Boyer, pp. 239–250. New York: Aronson.

—— (1975b). Therapeutic misalliances. *International Journal of Psychoanalytic Psychotherapy* 4: 77–105.

Lasegue, E.C. (1873). On hysterical anorexia. In *Evolution of Psychosomatic Concepts*, ed. M.R. Kaufman and M. Heiman, pp. 141–155. New York: International Universities Press, 1964.

Leonard, C.E. (1944). An analysis of a case of functional vomiting and bulimia. *Psychoanalytic Review* 31: 1–18.

Lewin, B.D. (1950). *The Psychoanalysis of Elation*. New York: Norton.

Limentani, A., (1985). The relationship of a psychoanalytic society to its institute-education committee. *Newsletter of the International Psychoanalytic Association* 17: 1, p. 1.

Loewenstein, R.M. (1969). Developments in the theory of transference in the last fifty years. *International Journal of Psycho-Analysis* 50: 583–588.

Lorand, S. (1943). Anorexia nervosa: report of a case. *Psychosomatic Medicine* 5: 282–292.

Lowenfeld, H., and Lowenfeld, Y. (1972). Our permissive society and the superego. In *Moral Values and the Superego Concept*, ed. S.C. Post, pp. 375–397. New York: International Universities Press.

Mahler, M.S. (1972). On the first three subphases of the separation-individuation process. *International Journal of Psycho-Analysis* 53: 333–338.

Mahler, M.S., and Furer, M. (1968). *On Human Symbiosis and the Vicissitudes of Individuation*. New York: International Universities Press.

Mahler, M.S., Pine, F., and Bergman, A. (1970). The mother's reaction to her toddler's drive for individuation. In *Parenthood: Its Psychology and Psychopathology*, ed. E.J. Anthony and T. Benedek. Boston: Little, Brown.

—— (1975). *The Psychological Birth of the Human Infant*. New York: Basic Books.

Margolis, P. M., and Jernberg, A. (1960). Anaclitic therapy in a case of extreme anorexia. *British Journal of Medical Psychology* 33: 291–300.

Masserman, J.H. (1941). Psychodynamics in anorexia nervosa and neurotic vomiting. *Psychoanalytic Quarterly* 10: 211–242.

Masterson, J. (1977). Primary anorexia nervosa in the borderline adolescent—an object relations review. In *Borderline Personality Disorders: The Concept, The Syndrome, The Patient*, ed. P. Horticollis, pp. 475–494. New York: International Universities Press.

McGrath, P.M., Quitkin, F.M., Stewart, J.W., et al. (1981). An open clinical trial of mianserin. *American Journal of Psychiatry* 138: 530–532.

McLaughlin, J.T. (1979). The sleepy analyst: some observations on states of consciousness in the analyst at work. *Journal of American Psychoanalytic Association* 23: 363–382.

Mendels, J. (1983). Eating disorders and antidepressants. *Journal of Clinical Psychopharmacology* 3: 59.

Meyer, B.C., and Weinroth, L.A. (1957). Observations on psychological aspects of anorexia nervosa: report of a case. *Psychosomatic Medicine* 19: 389–398.

Mintz, I.L. (1971). The anniversary reaction: a response to the unconscious sense of time. *Journal of the American Psychoanalytic Association* 19: 720–734.

—— (1980). Multideterminism in asthmatic disease. *International Journal of Psychoanalytic Psychotherapy* 8: 593–600.

Minuchin, S., Rosman, B.L., and Baker, L. (1978). *Psychosomatic Families: Anorexia Nervosa in Context.* Cambridge, Mass.: Harvard University Press.

Mitchell, J.E., and Pyle, R.L. (1982). The bulimic syndrome in normal weight individuals: a review. *International Journal of Eating Disorders* 1: 61–73.

Morton, R. (1689). *Pathisiologica or a Treatise of Consumption.* London: Smith and Walford.

Moulton, R. (1942). Psychosomatic study of anorexia nervosa including the use of vaginal smears. *Psychosomatic Medicine* 4: 62–72.

Mushatt, C. (1975). Mind-body environment: toward understanding the impact of loss on psyche and soma. *Psychoanalytic Quarterly* 44: 81–106.

—— (1980). Melitta Sperling Memorial Lecture. Presented at the Psychoanalytic Association of New York, February 25.

—— (1982). Anorexia nervosa: a psychoanalytic commentary. *International Journal of Psychoanalytic Psychotherapy* 9: 257–265.

Nemiah, J.C. (1976). Alexithymia: a view of the psychosomatic process. In *Modern Trends in Psychosomatic Medicine*, vol. 3, ed. O.W. Hill, pp. 430–439. New York: Appleton-Century-Crofts.

Nemiah, J.C., and Sifneos, P. (1970). Affect and fantasy in patients with psychosomatic disorders. In *Modern Trends in Psychosomatic Medicine*, vol. 2, ed. O.W. Hill, pp. 26–34. New York: Appleton-Century-Crofts.

Niederland, W.G. (1956). Clinical observations on the "little man" phenomenon. *Psychoanalytic Study of the Child* 11: 381–395.

—— (1965). Narcissistic ego impairment in patients with early physical malformations. *Psychoanalytic Study of the Child* 20: 518–534.

Ogden, T.H. (1978). A developmental view of identifications resulting from maternal impingements. *International Journal of Psychoanalytic Psychotherapy* 7: 486–506.

Orbach, S. (1978). *Fat is a Feminist Issue.* New York: Berkeley Publishing.

Orr, D. (1954). Transference and countertransference. *Journal of the American Psychoanalytic Association* 2: 621–670.

Palmer, H.A. (1939). Beriberi complicating anorexia nervosa. *Lancet* 1: 269.

Palmer, H.D., and Jones, M.S. (1939). Anorexia nervosa as a manifestation of compulsion neurosis: a study of psychogenic factors. *Archives of Neurology and Psychiatry* 41: 856–859.

Palmer, J.O., Mensh, I.O., and Matarazzo, J.S. (1952). Anorexia nervosa: case history and psychological examination data with implications for test validity. *Journal of Clinical Psychology* 8: 168–173.

Perestrello, M. (1963). Um caso de intensa identifacação projetiva. *Journal Brasileiro de Psiquiatria* 12: 425–441.

Pope, Jr., H.G., and Hudson, J.I. (1982). Treatment of bulimia with antidepressants. *Psychopharmacology* 78: 167–179.

Pope, Jr., H.G., Hudson, J.I., Jonas, J.M., et al. (1983). Bulimia treated with impramine: a placebo-controlled double-blind study. *American Journal of Psychiatry* 140: 554-558.

Pope, Jr., H.G., and Hudson, J.I. (1984). *New Hope for Binge-eaters: Advances in the Understanding and Treatment of Bulimia.* New York: Harper and Row.

Rank, B. (1948). The significance of "emotional climate" in early feeding difficulties. *Psychosomatic Medicine* 10: 279-283.

Reich, A. (1960). Further remarks on counter-transference. *International Journal of Psycho-Analysis* 41: 389-395.

Reich, W. (1933). *Character Analysis*, 3rd ed. New York: Orgone Institute Press, 1949.

Ribble, M.A. (1943). *The Rights of Infants: Early Psychological Needs and Their Satisfaction.* New York: Columbia University Press.

Ritvo, S. (1976a). Adolescent to woman. *Journal of the American Psychoanalytic Association* 24(Supplement): 127-137.

——— (1976b). Presentation to the panel on "The psychology of women: late adolescence and early adulthood," reported by E. Galenson. *Journal of the American Psychoanalytic Association* 24: 638.

——— (1977). Adolescent to woman. In *Female Psychology*, ed. H. Blum, pp. 127-137. New York: International Universities Press.

Riviere, J. (1936a). A contribution to the analysis of a negative therapeutic reaction. *International Journal of Psycho-Analysis* 17: 304-320.

——— (1936b). On the genesis of psychical conflict in earliest infancy. *International Journal of Psycho-Analysis* 17: 395-422.

Robertiello, R.D. (1976). "Acting out" or "working through." In *Acting Out*, 2nd ed., ed. L.E. Abt and S.L. Weissman, pp. 40-47. New York: Aronson.

Rosenfeld, D., and Mordo, E. (1973). Fusión, confusión, simbiosis e identificación. *Revista de Psicoanálisis* 30: 413-423.

Rosenfeld, H.A. (1952). Notes on the psycho-analysis of the superego conflict of an acute schizophrenic patient. *International Journal of Psycho-Analysis* 33: 111-131.

——— (1965). *Psychotic States: A Psycho-Analytical Approach.* New York: International Universities Press.

Ross, N., and Wilson, C.P. (1951). Psychotherapy in bronchial asthma. In *Treatment of Asthma*, ed. H. Abrahamson, Chapter 34. Baltimore: Williams and Wilkins.

Roussounis, S.H. (1971). Anorexia nervosa in a prepubertal male. *Proceedings of the Royal Society of Medicine* 64: 666-667.

Russell, G.F.M. (1975). Anorexia nervosa. In *Textbook of Medicine*, 14th ed., ed. P.B. Beeson and W. McDermott. Philadelphia: Saunders.

Sabine, E.J., Yonace, A., Farrington, A.J., et al. (1983). Bulimia nervosa: a placebo-controlled therapeutic trial of mianserin. *British Journal of Clinical Pharmacology* 15: 195S-202S.

Sandler, J., Dore, C., and Holder, A. (1973). *The Patient and the Analyst.* New York: International Universities Press.

Sandler, J., and Joffe, W.G. (1965). Notes on obsessional manifestations in children. *Psychoanalytic Study of the Child* 20: 425-438.

Sarnoff, C.A. (1970). Symbols and symptoms: phytophobia in a two-year-old girl. *Psychoanalytic Quarterly* 39: 550-562.

——— (1976). *Latency.* New York: Aronson.

Savitt, R.A. (1969). Transference, somatization, and symbiotic need. *Journal of the American Psychoanalytic Association* 17: 1030–1054.

────── (1977). Conflict and somatization: psychoanalytic treatment of the psychophysiological response in the digestive tract. *Psychoanalytic Quarterly* 46: 605–622.

Schlossman, H. (1979). Psychiatric meeting. Hackensack Hospital. *Bulletin of the New Jersey Psychoanalytic Society* 8: 1–2.

────── (1980). The role of swine in myth and religion. Paper presented at the New Jersey Psychoanalytic Society.

Schmale, A.H., Jr. (1958). Relationship of separation and depression to disease. *Psychosomatic Medicine* 20: 259–277.

Schur, M. (1955). Comments on the metapsychology of somatization. *Psychoanalytic Study of the Child* 10: 119–164.

Schwartz, H.L. (1980). Discussion of Chapter 1. *Bulletin of the Psychoanalytic Association of New York* 17(1): 9.

Screenivasan, U. (1978). Anorexia nervosa in boys. *Canadian Psychiatric: Association Journal* 23: 159–162.

Searles, H.F. (1965). *Collected Papers on Schizophrenia and Related Subjects.* New York: International Universities Press.

────── (1966). Feelings of guilt in the psychoanalyst. *Psychiatry* 28: 319–323.

Selvini Palazzoli, M. (1961). Emaciation as magic means for the removal of anguish in anorexia mentalis. *Acta Psychotherapica* 9: 37–45.

────── (1963). *L'Anoressia Mentale.* Milan: Felranelli.

────── (1965). Interpretation of mental anorexia. In *Anorexia Nervosa*, ed. J.E. Meyer and H. Feldmann, pp. 96–103. Stuttgart: Georg Thieme.

────── (1970). The families of patients with anorexia nervosa. In *The Child and His Family*, ed. E.J. Anthony and C. Koupernik. New York: Wilroy.

────── (1978). *Self-Starvation: From Individual to Family Therapy in the Treatment of Anorexia Nervosa.* New York: Aronson.

Sifneos, P. (1973). The prevalence of alexithymic characteristics in psychosomatic patients. In *Psychotherapy in Psychosomatics*, ed. J. Reusch, A. Schmale, and T. Spoerri, pp. 255–262. White Plains, N.Y.: Karger.

Silverman, J. (1974). Anorexia nervosa: clinical observations in a successful treatment plan. *Journal of Pediatrics* 8(1): 68–73.

Simmonds, M. (1914). Über hypophysisschwand mit tödlichem Ausgang. *Deutsche Medizinische Wochenschrift* 40: 322.

────── (1916). Über Kachexie hypophysaren. Ursprungs. *Deutsche Medizinische Wochenschrift* 42: 190.

Sours, J.A. (1968). Clinical studies in the anorexia nervosa syndrome. *New York State Journal of Medicine* 68: 1363–1365.

────── (1969). Anorexia nervosa: nosology, diagnosis, developmental patterns, and power-control dynamics. In *Adolescence: Psychosocial Perspectives*, ed. G. Caplan and S. Lebovici, pp. 185–212. New York: Basic Books.

────── (1974). The anorexia nervosa syndrome. *International Journal of Psycho-Analysis* 55: 567–576.

────── (1979). The primary anorexia nervosa syndrome. In *Basic Handbook of Child Psychiatry*, vol. 2, ed. J.D. Noshpitz, pp. 568–580. New York: Basic Books.

────── (1980). *Starving to Death in a Sea of Objects: The Anorexia Nervosa Syndrome.* New York: Aronson.

Sperling, M. (1946). Psychoanalytic study of ulcerative colitis in children. *Psychoanalytic Quarterly* 15: 302–329.

—— (1949). Neurotic sleep disturbances in children. *Nervous Child* 8: 28–46.

—— (1950a). Indirect treatment of psychoneurotic and psychosomatic disorders in children. *Quarterly Journal of Child Behavior* 2: 250–266.

—— (1950b). The structure of envy in depressions of women. In *Feminine Psychology*, pp. 17–23. New York Medical College, Symposium Proceedings.

—— (1952). Animal phobias in a two-year-old child. *Psychoanalytic Study of the Child* 7: 115–125.

—— (1953). Food allergies and conversion hysteria. *Psychoanalytic Quarterly* 22: 525–538.

—— (1955a). Observations from the treatment of children suffering from non-bloody diarrhea or mucous colitis. *Journal of the Hillside Hospital* 4: 25–31.

—— (1955b). Psychosis and psychosomatic illness. *International Journal of Psycho-Analysis* 36: 320–327.

—— (1957). The psychoanalytic treatment of ulcerative colitis. *International Journal of Psycho-Analysis* 38: 341–349.

—— (1959). Equivalents of depression in children. *Journal of the Hillside Hospital* 8: 138–148.

—— (1960). Symposium on disturbances of the digestive tract: II. Unconscious phantasy life and object-relationships in ulcerative colitis. *International Journal of Psycho-Analysis* 41: 450–455.

—— (1961). Psychosomatic disorders. In *Adolescents: Psychoanalytic Approach to Problems and Therapy*, ed. S. Lorand and H.I. Schneer, pp. 202–216. New York: Hoeber.

—— (1967). Transference neurosis in patients with psychosomatic disorders. *Psychoanalytic Quarterly* 36: 342–355.

—— (1968a). Acting-out behaviour and psychosomatic symptoms: clinical and theoretical aspects. *International Journal of Psycho-Analysis* 49: 250–253.

—— (1968b). Trichotillomania, trichophagy, and cyclic vomiting: a contribution to the psychopathology of female sexuality. *International Journal of Psycho-Analysis* 49: 682–690.

—— (1969). Ulcerative colitis in children: current views and therapies. *Journal of the American Academy of Child Psychiatrists* 8: 336–352.

—— (1970). The clinical effects of parental neurosis on the child. In *Parenthood: Its Psychology and Psychopathology*, ed. E.J. Anthony and T. Benedek, pp. 539–569. Boston: Little, Brown.

—— (1974). *The Major Neuroses and Behavior Disorders in Children.* New York: Aronson.

—— (1978). Anorexia nervosa (part 4). In *Psychosomatic Disorders in Childhood*, ed. O. Sperling, pp. 129–173. New York: Aronson.

Sperling, O. (1978a). The concept of psychosomatic disease. In *Psychosomatic Disorders in Childhood*, ed. O. Sperling, pp. 3–10. New York: Aronson.

—— (1978b). Discussion of Chapter 1 at the meeting of the Psychosomatic Study Group of the Psychoanalytic Association of New York, Inc., March 16.

Spitz, R.A. (1945). Hospitalism: an inquiry into the genesis of psychiatric conditions in early childhood. *Psychoanalytic Study of the Child* 1: 53–74.

—— (1955). The primal cavity: a contribution to the genesis of perception and its role for psychoanalytic theory. *Psychoanalytic Study of the Child* 10: 215–240.

Stangler, R.S., and Printz, A.M. (1980). Psychiatric diagnosis in a university population: DSM-III. *American Journal of Psychiatry* 137: 937-940.

Sterba, R.F. (1934). The fate of the ego in analytic therapy. *International Journal of Psycho-Analysis* 15: 117-126.

Stolorow, R., and Lachman, F. (1980). *Psychoanalysis of Developmental Arrests, Theory and Treatment.* New York: International Universities Press.

Stone, L. (1967). The psychoanalytic situation and transference: postscript to an earlier communication. *Journal of the American Psychoanalytic Association* 15: 3-58.

Strober, M. (1982). The significance of bulimia in juvenile anorexia nervosa: an exploration of possible etiologic factors. *International Journal of Eating Disorders* 1: 28-43.

Sydenham, A. (1946). Amenorrhea at Stanley Camp, Hong Kong, during internment. *British Medical Journal* 2: 159-165.

Sylvester, E. (1945). Analysis of psychogenic anorexia and vomiting in a four-year-old child. *Psychoanalytic Study of the Child* 1: 167-188.

Taipale, V., Larkio-Miettinen, K., Valanne, E., Moren, R., and Aukee, M. (1972). Anorexia nervosa in boys. *Psychosomatics* 13: 236-240.

Thomä, H. (1967). *Anorexia Nervosa*, trans. G. Brydone. New York: International Universities Press.

Tolstrup, K. (1965). Die Charakteristika de juengen faelle von Anorexia Nervosa. In *Anorexia Nervosa*, ed. J.E. Meyer and H. Feldman, pp. 51-59. Stuttgart: Georg Thieme.

Tucker, W.L. (1952). Lobotomy case histories: ulcerative colitis and anorexia nervosa. *Lahey Clinic Bulletin* 7: 239-243.

Volkan, V.D. (1965). The observation of the "little man" phenomenon in a case of anorexia nervosa. *British Journal of Medical Psychology* 38: 299-311.

—— (1976). *Primitive Internalized Object Relations: A Clinical Study of Schizophrenic, Borderline, and Narcissistic Patients.* New York: International Universities Press.

Waller, J.V., Kaufman, M.R., and Deutsch, F. (1940). Anorexia nervosa: a psychosomatic entity. *Psychosomatic Medicine* 2: 3-16.

Walsh, B.T., Stewart, J., Wright, L., et at. (1982). Treatment of bulimia with monoamine oxidase inhibitors. *American Journal of Psychiatry* 139: 1629-1630.

Walsh, B.T., Stewart, J., Wright, L., et al. (May, 1983). Treatment of bulimia with monamine oxidase inhibitors. Presented at the Annual Meeting, American Psychiatric Association.

Walsh, B.T., Stewart, J.W., Roose, S.P., Gladis, M., Glassman, A.H. (1984). Treatment of bulimia with phenelzine: a double-blind placebo controlled study. *Archives of General Psychiatry* 41: 1105-1109.

Wilson, C.P. (1967a). Stone as a symbol of teeth. *Psychoanalytic Quarterly* 36: 418-425.

—— (1967b). Symbolism of the umbrella. *Psychoanalytic Quarterly*, 36: 83-84.

—— (1968a). The boy friend—the girl friend: the detailed psychoanalytic investigation of a mannerism of speech. *Psychoanalytic Quarterly* 38: 519.

—— (1968b). Discussion of Little's paper on "Xerostomia" at the Fall Meeting of the American Psychoanalytic Association, New York, December 21.

—— (1968c). Psychosomatic asthma and acting out: a case of bronchial asthma that developed de novo in the terminal phase of analysis. *International Journal of Psycho-Analysis* 49: 330–335.

—— (1971). On the limits of the effectiveness of psychoanalysis: early ego and somatic disturbances. *Journal of the American Psychoanalytic Association* 19: 552–564.

—— (1973). The psychoanalytic treatment of hospitalized anorexia nervosa patients. Paper presented at the meeting of the Psychoanalytic Association of New York, November 19.

—— (1974). The psychoanalysis of an adolescent anorexic girl. Discussion group on "Late Adolescence," S. Ritvo, Chairman. Meeting of the American Psychoanalytic Association, December 12.

—— (1977). Group discussion on "The parent-child relationship in anorexia nervosa." Regional Psychoanalytic Meeting, Grossinger's Hotel, October 20.

—— (1978). The psychoanalytic treatment of hospitalized anorexia nervosa patients. Panel discussion on "Anorexia nervosa." *Bulletin of the Psychoanalytic Association of New York* 15: 5–7.

—— (1980a). The family psychological profile of anorexia nervosa patients. *Journal of the Medical Society of New Jersey* 77: 341–344.

—— (1980b). On the fear of being fat in female psychology and anorexia nervosa. *Bulletin of the Psychoanalytic Association of New York* 17: 8–9.

—— (1980c). Parental overstimulation asthma. *International Journal of Psychoanalytic Psychotherapy* 8: 601–621.

—— (1980d). The psychodynamic treatment of a hospitalized anorexic patient. Discussion group on "Psychoanalytic Considerations in Patients with Organic Disease or Major Physical Handicaps," P. Castelnuovo-Tedesco, Chairman. Meeting of the American Psychoanalytic Association, December 18.

—— (1981). Sand symbolism: the primary dream representation of the Isakower phenomenon and of smoking addictions. In *Clinical Psychoanalysis*, ed. S. Orgel and B.D. Fine, pp. 45–55. New York: Aronson.

—— (1982). The fear of being fat and anorexia nervosa. *International Journal of Psychoanalytic Psychotherapy* 9: 233–255.

Wilson, C.P. (1983). Fat phobia as a diagnostic term to replace a medical misnomer: anorexia nervosa. Meeting of the American Academy of Child Psychiatry, October, San Francisco, California. Tapes 96 and 97 by Instant Replay, 760 S. 23rd Street, Arlington, VA 22202.

Wilson, C.P., and Mintz, I.L. (1982). Abstaining and bulimic anorexics: two sides of the same coin. *Primary Care* 9: 459–472.

Wilson, C.P. (1985) The Treatment of Bulimic Depression; paper presented at Grand Rounds, Department of Psychiatry, St. Luke's Roosevelt Hospital Center, New York, March 6.

Wulff, M. (1932). An interesting oral symptom-complex and its relation to addiction. *Internationale Zeitschrift für Psychoanalyse* 18: 281–302.

Wurmser, L. (1980). Phobic core in the addictions and the paranoid process. *International Journal of Psychoanalytic Psychotherapy* 8: 311–335.

Zetzel, E.R. (1956). Current concepts of transference. *International Journal of Psycho-Analysis* 37: 369–376.

INDEX